THE

ONE YEAR

BIBLE

Companion

Tyndale House Publishers, Inc.
WHEATON, ILLINOIS

Library of Congress Cataloging-in-Publication Data

The One year Bible companion.
     p.   cm.
   ISBN 0-8423-4616-3
   1. Bible—Handbooks, manuals, etc. 2. Bible—Reading.
BS417.064   1992
220'.076—dc20   92-28480

Printed in the United States of America

06   05   04   03
12   11   10   9   8

THE **ONE YEAR**® BIBLE *Companion*

*I*ntroductions to each book of the Bible

GENESIS

Author: Moses

Date: 1420 or 1220 B.C.

Content: The book of Genesis was written to explain how everything began; in fact, the very title Genesis means "origin" or "beginning." It explains that God created the universe, how man was created and placed in a perfect environment, how sin began, and how God provided salvation for lost man. The beginning of human history is described, the beginning of human arts and crafts, how human languages began, and where the various nations came from. The focus then shifts to the beginning of the Hebrew people with Abraham, followed by the histories of Isaac, Jacob and his sons, and the book end with Joseph in Egypt.

Theme: The main idea that runs through the book is that although God made everything good and man's sin has spoiled it, God has not given up, but is now in search of man to save him. The overall control of God is stressed, and special attention is given to how God directs history for the good of his people and their salvation (Gen. 50:20).

EXODUS

Author: Moses

Date: 1420 or 1220 B.C.

Content: The book of Exodus deals with the significant facts surrounding Israel's emergence as a nation. Moses' great leadership is described as he accepted God's call to return to Egypt in order to lead God's people to freedom. God sent the ten devastating plagues upon Egypt because the Pharaoh refused to obey his command. The ceremony of Passover was established during the last plague and became a memorial of God's deliverance for all time to Israel. The Israelites crossed the sea and arrived at Mt. Sinai where God gave the Ten Commandments and the plan for the tabernacle, and the covenant was renewed with the nation.

Theme: The power of God over evil is clearly shown when God defeats the enemies of his people by delivering them from bondage, but God expects that we trust and obey him in return. Worship in the Tabernacle and adherence to the law were two aspects of Israel's obedience.

LEVITICUS

Author: Moses
Date: 1420 or 1220 B.C.
Content: The book of Leviticus was designed to be a handbook for the priests or Levites, hence the name Leviticus. It sets down the regulations that were to govern the life of Israel in general and specifically to give regulations concerning sacrifice and worship. All of the major sacrifices are described, as well as the way they were to be offered. All of the major festivals and holidays are discussed. There are also special sections devoted to the priesthood and regulations concerning ceremonial matters.

Theme: The central theme of this book is that God has provided a way for atonement to be made by the offering of sacrificial blood. This whole system found its fulfillment in the shedding of Christ's blood as the one great sacrifice for the sins of the world. Leviticus also shows that worship is to be orderly and is to follow a regular pattern.

NUMBERS

Author: Moses
Date: 1420 or 1220 B.C.
Content: This book deals with the journey of Israel from Mt. Sinai to the edge of Canaan and the Israelites' preparation to enter the Land. Because of sin and unbelief, however, they were not allowed by God to claim their inheritance but were condemned to wander in the wilderness for forty years. After the forty years they slowly made their way back to Canaan—this time ready to obey God's commands. After winning

some important battles to the east of the Jordan River, the Israelites prepared for the entrance into the land itself.

Theme: The book shows the continual faithfulness of God and the unbelievable sin of man. Israel rejected God but God remained true to his word, in leading the people through the wilderness and providing for their needs. In the New Testament the Christian life is likened to a wandering in the wilderness with the promise of a heavenly Canaan before us (Heb. 3:7-9; 4:8-11).

DEUTERONOMY

Author: Moses

Date: 1420 or 1220 B.C.

Content: The book consists of a series of addresses given by Moses in the plains of Moab prior to their entering into Canaan, as well as some specialized regulations and the appointment of Moses' successor, Joshua. In Moses' addresses he summarized the events that led up to that day, exhorted the people to faith and obedience, called the Israelites to rededicate themselves to the task God had given them, and then led them in worship and song. After the appointment of Joshua, Moses left the people and, after viewing the Holy Land from afar one last time, he died. With Moses' death the old order passed away and the destiny of Israel moved into the hands of the next generation.

Theme: The faithfulness and power of God to save are stressed throughout the book. A look at Israel's past shows that God led his people through their darkest days and gave them hope for the future. What God did in the past he could do again. The need for faith and obedience on the part of God's people is also stressed. God's richest blessings are given only to those who will use them for his glory.

JOSHUA

Author: Probably Joshua

Date: Either fourteenth century or twelfth century B.C.

Content: After the death of Moses, the leadership of the nation passed into the hands of Joshua and he was their commander-in-chief throughout the entire time of conquest when Israel was taking over the land.

While still in the plains of Moab, Joshua mobilized his forces and prepared them for battle. After this they crossed the Jordan River and the battle began. There were three campaigns fought, one in the north, one in the central region, and one in the south, and all are described, though not fully. After the initial victories, the land was divided among the various tribes of Israel. Joshua then exhorted the people and died in peace.

Theme: The book of Joshua shows that God is true to his promise. He had promised his people a land and they were now entering in to possess it. However, it was not automatic; God required of them that they actively engage in warfare in order to gain what he had given them. God's judgment upon the sin of the Canaanites in the form of Israel's armies is also a prominent feature.

JUDGES

Author: Unknown

Date: Eleventh century B.C.

Content: The book of Judges covers a period of several hundred years following the conquest of Canaan, during which time the people were ruled by individual leaders called judges or saviors. Their task was primarily military, being to expel the enemy from the land. Throughout this period of Israel's history there is a tragic cycle to be observed, that of rebellion against God, followed by the judgment of God, usually in the form of foreign invasion. The children of Israel then cry to God for help and a "judge" is sent to save them. This cycle is repeated numerous times throughout the book. Tragically, the people never seemed to learn that rebellion against God is a sure road to disaster.

Theme: The grim lesson of Judges is that "the wages of sin is death" (Rom. 6:23). Sin takes many forms, from the sophisticated sins of kings to the barbaric events that close the book, but the net result is always the same: when everyone does his own thing, chaos and destruction are the inevitable outcome (Judg. 21:25). Through it all, however, God in his faithfulness saves the people when they truly repent and turn to him.

RUTH

Author: Unknown

Date: During the time of the Judges

Content: The book of Ruth portrays another side to the chaotic time of the judges. In it there is a welcome relief from the bloodshed and mayhem that seemed to engulf the land because of Israel's sin. It is the story of Ruth, who decided to stay with her mother-in-law, Naomi, after tragedy struck that unfortunate woman. God returned good to Ruth in the form of a husband (Boaz) and a child, and also to Naomi in the form of grandchildren. From this family, eventually, came David the king.

Theme: The central point of this book is that even in times of crisis and despair, life may be lived according to the precepts of God and that God abundantly blesses those who do so live. The fundamental human values of love, faith, trust, and goodness are greater than the hatred and violence of men, and continue from generation to generation as a light to guide those who look for the true meaning of life.

1 SAMUEL

Author: Unknown

Date: Probably tenth century B.C.

Content: The books of First and Second Samuel comprise one book in the Hebrew Bible because they form one continuous history covering the lives of Samuel, Saul, and David. They were separated into two books for convenience in reading. First Samuel deals with the Philistine wars and Saul's ultimate failure to deal with the enemy. The book opens with Israel's being oppressed by the Philistines (a war-like neighboring nation) and the emergence of the two early leaders, Samuel and Saul. Samuel was the religious leader and Saul ultimately became the king. Saul's early victories are described, followed by his moral decline and tragic end. Balancing the decline of Saul is the rise of the youthful David who will assume leadership after the death of Saul.

Theme: The basic idea that pervades this book is that God does not make his people immune to the changes of human life, but gives them grace to see things through to a satisfactory conclusion. The rise and fall of kings, times of peace and war—throughout it all God stays the same and controls human events in such a way that those who trust him will find comfort and the courage to endure.

2 SAMUEL

Author: Unknown

Date: Probably tenth century B.C.

Content: Second Samuel covers approximately forty years, which is the bulk of David's reign as king. It begins with David's being proclaimed king and consolidating his position against others who claimed the throne. David moved the capital to Jerusalem, brought the sacred Ark of the Covenant there, and ultimately defeated the Philistines for all time. David's troubled career is described in some detail, including his family problems (his son Absalom) and his personal problems (adultery with Bathsheba). A summary of David's later years concludes the book.

Theme: The life of David is given as an example of good and of evil. The sins of David are exposed—so that too much trust will not be put in men, and the victories of David are recorded—so that it may be seen what God can do with someone who wholly trusts in him. God used David in spite of his faults because he found in David a willingness to repent and start again, no matter how far he had fallen.

1 KINGS

Author: Unknown

Date: Sixth century B.C.

Content: First and Second Kings form one book in the Hebrew Bible and are considered to be prophetic literature, probably because a prophet put the books together. The two books together cover a period of approximately 350 years, when kings ruled the land, hence the name of the book. First Kings begins with the death of David, followed by a description of Solomon's reign, including the building of the first Temple in Jerusalem. The split of the kingdom into Israel (North) and Judah (South) is described, ending with the great conflict between Elijah the prophet, and Ahab, the king of Israel.

Theme: The fact that a history book is considered to be prophetic is important. It shows that God speaks to us from the past, as well as from the present experience of others. These events are recorded so that we will not make the same mistakes again. The conflict between Elijah and Ahab shows God's immediate involvement in human life and his concern for human affairs. First Kings particularly shows the disastrous effects of social evil upon the spiritual life of a nation.

2 KINGS

Author: Unknown

Date: Sixth century B.C.

Content: Second Kings covers a period of approximately 250 years during which time two national tragedies occurred. In 722 B.C. the northern kingdom of Israel was destroyed by the Assyrians, and in 586 B.C. the southern kingdom of Judah was destroyed by the Babylonians. The reigns of the various kings are described in some detail with care being taken to show the spiritual significance of what they were doing. Throughout this whole time of good and bad kings, war and peace, prosperity and ruin, God is seen to be at work, in particular sending prophets to preach his word and warn of judgment to come.

Theme: God's control over the affairs of men and nations is constantly seen throughout this book. The rulers of men may think they are in control, but even the enemies of God's people fit into God's plan by executing judgment upon the wayward nations of Israel and Judah. It must be stressed that sin invariably brings judgment upon the people and righteousness brings God's blessing. Second Kings also shows that God never sends judgment without a warning first; in this instance, the warning came through the prophets who were sent.

1 CHRONICLES

Author: Unknown

Date: 5th century B.C.

Content: First and Second Chronicles form one book in the Hebrew Bible and are written from a priest's point of view. In this way they supplement the Books of Kings, which were written from a prophet's point of view. First Chronicles begins with a series of genealogies that record the family histories of David the king and the descendants of Levi the priest. This is followed by the death of Saul and the reign of David, with special emphasis being placed upon the religious affairs of the nation. It closes with Solomon's being made the king.

Theme: Because First Chronicles was written from a priestly point of view, many details about Judah's religion are given to supplement the history found in the Books of Kings. The stress is upon the supreme importance of worshiping God and the positive effect that has upon the life of a nation. God blesses those nations that trust in him.

The mention of so many unfamiliar names, while seemingly irrelevant, actually shows that God forgets no one. Those who go to their graves unknown by men are personally remembered by God.

2 CHRONICLES

Author: Unknown

Date: Fifth century B.C.

Content: Second Chronicles contains the history of Judah that was begun in First Chronicles. It deals with the glory of Solomon's reign, with a special emphasis being placed upon the glory of the temple. This emphasis is made because a priestly point of view pervades the book. The remaining kings of Judah are discussed, with a stress upon how the religious affairs of the nation were going. Hezekiah is given mention because during his reign an extended revival took place. The destruction of Jerusalem and the exile of the people to Babylon is described, and book ends with the Persian king's decree to let the people return home.

Theme: Judah's history is described from a religious point of view in this book. The righteous kings are commented on and the evil kings are named so that all can see who is responsible for the rise and fall of the nation. The religious leaders and their ultimate failure to remain true to God added to the sin of Judah—until God allowed his own chosen people to plunge themselves into ruin, as an example for all time that God will not tolerate sin.

EZRA

Author: Ezra

Date: Fifth century B.C.

Content: The book of Ezra deals with the return of the Israelites to the land of Palestine after their captivity in Babylon. After describing the first return and how the work on the Temple was begun, the author tells us the problems that arose. After a great deal of trouble and early failure, the Temple was finally finished and rededicated to the glory of God. The ministry of Ezra is described in some detail, stressing the intercession that he made to God for the wayward people of the restored community.

Theme: When the people of Israel returned home they saw this as the fulfillment of the promise of God. God had said he would never abandon his people, and although they were judged for their sin God never stopped loving them. That God should care for the world to this degree is the deepest of mysteries. God desires our worship in return for his love, however. This may be seen in that he sent the prophets Haggai and Zechariah to speed the rebuilding of the Temple after the people, in discouragement, had ceased to work upon it.

NEHEMIAH

Author: Nehemiah

Date: Fifth century B.C.

Content: The book of Nehemiah continues the story begun by Ezra and deals with life in the restored community. The major point of Ezra is the rededication of the Temple: the major point of Nehemiah is the rebuilding of the city walls of Jerusalem. The book begins by explaining the need Jerusalem had for the protection that walls would give. This is followed by a discussion of how the walls were built in spite of numerous problems both in the community and outside of it. A national day of repentance was called for and the project was completed.

Theme: The main theme of this book is the sad fact that people are slow to learn the lessons God wants to teach them. The Israelites had been carried into captivity because of their sin, but now the very same problems arose again. The people were neglecting worship, prayer, and Bible study, not to mention the fact that they were treating each other unjustly. But God in his patience continued to send his messengers to them to offer salvation and pardon.

ESTHER

Author: Unknown

Date: Fifth century B.C.

Content: The book of Esther deals with a momentous event that took place after the Persians had destroyed Babylon and while many Jews were still living in the land of their captivity. The story concerns a Jewess names Esther who had become the wife of the Persian King Ahasuerus. An evil adviser to the king, named Haman, sought the destruction of the Jews in order to gain control of their wealth, but Esther tactfully intervened and saved her people from this fate. Haman was executed, and after some civil strife things quieted down once more. This remarkable deliverance of the Jews was celebrated by a feast named Purim and it remains to this day.

Theme: The providence and power of God are the central points of this book. God was protecting his people even in their captivity and was working all things together for their good. God's power is seen in the overthrow of Israel's enemies. It is important to note that God used human beings to accomplish his purpose here, rather than doing it directly himself. We must be ready at all times to do God's will when he so directs.

JOB

Author: Unknown

Date: Tenth century B.C.

Content: This long narrative poem deals with one of the deepest problems of man: How do we explain sin and suffering, if there exists a God powerful enough to do something about them? The book begins with the suffering Job being given three sets of speeches by some friends of his: Eliphaz, Bildad, and Zophar, each of whom tries to explain Job's misery in a different way. A fourth man, Elihu, tries to summarize the situation, offering yet another explanation of why Job was suffering. Finally, the Lord himself speaks to Job, and Job recognizes that we do not so much need "answers" to life's problems, as we need God himself. Job is then healed and given material and spiritual blessings far beyond his former state.

Theme: The mystery that surrounds human existence and the need to trust in God runs throughout the book. Mankind simply does not have enough knowledge to explain why things happen the way they do. It is possible to rise above our limitations by faith in God, however, because God does know why everything happens and will work good for those who love him. We may thus learn the profound truth that when we have nothing left but God, God is enough.

PSALMS

Author: Principally David; also many others
Date: 10th century B.C. and later
Content: This favorite book of today was also a favorite in antiquity. In it may be seen the many different ways in which believers over several centuries related to God. Every human mood and feeling may be brought to God for him to bless. There are sorrow and joy, anger and calm, doubt and faith, repentance and praise. There are recollections of the past, the struggles of present existence, and visions of a glorious future. In numerous places God's Messiah, Jesus Christ, is portrayed in his suffering and in his glory. The book of Psalms was used in much the same way as a hymnbook is used today, for public and private worship.

Theme: The book of Psalms teaches principally that God has a personal concern for his people and that he wants us to come to him just as we are. We need not solve our problems before we go to him; we go to him for the solutions. Wherever we are, however we feel, whatever we have done—if we offer ourselves to God he is willing to help and give us the strength to live again. God's power and control of all things is also seen. Because God is in control of everything, he can help us when we turn to him for deliverance.

PROVERBS

Author: Principally Solomon; also many others
Date: Tenth century B.C. and later
Content: The book of Proverbs contains practical instructions for successful living, given by God to supplement the teaching of the prophets,

which was to call men to repentance, and the work of the priests, which was to direct the worship of the people. The book of Proverbs teaches that there is a divine wisdom given to man by God, but there is also a divinely given human wisdom, or common sense, and both must play a part in daily life. Practical sayings from many centuries are collected together in this book; it deals with such diverse matters as the discipline of children, social justice, foolish talk, and money. It ends significantly with a description of a truly good wife.

Theme: The theme of Proverbs is stated in 1:7—The first step to wisdom is to trust and reverence the Lord. This is to say that only when a man trusts in God will he be truly wise. Human wisdom is fine and necessary but no matter how skilled we might be, without humility in the presence of God and a willingness to learn from him, we will inevitably go astray. The book also teaches the sanctity of human life. Everything that pertains to successful living is a concern to God and he has made provision for it.

ECCLESIASTES

Author: Probably Solomon
Date: Probably tenth century B.C.
Content: This difficult book displays the dark philosophy of one who sought to find peace apart from God, but in the end realized that only futility is to be found there. The only possible solution to life's puzzle concludes the book: "Fear God and keep his commandments, for this is the whole duty of man" (Eccles. 12:13). Leading up to that positive statement is a series of pictures, each one portraying the futility of life without God. Wealth, wisdom, popularity, and pleasure are all put down as so much vanity. Only when a man turns from this world to God will he find true happiness.

Theme: There is a negative lesson to be learned from this book. It is a series of things not to do. It shows the emptiness of trying to live for oneself and to please oneself alone without considering the needs of others or considering God our Maker. There is a positive side, however. If one can see how not to live, perhaps then he will see what he ought to do and be spared the heartaches of living a wasted life.

THE SONG OF SOLOMON

Author: Solomon
Date: Tenth century B.C.
Content: This book, about the love of Solomon and a Shulamite woman, consists of a series of lyrics or songs, hence the designation in the

text: the Song of Songs. It is a simple but moving piece, describing the longing of two lovers for one another, of the struggles that need to be overcome, of the tender feelings that love awakens, and of the joy that the lovers find in being together. The young women of Jerusalem, who appear with Solomon and his beloved, add to the dramatic effect of the story by adding observations of their own.

Theme: The most obvious meaning of this narrative is that human love, which was ordained by God, is good and holy when enjoyed in obedience to the commands of God. Many interpreters have found a symbolic meaning in the book, however, and point to the love of God for Israel or the love of Christ for his Church. Seen in this way it underscores the teaching of the New Testament that God is love (1 John 4:8).

ISAIAH

Author: Isaiah

Date: Eighth century B.C.

Content: Isaiah's long ministry lasted almost sixty years and covered the reigns of four kings, the last one being Hezekiah, the reformer. Isaiah was sent primarily to Judah, although his message concerns the northern kingdom of Israel as well. He lived through the awful days of the civil war between Israel and Judah in 734–732 B.C. and saw the destruction of Israel by Assyria in 722 B.C.. The grim lesson taught by Israel's fall was not lost on Isaiah, and he used it to encourage Hezekiah to trust in the Lord. The Lord delivered Judah from the mighty Assyrian army by sending a plague to destroy the camp. Isaiah also looked beyond his own time to the coming exile of Judah and the deliverance that God would provide.

Theme: Isaiah was one of Jesus' favorite books and he quoted it frequently, because the central theme is salvation. God is seen as the Savior of his people, who redeemed them from Egypt, who will redeem them from their coming captivity, and who will send his beloved Servant to bear the sins of us all (Isa. 53:6). God freely offers to pardon all who will turn to him in repentance and faith. The future kingdom of God on earth is also described in exquisite detail as a time when men will lay down their swords and, in peace, sing praises to God their King.

JEREMIAH

Author: Jeremiah
Date: Sixth century B.C.
Content: Jeremiah's life covered the last forty years of Judah's existence. The burden of his message was for God's people to accept the judgment of God so that a new beginning could be made. He lived through the invasions by the Babylonian armies, the deportations of his people by the enemy, the slaughter of the inhabitants of Jerusalem, and the destruction of the Temple of God. He warned the people concerning these events, pleading with them to turn from their sins, but to no avail. He received only scorn and persecution. Jeremiah's life is described in some detail, thus making him the best known of the Old Testament prophets.
Theme: In the crisis days during which Jeremiah lived, he had but one message for the people: Repent and turn to God. All false hopes must be abandoned and God must be given his rightful place in the nation. Nothing can save the people—neither their wealth, their armies, their diplomats, nor even their religion—only God can save. The destruction of Jerusalem stands as a memorial for all time that when a nation rejects God, the inevitable result will be ruin. Jeremiah also has a message of hope. Although Judah had abandoned God, God had not abandoned them and would once again show himself mighty on their behalf.

LAMENTATIONS

Author: Jeremiah
Date: Sixth century B.C.
Content: The book of Lamentations is a funeral song, written for the fallen city of Jerusalem. It was composed by Jeremiah, who was an eye-witness of all he describes in such vivid detail. He shows the destruction in all its horror so that it could never again be asked, "Why did no one ever tell us the awful price we would have to pay for disobeying God?" There is very little of comfort, but Jeremiah's prayer in chapter 5 does look beyond the desolate ashes of the once glorious Jerusalem to God whose throne endures forever. Only there can Jeremiah find any solace.
Theme: Lamentations is a declaration of the wrath of God. It portrays the bitter truth that God had promised judgment upon sin, and Judah had been foolish enough to put God to the test. Bad as that was, the deeper tragedy was that it did not have to be. God's faithfulness is great, being renewed every morning, and his compassion never

fails (Lam. 3:22–23). Had Judah only known, it all could have been avoided. The warning and the promise found in this book should be emblazoned in the skies for all to see.

EZEKIEL

Author: Ezekiel
Date: Sixth century B.C.
Content: Ezekiel, who grew up as a priest, was carried off to Babylon with the Jewish exiles deported in 597 B.C., and there he became a prophet of God. His message was one of coming judgment for those remaining in Jerusalem, but his preaching was not well received by the Jews who were with him in captivity. When his dire predictions came true in 586 B.C. with the destruction of Jerusalem (see Ezek. 33:21), the people listened from then on with great earnestness. His message changed at this point from being one of unbending judgment to one of comfort and hope for the future. The worst had come; it was now time to make plans for beginning again. Ezekiel saw himself as a shepherd and watchman over Israel. As a shepherd, he was to protect the people, but as a watchman, he was to warn of danger ahead.
Theme: The message of Ezekiel is based upon the unchangeable holiness of God. This is both a promise and a warning. It is a warning because God has promised to remain faithful to his people and this will not change. The book of Ezekiel shows God's unbreakable promise fulfilled in both respects: the city fell according to promise because of Judah's sin, and the city would be restored according to promise because of God's faithfulness. The lives of God's people determined how God would treat them.

DANIEL

Author: Daniel
Date: Sixth century B.C.
Content: Daniel was carried off into captivity in Babylon as a young boy where, although he was a captive, he received an education and ultimately rose to a high position in Babylonian and later, Persian government. Because of his trust in God he was subjected to barbarous persecution, at one point being thrown to the lions. Three of his compatriots were thrown into a furnace, but they too survived by the power of God. The book deals with many historical events of Daniel's day, but it also contains prophecies concerning the future. Daniel saw the great world empires that were to come, but saw more

than just that. He also saw the power of God and the Messiah, Jesus, who was to come and undo the evil of this world, ultimately to establish a kingdom of righteousness that would never fade away.

Theme: Daniel's major theme is the sovereignty of God. God rules over the affairs of men, directing the course of history toward his own ends, working in and through the acts of men. The kingdoms of men rise and fall but God remains forever. God's will remains forever as well, and it is God's determination to bring salvation to men by the Messiah whom he will send. Ultimately evil will be overcome and good will triumph because God has willed it so.

HOSEA

Author: Hosea
Date: Eighth century B.C.
Content: The book of Hosea consists of two unequal parts, the first containing Hosea's life (1–3) and the second containing Hosea's messages (4–14). Hosea was a prophet to the northern kingdom of Israel prior to its fall in 722 B.C., and his ministry spanned some forty years. He was a contemporary of Amos, Isaiah, and Micah. Hosea's unhappy marriage life depicted symbolically the state of affairs in his nation. Just as his wife left home for a life of prostitution, so Israel had left God to seek after false gods. But as Hosea continued to love his wife and finally brought her home again, so God continued to love Israel and promised to restore her someday.

Theme: Two things stand in marked contrast in the book of Hosea: the love of God and the waywardness of Israel. God is depicted as faithful, caring, forgiving, kind, and loving. God's unfailing love is the theme of the book. Israel is seen as faithless, straying, sinful, rebellious, and wanton. She is characterized by ignorance of what God requires and total lack of desire to please God. However, just as Hosea's love triumphed in the end, so will God's love work a miracle of transformation in Israel.

JOEL

Author: Joel
Date: Ninth century B.C.
Content: This beautifully written book uses a plague of locusts to describe symbolically God's coming judgment on Jerusalem. Just as locusts devour the land, so will the enemy armies devour Jerusalem unless the nation repents of its sins. If the people do respond, there will be a time of prosperity and a return of God's favor. God's favor is seen as going beyond the immediate future to a time when God would

pour out his Holy Spirit upon all flesh (2:28-32). The New Testament sees this as being fulfilled at Pentecost (Acts 2:16-21).

Theme: Joel's message is one of coming judgment if Jerusalem does not repent. Just as surely as the locusts strip the trees bare, so will God strip bare the land. Joel also speaks of coming prosperity and final blessing, if the people respond in faith.

AMOS

Author: Amos

Date: Eighth century B.C.

Content: Amos was a contemporary of Hosea, Isaiah, and Micah, and like Hosea his message was directed to the northern kingdom of Israel, although he himself was from the south. He begins by pronouncing judgment upon the surrounding nations and finally centering on Israel itself. There follows a series of severe denunciations of Israel's sin, in particular the social sins of the day: injustice, official corruption, greed, and false worship. A series of visions continues the stern message and the book ends with the scantest hope that Israel will listen.

Theme: Amos's message is based upon the doctrine of God's eternal righteousness. Because God is righteous, he demands righteousness of his people. If they do not evidence their faith by the lives that they live, then it is God to whom they must answer. An offer of pardon is made, however (Amos 5:6), and Israel will some day be restored as of old by the power and mercy of God (Amos 15:11).

OBADIAH

Author: Obadiah

Date: Sixth century B.C.

Content: The book of Obadiah is a prophecy concerning the destruction of Edom, a nation that treacherously participated in the destruction of Jerusalem in 586 B.C. The Edomites were descendants of Esau, while the Israelites were the descendants of Jacob—Jacob and Esau being brothers. It is for this violence of brother (Edom) against brother (Israel) that Edom is condemned. Rather than render aid when the enemy was upon Israel, Edom helped in the destruction and took part in the plunder of the stricken city.

Theme: Edom's treachery and pride are visited by God's judgment. The point Obadiah wished us to see from this is God's hatred of sin. That God would stand idly by while brother watched brother being destroyed, and even take part in the slaughter, is unthinkable. God stepped in to judge the nation of Edom and it was finally destroyed.

JONAH

Author: Jonah

Date: Eighth century B.C.

Content: Jonah was a prophet who was born in Israel (2 Kings 14:25) and called by God to preach repentance to Assyria (the capital city was Nineveh)—the nation that was shortly going to destroy Israel in 722 B.C. On receiving the call, Jonah's nationalistic spirit would not allow him to offer salvation to the pagans, so he attempted to flee from God by ship. He was thrown overboard, swallowed by a great fish, disgorged on the shore, and finally obeyed God's command by going to Nineveh to preach. His success there angered him, however, and God taught him an object lesson by means of a plant. Jonah's experience in the fish is used in the New Testament (Matt. 12:38-41) as an example of Jesus' burial and resurrection.

Theme: The basic theme of Jonah is found in 4:11, where God declares his love for all men, whether Israelites or not. Jonah was unable to love the Assyrians properly, but God desired nothing for them but their good and their salvation, and he sent a prophet to offer repentance unto life. The book also shows the power of God and his control over the forces of nature.

MICAH

Author: Micah

Date: Eighth century B.C.

Content: Micah was a contemporary of Isaiah who preached to both Israel and Judah in the eighth century B.C. He lived in a small town (Moresheth) south of Jerusalem but directed his messages to the capital cities of Jerusalem and Samaria. He denounces their oppression, pride, greed, corruption, false piety and arrogance. As the leaders of the nation, the capital cities should take the lead in righteousness, not sin, and God the Righteous One will hold them responsible for their actions.

Theme: The righteousness of God and the demand of God for righteousness among men is the major idea in this book. God demands justice, humility, and love from his people and not outward show (Mic. 6:8). Those who persist in rebellion, oppression, and pride will be judged by God. Micah also predicts the coming of Christ as well as the place of his birth (Mic. 5:2). This prophecy was remembered by Herod's advisors when the Magi were seeking the infant Christ (Matt. 2:4-6).

NAHUM

Author: Nahum

Date: Seventh century B.C.

Content: The book of Nahum is a prophecy concerning the destruction of Nineveh, the capital city of Assyria. The Assyrians destroyed Samaria in 722 B.C. and for their pride and cruelty were in turn destroyed in 612 B.C. Nahum searingly describes the reasons for Nineveh's destruction: its idolatry, cruelty, murder, lies, treachery, superstition, and injustice. It is a city filled with blood (Nah. 3:1) and such a city cannot be allowed to endure.

Theme: The holiness, justice, and power of God underlie the message of this book. God rules over all the earth, even over those who do not acknowledge him. He sets the boundaries of the nations and those nations that transgress his laws are doomed to destruction. Through all of that, however, a message of hope shines through. God is slow to anger (Nah. 1:3) and good (Nah. 1:7) and offers good news to those who want the blessings instead of the judgment of God (Nah. 1:15).

HABAKKUK

Author: Habakkuk

Date: Seventh century B.C.

Content: Habakkuk preached during the last days of Judah before its fall in 586 B.C. He saw the impending doom and was troubled by two things—why God allowed evil to exist in the nation of Judah and how God could use a sinful nation like Babylon to punish Judah for its sins. God answered Habakkuk's perplexity and gave him far more than he asked, a vision of God himself. This new insight into the being of God and his own inadequacy gave Habakkuk the courage to live through those dark days with determination and strength.

Theme: The sovereignty of God and the need for man to trust him is the basic message of this marvelous book. God is in control of all nations and will do what is right. The proper attitude of man is trust, not doubt (Hab. 2:4). When a man does this, he may look beyond the unpleasant exterior of things into the deeper meaning of God and find strength to live no matter what might happen. We do not know the future but God does, and he may be fully trusted.

ZEPHANIAH

Author: Zephaniah

Date: Sometime before 621 B.C.

Content: Zephaniah was a prophet to Judah in the last decades of its existence, before it was destroyed in 586 B.C. Josiah was the king when Zephaniah preached and in part stirred by Zephaniah's message, he instituted some sweeping reforms in 621 B.C. But these reforms were in reality too little, too late. The people slid back into their evil ways and the city fell to the Babylonian invaders. Zephaniah's message is a stern one, based on the righteous judgment of God. Not only Judah, but all the surrounding nations, will feel God's heavy hand for their sins.

Theme: The people of Judah had hoped that in spite of their sin, when the "day of the Lord" (judgment day) arrived, God would go easy on them but hard on their enemies. Zephaniah tells them that when God judges sin, those who know the most suffer the most. Judgment will begin with Judah and end with the other nations. However, if Judah repents from the heart, God will turn aside this judgment and give them life and blessing.

HAGGAI

Author: Haggai

Date: 520 B.C.

Content: Haggai was a contemporary of Zechariah who was sent by God to preach to the restored community and to encourage them to finish the project of rebuilding the Temple. The messages are directed to the two leaders of the people, Zerubbabel the governor and Joshua the priest. The book consists of five prophetic utterances designed to speed the work along. This message had the desired effect, and the Temple was rededicated in 516 B.C.

Theme: The involvement of God in the life of his people and his desire that spiritual things matter is the basic theme of this book. The people had stopped work on the temple, turning to their own affairs, but God wanted them to see that a place of worship must be provided for the good of the nation. The complaint that the new temple would not be as glorious as the old is quieted by God's promise that he will fill it with his glory (Hag. 2:7).

ZECHARIAH

Author: Zechariah

Date: Beginning in 520 B.C.

Content: Zechariah was a contemporary of Haggai and was sent by God to the restored community to encourage the people to serve God without fear. The book begins with a series of eight visions that depict in highly graphic language the power of God, the control of God over the affairs of men, the importance of spiritual strength, the judgment of God on sin, and the promise of things to come. These visions are followed by a series of undated messages that contain general exhortation and judgment to come. The most important part of this material is the prophecies concerning the coming of Christ.

Theme: The provision of God, who is the Lord of all, for all the needs of his people is the central point of the book. God gives his people protection, prosperity, strength, and grace. Their greatest need, the need to know God better, will be met by the sending of the Messiah, the Lord Jesus Christ.

MALACHI

Author: Malachi

Date: 450–425 B.C.

Content: Malachi was sent as a prophet to the restored community at a time when the spiritual zeal of the people was at a dangerously low ebb. Nehemiah and Ezra had begun some necessary ritual and political reforms, and Malachi was directing the people to give serious attention to their spiritual problems. The basic problems that Malachi discusses concern the corruption of the priests, the neglect of God's Temple, and personal sins at home. He ends his book with a prophecy concerning the coming Messiah and his forerunner, John the Baptist (called Elijah here). Thus the Old Testament ends looking toward what God would do in the New Testament.

Theme: The people have not learned the lesson of the exile. They had been sent into captivity because of their sins and now they were doing the same things all over again. Divorce was common, the people were selfish and insincere, the temple was being neglected, and a general spiritual decline was to be noted everywhere. Malachi blames the religious leaders because they, of all people, should have known what God required. Malachi finds hope in the future coming of the Messiah who will make all things right because he comes with the power of God.

MATTHEW

Author:	Matthew
Place:	Perhaps Antioch
Date:	A.D. 60–70
Content:	Matthew was a tax-collector, called by Jesus to follow him early in his public ministry; hence, he was an eyewitness of most of the events he describes. He begins with a detailed account of Jesus' birth of the virgin Mary, his baptism and temptation in the wilderness. Jesus came preaching the kingdom of God, entrance into which meant eternal life. One entered by repentance and faith. Matthew blocks the teaching of Jesus together into five discourses in which may be seen the ethics, the proclamation, the parables, the fellowship, and the consummation of the kingdom. Jesus' death and resurrection end the Gospel with the command to go into all the world with the good news (gospel) of Jesus Christ.
Theme:	Matthew's main purpose in writing his Gospel is to show that Jesus fulfills the promise of God in the Old Testament. For this reason Jesus is introduced as "a descendant of King David and of Abraham" (Matt. 1:1), and Matthew makes use of numerous Old Testament prophecies and quotations to explain Jesus' life. Jesus came to be the Savior of the Jews (Matt. 1:21), the Gentiles (Matt. 4:13–16), and ultimately the world (Matt. 28:19). The ethics required by members of God's kingdom are found in the Sermon on the Mount (Matt. 5–7) where the world's values are rejected and the Kingdom of God and his righteousness become supreme (Matt. 6:33).

MARK

Author:	Mark
Place:	Rome
Date:	A.D. 60–65
Content:	John Mark was a companion of the apostle Paul. He finally settled in Rome where he wrote down the remembrances of the apostle Peter. Thus Mark's Gospel reflects the words of an eyewitness of the events he describes. Mark's purpose was to put together an expanded Gospel message. Hence it centers upon the acts of Jesus rather than his words and devotes a disproportionately large amount of material to the last week of Jesus' life. Mark's Gospel begins with Jesus' public ministry and preaching of the gospel of the Kingdom of God. Several explicit predictions of his coming death are made (Mark 8:31; 9:31; 10:33-34, 45) and then Jesus goes to the cross to die for the sins of the world.

Mark depicts Jesus as the Servant of God who came to do God's will. The miracles, healings, victory over demons, and personal power show the world that Jesus was no ordinary servant, but was truly the Son of God (Mark 15:39). Jesus' resurrection authenticated all that he did, and now we await his return in glory from heaven. Mark also wrote to encourage the Roman Christians in a time of persecution.

LUKE

Author: Luke

Place: Perhaps Caesarea

Date: A.D. 60–65

Content: Luke was a physician and a traveling companion of the Apostle Paul. He wrote his Gospel for a cultured Greek named Theophilus (Luke 1:3) in order to show the true humanity of Jesus and his place in history. For this reason Luke was careful to examine all the evidence very carefully and give precise dates for the events that took place. He begins with an account of Jesus' virgin birth, giving many details not found elsewhere. Jesus' Galilean ministry is described, followed by a lengthy account of Jesus' trip to Jerusalem. After Jesus' death and resurrection, the disciples are left rejoicing, waiting for the promised power of God from heaven to fill them.

Theme: Whereas Matthew shows Jesus to be the Jewish Messiah and Mark shows Jesus as the servant of God, Luke depicts Jesus as the perfect God-man whose genealogy may be traced back to Adam (Luke 3:23-38). Jesus is the greatest man in history and is placed within the flow of world events by Luke. He is the greatest man because of what he taught, what he did, why he died—and because he rose again from the dead. For this reason we ought to accept him as our Lord.

JOHN

Author: John

Place: Ephesus

Date: A.D. 85–95

Content: The Gospel of John was written many years after Jesus' death and resurrection by the apostle John so that those who read it might believe in Christ and thus have life through his name (John 20:31). John begins with a prologue unique to this Gospel where Jesus' preexistent life with the Father is depicted to show that Jesus was not simply a great man, but God. Miracles of Jesus as well as many of Jesus' teachings not found elsewhere are then described. A long section (John 14–17) describes Jesus' teaching to his apostles before his death. After Jesus' death and resurrection, special place is given to Jesus' appearances to his apostles.

Theme: The Gospel of John more than any other Gospel stresses the deity of Christ and provides us with an interpretation of his life. He is explained in figurative terms as light, truth, love, good shepherd, the door, the resurrection and the life, living water, true bread, and more. The beautiful material found in John 14–17 shows the deep love of Jesus for the believer and the peace that comes from faith in Christ.

ACTS

Author: Luke

Place: Uncertain

Date: A.D. 65–70

Content: The book of Acts is a continuation of the Gospel of Luke where Luke intends to show that what Jesus began on earth, he continues to do in the life of the church. The book begins with the apostles being filled with the power of God and preaching to great effect, three thousand being saved in one day (Acts 2:41). The life of the church in Jerusalem, the spread of the gospel to Samaria, the activities of the apostle Peter, and the persecution of the early Christians is then described. The focus then shifts to the apostle Paul and his missionary activity in Gentile territory. His three missionary journeys are treated in some detail, ending with Paul's trip to Rome where the book ends. Some scholars suggest that Luke intended to write a third volume that would have described Paul's release, further travels, arrest, and death.

Theme: Acts was written to show the spread of the gospel from Jewish to Gentile territory (Acts 1:8). The good news that Jesus died and rose again could not be confined to one corner of the world, but was intended by God for all. To that end God empowered his people so that they could accomplish their task. The Holy Spirit is that empowering agent. The sovereign control of God over all things is seen in the triumph of the gospel over paganism and persecution; and although it may cost many their very lives (even Peter and Paul, whose lives are described in Acts), ultimate victory is assured through Jesus our Lord.

ROMANS

Author:	Paul the apostle
Place:	Corinth
Date:	A.D. 57 or 58
Content:	Paul was in Corinth on his third missionary journey and was planning to go to Rome, but had never been there before. This letter was written to introduce himself to the church and to summarize his theological teachings. For the latter reason, it is the most systematically organized letter of Paul. He begins by showing the universal sin of man. Neither Gentile nor Jew has any legitimate claim upon God because sin has invalidated any appeal. But God in his mercy stepped in, while we were still sinners, and opened the way back to himself (Rom. 5:8). From this may come a victorious Christian life. Paul the deals with the place of the Jews in God's plan (Rom. 9–11), concluding with a series of ethical exhortations.
Theme:	The righteousness of God, his righteous dealings with the world, and the righteous plan of salvation are the focus of this book. God is seen to be the great and holy God of the universe who cannot relax his laws because they are based upon his nature. But consistent with those laws, he devised a plan of salvation for Jew and Gentile alike that sent his Son down from heaven to die for the sins of the world. Now anyone who trusts in Jesus will be saved (Rom. 10:9) and be given the power of God over sin in his life. From God and his love nothing can separate the believer (Rom. 8:38-39).

1 CORINTHIANS

Author:	Paul the apostle
Place:	Ephesus
Date:	A.D. 55
Content:	Paul had established a church in the Greek city of Corinth on his second missionary journey (Acts 18:1–8), but things had gone very badly after his departure. He felt it necessary to write them concerning the many problems that had arisen. They were challenging his apostleship, abusing the Lord's Supper, wondering about eating meat sacrificed to idols, going to court against one another, condoning immorality, denying the resurrection, arguing about marriage—to name a few of the problems. Paul felt that he had to deal with the situation, lest everything in Corinth fall to pieces. As Paul more or less systematically goes through these problems, he touches upon many of the fundamental teachings of the faith.

Theme: Paul's major purpose in writing this letter was to correct some glaring abuses in the church at Corinth, showing the importance of how we live. It is not enough to say that we are Christians, we must also act like Christians. Not to do so is to bring dishonor upon the name of Christ. Paul also stresses the all-sufficiency of Christ for the believer. In Christ we are made pure, holy, and acceptable to God (1 Cor. 1:30).

2 CORINTHIANS

Author: Paul the apostle
Place: Ephesus
Date: A.D. 57
Content: Paul's earlier letter to the Corinthians had not settled all of the problems. It had some good effect upon them but much more remained to be done. In particular, Paul had to settle the problem concerning his own authority. Deep suspicions had been aroused concerning him, for what reasons we do not fully understand, but in great anguish Paul writes to reestablish his own apostolic authority. He also attempts to deal with some more practical matters, like supporting the poor believers elsewhere.
Theme: Triumph over adversity is seen throughout this letter. It is a very personal one, written by one who loved his people but had been deeply wronged by them. As Paul catalogs the experiences of his life and the nature of the Christian ministry, it is possible to see the grace of God at work, bringing good from evil. Satan is active, seeking to destroy God's work, but God is greater still, establishing those who trust in him.

GALATIANS

Author: Paul the apostle
Place: Unknown
Date: A.D. 48 or 49
Content: Paul had preached to the inhabitants of Galatia on his first missionary journey (Acts 13:14–14:23). Shortly after his departure, a group of Jewish believers arrived to insist that the Gentile Christians submit to the laws of Moses in order to be saved. Paul writes to combat this error by showing that Abraham, who lived over four hundred years before the giving of the law, was saved by faith in the gospel— so how could it be argued that the law could either save a man or make a believer in Christ more perfect? Paul couples this with a

vigorous defense of himself as an apostle and with a discussion of how a Christian ought to live.

Theme: Paul energetically defends the truth of the gospel, which is that man is saved by the grace of God through faith in Christ and nothing else. Any other teaching is a perversion of the truth of God (Gal. 1:7). We are made right in the sight of God by faith (Gal. 2:16) and become the people of God (sons of Abraham) in the same way, by faith (Gal. 3:7). Because we are free in Christ, we must never allow anyone to drag us back to the idea of working for our salvation, but must live out of the gospel. This involves submission to the Spirit of God (Gal. 5:16) and loving our neighbor as ourselves (Gal. 5:14).

EPHESIANS

Author: Paul the apostle
Place: Rome
Date: A.D. 60 or 61
Content: Paul wrote this letter while a prisoner in Rome, his purpose being to comfort and encourage the believers in Asia Minor. He presents them with an overview of history, beginning in eternity past where God worked out his plans for the world, moving to the present where God is saving those who believe in Christ, and then to the future where all evil will be overcome. He points out that in the present there will be great conflict because our battle is with the forces of evil (Eph. 6:12), but because we are members of Christ's body, we have the power to withstand. Paul then deals with practical matters relating to living the Christian life: marriage, behavior, parents and children, and servants.

Theme: The basic idea in Ephesians is that God's eternal plan is being worked out through Christ and his body, the church. When a man believes, he is in Christ and finds salvation and safety. God had planned for this from all eternity and has given to the believer everything that he needs for his Christian life, but it is for him to avail himself of the resources at his command. Paul closes the book by describing the provision that God has made for the believer so that he may withstand the worst of Satan's attacks and when the battle is over, to be victorious.

PHILIPPIANS

Author: Paul the apostle
Place: Rome
Date: A.D. 61
Content: Paul wrote this letter from prison in Rome to some very dear friends in Philippi as a response to their sending some money to him in order to meet his needs. He begins by expressing his confidence in them and then describes some of the problems he faces in Rome. Whether he will die or not he does not know, but if death does come, he will rejoice in the presence of Christ. If he remains, he will continue to serve God by serving the churches. The example of Christ's humility is set before the Philippians as an example to follow. False teachings are to be vigorously rejected. Two quarreling sisters are admonished to make up and all believers are admonished to set high ideals for themselves because God will supply all that one needs in life.
Theme: In this very personal letter of Paul the theme of rejoicing may be seen throughout. If one lives, he may rejoice because God loves him, Christ died for him, and all things are given to him by God for his life. If one dies, then he may rejoice by being in Christ's presence for evermore. This does not mean that Christians will have no problems, however. Even as Jesus had to endure the cross, so we must be ready to follow that example of submission to God, if it must be. But we are citizens of heaven (Phil. 3:20) and should live with that thought constantly before us.

COLOSSIANS

Author: Paul the apostle
Place: Rome
Date: A.D. 60 or 61
Content: Paul wrote this letter while a prisoner in Rome to a city he had never visited. He had come to know of these believers while living in Ephesus on his second missionary journey, and now he was concerned because he had heard of some strange pagan theories that were creeping into the church. The views that were troubling the Colossians were a mixture of astrology, magic, and Judaism, which downgraded Christ to being just some sort of angel. Paul wrote to correct this error by showing that Christ is none other than God and possesses the fullness of the eternal God (Col. 2:9). Instructions follow concerning Christian living.

Theme: In this important letter of Paul we are presented with a carefully worked-out defense of Christ's deity and glory. He is all in all and the believer has everything he needs in Christ. Paul warns that believers ought not to be led astray by the foolishness and false wisdom of men (Col. 2:8). Instructions for Christian living stress the power of God for men and the joy that believers may have by making use of all the resources that are theirs in Christ.

1 THESSALONIANS

Author: Paul the apostle
Place: Corinth
Date: A.D. 50 or 51
Content: On Paul's second missionary journey he visited Thessalonica but was forced to flee because of the intense persecution that arose there (Acts 17:1-9). After making his way to Athens and finally to Corinth, Paul heard from Timothy, whom he had sent to inquire about the Thessalonians, that they were standing fast in spite of their suffering. Paul wrote this letter to comfort and encourage the young believers in the Lord. He also wrote to confirm their faith in the basic doctrines of the church concerning God, the Holy Spirit, Christ, Christian living, but especially concerning Christ's second coming. Apparently because some believers had died, the remaining Christians were concerned lest the believing dead miss out on the resurrection. Paul writes to assure them that the dead in Christ rise first (1 Thess. 4:16).
Theme: Paul comforts the persecuted believers with the assurance that God is with us and has assured us of ultimate victory. The final victory will occur at Christ's return, when the Lord himself shall descend from heaven and gather us to himself, ever to be with him (1 Thess. 4:17). In the light of this we should bear up under persecution, living lives that are godly and above reproach.

2 THESSALONIANS

Author: Paul the apostle
Place: Corinth
Date: A.D. 51
Content: Either Paul's first letter or a forged letter purporting to be from him had disturbed the Thessalonians concerning the second coming of Christ. Perhaps adding to the confusion was the continued persecution that they were enduring. Paul writes to assure the believers that Christ will certainly return to comfort the believers and to punish

those who are troubling them (2 Thess. 1:7-8). He also tells them that the great day of judgment (the day of the Lord) will not take them by surprise but will be preceded by a series of events (2 Thess. 2:3). In the light of Christ's sure return, Christians are to live above reproach.

Theme: Throughout this short letter the promise of God's victory over evil is stressed. Believers may suffer now, but God has planned comfort and reward for them. For those who refuse to obey God, however, there will be distress and judgment. Paul also stresses the need for living in such a way that God is honored. Some people at Thessalonica may have stopped working because they believed Christ would return soon. This does not honor God and Paul says concerning it, "He who does not work shall not eat" (2 Thess. 3:10).

1 TIMOTHY

Author: Paul the apostle
Place: Uncertain
Date: A.D. 64
Content: This letter was written by Paul near the end of his life and he addressed it to his associate Timothy, whom he had left in Ephesus to correct some problems in the church. By this time problems had arisen concerning doctrine, church practice, church government, and various aspects of Christian living. Paul wrote to instruct Timothy concerning these matters so that the church would function properly. He also wrote to encourage Timothy so that he would not become weary in his Christian life, but would live wholly to the glory of God. There are some specific regulations given for the ordination of church officers as well.

Theme: The importance of right belief and right behavior form the theme of this book. Paul stresses that we must know the truth and defend it against the false doctrines that arise. We must also be very careful to live lives that are consistent with that doctrine so that Satan will not get an advantage over the people of God. The importance of dedicated and pure-hearted men to lead the church is also stressed.

2 TIMOTHY

Author: Paul the apostle
Place: Probably Rome
Date: A.D. 66 or 67
Content: This letter was probably the last letter that Paul ever wrote, and he addressed it to his former associate Timothy. It is a personal letter

that expresses Paul's deepest feelings and the assurance that though his earthly life might end, God had eternal life waiting for him in heaven (2 Tim. 1:10–12). Paul also reflects upon the faithfulness of God (who led him throughout his entire life) and upon the coming desperate days when men would depart from the truth, refusing to acknowledge God as Lord. He exhorts Timothy to stand firm in the face of the coming persecutions.

Theme: The sovereign control of God over all things is the basic theme of this book. Although distress has come and will continue to increase, God is in control and those who trust him will have nothing to fear. Paul also adds his own testimony of faith, describing how he fought for the truth and will be rewarded by God in the end (2 Tim. 4:6-8).

TITUS

Author: Paul the apostle
Place: Uncertain
Date: A.D. 64 or 65
Content: Paul addressed this letter to an earlier associate of his whom he had left on the island of Crete to help strengthen the churches there. Titus' task was to ordain elders and to instruct the believers in the basic doctrines of the faith. It was necessary for Paul to go into some detail regarding the qualifications for the office of elder, and to give instructions for others in the church as well. During the course of these instructions, Paul touches upon the problems that face the servant of God and how these problems may be met.
Theme: The need for proper Christian living in the midst of the evil of the world is stressed by Paul in this letter. Around us we see the hostility and corruption of the world, but we must show by our lives what the grace of God can do. Such a life will have an impact, whereas mere words will do little or nothing.

PHILEMON

Author: Paul the apostle
Place: Rome
Date: A.D. 60 or 61
Content: A slave named Onesimus, who was owned by a Christian in Colosse named Philemon, had run away, ultimately making his way to Rome. Here he heard the gospel from Paul and became a believer. This letter was written by Paul to encourage Philemon to take Onesimus back, this time as more than a servant, indeed, as a Christian brother. There is a play on words in verse 11 where Paul says that now

Onesimus (the word means "useful") will in fact *be* Onesimus—useful both to Philemon and the ministry.

Theme: This short book is quite important in many ways. Two things stand out. First, we see the way in which the gospel worked. No one, not even a runaway slave, is beyond the reach of God. If anyone will trust in Christ, he will become a new person. Second, the ancient barriers of class hatred are being broken down by the gospel—Philemon and Onesimus are now Christian brothers.

HEBREWS

Author: Uncertain
Place: Uncertain
Date: A.D. 60–69
Content: This important letter was written to Jewish Christians who were perhaps thinking of returning to their old ways in Judaism. It was designed to show that now because Christ has come, there remains nothing in Judaism for the believer. The time of fulfillment has arrived and it would be futile to return to the old life which was inherently inferior to the new life found in the gospel. This is justified by showing that in every way Christ is better—he is superior to angels, to Moses, and to the Old Testament priest. He mediates a better covenant and offers a better sacrifice. The life of faith that the Christian lives is also better than the old life, proof of this coming from the lives of Old Testament saints who showed the way by their lives of faith.

Theme: The overall superiority of Christ and the Christian life is the central theme of this book. Other religious systems have value, no doubt, but they cannot compare with the work that God has done in Christ. Not even Judaism, which has the Old Testament, can compare, great as it was. Christ is the very essence of God, who did God's work on earth by dying for our sins. What God requires of us now is trust in him. If we have faith we have entered into the promises of God—fullness of life now and eternal life to come.

JAMES

Author: James, a brother of Jesus
Place: Uncertain
Date: A.D. 45–49
Content: The book of James was written to Jewish Christians in order to provide them with some practical instructions in the Christian life. It contains many short proverbial sayings and reflects in a remarkable

way the teachings of Jesus and the Sermon on the Mount. The problems addressed show the kinds of difficulties that were troubling the church. We read of pride, discrimination, greed, lust, hypocrisy, worldliness, and backbiting. James writes to correct these evils by showing that faith without works is dead (James 2:26); that is, mere profession of faith is not enough. True faith will issue forth in a good life as surely as a good tree bears good fruit and not thistles.

Theme: James stresses the need for Christian living both to show the reality of one's inner faith and to show the world that the gospel does in fact change lives. If a person says he is a Christian but is no different than when he was an unbeliever, what benefit has there been either for him or for the needy world? But in fact the gospel does change lives and if we will commit ourselves to Christ, we will find that from our living faith will flow living deeds of love and kindness.

1 PETER

Author: Peter the apostle
Place: Uncertain, perhaps Rome
Date: A.D. 63 or 64
Content: The apostle Peter wrote this letter near the end of his life to comfort and encourage the Jewish Christians who were living in Asia Minor. He points out that suffering is part of the Christian life and that God has an imperishable reward reserved for those who trust him. In case any were thinking of returning to Judaism to escape from persecution, Peter points out that the church is now the chosen nation and the priesthood of God (1 Pet. 2:9). Hence any thoughts of returning to Judaism were futile. Peter then presents the example of Christ who suffered and admonished the believers to be prepared for the same experience.

Theme: The theme of 1 Peter is triumph through suffering. Early Christians lived difficult lives, often paying for their faith with their lives, but this letter shows us that it is worth it, no matter what the price. God knows all that is occurring and in his eternal plan will work everything out for the best.

2 PETER

Author: Peter the apostle
Place: Uncertain, perhaps Rome
Date: A.D. 67
Content: This letter was written by Peter shortly before his death and deals with the problems that the church would face after his departure. He encourages the believers to continue in their spiritual growth, realizing the truth of the Christian gospel. It does not consist of fable but fact. He warns them of false teachers who would destroy the truth by exalting their own ideas over those of the church. Finally, he points out that Christ will return some day to destroy the old order of this world; as a result, we ought not to become too attached to it.
Theme: Second Peter is a call to steadfastness in the midst of numerous pressures to drift from the truth. The world is seeking to undo the work of God, but we must resist all such pressure by living godly lives, believing the truth, enduring persecution, trusting God, and looking for Christ's return.

1 JOHN

Author: John the apostle
Place: Uncertain, probably Ephesus
Date: A.D. 85–95
Content: This very personal letter was written by the apostle John in his old age to believers who were very dear to him. He addresses them as his little children and gives them practical instructions for Christian living. He begins by stressing Jesus' incarnation and builds his commands upon the truth that those who know Jesus know the Father as well. Those who do not know Jesus do not know the Father, nor do they know the love of the Father. Christians, however, have experienced the love of God in their lives, for God is love, and have no need to fear either in this life or in the life to come.
Theme: John stresses the basic truths of the Christian faith in this letter in order to comfort and encourage his children in the faith. The themes of love, forgiveness, fellowship, victory over sin, assurance, purity, and eternal life are woven together in a marvelous document that shines with the light of God in the darkness of the world.

2 JOHN

Author: John the apostle
Place: Uncertain, probably Ephesus
Date: A.D. 85–95
Content: This short letter was written either to a Christian woman whom John knew or to a church personified as a woman. In any case, it was written to encourage true Christian love and to warn against the deceivers who were coming into the world. John charges the believers not to participate in their evil, but to stand for the truth no matter what the cost.
Theme: The need for Christians to be alert and diligent when it comes to false doctrine is the theme of this letter. We must be aware that false doctrine exists and we must be ready to deal with it, if confronted. All the while, however, we must live out the love of God in our lives.

3 JOHN

Author: John the apostle
Place: Uncertain, probably Ephesus
Date: A.D. 85–95
Content: This short letter is a personal note from John the apostle to his friend Gaius, encouraging him to support the traveling evangelists who are preaching the truth. He warns Gaius against such men as Diotrephes who refuse to help in spreading the gospel and commends others, such as Demetrius, for helping.
Theme: Christians are to support one another in the work of Christ. Not to do so is to do the work of Satan, who seeks to destroy the believers. John stresses that all believers are bound together as Christians and should work for the common good of all.

JUDE

Author: Jude, a brother of Jesus
Place: Uncertain
Date: A.D. 65–70
Content: It is not known to whom this letter was addressed, but the problem that Jude confronts is very clear. Jude is urging the believers to stand firm against some false teachers and the false doctrine that they bring. In a lengthy passage Jude gives examples of judgment in the past that God visited upon sin, as well as a devastating description of the evil lives of those false teachers. Jude closes with an

exhortation to the Christians to stand fast in the power of God who will keep us from falling.

Theme: The danger of false doctrine and the need for constant vigilance by the church is the theme of this book. Jude admonishes us to examine what people say and the kind of lives that they live so that we may approve what is pleasing in the sight of God. We may call upon God to help us in this with full assurance that he will hear and answer our prayer.

REVELATION

Author: John the apostle
Place: Patmos
Date: A.D. 90–95
Content: There are two major sections in this complex book, the first being letters to seven churches in Asia Minor (Rev. 1–3) and the second being a series of visions dealing with the life and persecutions of the people of God, the overthrow of evil, the return of Christ, the last judgment, the millennial state, and heaven (Rev. 4–22). The major portion of the visions deals with a series of devastations poured out on the earth (the seals, trumpets, and bowls), in which the wrath of the Lamb (Jesus) is displayed. Mingled in with these visions are visions of the martyred people of God in heaven and the persecuted saints upon earth. The visions surge forward to a final confrontation between the Prostitute of Babylon and the triumphant Word of God, who is King of kings and Lord of lords (Rev. 19:16), come to destroy evil and prepare a feast for the believers. There follow scenes of judgment and glory, with a closing prayer: "Amen! Come, Lord Jesus" (Rev. 22:20).

Theme: This glorious book shows the once humiliated Jesus, the Lamb of God slain for the sins of the world, taking control of history at the time of the end and bringing eternal good to pass by destroying evil and establishing righteousness forever and ever. It is the Christian's certain hope that someday all will be well and God shall be all in all. Tears shall be wiped away and death, sorrow, crying, and pain shall be gone forever (Rev. 21:4). This comforting message is for all believers of all time.

JANUARY 1

Genesis 1:1–2:25; Matthew 1:1–2:12; Psalms 1:1-6; Proverbs 1:1-6

GENESIS 1:3–2:27
How long did it take God to create the world?

There are two basic views about the days of creation: (1) each day was a literal 24-hour period; (2) each day represents an indefinite period of time (even millions of years). In response to the claim of scientists that the earth is millions or billions of years old, some Christians say there is a gap between Genesis 1:1 and 1:2. In this view the first creation was wrecked by Satan's fall; the six days were really a re-creation.

GENESIS 2:9, 16-17
Were the tree of life and the tree of the knowledge of good and evil real trees?

Two views are often expressed: (1) The trees were real, but symbolic. Eating from the tree of life was a symbol of receiving eternal life from God. (2) The trees were real, possessing special properties. By eating the fruit from the tree of life, Adam and Eve could have had eternal life, enjoying a permanent relationship as God's children. Interestingly, the tree of life again appears in a description in Revelation 22 of people enjoying eternal life with God.

MATTHEW 1:18
Why is the virgin birth important to the Christian faith?

Jesus Christ, God's Son, had to be free from the sinful nature passed on to all other human beings by Adam. Because Jesus was born of a woman, he was a human being; but as the Son of God, Jesus was born without any trace of human sin. The sinless Savior lived a sinless life and died on the cross for the sins of the world.

MATTHEW 1:20
Why did an angel come to Joseph?

The conception and birth of Jesus Christ were supernatural events beyond human logic or reasoning. Because of this, God sent angels to help certain people understand the significance of what was happening (see Matt. 2:13, 19; Luke 1:11, 26; 2:9). Angels are spiritual beings created by God who help carry out his work on earth. They bring God's messages to people (Luke 1:26), protect God's people (Dan. 6:22), offer encouragement (Gen. 16:7ff.), give guidance (Exodus 14:19), carry out punishment (2 Samuel 24:16), patrol the earth (Zech. 1:9-14), and fight the forces of evil (2 Kings 6:16-18; Rev. 20:1-2). There are both good and bad angels (Rev. 12:7), but because bad angels are allied with the devil, or Satan, they have considerably less power and authority than good angels.

JANUARY 2

Genesis 3:1–4:26; Matthew 2:13–3:6; Psalms 2:1-12; Proverbs 1:7-9

 **GENESIS 3:14-19**
What was the result of the serpent's temptation of Adam and Eve?

After the fall God changed the life of Adam and Eve and their descendants in the following ways: (1) The serpent was cursed for his evil work; (2) the Redeemer was promised for the salvation of humanity; (3) women were promised multiplied pain in childbirth and were placed in subjection to their husbands; (4) the ground was cursed to produce thorns and thistles; (5) men were to eke out a living by the sweat of their brow; (6) physical death was to be the lot of all humanity.

 **GENESIS 4:14-17**
The Bible has recorded only four people so far: Adam, Eve, Cain, and Abel. Why was Cain worried about being killed by others, and where did he get his wife?

Adam and Eve had numerous children; they had been told to "fill the earth" (Gen. 1:28). Cain's guilt and fear over killing his brother were heavy, and he probably feared repercussions from his family. If he was capable of killing, so were they. The wife Cain chose may have been one of his sisters or a niece. The human race was still genetically pure, and there was no fear of side-effects from marrying relatives.

MATTHEW 2:14-15
Why did Joseph choose to go to Egypt?

Going to Egypt was not unusual because there were colonies of Jews in several major Egyptian cities. These colonies had developed during the time of the great captivity (see Jer. 43–44). There is an interesting parallel between this flight to Egypt and Israel's history. As an infant nation, Israel went to Egypt, just as Jesus did as a child. God led Israel out (Hos. 11:1); God brought Jesus back. Both events show God working to save his people.

MATTHEW 2:16
Why did Herod kill all the children in Bethlehem?

Herod, the king of the Jews, killed all the boys under two years of age in an obsessive attempt to kill Jesus, the newborn King. He stained his hands with blood, but he did not harm Jesus. Herod was king by a human appointment; Jesus was King by a divine appointment.

JANUARY 3

Genesis 5:1–7:24; Matthew 3:7–4:11; Psalms 3:1-8; Proverbs 1:10-19

Q GENESIS 5:25-27
How did these people live so long?

Some believe that the ages listed here were lengths of family dynasties rather than ages of individual men. Those who think these were actual ages offer three explanations: (1) the human race was more genetically pure in this early time period, so there was less disease to shorten life spans; (2) no rain had yet fallen on the earth, and the expanse of water "above" (Gen. 1:7) kept out harmful cosmic rays and shielded people from environmental factors that hasten aging; (3) God gave people longer lives so they would have time to "fill the earth" (Gen. 1:28).

Q GENESIS 7:17-24
Was the flood a local event, or did it cover the entire earth?

A universal flood was certainly possible. There is enough water on the earth to cover all dry land (the earth began that way; see Gen. 1:9-10). Afterward, God promised never again to destroy the earth with a flood. Thus this flood must have either covered the entire earth or destroyed all the inhabitants of the earth. God's reason for sending the flood was to destroy all the earth's wickedness. It would have taken a major flood to accomplish this.

Q MATTHEW 3:16-17
What is the doctrine of the Trinity?

The doctrine of the Trinity means that God is three persons and yet one in essence. In this passage, all three persons of the Trinity are present and active. God the Father speaks; God the Son is baptized; God the Holy Spirit descends on Jesus. God is one, yet in three persons at the same time. This is one of God's incomprehensible mysteries. Other Bible references that speak of the Father, Son, and Holy Spirit are Matthew 28:19; John 15:26; 1 Corinthians 12:4-13; 2 Corinthians 13:14; Ephesians 2:18; 1 Thessalonians 1:2-5; and 1 Peter 1:2.

Q MATTHEW 4:8-9
Did the devil have the power to give Jesus the kingdoms of the world, or did God, the creator of the world, have control over these kingdoms?

The devil may have been lying about his implied power, or he may have based his offer on his temporary control and free reign over the earth because of humanity's sinfulness. Jesus' temptation was to take the world as a political ruler right then, without carrying out his plan to save the world from sin. Satan was trying to distort Jesus' perspective by making him focus on worldly power and not on God's plans.

JANUARY 4

Genesis 8:1–10:32; Matthew 4:12-25; Psalms 4:1-8; Proverbs 1:20-23

GENESIS 9:1-17
Did God change his relationship with humanity after the flood?

Following the flood, God made a covenant with Noah. According to Genesis, the agreement specified that: (1) there would always be the seasons of the year with planting and harvest (8:22); (2) Noah and his family would replenish the earth (9:1); (3) law and government were to be reinstituted (9:1-6); (4) meat, except for the blood, and vegetables were to be given to humanity for food (9:3-4); and (5) there would never again be a universal flood (9:15).

GENESIS 9:25
Does Genesis 9:25 support racial prejudice and slavery?

Noah's curse wasn't directed toward any particular race, but rather at the Canaanite nation—a nation God knew would become wicked. The curse was fulfilled when the Israelites entered the promised land and drove the Canaanites out (see Joshua).

GENESIS 10:8-9
Who was Nimrod?

Not much is known about him except that he was a warrior, mighty hunter, and hero, the son of Cush. Although he was called "blessed of God," he is also considered by some to be the founder of the great, godless Babylonian Empire (Gen. 10:11-12). This was the land adjacent to Assyria later called "the land of Nimrod" (Mic. 5:6).

MATTHEW 4:17
What is the difference between the "Kingdom of Heaven" and the "Kingdom of God"?

The "Kingdom of Heaven in Matthew has the same meaning as the "Kingdom of God" in Mark and Luke. Matthew uses this phrase because he was writing to the Jews, and they, out of their intense reverence and respect, did not pronounce God's name. Since heaven is God's dwelling place, the word "heaven" is a circumlocution for "God."

MATTHEW 4:23
Why did Jesus teach in the synagogues?

Most towns that had ten or more Jewish families had a synagogue. The building served as a religious gathering place and as a school. It was customary for the leader of a synagogue to invite visiting rabbis like Jesus to speak.

JANUARY 5

Genesis 11:1–13:4; Matthew 5:1-26; Psalms 5:1-12; Proverbs 1:24-28

GENESIS 11:3-4
What was this tower?

The tower of Babel was most likely a ziggurat, a common structure in Babylonia at this time. Most often built as temples, ziggurats looked like pyramids with steps or ramps leading up the sides. Ziggurats stood as high as three hundred feet and were often just as wide; thus they were the focal point of the city.

GENESIS 12:11-13
Why did Abram want to deceive the Egyptians?

Abram was acting out of fear when he asked Sarai to tell a half-truth and say she was his sister. She *was* his half sister, but she was also his wife (see Gen. 20:12). Abram's intent was to deceive the Egyptians. He feared that if they knew the truth, they would kill him to get Sarai. She would have been a desirable addition to Pharaoh's harem because of her wealth, beauty, and potential for political alliance. As Sarai's brother, Abram would have been given a place of honor. As her husband, however, his life would be in danger, because Sarai could not enter Pharaoh's harem unless Abram was dead. So Abram told only half the truth and lost faith in God's protection, even after all God had promised him.

MATTHEW 5:17-20
If Jesus did not come to abolish the law, does the Old Testament law still apply to us today?

In the Old Testament, there were three categories of law: ceremonial, civil, and moral. (1) The *ceremonial law* related specifically to Israel's worship (see Lev. 1:2-3). Its primary purpose was to point forward to Jesus Christ; these laws, therefore, were no longer necessary after Jesus' death and resurrection. While we are no longer bound by ceremonial laws, the principles behind them—to worship and love a holy God—still apply. (2) The "civil law" applied to daily living in Israel (see Deut. 24:10-11). Because modern society and culture are so radically different from that time and setting, all of these guidelines cannot be followed specifically. But the principles behind the commands are timeless and should guide our conduct. (3) The *moral law* (such as the Ten Commandments) is the direct command of God, and it requires strict obedience (see Exod. 20:13, for example). The moral law reveals the nature and will of God, and it still applies today.

JANUARY 6

Genesis 13:5–15:21; Matthew 5:27-48; Psalms 6:1-10; Proverbs 1:29-33

GENESIS 14:18
Who was Melchizedek?

He was obviously a God-fearing man, for his name means "king of righteous-ness," and king of Salem means "king of peace." He was a "priest of God Most High" (Heb. 7:1-2). He recognized God as Creator of heaven and earth. What else is known about him? Four main theories have been suggested. (1) Melchizedek was a respected king of that region. Abram was simply showing him the respect he deserved. (2) The name Melchizedek may have been a standing title for all the kings of Salem. (3) Melchizedek was a type of Christ (Heb. 7:3). A type is an Old Testament event or teaching that is so closely related to what Christ did that it illustrates a lesson about Christ. (4) Melchizedek was the appearance on earth of the preincarnate Christ in a temporary bodily form.

MATTHEW 5:27-28
Did Jesus teach that we should not be interested in the opposite sex?

The Old Testament law said that it is wrong for a person to have sex with someone other than his or her spouse (Exodus 20:14). But Jesus said that the "desire" to have sex with someone other than your spouse is mental adultery and thus sin. Jesus emphasized that if the "act" is wrong, then so is the "intention." To be faithful to your spouse with your body but not your mind is to break the trust so vital to a strong marriage. Jesus is not condemning natural interest in the opposite sex or even healthy sexual desire, but the deliberate and repeated filling of one's mind with fantasies that would be evil if acted out.

MATTHEW 5:29-30
Did Jesus teach that people should disfigure themselves?

When Jesus said to get rid of your hand or your eye, he was speaking figura-tively. He didn't mean literally to gouge out your eye, because even a blind person can lust. But if that were the only choice, it would be better to go into eternity with one eye or hand than to go to hell with two. We sometimes tolerate sins in our lives that, left unchecked, could eventually destroy us. It is better to experience the pain of removal (getting rid of a bad habit or something we treasure, for instance) than to allow the sin to bring judgment and condemna-tion.

JANUARY 7

Genesis 16:1–18:19; Matthew 6:1-24; Psalms 7:1-17; Proverbs 2:1-5

GENESIS 17:2-8
Why did God repeat his covenant to Abram?

Twice before, he had mentioned this agreement (Gen. 12 and 15). Here, however, God was bringing it into focus and preparing to carry it out. He revealed to Abram several specific parts of his covenant: (1) God would make Abram the father of a mighty nation; (2) many nations and kings would descend from him; (3) God would continue to reveal himself to Abram's descendants; (4) God would give Abram's descendants the land of Canaan.

GENESIS 17:9-10
Why did God require circumcision?

(1) As a sign of obedience to him in all matters. (2) As a sign of belonging to his covenant people. Once circumcised, there was no turning back. The man would be identified as a Jew forever. (3) As a symbol of "cutting off" the old life of sin, purifying one's heart and dedicating oneself to God. (4) Possibly as a health measure. Circumcision more than any other practice separated God's people from their pagan neighbors. In Abraham's day, this was essential to develop the pure worship of the one true God.

MATTHEW 6:2
What is a hypocrite?

The original Greek word means a play-actor. The English meaning is usually someone who deliberately claims to be what he or she is not. In the New Testament only Christ used the term applying it to scribes and Pharisees where they were blind to their own faults (Matt. 7:5), God's workings (Luke 12:56), and true values (Luke 13:15), overvaluing tradition (Matt. 15:7) and loving display (Matt. 6:2, 5, 16). The term "hypocrites," as used here, describes people who do good acts for appearances only—not out of compassion or other good motives. Their actions may be good, but their motives are hollow.

MATTHEW 6:24
What is mammon?

This word occurs only in Matthew 6:24, (KJV); Luke 16:9, 11, 13, and is a transliteration of an Aramaic word meaning wealth or profit. Jesus sees in it a self-centered covetousness which claims people's hearts and thus alienates them from God. When a person owns something, in reality it owns him. Since humanity belongs to its creator, mammon here seems to be a rival to God. Thus the servant of mammon is an idol-worshiper and wealth is the object of his worship.

JANUARY 8

Genesis 18:20–19:38; Matthew 6:25–7:14; Psalms 8:1-9; Proverbs 2:6-15

GENESIS 19:1
Where was Sodom?

Sodom, Gomorrah, Admah, Zeboiim, and Bela or Zoar (Gen. 14:2) were called the Cities of the Plain. Scholars say they were located either north of the Dead Sea, or lie buried beneath the southern tip of the Dead Sea. The cities were probably destroyed by an earthquake accompanied by an explosion of gaseous deposits.

GENESIS 19:1
Why was Lot sitting in the gate of Sodom?

The gateway of the city was the meeting place for city officials and other men to discuss current events and transact business. It was a place of authority and status where a person could see and be seen. Evidently Lot held an important position in the government or was associated with those who did, because the angels found him at the city gate. Perhaps Lot's status in Sodom was one reason he was so reluctant to leave (Gen. 19:16, 18-22).

GENESIS 19:30-38
Why doesn't the Bible openly condemn Lot's daughters for what they did?

In many cases, the Bible does not judge people for their actions. It simply reports the events. However, incest is clearly condemned in other parts of Scripture (Lev. 18:6-18; 20:11, 12, 17, 19-21; Deut. 22:30; 27:20-23; Ezek. 22:11; 1 Cor. 5:1). Perhaps the consequence of their action—Moab and Ammon became enemies of Israel—was God's way of judging their sin.

MATTHEW 7:6
What does the swine represent in Matthew 7:6?

Pigs were unclean animals according to God's law (Deut. 14:8). Anyone who touched an unclean animal became "ceremonially unclean" and could not go to the temple to worship until the uncleanness was removed. Jesus says that we should not entrust holy teachings to unholy or unclean people. It is futile to try to teach holy concepts to people who don't want to listen and will only tear apart what we say.

JANUARY 9

Genesis 20:1–22:24; Matthew 7:15-29; Psalms 9:1-12; Proverbs 2:16-22

GENESIS 21:18
What happened to Ishmael, and who are his descendants?

Ishmael became ruler of a large tribe or nation. The Ishmaelites were nomads living in the Desert of Sinai and Paran, south of Israel. One of Ishmael's daughters married Esau, Ishmael's nephew (Gen. 28:9). The Bible pictures the Ishmaelites as hostile to Israel and to God (Ps. 83:6).

GENESIS 22:7-8
Why did God ask Abraham to perform human sacrifice?

Pagan nations practiced human sacrifice, but God condemned this as a terrible sin (Lev. 20:1-5). God did not want Isaac to die, but he wanted Abraham to sacrifice Isaac in his heart so it would be clear that Abraham loved God more than he loved his promised and long-awaited son. Isaac is a type of Christ. He was an only son. His father offered him up as a sacrifice. Through Isaac came the descendants of Abraham. Abraham believed that if he offered Isaac as a sacrifice, God would raise Isaac from the dead (Heb. 11:17-19). Like Isaac, Christ was an only Son who was offered and who was raised from the dead. Through his death and resurrection came the children of God.

MATTHEW 7:15, KJV
What is a false prophet?

False prophets were common in Old Testament times. They prophesied only what the king and the people wanted to hear, claiming it was God's message. Scripture abounds with warnings against false prophets. They are called treacherous, covetous, crafty, drunken, immoral, and profane. False teachers are just as common today. Jesus says to beware of those whose words sound religious but who are motivated by money, fame, or power. You can tell who they are because in their teaching they minimize Christ and glorify themselves.

MATTHEW 7:21
What does the word "Lord" mean?

The title "Lord" (Greek *kyrios*) is applied to Jesus Christ nearly seven hundred times in the New Testament. The word *kyrios* was used as the equivalent of *Yahweh* in the ancient Greek translation of the Old Testament, the Septuagint. It is so used in the New Testament, too. Thus Jesus Christ is identified with Yahweh in the use of *kyrios* (Lord). Jesus the Christ is called *Lord* because he is Yahweh, or God.

JANUARY 10

Genesis 23:1–24:51; Matthew 8:1-17; Psalms 9:13-20; Proverbs 3:1-6

GENESIS 23:9
Why did Abraham buy a cave to bury Sarah?

In patriarchal times, successive generations were buried in cave or rock-cut family tombs: Sarah, Abraham, Isaac, Rebekah, Leah, and Jacob were all buried in this cave at Machpelah. This name is applied to the field, cave, and surrounding land bought by Abraham. The modern site at Hebron is venerated by Jews, Christians, and Muslims, but the authenticity of the cave is unconfirmed. In ancient days mourning might last seven days and included weeping, tearing clothes, and wearing sackcloth (Gen. 37:34).

GENESIS 24:10
Where is Mesopotamia?

Mesopotamia (Hebrew *Aram-naha-raim,* meaning "between the two rivers") in the time of Abraham was a fertile land covering the upper and middle Euphrates valley, modern Eastern Syria and Northern Iraq. It was also called *Paddan-aram* (Gen. 25:20; 28:2). It was the original home of Balaam (Deut. 23:4), and provided charioteers and cavalry for David (1 Chron. 19:6). The town of *Nahor* mentioned here was near Haran; its Hebrew spelling is slightly different from Nahor the brother of Abraham (Gen. 24:15).

MATTHEW 8:2-3
What is leprosy?

Leprosy was a feared disease because there was no known cure. In Jesus' day, the Greek word for *leprosy* was used for a variety of similar diseases, and some forms were contagious. If a person contracted the contagious type, a priest declared him a leper and banished him from his home and city. The leper was sent to live in a community with other lepers until he either got better or died. When this leper begged Jesus to heal him, Jesus reached out and touched him, even though his skin was covered with the dread disease. During the days immediately before his crucifixion Jesus stayed in a house belonging to Simon the leper (Matt. 26:6) who may have been one of those cured of this disease by the Lord.

MATTHEW 8:4
Why did Jesus send the healed leper to a priest?

The law required a healed leper to be examined by a priest (Lev. 14). Jesus wanted this man to give his story firsthand to the priest to prove that his leprosy was completely gone so that he could be restored to his community.

JANUARY 11

GENESIS 25:6
What happened to Abraham's other children?

Hagar bore one son to Abraham; Keturah gave him six sons. Before his death Abraham distributed a portion of his wealth to these children and sent them "eastward, unto the east country." These descendants of Abraham were called *the children of the east.* They are mentioned in Judges 6:3, 33, where they are said to be very numerous. They were enemies of the people of Israel. Today there may be multitudes of people in the Middle East who are lineal descendants of Abraham through these two concubines. Especially interesting is the fact that 25:16 speaks of these children of Abraham through Ishmael, calling them "twelve princes according to their nations." Thus there were the twelve tribes of Israel through Isaac and Jacob and twelve princes through Ishmael.

GENESIS 25:31
What is a birthright?

A birthright was a special honor given to the firstborn son. It included a double portion of the family inheritance along with the honor of one day becoming the family's leader. The oldest son could sell his birthright or give it away if he chose, but in so doing, he would lose both material goods and his leadership position. By trading his birthright, Esau showed complete disregard for the spiritual blessings that would have come his way if he had kept it. In effect, Esau "despised" his birthright (Gen. 25:34).

MATTHEW 8:28
What is a demon?

Demons are probably fallen angels who joined Satan in his rebellion against God and are now evil spirits under Satan's control. People possessed by demons display such symptoms as dumbness (Luke 11:14), epilepsy (Mark 9:17), and strange behavior (Luke 8:27-29). The New Testament clearly distinguishes between demon-possession and ordinary physical or mental sickness (see Matt. 4:24). These demons recognized Jesus as God's Son (Matt. 8:29), but they didn't think they had to obey him.

MATTHEW 8:34
Why did the people ask Jesus to leave?

Unlike their own pagan gods, Jesus could not be contained, controlled, or appeased. They feared Jesus' supernatural power, a power that they had never before witnessed. And they were upset about losing a herd of pigs more than they were glad about the deliverance of the demon-possessed men.

JANUARY 12

GENESIS 26:17-22
Why were they arguing over these wells?

The desolate Gerar area was located on the edge of a desert. Water was as precious as gold. If someone dug a well, he was staking a claim to the land. Some wells had locks to keep thieves from stealing the water. To "stop" or plug up someone's well was an act of war; it was one of the most serious crimes in the land. Isaac had every right to fight back when the Philistines ruined his wells, and yet he chose to keep the peace. In the end, the Philistines respected him for his patience.

GENESIS 27:8-38
If Jacob already had the birthright (Gen. 25:31-34), why was he trying to get it?

Before a father died, he performed a ceremony of blessing, in which he officially handed over the birthright to the rightful heir. Although the firstborn son was entitled to the birthright, it was not actually his until the blessing was pronounced. Before the blessing was given, the father could take the birthright away from the oldest son and give it to a more deserving son. But after the blessing was given, the birthright could no longer be taken away. This is why fathers usually waited until late in life to pronounce the blessing. Although Jacob had been given the birthright by his older brother years before, he still needed his father's blessing to make it binding.

MATTHEW 9:9
Who was Matthew?

Matthew was a Jew who was appointed by the Romans to be the area's tax collector. He collected taxes from the citizens as well as from merchants passing through town. Tax collectors were expected to take a commission on the taxes they collected, but most of them overcharged and kept the profits. Thus, tax collectors were hated by the Jews because of their reputation for cheating and because of their support of Rome. The authorship of the Gospel of Matthew is attributed to this man.

MATTHEW 9:17
What is a wineskin?

In Bible times, wine was not kept in glass bottles but in goatskins sewn around the edges to form watertight bags. New wine expanded as it fermented, stretching its wineskin. After the wine had aged, the stretched skin would burst if more new wine was poured into it. New wine, therefore, was always put into new wineskins.

JANUARY 13

Genesis 28:1–29:35; Matthew 9:18-38; Psalms 11:1-7; Proverbs 3:11-12

GENESIS 28:19
Where is Bethel?

Bethel was about ten miles north of Jerusalem and 60 miles north of Beersheba, where Jacob had left his family. The meaning of the name is "house of god." It was probably established in the Middle Bronze Age (2200–1550 B.C.). This was where Abraham made one of his first sacrifices to God when he entered the land (Gen. 12:8). At first, Bethel became an important center for worship; later, it was a center of idol worship. The prophet Hosea condemned its evil practices.

GENESIS 29:18-28
Why did Jacob work for a wife?

It was the custom of the day for a man to present a dowry, or substantial gift, to the family of his future wife. This was to compensate the family for the loss of the girl. Jacob's dowry was not a material possession, for he had none to offer. Instead he agreed to work seven years for Laban. But there was another custom of the land that Laban did not tell Jacob. The older daughter had to be married first. By giving Jacob Leah and not Rachel, Laban tricked him into promising another seven years of hard work.

MATTHEW 9:11, KJV
Why did the Pharisees call these people "publicans and sinners"?

Publicans were the tax collectors who were hated by the Jews because of their reputation for cheating and because of their support of Rome. Sinners were ordinary people who did not keep all the minute prescriptions of the ceremonial laws—especially those dealing with food and social customs—that the Pharisees prized so highly. Because they were self-righteous the Pharisees criticized Jesus for eating and drinking with both kinds of people, and for befriending them as well.

MATTHEW 9:34
Why did the Pharisees say Jesus was working with Satan?

In chapter 9, the Pharisees accuse Jesus of four different sins: blasphemy (v. 3), befriending outcasts (v. 11), impiety (v. 14), and serving Satan (v. 34). Matthew shows how Jesus was maligned by those who should have received him most gladly. The Pharisees did this because: (1) Jesus bypassed their religious authority. (2) He weakened their control over the people. (3) He challenged their cherished beliefs. (4) He exposed their insincere motives.

JANUARY 14

GENESIS 30:6
What are the meanings of the names of Jacob's sons?

Dan means "justice." The meaning is not of the actual Hebrew name, but of a Hebrew word sounding like the name. The name is a Hebrew pun. An example in English might be, "Because of the large hospital bill the child was named 'Bill.'" *Naphtali* (Gen. 30:8) means "wrestling"; *Gad* (Gen. 30:11) means "fortune"; *Asher* (Gen. 30:13) means "happy"; *Issachar* (Gen. 30:18) means "reward"; *Zebulun* (Gen. 30:20) means "dwelling" or "honor"; *Joseph* (Gen. 30:24) means "he adds."

GENESIS 30:14
What are mandrakes?

Mandrakes were leafy plants eaten by peasant women who supposed this would aid them in becoming pregnant. Rachel wanted to eat some in the hope she would have a child. She acquired some of the mandrakes from Leah by promising to allow her to go to bed with Jacob. Leah then had two more sons. Rachel, at last, did have a son, Joseph, then later died upon giving birth to Benjamin.

MATTHEW 10:5-6
Why didn't Jesus send the disciples to the Gentiles or the Samaritans?

A Gentile is anyone who is not a Jew. The Samaritans were a race that resulted from intermarriage between Jews and Gentiles after the Old Testament captivities (see 2 Kings 17:24). Jesus asked his disciples to go only to the Jews because he came *first* to the Jews (Romans 1:16). God chose them to tell the rest of the world about him. Jewish disciples and apostles preached the gospel of the risen Christ all around the Roman empire, and soon Gentiles were pouring into the church. The Bible clearly teaches that God's message of salvation is for *all* people, regardless of race, sex, or national origin (Acts 10:34-35; Rom. 3:29-30; Gal. 3:28).

MATTHEW 10:14
Why did Jesus tell his disciples to shake the dust off their feet if a city or home didn't welcome them?

When leaving Gentile cities, pious Jews often shook the dust from their feet to show their separation from Gentile practices. If the disciples shook the dust of a *Jewish* town from their feet, it would show their separation from Jews who rejected their Messiah.

JANUARY 15

GENESIS 31:19, KJV
Why did these people have images?

Many people kept small wooden or metal idols ("gods") in their homes. These idols were called *teraphim,* and they were thought to protect the home and offer advice in times of need. They had legal significance as well, for when they were passed on to an heir, the person who received them could claim the greatest part of the family inheritance. No wonder Laban was concerned when he realized his idols were missing (Gen. 31:30). Most likely Rachel stole her father's idols because she was afraid Laban would consult them and learn where she and Jacob had gone, or perhaps she wanted to claim the family inheritance.

MATTHEW 10:34-39
Does Matthew 10:34-39 mean that Jesus came to bring war and disagreement?

Jesus did not come to bring the kind of peace that glosses over deep differences just for the sake of superficial harmony. Conflict and disagreement will arise between those who choose to follow Christ and those who don't. (For more on Jesus as peacemaker, see Isa. 9:6; Matt. 5:9; John 14:27.) Christian commitment may separate friends and loved ones. In these verses Jesus was not encouraging disobedience to parents or conflict at home. Rather, he was showing that his presence demands a decision. Because some will follow Christ and some won't, conflict will inevitably arise. As we take up our cross and follow him, our different values, morals, goals, and purposes will set us apart from others.

MATTHEW 11:3-6
Why did John ask Jesus this question, and what does Jesus' answer mean?

John had baptized Jesus. He had seen the endorsement of Jesus as Messiah by the Father and the Holy Spirit. Now he is in jail, despondent, and without the help of the Messiah whom he had announced to all men. Doubtless he expected the Messiah to deliver him. Thus he sends his disciples with the question addressed to Jesus, so that he might be reassured that indeed he is the Messiah. Jesus answered John's doubts by pointing to his own acts of healing the blind, lame, and deaf, curing the lepers, raising the dead, and preaching the good news to the poor. With so much evidence, Jesus' identity was obvious.

JANUARY 16

Genesis 32:13–34:31; Matthew 11:7-30; Psalms 14:1-7; Proverbs 3:19-20

Q GENESIS 32:24
Who was the man with whom Jacob wrestled?

Some think the man was the preincarnate Christ. Others think it was probably Michael, one of the highest of the angelic host. Whoever it was, we can be certain that God was with him because Jacob thought he had seen God face to face.

Q GENESIS 32:27-29
Why was Jacob's name changed?

According to the Bible God gave many people new names (Abraham, Sarah, Peter). Their new names were symbols of how God had changed their lives. Here we see how Jacob's character had changed. "Jacob," the ambitious deceiver, had now become "Israel"—meaning "the one who struggles with God and overcomes."

Q GENESIS 33:11
Why did Jacob send gifts ahead for Esau?

In Bible times, gifts were given for several reasons. (1) This may have been a bribe. Gifts are still given to win someone over or buy his or her support. Esau may first have refused Jacob's gifts (Gen. 33:9) because he didn't want or need a bribe. He had already forgiven Jacob and he had ample wealth of his own. (2) This may have been an expression of affection. (3) It may have been the customary way of greeting someone before an important meeting. Such gifts were often related to a person's occupation. This explains why Jacob sent Esau, who was a herdsman, sheep, goats, and cattle.

Q MATTHEW 11:12, KJV
What does it mean that "the violent take it by force"?

There are three common views about the meaning of this verse. (1) Jesus may have been referring to a vast movement toward God, the momentum of which began with John's preaching. (2) A more literal translation of this verse reads, "the Kingdom of Heaven suffers violence, and violent men take it by force" (NASB). Most of the Jews in Jesus' day expected God's Kingdom to come through a violent overthrow of Rome. They wanted a kingdom, but not Jesus' kind. (3) A third translation reads, "the Kingdom of Heaven has been forcefully advancing, and forceful men lay hold of it" (NIV). The emphasis of this alternative rendering is that entering God's kingdom takes courage, unwavering faith, determination, and endurance because of the growing opposition leveled at Jesus' followers.

JANUARY 17

Genesis 35:1–36:43; Matthew 12:1-21; Psalms 15:1-5; Proverbs 3:21-26

GENESIS 35:2
Why did the people have these idols ("foreign gods")?

Idols were sometimes seen more as good-luck charms than as gods. Some Israelites, even though they worshiped God, had idols in their homes, just as some Christians today own good-luck trinkets. Jacob believed that idols should have no place in his household. He was on his way to Bethel where he was to build an altar and worship the true God with his family and wanted nothing to divert their spiritual focus.

GENESIS 35:4
Why did the people give Jacob their earrings?

Jewelry in itself was not evil, but in Jacob's day earrings were often worn as good-luck charms to ward off evil. The people in his family had to cleanse themselves of all pagan influences including reminders of foreign gods.

GENESIS 35:13-14
Why did Jacob pour oil on the pillar?

This oil used to anoint the pillar was olive oil of the finest grade of purity. It was expensive, so using it showed the high value placed on the anointed object. Jacob was showing the greatest respect for the place where he met with God.

MATTHEW 12:14
Why did the Pharisees want to kill Jesus?

The Pharisees plotted Jesus' death because they were outraged (Luke 6:11). Jesus had overruled their authority and had exposed their evil attitudes in front of the crowd in the synagogue. He showed that the Pharisees placed their laws above human need. They were so concerned about Jesus' breaking one of their rules that they did not care about the man's shriveled hand. Jesus showed that the Pharisees were more loyal to their religious system than to God.

MATTHEW 12:17-21
Why does Matthew quote the Old Testament so often?

Matthew quoted the Old Testament Scriptures often because he wanted to prove to his Jewish audience that Jesus was the Messiah. The Jews held the Bible as their highest authority. They believed it pointed to a coming Messiah, but they didn't believe Jesus was the one. Matthew showed that Jesus was, in fact, the Messiah prophesied by Old Testament prophets. This particular prophecy teaches that Jesus was not to be the high-profile Messiah the Jews were expecting. Instead, the Messiah would come as a servant, helping and healing, not leading into battle (Isa. 42:1-4).

JANUARY 18

Genesis 37:1–38:30; Matthew 12:22-45; Psalms 16:1-11; Proverbs 3:27-32

GENESIS 37:3
What was so special about Joseph's coat?

In Joseph's day, everyone had a robe or cloak. Robes were used to warm oneself, to bundle up belongings for a trip, to wrap babies, to sit on, or even to serve as security for a loan. Most robes were knee-length, short-sleeved, and plain. In contrast, Joseph's robe was probably of the kind worn by royalty—long-sleeved, ankle-length, and colorful. The robe became a symbol of Jacob's favoritism toward Joseph, and it aggravated the already strained relations between Joseph and his brothers.

GENESIS 38:8-10
Why did Judah want Onan to marry Er's wife, Tamar?

The custom of marrying a widow in a family is explained in Deuteronomy 25:5-10. Its purpose was to ensure that a childless widow would have a son who would receive her late husband's inheritance and who, in turn, would care for her. Because Judah's son (Tamar's husband) had no children, there was no family line through which the inheritance and the blessing of the covenant could continue. God killed Onan because he refused to fulfill his obligation to his brother and to Tamar. This event shows Tamar's persistence to have a child and inherit the birthright. It resulted in the continuation of the genealogy of Jesus Christ (Matt. 1:3).

MATTHEW 12:39-41
What is the "sign of the prophet Jonah"?

Jonah was a prophet sent to the Assyrian city of Nineveh (see the book of Jonah). Because Assyria was such a cruel and warlike nation, Jonah tried to run from his assignment and ended up spending three days in the belly of a huge fish. When Jonah got out, he grudgingly went to Nineveh, preached God's message, and saw the city repent. By contrast, when Jesus came to his people, they refused to repent. Here Jesus is clearly saying that his resurrection will prove he is the Messiah. Three days after his death Jesus would come back to life, just as Jonah was given a new chance at life after three days in the fish.

MATTHEW 12:42, KJV
Who was the queen of the south?

Also called the Queen of Sheba, she traveled far to see Solomon, king of Israel, and learn about his great wisdom (1 Kings 10:1-10). She was a Gentile who recognized the truth about God when it was presented to her, unlike the Jewish religious leaders who ignored the truth even though it stared them in the face.

JANUARY 19

Genesis 39:1–41:16; Matthew 12:46–13:23; Psalms 17:1-15; Proverbs 3:33-35

GENESIS 40:1
Who was the king of Egypt?

"Pharaoh" was the general name for all the kings of Egypt. It was a title like "Mr. President," used to address the country's leader. The Pharaohs in Genesis and Exodus were not the same man. Many scholars believe Joseph arrived in Egypt during the period of the Hyksos rulers, foreigners who came from the region of Canaan. They invaded Egypt and controlled the land for almost 150 years.

GENESIS 41:8
Why did Pharaoh consult magicians?

Magicians and wise men were common in the palaces of ancient rulers. Their job included studying sacred arts and sciences, reading the stars, interpreting dreams, predicting the future, and performing magic. These men had power (see Exod. 7:11-12), but their power was satanic. They were unable to interpret Pharaoh's dream, but God had revealed its meaning to Joseph in prison.

MATTHEW 12:46-50
Did Jesus turn against his family?

Jesus was not denying his responsibility to his earthly family. On the contrary, he criticized the religious leaders for not following the Old Testament command to honor their parents (Matt. 15:1-9). He provided for his mother's security as he hung on the cross (John 19:25-27). His mother and brothers were present in the upper room at Pentecost (Acts 1:14). Jesus was pointing out that spiritual relationships are as binding as physical ones, and he was paving the way for a new community of believers (the church).

MATTHEW 13:2-3, KJV
What is a parable?

Jesus used many illustrations or *parables,* when speaking to the crowds. A parable compares something familiar to something unfamiliar. It helps us understand spiritual truth by using everyday objects and relationships. Parables compel listeners to discover truth, while at the same time concealing the truth from those too lazy or too stubborn to see it. To those who are honestly searching, the truth becomes clear.

MATTHEW 13:9
Everyone has ears, so what does Jesus mean in Matthew 13:9?

Human ears hear many sounds, but there is a deeper kind of listening that results in spiritual understanding. A person who honestly seeks God's will, has spiritual hearing to understand these parables.

JANUARY 20

GENESIS 41:45
Did Pharaoh want to make Joseph into an Egyptian?

Pharaoh may have been trying to make Joseph more acceptable by giving him an Egyptian name and wife to (1) play down the fact that Joseph was a nomadic shepherd, an occupation disliked by the Egyptians, (2) make Joseph's name easier for Egyptians to pronounce and remember, and (3) show how highly he was honored by giving him the daughter of a prominent Egyptian official.

GENESIS 41:46
How old was Joseph at this time?

Joseph was 30 years old when he became governor of Egypt. He was 17 when he was sold into slavery by his brothers, thus he must have spent 11 years as an Egyptian slave and two years in prison.

GENESIS 42:4
Why did Jacob protect Benjamin but not his other sons?

Jacob was especially fond of Benjamin because (1) he was Joseph's only full brother and (2) the only other son of his beloved wife, Rachel. Benjamin was Jacob's youngest son and a child of his old age.

GENESIS 42:15
Why did Joseph want to see Benjamin?

Joseph was testing his brothers to make sure they had not been as cruel to Benjamin as they had been to him. Benjamin was his only full brother, and he wanted to see him face to face.

MATTHEW 13:33
What does leaven mean in the Bible?

Yeast, or leaven, was usually what is now referred to as "sourdough." It was produced from bread flour kneaded without salt and kept until it began to ferment. In ordinary bread-making leaven was probably a piece of dough left over from one baking, allowed to ferment, and then kneaded into the next batch. In the Bible it is generally referred to in an evil sense. In the New Testament it signifies (1) the doctrines of the Pharisees and Sadducees (16:6, 12); (2) ungodly professors of the true faith (1 Cor. 5:6-7); (3) false teachers (Gal. 5:8-9); and (4) malice and evil (1 Cor. 5:8). Leaven here suggests its silent permeating power that requires only a small amount in the dough to be effective. Leaven, or yeast, was generally forbidden in the Old Testament except for use with thank-offerings (Lev. 7:13) and with the presentation of the first fruits of wheat (Lev. 23:17).

JANUARY 21

Genesis 42:18–43:34; Matthew 13:47–14:12; Psalms 18:16-36; Proverbs 4:7-10

Q GENESIS 43:32
Why did Joseph eat by himself?

The Egyptians had a caste system. They considered themselves highly intelligent and sophisticated, looking upon shepherds and nomads as uncultured and even vulgar. As a Hebrew, Joseph could not eat with Egyptians even though he outranked them. As foreigners and shepherds, his brothers were lower in rank than any Egyptian citizens, so they had to eat separately too.

Q GENESIS 43:29-30
Why did Joseph weep?

Except for Benjamin, all Joseph's brothers were born of different mothers than he. He and Benjamin were the sons of Rachel, Jacob's beloved. He had not seen Benjamin for more than twenty years. Great changes in his appearance would have taken place. Joseph probably would not have recognized Benjamin in a crowd of people. This meeting was a touching reminder to him of their dead mother and of his love for his full brother.

Q PSALM 18:13, KJV
What does the term "the Highest" mean?

"The Highest" was an important designation for David to make. Pagan idol worship was deeply rooted in the land, and each region had its own deity. But these images of wood and stone were powerless. David was placing the Lord alone in a superior category: he is by far the Most High.

Q MATTHEW 13:55-58
Why did the people in Jesus' hometown reject him?

The residents of Jesus' hometown had known Jesus since he was a young child and knew his family; they could not bring themselves to believe in his message. They were too close to the situation. Jesus had come to them as a prophet, one who challenged them to respond to unpopular spiritual truth. They did not listen to the timeless message because they could not see beyond the man.

Q MATTHEW 14:1
Who was Herod?

Herod was a tetrarch—one of four rulers over the four districts of Palestine. His territory included the regions of Galilee and Perea. He was the son of Herod the Great, who ordered the killing of the babies in Bethlehem (2:16). Also known as Herod Antipas, he heard Jesus' case before Jesus' crucifixion (Luke 23:6-12).

JANUARY 22

Genesis 44:1–45:28; Matthew 14:13-36; Psalms 18:37-50; Proverbs 4:11-13

GENESIS 44:2-13
What was so important about Joseph's cup?

Joseph's silver cup was a symbol of his authority. It was thought to have supernatural powers, and to steal it was a serious crime. Such goblets were used for predicting the future. A person poured water into the cup and interpreted the reflections, ripples, and bubbles. Joseph wouldn't have needed his cup, since God told him everything he needed to know about the future.

GENESIS 45:10
Where is Goshen?

In Genesis 47:6 Pharaoh tells Joseph to settle his father and his kin in Goshen. This was fertile grazing land located in the eastern section of the Nile Delta near the city of Raamses and the royal court at Memphis (near Cairo). This is not the Goshen of Joshua 10:41 and 11:16 which was a district in South Palestine near Hebron.

PSALM 18:40-42
Isn't David being very cruel to his enemies?

David was a merciful man. He spared the lives of Saul (1 Sam. 24:1-8), Nabal (1 Sam. 25:21-35), and Shimei (2 Sam. 16:5-12) and showed great kindness to Mephibosheth (2 Sam. 9). In asking God to destroy his enemies, David was simply asking him to give the wicked the punishment they deserved.

MATTHEW 14:21
If there were five thousand men present, how many women and children were fed?

The text states that there were five thousand men present, *besides* women and children. Therefore, the total number of people Jesus fed could have been ten to fifteen thousand. The number of men is listed separately because in the Jewish culture of the day, men and women usually ate separately when in public. The children ate with the women.

MATTHEW 14:36, TLB
Why did people want to touch the tassel of Jesus' robe?

Jewish men wore tassels on the lower edges of their robes according to God's command (Deut. 22:12). By Jesus' day, these tassels were seen as signs of holiness (Matt. 23:5). It was natural that people seeking healing should reach out and touch these. But as one sick woman learned, healing came from faith and not from Jesus' cloak (Matt. 9:19-22).

JANUARY 23

Genesis 46:1–47:31; Matthew 15:1-28; Psalms 19:1-14; Proverbs 4:14-19

GENESIS 46:31-34
Is Joseph trying to control Pharaoh's decisions?

Jacob moved his whole family to Egypt, but wanted to live apart from the Egyptians. Thus, Joseph told him to let Pharaoh know they were shepherds. Although Pharaoh may have been sympathetic to shepherds (for he was probably descended from the nomadic Hyksos line), the Egyptian culture would not willingly accept shepherds among them. The strategy worked, and Jacob was able to benefit from Pharaoh's generosity as well as from the Egyptians' prejudice.

PSALM 19:12-13, TLB
What is the difference between "hidden faults" and "deliberate wrongs"?

Hidden faults are sins committed unknowingly or in ignorance of God's laws. Deliberate wrongs are sins committed in defiant rebellion against God. David asked forgiveness for both and realized that even his dreadful sins of murder and adultery (2 Sam. 11–12) were covered by God's mercy.

MATTHEW 15:1-2
Aren't religious traditions good?

The Pharisees came from Jerusalem, the center of Jewish authority, to scrutinize Jesus' activities. Over the centuries since the Jews' return from Babylonian captivity, hundreds of religious traditions had been added to God's laws. The Pharisees and teachers of the law considered them all equally important. Many traditions are not bad in themselves. They can add richness and meaning to life. But we must not assume that because our traditions have been practiced for years they should be elevated to a sacred standing. God's principles never change, and his law doesn't need additions. Traditions should help us understand God's laws better, not become laws themselves.

MATTHEW 15:5-6
Didn't the Pharisees teach to honor your mother and father?

Yes, but here Jesus gives an example of a tradition that supplanted God's law. This was the practice of *Corban.* Anyone who made a Corban vow was required to dedicate money to God's temple that otherwise would have gone to support his parents. Corban had become a religiously acceptable way to neglect parents, circumventing the child's responsibility to them. Although the action—giving money to God—seemed worthy and no doubt conferred prestige on the giver, many people who took the Corban vow were disregarding God's command to care for needy parents. These religious leaders were ignoring God's clear command to honor their parents.

JANUARY 24

Genesis 48:1–49:33; Matthew 15:29–16:12; Psalms 20:1-9; Proverbs 4:20-27

GENESIS 49:8-12
Why was Judah—known for selling Joseph into slavery and trying to defraud his daughter-in-law—so greatly blessed?

God had chosen Judah to be the ancestor of Israel's royal line of kings (referred to as the "scepter" in these verses). This may have been due to Judah's dramatic change of character (44:33-34). Judah's line would produce the promised Messiah, Jesus who was the "Lion of the Tribe of Judah" (Rev. 5:5).

GENESIS 49:10
What is does Shiloh mean?

This is a difficult passage to understand and its meaning is disputed. Shiloh may be another name for the Messiah, because its literal meaning is "until he to whom it belongs comes, whom all people shall obey." Shiloh might also refer to the Tent of Meeting (Tabernacle) set up at the city of Shiloh (Josh. 18:1).

GENESIS 49:22
Why is Joseph called a "fruitful vine"?

Joseph was indeed fruitful, with some heroic descendants. Among them were Joshua, who would lead the Israelites into the promised land (Joshua 1:10-11); Deborah, Gideon, and Jephthah, judges of Israel (Judges 4:4; 6:11-12; 11:11); and Samuel, a great prophet (1 Sam. 3:19).

MATTHEW 16:1
Who were the Pharisees and Sadducees?

The Pharisees and Sadducees were Jewish religious leaders of two different parties, and their views were diametrically opposed on many issues. The Pharisees carefully followed their religious rules and traditions, believing that this was the way to God. They also believed in the authority of all Scripture and in the resurrection of the dead. The Sadducees accepted only the books of Moses as Scripture and did not believe in life after death. These two groups were wholly in disagreement with each other on virtually every matter. But they were companions in crime by becoming friends in their opposition to Jesus Christ.

MATTHEW 15:32-39
This feeding of the multitude sounds just like the one in chapter 14.

Although similar, this feeding of four thousand is a separate event from the feeding of the five thousand (14:13-21), confirmed by Mark 8:19-20. This was the beginning of Jesus' expanded ministry to the Gentiles.

JANUARY 25

Genesis 50:1–Exodus 2:10; Matthew 16:13–17:9; Psalms 21:1-13; Proverbs 5:1-6

 GENESIS 50:2-3
Did the Israelites usually embalm their dead?
Embalming was typical for Egyptians but unusual for these nomadic shepherds. Believing that the dead went to the next world in their physical bodies, the Egyptians embalmed bodies to preserve them so they could function in the world to come. Jacob's family allowed him to be embalmed as a sign of courtesy and respect to the Egyptians.

 EXODUS 1:1
What was the difference between the Egyptians and the Hebrews?
The children of Israel, or Israelites, were the descendants of Jacob, whose name was changed to Israel after he wrestled with the angel (see Gen. 32:24-30). Jacob's family had moved to Egypt at the invitation of Joseph, one of Jacob's sons, who had become a great ruler under Pharaoh. Jacob's family grew into a large nation. But, as foreigners and newcomers, their lives were quite different from the Egyptians. The Hebrews worshiped one God; the Egyptians worshiped many gods. The Hebrews were wanderers; the Egyptians had a deeply rooted culture. The Hebrews were shepherds; the Egyptians were builders. The Hebrews were also physically separated from the rest of the Egyptians. They lived in Goshen, north of the great Egyptian cultural centers.

MATTHEW 16:18
What is the "rock" in Matthew 16:18?
The rock on which Jesus would build his church refers to either (1) Jesus himself (his work of salvation by dying for us on the cross); (2) Peter (the first great leader in the church at Jerusalem); (3) the confession of faith that Peter gave and that all subsequent true believers would give. Peter later reminds Christians that they are the church built on the foundation of the apostles and prophets, with Jesus Christ as the chief cornerstone (1 Pet. 2:4-6). All believers are joined into this church by faith in Jesus Christ as Savior, the same faith that Peter expressed here (see also Eph. 2:20-21). Jesus praised Peter for his confession of faith. It is faith like Peter's that is the foundation of Christ's kingdom.

JANUARY 26

Exodus 2:11–3:22; Matthew 17:10-27; Psalms 22:1-18; Proverbs 5:7-14

EXODUS 3:2-4
Why was God in a burning bush?

Moses "saw" God in a burning bush and spoke with him. Many people in the Bible experienced God in visible (not necessarily human) form. Abraham saw the smoking firepot and blazing torch (Gen. 15:17); Jacob wrestled with a man (Gen. 32:24-29). When the slaves were freed from Egypt, God led them by pillars of cloud and fire (13:17-22). God made such appearances to encourage his new nation, to guide them, and to prove the reliability of his verbal message. The call of Moses to be Israel's deliverer from Egypt came when he saw a bush which was in flame but was not being burnt up. It revealed to him a living, self-sufficient, holy God who promised to be with Moses and to fulfill his past promises.

EXODUS 3:13-15
Why would the children of Israel want to know God's name?

The Egyptians had many gods by many different names. Moses wanted to know God's name so the Hebrew people would know exactly who had sent him to them. God called himself, *I Am,* a name describing his eternal power and unchangeable character. Jehovah or Yahweh is the *I Am.* God was reminding Moses of his covenant promises to Abraham (Gen. 12:1-3; 15; 17), Isaac (Gen. 26:2-5), and Jacob (Gen. 28:13-15). When Moses later used this name with the elders (Exod. 4:29-31), he was invoking national pride in a promise given to the patriarchs almost five hundred years before.

MATTHEW 17:24-27
Why did Jesus pay the temple tax?

All Jewish males had to pay a temple tax to support temple upkeep (Exod. 30:11-16). Tax collectors set up booths to collect these taxes. Only Matthew records this incident—perhaps because he had been a tax collector himself. Jesus used this situation to emphasize his kingly role. Just as kings pay no taxes and collect none from their family, Jesus, the King, owed no taxes. But Jesus supplied the tax payment for both himself and Peter rather than offend those who didn't understand his kingship. Although Jesus supplied the tax money, Peter had to go and get it.

JANUARY 27

EXODUS 4:24-26
Why did God want to kill Moses?

God threatened to kill Moses because Moses had not circumcised his son. Why hadn't Moses done this? Remember that Moses had spent half his life in Pharaoh's palace and half his life in the Midianite desert. He might not have been familiar with God's laws, especially since all the requirements of God's covenant with Israel (Gen. 17) had not been actively carried out for over four hundred years. In addition, Moses' wife, due to her Midianite background, may have opposed circumcision. But Moses could not effectively serve as deliverer of God's people until he had fulfilled the conditions of God's covenant, and one of those conditions was circumcision. Before they could go any further, Moses and his family had to follow God's commands completely. Under Old Testament law, failing to circumcise your son was to remove yourself and your family from God's blessings. Moses learned that disobeying God was even more dangerous than tangling with an Egyptian pharaoh.

MATTHEW 18:9
What is the "fire of hell"?

The word translated *hell* here is *gehenna,* which is the Aramaic form of the Hebrew *Gehinnom,* meaning "the Valley of Hinnom." *Gehenna* is the word used to describe the place to which unrepentant sinners go. Its fire is unquenchable and the torment unending. In the Old Testament the Valley of Hinnom (Topheth) was the place where infants were killed as sacrifices and where the repulsive idol of Molech was worshipped. These perversions occurred during the reigns of Ahaz and Manasseh. King Josiah converted the area into a city dump where fire smoldered continually. Gehenna was used by Jeremiah as a symbol of judgment (Jer. 7:31-34). The general idea of fire expressing God's judgment is also found in the Old Testament (Deut. 32:22; Dan. 7:10).

In the New Testament hell is pictured as a place of unending fire and the undying worm (Mark 9:43-49), of outer darkness with weeping and gnashing of teeth (Matt. 8:12), and as a lake of fire (Rev. 19:20). It is the "second death" (Rev. 20:14), destroying body and soul (Matt. 10:28). Hell has been prepared for the devil and his angels (Matt. 25:41); it becomes the destiny of people only because they have refused their true destiny which God offers them in Christ. God desires everyone's salvation (1 Tim. 2:4) but not all accept his gracious offer.

JANUARY 28

Exodus 5:22–7:24; Matthew 18:23–19:12; Psalms 23:1-6; Proverbs 5:22-23

EXODUS 7:11
How were these sorcerers and magicians able to duplicate Moses' miracles?

Some of their feats involved trickery or illusion, and some may have used satanic power, since worshiping gods of the underworld was part of their religion. Ironically, whenever the sorcerers duplicated one of Moses' plagues, it only made matters worse. If the magicians had been as powerful as God, they would have reversed the plagues, not added to them.

EXODUS 7:20
Was the Nile River important to Egypt?

Egypt was a large country, but most of the population lived along the banks of the Nile River. This three-thousand-mile waterway was truly a river of life for the Egyptians. It made life possible in a land that was mostly desert by providing water for drinking, farming, bathing, and fishing. Egyptian society was a ribbon of civilization lining the banks of this life source, rarely reaching very far into the surrounding desert. Without the Nile's water, Egypt could not have existed. Imagine Pharaoh's dismay when Moses turned this sacred river to blood!

MATTHEW 18:30
Was the man in Matthew 18:30 put in jail just because he couldn't pay his debts?

In Bible times, serious consequences awaited those who could not pay their debts. The lender could seize the borrower and force him or his family to work until the debt was paid. The debtor could also be thrown into prison, or his family could be sold into slavery to help pay off the debt. It was hoped that the debtor, while in prison, would sell off his landholdings or that relatives would pay the debt. If not, the debtor could remain in prison for life.

MATTHEW 19:3-12
Why did the Pharisees want to talk about divorce?

John was put in prison and killed, at least in part, for his public opinions on marriage and divorce, so the Pharisees hoped to trap Jesus too. They were trying to trick Jesus by having him choose sides in a theological controversy. Two schools of thought represented two opposing views of divorce. One group supported divorce for almost any reason. The other believed that divorce could be allowed only for marital unfaithfulness. This conflict hinged on how each group interpreted Deuteronomy 24:1-4. In his answer, however, Jesus focused on marriage rather than divorce. He pointed out that God intended marriage to be permanent and gave four reasons for the importance of marriage (19:4-6).

JANUARY 29

Exodus 7:25–9:35; Matthew 19:13-30; Psalms 24:1-10; Proverbs 6:1-5

EXODUS 8:7
How were these sorcerers and magicians able to duplicate Moses' miracles?

Some of their feats involved trickery or illusion, and some may have used satanic power, since worshiping gods of the underworld was part of their religion. Ironically, whenever the sorcerers duplicated one of Moses' plagues, it only made matters worse. If the magicians had been as powerful as God, they would have reversed the plagues, not added to them. In Exodus 7:11, 22, and 8:7 the magicians of Egypt replicated the miracles of Moses and Aaron. But in 8:18 they failed to do so. Paul explains these kinds of phenomena when he speaks about "the working of Satan with all power and signs and lying wonders" in 2 Thessalonians 2:9 (KJV).

EXODUS 9:1; 10:3
Why did God identify himself in detail as "Jehovah, the God of the Hebrews"?

As each gloomy plague descended upon the land, the Egyptian people realized how powerless their own gods were to stop it. Hapi, the god of the Nile River, could not prevent the waters from turning to blood (7:20). Hathor, the crafty cow-goddess, was helpless as Egyptian livestock died in droves (9:6). Amon-Re, the sun-god and chief of the Egyptian gods, could not stop an eerie darkness from covering the land for three full days (10:21-22). The Egyptian gods were (1) centered around nonpersonal images like the sun or the river; (2) many in number; (3) worshiped along with many other gods. By contrast, the God of the Hebrews was (1) a living personal Being, (2) the only true God, and (3) the only God who should be worshiped. God was proving to both the Hebrews and the Egyptians that he alone is the living and all-powerful God.

MATTHEW 19:13-15
Is the kingdom of heaven only for little children?

The disciples must have forgotten what Jesus had said about children (18:4-6). Jesus wanted little children to come because he loved them and because they had the kind of attitude needed to approach God. He didn't mean that heaven is only for children, but that people need childlike attitudes of trust in God. The receptiveness of little children was a great contrast to the stubbornness of the religious leaders, who let their education and sophistication stand in the way of the simple faith needed to believe in Jesus.

JANUARY 30

Exodus 10:1–12:13; Matthew 20:1-28; Psalms 25:1-15; Proverbs 6:6-11

EXODUS 12:3-4
Why did the Hebrews sacrifice a lamb?

The significance of the sacrifice was that innocent blood was shed. For the Israelites to be spared from the plague of death, a lamb with no defects had to be killed and its blood placed on the doorposts of their homes. What was the significance of the lamb? In killing the lamb, the Israelites shed innocent blood. The lamb was a sacrifice, a substitute for the person who was to die. From this point on, the Hebrew people would clearly understand that for them to be spared from death, an innocent life had to be sacrificed in their place.

EXODUS 12:6-14
What was the significance of the Passover?

The Feast of the Passover was to be an annual holiday in honor of the night when the Lord "passed over" the homes of the Israelites. The Hebrews followed God's instructions by placing the blood of a lamb on the doorpost of their homes. That night the firstborn son of every family who did not have blood on the doorpost was killed. The lamb had to be killed in order to get the blood that would protect them. (This foreshadowed the blood of Christ, the Lamb of God, who gave his blood for the sins of all people.) Inside their homes, the Israelites ate a meal of roast lamb, bitter herbs, and bread made without yeast. Unleavened bread could be made quickly because the dough did not have to rise. Thus they could leave at any time. Bitter herbs signified the bitterness of slavery. Eating the Passover feast while dressed for travel was a sign of the Hebrews' faith. Although they were not yet free, they were to prepare themselves, for God had said he would lead them out of Egypt. Their preparation was an act of faith.

MATTHEW 20:28
What is a ransom?

A ransom was the price paid to release a slave from bondage. Jesus often told his disciples that he must die, but here he told them why—to redeem all people from the bondage of sin and death. The disciples thought that as long as Jesus was alive, he could save them. But Jesus revealed that only his death would save them and the world.

JANUARY 31

EXODUS 12:28-30
Why were the firstborn of the Israelites not killed by Jehovah?

Every firstborn child of the Egyptians died, but all the Israelite children were spared. Because the blood of the lamb had been placed on their doorposts, the people were saved. So began the story of redemption, the central theme of the Bible. Redemption, as it is used in the Bible, means to be freed from our slavery to sin. All of us have sinned and will sin again; that makes us slaves to sin. We cannot deliver ourselves from its consequences. That is where redemption comes in. It involves two parts: (1) a ransom, a cost paid for the penalty of sin, and (2) a substitute who pays the penalty for us. In this story, the lamb was sacrificed as a substitute for the lives of the Israelites. Its life was the penalty paid. In the Old Testament, animal sacrifice was the method used by God to forgive and take away one's sin. The individual sacrificed a valuable animal to demonstrate that sin's penalty must be paid.

In the New Testament, Jesus performed the ultimate act of redemption by sacrificing his life on the cross for our sins. This made animal sacrifice no longer necessary. He was the substitute and his blood was the cost paid for the penalty of our sins (1 Pet. 1:18-19). Only Jesus could redeem all people from slavery to sin because only he had lived a life that was perfect in every way (Heb. 7:27; 1 John 3:5). Since only he lived up to the demands of God, only he had the right to release us from our "sentence," which was death due to our sin. Jesus substituted his life for ours so that we could be restored to God.

We must recognize that if we want to be freed from the deadly consequences of our sins, a tremendous price must be paid. But *we* don't have to pay it. Jesus Christ (our substitute) has already redeemed us by his death on the cross. Our part is to trust him and accept his gift of eternal life. Our sins have been paid for, and the way has been cleared for us to begin a bright new relationship with God (Tit. 2:14; Heb. 9:13-15, 23-26).

FEBRUARY 1

Exodus 13:17–15:18; Matthew 21:23-46; Psalms 26:1-12; Proverbs 6:16-19

EXODUS 13:17-18
When did the Hebrews leave Egypt?

There are two theories. The "early" theory says the exodus occurred around 1446–1445 B.C. The "late" theory suggests the exodus happened between 1300 and 1200 B.C. Those who hold to the earlier date point to 1 Kings 6:1, where the Bible clearly states that Solomon began building the temple 480 years after the Hebrews left Egypt. Since almost all scholars agree that Solomon began building the temple in 966, this puts the exodus in the year 1446. But those who hold to the later date suggest that the 480 years cannot be taken literally. They point to Exodus 1:11, which says that the Hebrews built the cities of Pithom and Rameses, named after Pharaoh Rameses II, who reigned around 1290 B.C. Regardless of which date is correct, the fact is that God led the Hebrews out of Egypt, just as he had promised.

EXODUS 15:1
Did the ancient Israelites often sing and enjoy music?

Music played an important part in Israel's worship and celebration. Singing was an expression of love and thanks, and it was a creative way to pass down oral traditions. Some say this song of Moses is the oldest recorded song in the world. It was a festive epic poem celebrating God's victory, lifting the hearts and voices of the people outward and upward. After having been delivered from great danger, they sang with joy!

MATTHEW 21:42
What stone is Jesus talking about in Matthew 21:42?

This verse, taken from Psalm 118:22, refers to a stone for the temple that was discarded when no place could be found for it. Then it was discovered that it was the chief cornerstone of the building. Jesus is also quoting several other Old Testament texts: Isaiah 8:14-15; Isaiah 28:16; Daniel 2:34, 44-45. He uses this metaphor to show that one stone can affect people in different ways, depending on how they relate to it. Ideally they will build on it; many, however, will trip over it. And at the last judgment it will crush God's enemies. In the end, Christ, the "building block," will become the "crushing stone." He offers mercy and forgiveness *now* and promises judgment later.

FEBRUARY 2

Exodus 15:19–17:7; Matthew 22:1-33; Psalms 27:1-6; Proverbs 6:20-26

EXODUS 16:14-16
What was manna like and how was it used?

Manna was the Israelites' chief food during their 40-year stay in the desert. It was found on the ground each morning. It did not keep overnight, but a double portion was collected on the sixth day and cooked, because none appeared on the Sabbath. It was a fresh white grain the size of a pearl or coriander seed. The people gathered it, ground it like grain, and made it into honey-tasting pancakes. For the Israelites the manna was a free gift—it came every day and was just what they needed. It satisfied their temporary physical need. Manna was used to teach the Israelites the spiritual lesson of dependence on God (Deut. 8:3, 16). The word "manna" is used by Christ in John 6:48-49 to portray his own person, the bread of life from heaven. In Revelation 2:17 it represents the spiritual sustenance he gives his followers.

EXODUS 17:6
What is the significance of the rock in Horeb?

The rock which Moses struck and from which water flowed is a type of Christ. This is the rock of which Paul wrote in 1 Corinthians 10:4 "and all drank the same spiritual drink. For they drank from the spiritual rock that followed them, and the rock was Christ" (NRSV).

MATTHEW 22:15-17
Why were the Pharisees and Herodians concerned about what Jesus thought about paying taxes?

The Pharisees, a religious group, opposed the Roman occupation of Palestine. The Herodians, a political party, supported Herod Antipas and the policies instituted by Rome. Normally these two groups were bitter enemies, but here they united against Jesus. Thinking they had a foolproof plan to corner him, together their representatives asked Jesus about paying Roman taxes. If Jesus agreed that it was right to pay taxes to Caesar, the Pharisees would say he was opposed to God, the only King they recognized. If Jesus said the taxes should not be paid, the Herodians would hand him over to Herod on the charge of rebellion. In this case the Pharisees were not motivated by love for God's laws, and the Herodians were not motivated by love for Roman justice. Jesus' answer exposed their evil motives and embarrassed them both.

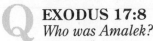

FEBRUARY 3

Exodus 17:8–19:15; Matthew 22:34–23:12; Psalms 27:7-14; Proverbs 6:27-35

EXODUS 17:8
Who was Amalek?

The Amalekites were descendants of Amalek, a grandson of Esau. They were a fierce nomadic tribe that lived in the desert region of the Dead Sea. They made part of their livelihood by conducting frequent raids on other settlements and carrying off booty. They killed for pleasure. One of the greatest insults in Israelite culture was to call someone "a friend of Amalek." When the Israelites entered the region, the Amalekites saw this as a perfect opportunity for both pleasure and profit. For the Israelites, former slaves, to defeat such a warlike nation was more than enough proof that God was with them as he had promised.

EXODUS 8:7
What was Moses' tent like?

Tents were the homes of shepherds. In shape and design, they resembled the tents in the Mideast today, but they were very large and made of a thick cloth woven from goat or camel hair. This fabric breathed in warm weather and contracted in stormy weather to offer protection from the winter winds and rains. The floor was often covered with animal-skin rugs, while curtains divided the inside space into rooms.

MATTHEW 23:2-3
What did Jesus mean when he said "the scribes and the Pharisees sit in Moses' seat"?

The Pharisees' traditions and their interpretations and applications of the laws had become as important to them as God's law itself. Therefore they were putting themselves in the place of Moses who had originally brought the law to Israel. Their laws were not all bad—some were beneficial. The problem arose when the religious leaders (1) took man-made rules as seriously as God's laws, (2) told the people to obey these rules but did not do so themselves, or (3) obeyed the rules not to honor God but to make themselves look good. Usually Jesus did not condemn what the Pharisees taught, but what they *were*—hypocrites.

MATTHEW 23:5, TLB
What were the "little prayer boxes"?

These little prayer boxes, called *phylacteries,* contained Bible verses. The Pharisees wore them because Exodus 13:9 and 16 command people to keep God's Word close to their hearts, and they took this literally. But these little prayer boxes had become more important for the status they gave than for the truth they contained.

FEBRUARY 4

Exodus 19:16–21:21; Matthew 23:13-39; Psalms 28:1-9; Proverbs 7:1-5

Q EXODUS 20:24-26
Why were specific directions given for building altars?

God's people had no Bible and few religious traditions to learn from. God had to start from scratch and teach them how to worship him. God gave specific instructions about building altars because he wanted to control the way sacrifices were offered. To prevent idolatry from creeping into worship, God did not allow the altar stones to be cut or shaped into any form. Nor did God let the people build an altar just anywhere. This was designed to prevent them from starting their own religions or making changes in the way God wanted things done. God is not against creativity, but he is against us creating our own religion.

Q EXODUS 21:2
Did the Hebrews own slaves?

The Hebrews, though freed from slavery, had slaves themselves. A person could become a slave because of poverty, debt, or even crime. But Hebrew slaves were treated as humans, not property, and were allowed to work their way to freedom. The Bible acknowledges the existence of slavery but never encourages it.

Q MATTHEW 23:34-36, NRSV
Who are the prophets, sages, and scribes?

These could be the disciples, Stephen, Paul, and other leaders in the early church who were persecuted, scourged, and killed, as Jesus predicted. The people of Jesus' generation said they would not act as their fathers did in killing the prophets whom God had sent to them (23:30), but they were about to kill the Messiah himself and his faithful followers. Thus they would become guilty of all the righteous blood shed through the centuries.

Q MATTHEW 23:35
What is "all the righteous blood that has been shed on earth"?

Here Jesus was alluding to the history of Old Testament martyrdom. Abel was the first martyr (Gen. 4); Zechariah was the last mentioned in the Hebrew Bible, which ended with 2 Chronicles (24:20-21). The phrase *from the blood of righteous Abel to the blood of Zechariah* means "from the first to the last murder in the Old Testament."

FEBRUARY 5

Exodus 21:22–23:13; Matthew 24:1-28; Psalms 29:1-11; Proverbs 7:6-23

EXODUS 21:24-25
Should I practice "an eye for an eye" in my personal life?

The "eye for eye" rule was instituted as a guide for judges, not as a rule for personal relationships or to justify revenge. This rule made the punishment fit the crime, thereby preventing the cruel and barbaric punishments that characterized many ancient countries. Jesus referred to this principle when he taught us not to retaliate at all (Matt. 5:38-48).

EXODUS 22:18
Why did God's laws speak so strongly against sorcery?

Sorcery was punishable by death because it was a crime against God himself. To invoke evil powers violated the first commandment to "have no other gods." Sorcery was rebellion against God and his authority. In essence, it was teaming up with Satan instead of with God. (See also Lev. 19:31; 20:6, 27; Deut. 18:10-12.)

MATTHEW 24:1-2
What did the temple look like in Jesus' time?

No one knows what this temple looked like, but it must have been beautiful. Solomon's porch alone was 1,562 feet long; the royal portico was decorated with 160 columns stretching along its 921-foot length. Gazing at this massive structure, the disciples found Jesus' words about its destruction difficult to believe. But the temple was indeed destroyed only forty years later when the Romans sacked Jerusalem in A.D. 70.

MATTHEW 24:15-16
What is this "abomination that causes desolation" mentioned by both Daniel and Jesus?

Rather than one specific object, event, or person, it could be seen as any deliberate attempt to mock and destroy God's presence. Daniel's prediction came true in 168 B.C. when Antiochus Epiphanes sacrificed a pig to Zeus on the sacred temple altar (Dan. 9:27; 11:30-31). Jesus' words were remembered in A.D. 70, when Titus placed an idol on the site of the burned temple after destroying Jerusalem. In the end times the antichrist will set up an image of himself and order everyone to worship it (2 Thess. 2:4; Rev. 13:14-15). These are all "abominations" that seek to desecrate that which is holy.

FEBRUARY 6

EXODUS 24:6-8, TLB
Why did Moses throw the blood toward the people, and how did this blood "confirm and seal the covenant" God had made with them?

God is the sovereign judge of the universe. He is also absolutely holy. As the holy judge of all, he condemns sin and judges it worthy of death. In the Old Testament, God accepted the death of an animal as a substitute for the sinner. The animal's blood was shed as proof that one life had been given for another. So on the one hand, blood symbolized the death of the animal, but it also symbolized the life that was spared as a result. Of course the death of the animal that brought forgiveness in the Old Testament was only a temporary provision, looking forward to the death of Jesus Christ (Heb. 9:9–10:24). In the ceremony described here, Moses sprinkled half the blood from the sacrificed animals on the altar to show that the sinner could once again approach God because something had died in his place. He sprinkled the other half of the blood on the people to show that the penalty for their sin had been paid and they could be reunited with God. Through this symbolic act God's promises to Israel were reaffirmed and lessons are taught to us about the future sacrificial death (or atonement) of Jesus Christ.

MATTHEW 24:34
What generation is Jesus speaking of in Matthew 24:34?

A generation in the Old Testament was measured as forty years. There is a question about whether Jesus was talking about the generation of people who were alive then, or the generation of people who would be living at the time of the second coming. If the former is correct, then Jesus was saying that his second coming would come not more than forty years after his death and resurrection. Since the temple was destroyed in A.D. 70, Christ's contemporaries *did* live to see the fulfillment of *these things*. In the latter case, the generation refers to those living at the time of the beginning of the signs characterizing the end times—they will live to see the fulfillment of them all.

FEBRUARY 7

Exodus 26:1–27:21; Matthew 25:1-30; Psalms 31:1-8; Proverbs 8:1-11

EXODUS 26:31-33
Why was there a curtain inside the Tabernacle?

This curtain separated the two sacred rooms in the tabernacle—the Holy Place and the Most Holy Place. The priest entered the Holy Place each day to commune with God and to tend to the altar of incense, the lampstand, and the table with the bread of the Presence. The Most Holy Place was where God himself dwelt, his presence resting on the atonement cover, which covered the ark of the Testimony. Only the high priest could enter the Most Holy Place. Even he could do so only once a year (on the Day of Atonement) to make atonement for the sins of the nation as a whole. When Jesus Christ died on the cross, the curtain in the temple (which had replaced the tabernacle) tore open from top to bottom (Mark 15:38), symbolizing our free access to God because of Jesus' death. No longer did people have to approach God through priests and sacrifices.

MATTHEW 25:1-13, TLB
Why did the ten bridesmaids have lamps? What kind of lamps were they?

The standard pottery lamp in New Testament times was round, plain, with a fairly wide flanged filling hole and a flared nozzle for the wick, sloping downwards. Lamps burned coarse olive oil or fat, and could stay lit for two to four hours. The wick was made from flax, other fiber, or rags.

This parable is about a wedding. In Jewish culture a couple was engaged for a long time before the actual marriage, and an engagement promise was just as binding as the marriage vows. On the wedding day the bridegroom went to the bride's house for the ceremony; then the bride and groom, along with a great procession, returned to the groom's house where a feast took place, often lasting a full week.

These bridesmaids were waiting with lamps to carry in the procession, and they hoped to take part in the wedding banquet. But when the groom didn't come at the expected time, five of them let their lamps run out of oil. By the time they had purchased extra oil, it was too late to join the feast.

This teaches Christians that they must be watchful and ready for the coming of the Lord. The foolish virgins were careless, assuming they had plenty of time to get ready when the event approached.

FEBRUARY 8

Exodus 28:1-43; Matthew 25:31–26:13; Psalms 31:9-18; Proverbs 8:12-13

EXODUS 28:6
What is an ephod?

The ephod, a priestly garment, was a close-fitting outer vest which generally extended down to the hips. The high priestly ephod was ornate with onyx stones and a lovely woven girdle.

EXODUS 28:30
What were the Urim and Thummim?

Urim and Thummim signify "lights" and "perfections." What they looked like is not known. The were perhaps two gemstones located in the breastplate of the high priest. They were specially marked, so that when they were cast to the ground, their markings and positions could be interpreted; by such decipherment, the high priest could know God's answers to questions involving national interest. In 1 Samuel 14, Urim and Thummim were used by Saul to uncover Jonathan's guilt. No mention is made of the use of the Urim and Thummim after the kingship of David. Ezra 2:63 and Nehemiah 7:65 indicate that, after the Babylonian exile, Israel had no priest with Urim and Thummim. The Bible does not refer to them after this.

MATTHEW 25:32
What is the significance of the sheep and the goats in Matthew 25:32?

Jesus used sheep and goats to picture the division between believers and unbelievers. Sheep and goats often grazed together but were separated when it came time to shear the sheep. Ezekiel 34:17-24 also refers to the separation of sheep and goats.

MATTHEW 26:6-13
Why does Matthew (and Mark) place the event in Matthew 26:6-13 just before the Last Supper, while John has it a week earlier before the Triumphal Entry?

Of the three, John places this event in the most likely chronological order (John 12:3-8). We must remember that the main purpose of the Gospel writers was to give an accurate record of Jesus' message, not to present an exact chronological account of his life. Matthew and Mark may have chosen to place this event here to contrast the complete devotion of Mary with the betrayal of Judas, the next event they record in their Gospels.

FEBRUARY 9

Exodus 29:1–30:10; Matthew 26:14-46; Psalms 31:19-24; Proverbs 8:14-26

EXODUS 29:1-26
Why did God set up the priesthood?

God had originally intended that his chosen people be a "kingdom of priests" with both the nation as a whole and each individual dealing directly with God. But the people's sin prevented this from happening, because a sinful person is not worthy to approach a perfect God. God then appointed priests from the tribe of Levi to carry out the intent of his original desire. The people could only approach God now through the priests and the system of sacrifices. Sacrifices had to be made in order to forgive the people's sin. Through these priests and their work, God wished to prepare all people for the coming of Jesus Christ, who would once again provide a direct relationship with God for anyone who would come to him. But until Christ came, the priests were the people's representatives before God. Through this Old Testament system, we can better understand the significance of what Christ did for us (see Heb. 10:1-14).

MATTHEW 26:14-15
Why would Judas want to betray Jesus?

Like the other disciples, Judas expected Jesus to start a political rebellion and overthrow Rome. As the treasurer among the Twelve (John 12:6), Judas certainly assumed (as did the other disciples—see Mark 10:35-37) that he would be given an important position in Jesus' new government. But when Jesus praised Mary for pouring out perfume worth a year's salary, Judas may have realized that Jesus' kingdom was not physical or political, but spiritual. Judas's greedy desire for money and status could not be realized if he followed Jesus, so he betrayed Jesus in exchange for money and favor from the religious leaders.

MATTHEW 26:28
Why is Jesus' blood called "the blood of the New Covenant"?

People under the Old Covenant could approach God only through a priest and an animal sacrifice. Now all people can come directly to God through faith because Jesus' death has made us acceptable in God's eyes (Rom. 3:21-25).

The Old Covenant was a shadow of the New (Jer. 31:31; Heb. 8:1ff.), pointing to the day when Jesus himself would be the final and ultimate sacrifice for sin. Rather than a lamb slain on the altar, the perfect Lamb of God was slain on the cross, a sinless sacrifice so that our sins could be forgiven once and for all. All those who believe in Christ receive that forgiveness.

FEBRUARY 10

Exodus 30:11–31:18; Matthew 26:47-68; Psalms 32:1-11; Proverbs 8:27-32

EXODUS 30:34-38
Why did the priests burn incense?

The incense was made of frankincense, salt, and equal parts of galbanum, stacte, and onycha. This comprised the holy incense, and was not to be used for non-religious purposes. The burning of the incense was to honor God, and represented prayer. In Revelation 5:8 and 8:3-4 the burning incense or perfume is said to represent the prayers of the saints. In Luke 1:10 we read that it was at the hour of prayer and incense that the angel appeared to Zechariah to tell him that his prayer had been heard and that John would be conceived in the womb of his elderly wife, Elizabeth.

EXODUS 31:18
Were the Ten Commandments the first laws in the ancient world?

The Ten Commandments were not the only code of laws at that time. Other law codes had come into existence when cities or nations decided that there must be standards of judgment, ways to correct specific wrongs. But God's laws for Israel were unique in that: (1) they alleviated the harsh judgments typical of the day; (2) they were egalitarian—the poor and the powerful received the same punishment; and (3) they did not separate religious and social law. All law rested on God's authority.

MATTHEW 26:48-49
Why did Judas kiss Jesus when he betrayed him?

A kiss is the common form of greeting used among men in Eastern lands to this day. Judas had told the temple guards to arrest the man he kissed. This was not an arrest by Roman soldiers under Roman law, but an arrest by the religious leaders. Judas pointed Jesus out not because Jesus was hard to recognize, but because Judas had agreed to be the formal accuser in case a trial was called. Judas was able to lead the group to one of Jesus' retreats where no onlookers would interfere with the arrest.

MATTHEW 26:59
What is the "Sanhedrin"?

The Sanhedrin was the most powerful religious and political body of the Jewish people. Although the Romans controlled Israel's government, they gave the people power to handle religious disputes and some civil disputes, so the Sanhedrin made many of the local decisions affecting daily life. But a death sentence had to be approved by the Romans (John 18:31).

FEBRUARY 11

Exodus 32:1–33:23; Matthew 26:69–27:14; Psalms 33:1-11; Proverbs 8:33-36

Q EXODUS 32:4-5
Why did the Israelites make their image in the form of a calf?

Two popular Egyptian gods, Hapi (Apis) and Hathor, were thought of as a bull and a heifer. The Canaanites around them worshiped Baal, thought of as a bull. Baal was their sacred symbol of power and fertility and was closely connected to immoral sexual practices. No doubt the Israelites, fresh from Egypt, found it quite natural to make a golden calf to represent the God that had just delivered them from their oppressors. They were weary of a god without a face. But in doing so, they were ignoring the command he had just given them: "You shall not make for yourself an idol in the form of anything in heaven above or on the earth beneath or in the waters below" (Exod. 20:4). They may even have thought they were worshiping God. Their apparent sincerity was no substitute for obedience or excuse for disobedience.

Q EXODUS 33:5-6
Does Exodus 33:5-6 mean that I should not wear jewelry?

This ban on jewelry was not a permanent law, but a symbol of repentance and mourning. In Exodus 35:22 the people still had their jewelry.

Q MATTHEW 26:72-74
Did Peter use foul language when he denied the Lord?

That Peter denied that he knew Jesus, using an oath and calling down curses, does not mean he used foul language. This was the kind of swearing that a person does in a court of law. Peter was swearing that he did not know Jesus and was invoking a curse on himself if his words were untrue. In effect he was saying, "May God strike me dead if I am lying."

Q MATTHEW 27:2
Who was Pilate and why was he involved in the Jews' affairs?

Pilate was the Roman governor for the regions of Samaria and Judea from A.D. 26–36. Jerusalem was located in Judea. Pilate took special pleasure in demonstrating his authority over the Jews; for example, he impounded money from the temple treasuries to build an aqueduct. Pilate was not popular, but the religious leaders had no other way to get rid of Jesus than to go to him. Ironically, when Jesus, a Jew, came before him for trial, Pilate found him innocent. He could not find a single fault in Jesus, nor could he contrive one.

FEBRUARY 12

Exodus 34:1–35:9; Matthew 27:15-31; Psalms 33:12-22; Proverbs 9:1-6

EXODUS 34:1
Did God actually write on the stone tablets?

The Ten Commandments were engraved on the stone tablets by God himself. Exodus 32:16 says, "the writing was the writing of God"; here, when the second set of the Commandments were made, Moses quotes God as saying: "I will write upon these tables the words that were in the first tables." This constitutes a miracle from the human perspective but something hardly extraordinary from the divine vantage point.

EXODUS 34:14
What does it mean that the Lord is a "jealous God"?

Here and in Exodus 20:5 God is called *jealous.* "Jealous" can be understood two ways: (1) Envious, resentful, suspicious, or distrustful; (2) solicitous in maintaining or guarding something, sleepless, scrupulous, or alert. It is in the second sense that God is jealous. He will maintain his holiness, justice, and integrity and will not suffer anyone to malign or denigrate the divine person.

MATTHEW 27:15
Who was Barabbas?

Barabbas was a well-known revolutionary who may have led the revolt mentioned in Luke 23:18-19, 25. In John 18:40 he is called a "robber," a word used by Josephus the historian to describe rebels against Roman authority. The same word is used to describe the two thieves crucified on either side of Jesus. Although an enemy to Rome, he may have been a hero to the Jews. Ironically, Barabbas was guilty of the crime for which Jesus was accused. *Barabbas* means "son of the father," which was actually Jesus' position with God.

MATTHEW 27:24
Why did Pilate wash his hands?

In making no decision, Pilate made the decision to let the crowd have its way. Although he washed his hands, his responsibility remained. At first Pilate hesitated to give the religious leaders permission to crucify Jesus. He thought they were simply jealous of a teacher who was more popular with the people than they were. But when the Jews threatened to report Pilate to Caesar (John 19:12), Pilate became afraid. Historical records indicate that the Jews had already threatened to lodge a formal complaint against Pilate for his stubborn flouting of their traditions—and such a complaint would most likely have led to his recall by Rome. His job was in jeopardy. The Roman government could not afford to put large numbers of troops in all the regions under their control, so one of Pilate's main duties was to do whatever was necessary to maintain peace.

FEBRUARY 13

Exodus 35:10–36:38; Matthew 27:32-66; Psalms 34:1-10; Proverbs 9:7-8

EXODUS 35:20-24
Where did the Israelites, who were once Egyptian slaves, get all this gold and jewelry?

When the Hebrews left Egypt, they took with them the spoils from the land—all the booty they could carry (12:35-36). This included gold, silver, jewels, linen, skins, and other valuables.

EXODUS 36:8-9
How did the Israelites weave so much cloth?

Making cloth (spinning and weaving) took a great deal of time in Moses' day. To own more than two or three changes of clothes was a sign of wealth. The effort involved in making enough cloth for the tabernacle was staggering. The tabernacle would never have been built without tremendous community involvement.

MATTHEW 27:51
Why was the curtain in the temple "split apart from top to bottom"?

The temple had three main parts—the courts, the Holy Place (where only the priests could enter), and the Most Holy Place (where only the high priest could enter, and only once a year, to atone for the sins of the nation—Leviticus 16:1-35). The curtain separating the Holy Place from the Most Holy Place was torn in two at Christ's death, symbolizing that the barrier between God and humanity was removed. Now all people are free to approach God because of Christ's sacrifice for our sins (see Heb. 9:1-14; 10:19-22).

MATTHEW 27:52
What happened to the "godly men and women" in Matthew 27:52?

Only Matthew records this miracle of the resurrection of some dead believers. We do not know how many were raised, nor do we know whether they died later and were reburied or whether they ascended into heaven in their bodies with Jesus in his ascension. As it is translated in the KJV, RSV, and NIV, this verse makes it appear that these dead came out of their graves *after* the Lord's resurrection, then went into Jerusalem and appeared to many believers.

FEBRUARY 14

EXODUS 37:1
What was the ark used for?

The ark (also called the ark of the Testimony or ark of the covenant) was built to hold the Ten Commandments. It symbolized God's covenant with his people. Two gold angels called cherubim were placed on its top. The ark was Israel's most sacred object and was kept in the Most Holy Place in the tabernacle. Only once each year, the high priest entered the Most Holy Place to sprinkle blood on the top of the ark (called the atonement cover) to atone for the sins of the entire nation.

EXODUS 38:24-25
How much was the gold and silver in the tabernacle worth?

The value of the gold given by God's people was worth approximately $10 million in today's money. The value of the silver probably was worth in excess of one million dollars.

MATTHEW 28:5-6
Why is Jesus' resurrection the key to the Christian faith?

The resurrection is the fulfillment of Old Testament prophecy (Ps. 16:10) and of Jesus' own statements (Matt. 20:19; John 10:18). While there is no record of his having been seen by nonbelievers, it attested to in a variety of ways: (1) by the eleven apostles (Acts 1:3); he thus "proved to them in many ways that it was really he himself . . ." (TLB); (2) by the apostle Paul (Acts 9:3-8; 1 Cor 15:8; Gal. 1:12); (3) by the five hundred Christian brothers (1 Cor. 15:6); and (4) by Thomas the doubter who had to see for himself (John 20:24-29). According to Paul in 1 Corinthians 15, the Christian faith stands or falls on the bodily resurrection of Jesus, for it guarantees that (1) Jesus was truly the Son of God (Rom. 1:4); (2) God the Father accepted what Jesus did at Calvary on the basis of the resurrection (Rom. 4:25); (3) the risen Christ pleads for his people before the Father (Rom. 8:34); (4) believers have the hope of eternal life (1 Pet. 1:3-5); and (5) believers will also rise and have resurrected bodies like that of Jesus (1 Cor. 15:49; Phil. 3:21; 1 John 3:2).

FEBRUARY 15

EXODUS 40:34
Why did God's glory fill the tabernacle?

The tabernacle was God's home on earth. He filled it with his presence and glory. Almost five hundred years later, Solomon built the temple, which replaced the tabernacle as the central place of worship. God also filled the temple with his glory (2 Chron. 5:13-14). But when Israel turned from God, his glory and presence departed from the temple and it was destroyed by invading armies (2 Kings 25). The temple was rebuilt in 516 B.C. The Scriptures promised that the second temple would surpass the first one in glory. This occurred nearly five centuries later when Jesus Christ came to cleanse the temple and to teach in it. When Jesus was crucified, God's glory again left the temple and the building was destroyed in A.D. 70. God no longer needed a physical building after Jesus rose from the dead. God's temple now is the New Testament church.

MARK 1:2
Why did Jesus come at this time in history?

The entire Mediterranean world was relatively peaceful under Roman rule, travel was easy, and there was a common language. The news about Jesus' life, death, and resurrection could spread quickly throughout the vast Roman empire. In Israel, common men and women were ready for Jesus too. There had been no God-sent prophets for four hundred years, since the days of Malachi (who wrote the last book of the Old Testament). There was growing anticipation that a great prophet, or the Messiah mentioned in the Old Testament, would soon come (see Luke 3:15).

MARK 1:9
If John's baptism was for repentance from sin, why was Jesus baptized?

While even the greatest prophets (Isaiah, Jeremiah, Ezekiel) had to confess their sinfulness and need for repentance, Jesus didn't need to admit sin—he was sinless. Although Jesus didn't need forgiveness, he was baptized for the following reasons: (1) to begin his mission to bring the message of salvation to all people; (2) to show support for John's ministry; (3) to identify with our humanness and sin; (4) to give us an example to follow. We know that John's baptism was different from Christian baptism in the church because Paul had John's followers baptized again (see Acts 19:2-5).

FEBRUARY 16

Leviticus 1:1–3:17; Mark 1:29–2:12; Psalms 35:17-28; Proverbs 9:13-18

LEVITICUS 1:2-3
Why did God place so much emphasis on sacrifices?

Sacrifices were God's way in the Old Testament for people to ask forgiveness for their sins. Since creation, God has made it clear that sin separates people from him, and that those who sin deserve to die. Because "all have sinned" (Rom. 3:23), God designed sacrifice as a way to seek forgiveness and restore a relationship with him. Because he is a God of love and mercy, God decided from the very first that he would come into our world and die to pay the penalty for all humans. This he did in his Son who, while still God, became a human being. In the meantime, before God made this ultimate sacrifice of his Son, he instructed people to kill animals as sacrifices for sin. Animal sacrifice accomplished two purposes: (1) the animal symbolically took the sinner's place and paid the penalty for sin, and (2) the animal's death represented one life given so that another life could be saved. This method of sacrifice continued throughout Old Testament times. It was effective in teaching and guiding the people and bringing them back to God. But in New Testament times, Christ's death became the last sacrifice needed. He took our punishment once and for all. Animal sacrifice is no longer required. Now, all people can be freed from the penalty of sin by simply believing in Jesus and accepting the forgiveness he offers.

MARK 1:34
Why didn't Jesus want the demons to reveal who he was?

(1) By commanding the demons to remain silent, Jesus proved his authority and power over them. (2) Jesus wanted the people to believe he was the Messiah because of what he said and did, not because of the demons' words. (3) Jesus wanted to reveal his identity as the Messiah according to his timetable, not according to Satan's timetable. Satan wanted the people to follow Jesus around based on his popularity, not because he was the Son of God.

MARK 2:9-11
What does the title "Son of Man" mean?

This is the first time in Mark that Jesus is referred to as the "Son of Man." The title *Son of Man* emphasizes that Jesus is fully human, while *Son of God* (see, for example, John 20:31) emphasizes that he is fully God. As God's Son, Jesus has the authority to forgive sin. As a man, he can identify with our deepest needs and sufferings and help us overcome sin.

FEBRUARY 17

Q LEVITICUS 4:2
What kind of sins were covered by the sin offering?

Sins which were intended to reject God's sovereignty were to be punished by executing the offender (Num. 15:30-31). The sin offering was for those who (1) committed a sin without realizing it or (2) committed a sin out of weakness or negligence as opposed to outright rebellion against God. Different animals were sacrificed for the different kinds of sin. The death of Jesus Christ was the final sin offering in the Bible (2 Cor. 5:21).

Q LEVITICUS 5:14-19
Is the guilt offering different from the sin offering?

The guilt offering was another way of taking care of sin committed unintentionally. It was for those who sinned in some way against "holy things"—the tabernacle or the priesthood—as well as for those who unintentionally sinned against someone. In either case, a ram with no defects had to be sacrificed, plus those harmed by the sin had to be compensated for their loss, plus a 20 percent penalty. Even though Christ's death has made guilt offerings unnecessary for us today, we still need to make things right with those we hurt.

Q MARK 2:18-22
Is fasting a part of the old way of doing things (the old wine)?

John had two goals: to lead people to repent of their sin, and to prepare them for Christ's coming. John's message caused sober reflection, so he and his followers fasted. Their fasting was an outward sign of humility and regret for sin. Jesus' disciples did not need to fast to prepare for his coming because he was with them. Jesus did not condemn fasting, however. He himself fasted for forty days (Matt. 4:2). Nevertheless, Jesus emphasized fasting with the right motives. The Pharisees fasted twice a week to show others how holy they were. Jesus explained that if people fast only to impress others, they will be twisting the purpose of fasting.

Q MARK 2:23-28
Was Jesus stealing the grain in Mark 2:23?

Jesus and his disciples were not stealing when they picked the grain. Leviticus 19:9-10 and Deuteronomy 23:25 say that farmers were to leave the edges of their fields unharvested so that some of their crops could be picked by travelers and by the poor.

FEBRUARY 18

Leviticus 6:1–7:27; Mark 3:7-30; Psalms 37:1-11; Proverbs 10:3-4

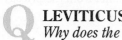

LEVITICUS 6:12-13
Why did the fire on the altar have to keep burning?

The holy fire on the altar had to keep burning because God had started it. It had come down from God supernaturally. The supernatural origin of the altar fire represented God's eternal presence in the sacrificial system, and meant, in effect, that only by the grace of God were sacrifices acceptable for atonement. Man-made fire was forbidden. The sin of bringing unholy (man-made) fire to the altar resulted in the deaths of Nadab and Abihu (Lev. 10:1-2).

LEVITICUS 7:26, KJV
Why does the Bible say to "eat no manner of blood"?

The prohibition against eating blood can be traced all the way back to Noah (Gen. 9:4). God prohibited eating or drinking blood for several reasons. (1) To discourage pagan practices. Israel was to be separate and distinct from the foreign nations around them. Eating blood was a common pagan practice. It was often done in hopes of gaining the characteristics of the slain animal (strength, speed, etc.). God's people were to rely on him, not on ingested blood, for their strength. (2) To preserve the symbolism of the sacrifice. Blood symbolized the life of the animal that was sacrificed in the sinner's place. To drink it would change the symbolism of the sacrificial penalty and destroy the evidence of the sacrifice. (3) To protect the people from infection, because many deadly diseases are transmitted through the blood. The Jews took this prohibition seriously, and that is why Jesus' hearers were so upset when Jesus told them to drink his blood (John 6:53-56). However Jesus, as God himself and the last sacrifice ever needed for sins, was asking believers to identify with him completely. He wants us to take his life into us, and he wants to participate in our lives as well.

MARK 3:14-15
Why did Jesus choose twelve men?

The number twelve corresponds to the twelve tribes of Israel (Matt. 19:28), showing the continuity between the old religious system and the new one based on Jesus' message. Many people followed Jesus, but these twelve received the most intense training. We see the impact of these men throughout the rest of the New Testament.

FEBRUARY 19

Leviticus 7:28–9:6; Mark 3:31–4:25; Psalms 37:12-29; Proverbs 10:5

LEVITICUS 8:1-3
Why did Aaron and his sons need to be cleansed and set apart?

Although all the men from the tribe of Levi were dedicated for service to God, only Aaron's descendants could be priests. They alone had the honor and responsibility of performing the sacrifices. These priests had to cleanse and dedicate themselves before they could help the people do the same. The ceremony described in Leviticus 8 and 9 was their ordination ceremony. Blood was placed on the priests to show that the entire person was set apart for service to God. This showed that holiness came from God alone, not from the priestly role.

LEVITICUS 8:12
What was the significance of anointing Aaron as high priest?

The high priest had special duties that no other priest had. He alone could enter the Most Holy Place in the tabernacle on the yearly Day of Atonement to atone for the sins of the nation. Therefore he was in charge of all the other priests. The high priest was a picture of Jesus Christ, who is our High Priest (Hebrews 7:26-28).

MARK 3:31-35
Did Jesus have brothers and sisters?

Jesus' mother was Mary (Luke 1:30-31), and his brothers were probably the other children Mary and Joseph had after Jesus. His sisters and brothers are mentioned in Mark 6:3. Some Christians, however, believe the ancient tradition that Jesus was Mary's only child. If this is true, the "brothers" were possibly cousins (cousins were often called brothers in those days). Some have offered yet another suggestion: when Joseph married Mary, he was a widower, and these were his children by his first marriage. Most likely, these were Jesus' half brothers.

MARK 4:3
Why did the farmer's seed fall outside of the field?

Seed was planted, or sowed, by hand. As the farmer walked across the field, he threw handfuls of seed onto the ground from a large bag slung across his shoulders. The plants did not grow in neat rows as with today's machine planting. No matter how skillful, no farmer could keep all of his seed from falling by the wayside, from being scattered among rocks and thorns, or from being carried off by the wind. So the farmer would throw the seed liberally, and enough would fall on good ground to ensure the harvest.

FEBRUARY 20

Leviticus 9:7–10:20; Mark 4:26–5:20; Psalms 37:30-40; Proverbs 10:6-7

LEVITICUS 10:1-2, TLB
What was the unholy fire that Nadab and Abihu offered before the Lord?

Leviticus 6:12-13 mentions that the fire on the altar of burnt offering was never to go out, implying that it was holy. It is possible that Nadab and Abihu brought coals of fire to the altar from another source, making the sacrifice unholy. It has also been suggested that the two priests gave an offering at an unprescribed time. Whatever explanation is correct, the point is that Nadab and Abihu abused their office as priests in a flagrant act of disrespect to God, who had just reviewed with them precisely how they were to conduct worship. As leaders, they had special responsibility to obey God. In their position, they could easily lead many people astray. Aaron's sons were careless about following the laws for sacrifices. In response, God destroyed them with a blast of fire. Performing the sacrifices was an act of obedience. Doing them correctly showed respect for God.

MARK 37-38
Why were experienced fishermen on the sea in a storm?

The Sea of Galilee is an unusual body of water. It is relatively small (13 miles long, 7 miles wide), but it is 150 feet deep, and the shoreline is 680 feet below sea level. Sudden storms can appear over the surrounding mountains with little warning, stirring the water into violent 20-foot waves. This was an open fishing boat large enough to hold Jesus and his 12 disciples and was powered both by oars and sails. During a storm, however, the sails were taken down to keep them from ripping and to make the boat easier to control. The disciples had not foolishly set out in a storm. They had been caught without warning, and their danger was great.

MARK 5:19
Why did Jesus instruct this man to tell his friends about the miraculous healing?

Most of the time, Jesus urged those he healed to keep quiet. Why the change? Here are possible answers: (1) The demon-possessed man had been alone and unable to speak. Telling others what Jesus did for him would prove that he was healed. (2) This was mainly a Gentile and pagan area, so Jesus was not expecting great crowds to follow him or religious leaders to hinder him. (3) By sending the man away with this good news, Jesus was expanding his ministry to the Gentiles.

FEBRUARY 21

Leviticus 11:1–12:8; Mark 5:21-43; Psalms 38:1-22; Proverbs 10:8-9

Q LEVITICUS 11:47
Why did God restrict the diet of the Israelites?

The designations "clean" and "unclean" were used to define the kind of animals the Israelites could and could not eat. There were several reasons for this restricted diet: (1) To insure the health of the nation. The forbidden foods were usually scavenging animals that fed on dead animals; thus disease could be transmitted through them. (2) To visibly distinguish Israel from other nations. The pig, for example, was a common sacrifice of pagan religions. (3) To avoid objectionable associations. The creatures that move about on the ground, for example, were reminiscent of serpents, which often symbolized sin.

Q LEVITICUS 12:1-4
Why was a woman considered unclean after the wonderful miracle of birth?

It was due to the bodily secretions occurring during and after childbirth. These were considered unclean and made the woman unprepared to enter the pure surroundings of the tabernacle. *Unclean* did not mean sinful or dirty. God created us male and female, and he ordered us to be fruitful and multiply (Gen. 1:27-28). He did not change his mind and say that sex and procreation were now somehow unclean. Instead, he made a distinction between his worship and the popular worship of fertility gods and goddesses. Canaanite religions incorporated prostitution and immoral rites as the people begged their gods to make their crops, herds, and families increase. By contrast, God kept worship and sex entirely separate, helping the Israelites avoid confusion with pagan rites. The Israelites worshiped God as their loving Creator and Provider, and they thanked him for bountiful crops and safe childbirth.

Q MARK 5:32-34
Was Jesus angry with this woman for touching him?

He knew she had touched him, but he stopped and asked who did it in order to teach her something about faith. Although the woman was healed when she touched him, Jesus said her faith caused the cure.

Q MARK 5:38, TLB
Why were the people "weeping and wailing" so loud?

Loud weeping and wailing was customary at a person's death. Lack of it was the ultimate disgrace and disrespect. There were some people, usually women, who made mourning a profession and were paid by the dead person's family to weep over the body. On the day of death, the body was carried through the streets, followed by mourners, family members, and friends.

FEBRUARY 22

Leviticus 13:1-59; Mark 6:1-29; Psalms 39:1-13; Proverbs 10:10

PSALM 39:10, NRSV
What did David mean when he asked God, "Remove your stroke from me"?

This is a metaphor of the discipline a parent should give to a disobedient child. It may also be a picture of the difficulties David was facing that caused him to feel as if he were being struck. Just as a loving father carefully disciplines his children, so God corrects us (Heb. 12:5-9).

MARK 6:7, KJV
Why were the disciples sent "by two and two"?

Jesus sent forth the twelve in pairs. This meant that his own ministry was increased sixfold. Individually they could have reached more areas of the country, but this was not Christ's plan. One advantage in going out by twos was that they could strengthen and encourage each other, especially when they faced rejection.

MARK 6:14
How could Herod think that Jesus was "John the Baptist come back to life again"?

Herod, along with many others, wondered who Jesus really was. Unable to accept Jesus' claim to be God's Son, many people made up their own explanations for his power and authority. Herod thought that Jesus was John the Baptist come back to life, while those who were familiar with the Old Testament thought he was Elijah (Mal. 4:5). Still others believed that Jesus was a teaching prophet in the tradition of Moses, Isaiah, or Jeremiah.

MARK 6:17-29
Who were Herod, Herodias, and Philip? And why did Herod kill John?

Palestine was divided into four territories, each with a different ruler. Herod Antipas, called Herod in the Gospels, was ruler over Galilee; his brother Philip ruled over Traconitis and Idumea. Philip's wife was Herodias, but she left him to marry Herod Antipas. When John confronted the two for committing adultery, Herodias formulated a plot to kill him. Instead of trying to get rid of her sin, Herodias tried to get rid of the one who brought it to public attention. This is exactly what the religious leaders were trying to do to Jesus. Herod arrested John the Baptist under pressure from his wife and advisers. Though Herod respected John's integrity, in the end Herod had John killed because of pressure from his peers and family.

FEBRUARY 23

LEVITICUS 14:8-42
Could leprosy really infect one's clothing or house?

The Hebrew word for "leprosy" included a variety of skin diseases as well as other molds and fungi. The "leprosy" found on clothing or house walls was more like a mold, fungus, or bacteria. Like mildew, this fungus could spread rapidly and promote disease. It was therefore important to check its spread as soon as possible.

LEVITICUS 14:54-57
Are we to follow the Old Testament health and dietary restrictions today?

These laws were given for the people's health and protection and helped the Israelites avoid diseases that were serious threats in that time and place. In general, the basic principles of health and cleanliness are still healthful practices, but it would be legalistic, if not wrong, to adhere to each specific restriction today. Some of these regulations were intended to mark the Israelites as different from the wicked people around them. Others were given to prevent God's people from becoming involved in pagan religious practices, one of the most serious problems of the day. Still others related to quarantines in a culture where exact medical diagnosis was impossible. Today, for example, physicians can diagnose the different forms of leprosy, and they know which ones are contagious. Treatment methods have greatly improved, and quarantine for leprosy is rarely necessary.

MARK 6:30
What is an apostle?

Mark uses the word *apostles* only once. *Apostle* means "one sent" as messenger or missionary. The word became an official title for Jesus' twelve disciples after his death and resurrection (Acts 2:14; Eph. 2:20).

MARK 6:52
What does it mean that the disciples "hearts were hardened"?

This means that the disciples didn't want to believe. This may have been because (1) they couldn't accept the fact that this human named Jesus was really the Son of God; (2) they dared not believe that the Messiah would choose them as his followers—it was too good to be true; (3) they still did not understand the real purpose for Jesus' coming to earth. Their disbelief took the form of misunderstanding.

FEBRUARY 24

Leviticus 15:1–16:28; Mark 7:1-23; Psalms 40:11-17; Proverbs 10:13-14

 LEVITICUS 15:18
Is Leviticus 15:18 implying that sex is dirty or disgusting?

God created sex for the enjoyment of married couples as well as for continuing the race and continuing the covenant. Everything must be seen and done with a view toward God's love and control. Sex is not separate from spirituality and God's care. God is concerned about our sexual habits. We tend to separate our physical and spiritual lives, but there is an inseparable intertwining. God must be Lord over our whole selves—including our private lives.

 LEVITICUS 16:5-28
What do the two goats represent?

This event occurred on the Day of Atonement. The two goats represented the two ways God was dealing with the Israelites' sin: (1) he was forgiving their sin through the first goat, which was sacrificed, and (2) he was removing their guilt through the second goat, the scapegoat that was sent into the wilderness. This symbolized how God carried away the sins of the people. The same ritual had to be repeated every year. Jesus Christ's death replaced this system once and for all. At any time we can have our sins forgiven and guilt removed by placing our trust in Christ, our permanent "scapegoat" (Heb. 10:1-18).

MARK 7:1
What did the Pharisees believe?

The Pharisees were the most influential sect of the day. They believed in rigid separation from anything non-Jewish. Their theology included (1) the most careful keeping of the law; (2) a belief on the immortality of the soul, the resurrection of the body, and retribution in the afterlife; (3) a belief in the reality of angels and spirits; (4) a belief that God would deliver Israel and restore her earlier glory; and (5) a belief in the doctrine of providence along with free will. Overriding all of this was their belief that Jews earned merit by keeping all the major and minor points of the law.

 MARK 7:3-4
Why did Mark explain the Jewish rituals?

Mark explained these Jewish rituals because he was writing to a non-Jewish audience. Before each meal, devout Jews performed a short ceremony, washing their hands and arms in a specific way. The disciples did not have dirty hands, but they were simply not carrying out this traditional cleansing. The Pharisees thought this ceremony cleansed them from any contact they might have had with anything considered unclean. Jesus said they were wrong in thinking they were acceptable to God just because they were clean on the outside.

FEBRUARY 25

Leviticus 16:29–18:30; Mark 7:24–8:10; Psalms 41:1-13; Proverbs 10:15-16

 ### LEVITICUS 17:3-9
Why were the Israelites prohibited from sacrificing outside the tabernacle area?

God had established specific times and places for sacrifices, and each occasion was permeated with symbolism. If people sacrificed on their own, they might easily add to or subtract from God's laws to fit their own life-styles. Many pagan religions allowed every individual priest to set his own rules; God's command helped the Israelites resist the temptation to follow the pagan pattern. It is interesting that when the Israelites slipped into idolatry, it was because "everyone did as he saw fit" (Judg. 17:6).

LEVITICUS 17:11-14
How does blood make atonement for sin?

On the one hand, blood represented the sinner's life, infected by his sin and headed for death. On the other hand, the blood represented the innocent life of the animal that was sacrificed in place of the guilty person making the offering. The death of the animal (of which the blood was proof) fulfilled the penalty of death. God therefore granted forgiveness to the sinner. It is God who forgives based on the faith of the person doing the sacrificing.

MARK 7:24
How far was Tyre and Sidon from Galilee?

Jesus traveled about 50 miles to Tyre and then went to Sidon. These were port cities on the Mediterranean Sea north of Israel. Both cities had flourishing trade and were very wealthy. They were proud, historic Canaanite cities. In David's day, Tyre was on friendly terms with Israel (2 Sam. 5:11), but soon afterward the city became known for its wickedness. Its king, Ethbaal, even claimed to be God (Ezek. 28:1ff.). Tyre rejoiced when Jerusalem was destroyed in 586 B.C., because without Israel's competition, Tyre's trade and profits would increase. It was into this evil and materialistic culture that Jesus brought his message.

MARK 7:26
What is a "Syrophoenician"?

This woman is called a *Syrophoenician* in Mark and a *Canaanite* in Matthew. Mark's designation refers to her political background. His Roman audience would easily identify her by the part of the empire that was her home. Matthew's description was designed for his Jewish audience, who remembered the Canaanites as bitter enemies when Israel was settling the promised land.

FEBRUARY 26

Leviticus 19:1–20:21; Mark 8:11-38; Psalms 42:1-11; Proverbs 10:17

Q **LEVITICUS 20:10-21**
The list of commands against sexual sins in Leviticus 20:10-21 includes extremely harsh punishments. Why?

The detestable acts listed here were very common in the pagan nations of Canaan; their religions were rampant with sex goddesses, temple prostitution, and other gross sins. The Canaanites' immoral religious practices reflected a decadent culture that tended to corrupt whoever came in contact with it. By contrast, God was building a nation to make a positive influence on the world. So he prepared the people for what they would face in the promised land and commanded them against falling into the trap of such sexual sins.

Sexual sins were dealt with swiftly and harshly in the Old Testament. God had no tolerance for such acts for the following reasons: (1) they shatter the mutual commitment of married partners; (2) they destroy the sanctity of the family; (3) they twist people's mental well-being; and (4) they spread disease. Sexual sin has always been widely available, but the glorification of sex between people who are not married to each other often hides deep tragedy and hurt behind the scenes. When society portrays sexual sins as attractive, it is easy to forget the dark side. God had good reasons for prohibiting sexual sins: He loves us and wants the very best for us.

Q **MARK 8:11**
Why were the Pharisees seeking a "sign from heaven"?

The Pharisees had tried to explain away Jesus' previous miracles by claiming they were done by luck, coincidence, or evil power. Here they demanded a sign from heaven—something only God could do. Jesus refused their demand because he knew that even this kind of miracle would not convince them. They had already decided not to believe. Hearts can become so hard that even the most convincing facts and demonstrations will not change them.

Q **MARK 8:27**
What kind of place was Caesarea Philippi?

Caesarea Philippi was an especially pagan city known for its worship of Greek gods and its temples devoted to the ancient god Baal. Herod Philip, mentioned in Mark 6:18, changed the city's name from Caesarea to Caesarea Philippi so that it would not be confused with the coastal city of Caesarea (Acts 8:40), the capital of the territory ruled by his brother Herod Antipas. This pagan city where many gods were recognized was a fitting place for Jesus to ask the disciples to recognize him as the Son of God.

FEBRUARY 27

Leviticus 20:22–22:16; Mark 9:1-29; Psalms 43:1-5; Proverbs 10:18

Q LEVITICUS 21:16-23
Was God unfairly discriminating against handicapped people when he said they were unqualified to offer sacrifices?

Just as God demanded that no imperfect animals be used for sacrifice, he required that no handicapped priests offer sacrifices. This was not meant as an insult; rather, it had to do with the fact that the priest must match as closely as possible the perfect God he served. Of course, such perfection was not fully realized until Jesus Christ came. As Levites, the handicapped priests were protected and supported with food from the sacrifices. They were not abandoned, because they still performed many essential services within the tabernacle.

Q LEVITICUS 21:44
Why did the high priest have to marry a virgin?

The high priest could not marry a widow (as other priests could), much less one divorced, or a harlot. High priests were a type of Christ. As the church is to be presented as a chaste virgin to Christ (2 Cor. 11:2), so the high priest could marry only a virgin.

Q MARK 9:2
Why did Jesus only take Peter, James, and John to the mountain?

We don't know why Jesus singled out Peter, James, and John for this special revelation of his glory and purity. Perhaps they were the ones most ready to understand and accept this great truth. These three disciples were the inner circle of the group of 12. They were among the first to hear Jesus' call (Mark 1:16-19). They headed the Gospel lists of disciples (Mark 3:16). And they were present at certain healings where others were excluded (Luke 8:51).

Q MARK 9:3-8
What was the significance of the transfiguration?

The transfiguration revealed Christ's divine nature as God's Son. God's voice singled Jesus out from Moses and Elijah as the long-awaited Messiah with full divine authority. Moses represented the law, and Elijah, the prophets. With their appearance, Jesus was shown as the fulfillment of both the Old Testament law and the prophetic promises. Jesus was not a reincarnation of Elijah or Moses. He was not merely one of the prophets. As God's only Son, he far surpasses their authority and power.

FEBRUARY 28

Leviticus 22:17–23:44; Mark 9:30–10:12; Psalms 44:1-8; Proverbs 10:19

Q LEVITICUS 23:6
What was the significance of the feast of unleavened bread?

The Feast of Unleavened Bread reminded Israel of their escape from Egypt. For seven days they ate unleavened bread, just as they had eaten it back then (Exod. 12:14-15). The symbolism of this bread made without yeast was important to the Israelites. First, because the bread was unique, it illustrated Israel's uniqueness as a nation. Second, because yeast was a symbol of sin, the bread represented Israel's moral purity. Third, the bread reminded them to obey quickly. Their ancestors left the yeast out of their dough so they could leave Egypt quickly without waiting for the dough to rise.

Q MARK 9:2
Why were the disciples afraid to ask Jesus about his prediction of his death?

Perhaps it was because the last time they reacted to Jesus' sobering words they were scolded (Mark 8:32-33). In their minds, Jesus seemed morbidly preoccupied with death. Actually it was the disciples who were wrongly preoccupied—constantly thinking about the kingdom they hoped Jesus would bring and their positions in it. They were worried what would happen to them if Jesus died and the kingdom as they imagined it could not come. Consequently they preferred not to ask him about his predictions.

Q MARK 9:49
What did Jesus mean when he said, "For everyone will be salted with fire"?

Numerous explanations have been given for this phrase. Many commentators perceive this as an allusion to Leviticus 2:13, which states that cereal offerings are to be offered with the salt of the covenant (literal translation). Since salt is a preservative and fire is often used as a purifier, the metaphor speaks of preserving and purifying.

Q MARK 10:3-9
Why did God permit divorce?

God allowed divorce as a concession to people's sinfulness. Divorce was not approved, but it was instituted to protect the injured party in a bad situation. Unfortunately, the Pharisees used Deuteronomy 24:1 as a prooftext for divorce. Jesus explained that this was not God's intent; instead, God wants married people to consider their marriage permanent.

MARCH 1

LEVITICUS 25:8-16
What was the "year of jubilee"?

The *year of jubilee* occurred every fiftieth year. It commenced on the day of atonement. It was called by different names, such as the *year of release* (Ezek. 46:17), the *time of God's favor* (Isa. 61:2), and the *year of redemption* (Isa. 63:4). It was introduced with the blowing of trumpets. All field labor ceased for that year. Nonurban property came back to the original owner, inheritances were restored, and slaves were freed. There is no indication in the Bible that the year of jubilee was ever carried out. If the Israelites had followed this practice faithfully, they would have been a society without permanent poverty. The year of jubilee is said to be fulfilled in the gospel (Luke 4:18-19) when people are set free from their bondage and brought into the glorious liberty of the sons of God through Jesus Christ.

LEVITICUS 25:44
Why did God allow the Israelites to purchase slaves?

Under Hebrew laws, slaves were treated differently from slaves in other nations. They were seen as human beings with dignity, and not as animals. Nowhere does the Bible condone slavery, but it recognizes its existence. God's laws offered many guidelines for treating slaves properly. Hebrew slaves, for example, took part in the religious festivals and rested on the Sabbath.

MARK 10:13-16
Why did Jesus' disciples rebuke the people who brought the children to Jesus?

Jesus was often criticized for spending too much time with the wrong people—children, tax collectors, and sinners (Matt. 9:11; Luke 15:1-2; 19:7). Some, including the disciples, thought Jesus should be spending more time with important leaders and the devout, because this was the way to improve his position and avoid criticism. But Jesus didn't need to improve his position. He was God, and he wanted to speak to those who needed him most.

MARK 10:25
How can a camel pass through the eye of a needle?

This figure of speech indicates how difficult it is for a rich person who prides himself on his material possessions to repent and accept Christ as his Savior. There is no evidence to support the idea that Jesus was referring to a certain narrow gateway in Jerusalem.

MARCH 2

Leviticus 25:47–27:13; Mark 10:32-52; Psalms 45:1-17; Proverbs 10:22

Q LEVITICUS 26:46
Does the Old Testament law apply to the New Testament age?

The Law of Moses takes in the total economy in which the people of Israel moved and lived. The Law can be divided into three segments: (1) the moral law of the Ten Commandments (Deut. 5:22; 10:4); (2) the ceremonial law which set forth the proper approach to God in worship (Lev. 7:37-38); (3) the civil law under which the people lived and were governed (Deut. 17:9-11). The ceremonial law, having been fulfilled by Jesus Christ, is no longer binding on people under the new covenant. The civil law was designed for the Old Testament theocracy, so other nations living under other conditions are not bound by it. The basic moral law, however, applies to all people of all eras and has for its purposes: (1) showing all men their need for a Savior; (2) laying down the rules which men of faith can follow in order to please him who has saved them; and (3) a restraining influence on all of mankind so that a government of law and not of men is made possible.

Q MARK 10:46
Were beggars aided by the government or religion of Israel?

Beggars were a common sight in most towns. Because most occupations of that day required physical labor, anyone with a crippling disease or disability was at a severe disadvantage and was usually forced to beg, even though God's laws commanded care for such needy people (Lev. 25:35-38). Blindness was considered a curse from God for sin (John 9:2), but Jesus refuted this idea when he reached out to heal the blind.

Q MARK 10:47
Why did the beggar call Jesus "Son of David"?

"Son of David" was a popular way of addressing Jesus as the Messiah, because it was known that the Messiah would be a descendant of King David (Isa. 9:7). Jesus was "made of the seed of David" (Rom. 1:4, KJV), and David appears in the genealogy of Jesus Christ (Matt. 1:1). Luke 1:32 says that Jesus will inherit the throne of David. The fact that Bartimaeus called Jesus the Son of David shows that he recognized Jesus as the Messiah. His faith in Jesus as the Messiah brought about his healing.

MARCH 3

NUMBERS 1:2-15
What was the use of taking a census of Israel?

Taking a census was long and tedious, but it was an important task. The fighting men had to be counted to determine Israel's military strength before entering the promised land. In addition, the tribes had to be organized to determine the amount of land each would need, as well as to provide genealogical records. Without such a census, the task of conquering and organizing the promised land would have been more difficult.

EXODUS 1:7
How could such a large population grow from Jacob's family of 70 who moved down to Egypt?

The book of Exodus tells us that the Israelites who descended from Jacob's family "multiplied greatly". Because they remained in Egypt more than four hundred years, they had plenty of time to grow into a large group of people. After leaving Egypt, they were able to survive in the desert because God miraculously provided the food and water they needed. The leaders of Moab were terrified because of the large number of Israelites (Num. 22:3).

MARK 11:11-24
Why was the fig tree withered after Jesus cleared the temple?

There are two parts to this unusual incident: the cursing of the fig tree and the clearing of the temple. The cursing of the fig tree was an acted-out parable related to the clearing of the temple. The temple was supposed to be a place of worship, but true worship had disappeared. The fig tree showed promise of fruit, but it produced none. Jesus was showed his anger at religious life without substance.

MARK 11:13-25
What was the significance of the fig tree?

Fig trees require three years from the time they are planted until they can bear fruit. Each tree yields a great amount of fruit twice a year, in late spring and in early autumn. This incident occurred early in the spring fig season. The figs normally grow as the leaves fill out; but this tree, though full of leaves, had none. The tree looked promising but offered no fruit. Jesus' harsh words to the fig tree could be applied to the nation of Israel. Fruitful in appearance only, Israel was spiritually barren.

MARCH 4

NUMBERS 2:2
Why was the nation of Israel organized according to tribes?

This was done for several reasons. (1) It was an effective way to manage and govern a large group. (2) It made dividing the promised land easier. (3) It was part of their culture and heritage (people were not known by a last name, but by their family, clan, and tribe). (4) It made it easier to keep detailed genealogies, and genealogies were the only way to prove membership in God's chosen nation. (5) It made travel much more efficient. The people followed the tribe's standard (a kind of flag), and thus stayed together and kept from getting lost. This must have been one of the biggest campsites the world has ever seen! It would have taken about twelve square miles to set up tents for just the 600,000 fighting men—not to mention the women and children.

MARK 12:1-12
What is the meaning of the parable in Mark 12:1-12?

In this parable, the man who planted the vineyard is God; the vineyard is the nation Israel; the tenants are Israel's religious leaders; the servants are the prophets and priests who remained faithful to God; the son is Jesus; and the others are the Gentiles. By telling this story, Jesus exposed the religious leaders' plot to kill him and warned that their sins would be punished. Israel, pictured as a vineyard, was the nation that God had cultivated to bring salvation to the world. The religious leaders not only frustrated their nation's purpose; they also killed those who were trying to fulfill it. They were so jealous and possessive that they ignored the welfare of the very people they were supposed to be bringing to God.

MARK 12:10
Why did Jesus refer to himself as the stone rejected by the builders?

Jesus knew he would be rejected by most of the Jewish leaders, but he would become the cornerstone of a new "building," the church (Acts 4:11-12). A cornerstone was used as a base to make sure the other stones of the building were straight and level. Likewise, Jesus' life and teaching would be the church's foundation.

MARCH 5

NUMBERS 5:11-30
What is the purpose of this test for adultery?

This "Law of Jealousy" served to remove a jealous husband's suspicion. Trust between husband and wife had to be completely eroded, however, for a man to bring his wife to the priest for this type of test. Whether justified or not, suspicion must be removed for a marriage to survive and trust to be restored. This law was instituted so that God himself could determine the guilt of innocence of a wife whose conduct was suspect but for whose guilt there was no proof. It was to the advantage of an innocent party to go through the ordeal and have her name cleared and her husband reassured. The Scriptures afford no example of the use of this provision. Today we are unsure what the bitter water and the rotting thigh were. But the intent of the procedure is still clear. In the absence of positive proof, the procedure was an appeal to God to determine the guilt or innocence of the accused person. The passage does not say what should be done if a wife suspected her husband of adultery but had no certainty that he had been unfaithful.

MARK 12:31-33, NRSV
Why did Jesus say that loving one's God and neighbor is "much more important than all whole burnt offerings and sacrifices"?

God's laws are not burdensome. They can be reduced to two simple rules for life: love God and love others. These commands are from the Old Testament (Lev. 19:18; Deut. 6:5). When you love God completely and care for others as you care for yourself, then you have fulfilled the intent of the Ten Commandments and the other Old Testament laws. According to Jesus, these two commandments summarize all God's laws.

MARK 12:35-37
Why did David call his descendant "Lord"?

Jesus quoted Psalm 110:1 to show that David considered the Messiah to be his Lord, not just his son. The religious leaders did not understand that the Messiah would be far more than a human descendant of David; he would be God himself in human form. The scribes did teach that the Messiah was to be the Son of David. But they did not explain how and why David called that Son "Lord." Obviously, by calling him Lord, David meant that the Son of David was the Son of God and as such was worthy of being his Lord.

MARCH 6

Numbers 6:1–7:89; Mark 12:38–13:13; Psalms 49:1-20; Proverbs 10:27-28

NUMBERS 6:1-2
What is a "Nazirite"?

God instituted the Nazirite vow for people who wanted to devote some time exclusively to serving him. This vow could be taken for as little as thirty days or as long as a lifetime. It was voluntary, with one exception—parents could take the vow for their young children, making them Nazirites for life. The vow included three distinct restrictions: (1) he must abstain from wine and fermented drink; (2) the hair could not be cut, and the beard could not be shaved; and (3) touching a dead body was prohibited. The purpose of the Nazirite vow was to raise up a group of leaders devoted completely to God. Samson, Samuel, and John the Baptist were probably Nazirites for life.

NUMBERS 6:24-26
What is the purpose of the blessing in Numbers 6:24-26?

A blessing was one way of asking for God's divine favor to rest upon others. The ancient blessing in these verses helps us understand what a blessing was supposed to do. Its five parts conveyed hope that God would bless and keep them (favor and protect); (2) make his face shine upon them (be pleased); (3) be gracious (merciful and compassionate); (4) turn his face toward them (give his approval); (5) give peace. Some say that this blessing was given at the close of the morning sacrifice, in order to show that when the Messiah came, in the evening of the world, the gospel would replace the law, and the blessing of Christ would be instituted.

MARK 13:3-4
Where is the Mount of Olives?

The Mount of Olives rises above Jerusalem to the east. From its slopes a person can look down into the city and see the temple. Zechariah 14:1-4 predicts that the Messiah will stand on this very mountain when he returns to set up his eternal kingdom.

MARK 13:5-7
What are the signs of the end times?

There have been people in every generation since Christ's resurrection claiming to know exactly when Jesus would return. No one has been right yet, however, because Christ will return on God's timetable, not ours. Jesus predicted that before his return, many believers would be misled by false teachers claiming to have revelations from God. According to Scripture, the one clear sign of Christ's return will be his unmistakable appearance in the clouds, which will be seen by all people (Mark 13:26; Rev. 1:7).

MARCH 7

NUMBERS 8:23-24
Why were the Levites supposed to retire at age 50?

The reasons were probably more practical than theological. (1) Moving the tabernacle and its furniture through the desert required strength. The younger men were more suited for the work of lifting the heavy articles. (2) The Levites over 50 did not stop working altogether. They were allowed to assist with various light duties in the tabernacle. This helped the younger men assume more responsibilities, and it allowed the older men to be in a position to advise and counsel them.

NUMBERS 9:15-22
What was the pillar of cloud and pillar of fire?

A pillar of cloud by day and a pillar of fire by night guided and protected the Israelites as they traveled across the desert. Some have said this pillar may have been a burning bowl of pitch whose smoke was visible during the day and whose fire could be seen at night. However, a bowl of pitch would not have lifted itself up and moved ahead of the people, and the Bible is clear that the cloud and fire moved in accordance with the will of God. The cloud and the fire were not merely natural phenomena; they were the vehicle of God's presence and the visible evidence of his moving and directing his people.

MARK 13:32
Why didn't Jesus know the time the end would come?

When Jesus said that even he did not know the time of the end, he was affirming his humanity. Of course God the Father knows the time, and Jesus and the Father are one. But when Jesus became a man, he voluntarily gave up the unlimited use of his divine attributes. The emphasis of this verse is not on Jesus' lack of knowledge, but rather on the fact that no one knows. It is God the Father's secret to be revealed when he wills. "The day of the Lord is surely coming" (2 Pet. 3:10, TLB) and he will come "unexpectedly like a thief in the night" (1 Thess. 5:2) No one can predict by Scripture or science the exact day of Jesus' return. Jesus is teaching that preparation, not calculation, is needed. "Therefore you also must be ready, for the Son of Man is coming at an unexpected hour" (Matt. 24:44, NRSV).

MARCH 8

Numbers 10:1–11:23; Mark 14:1-21; Psalms 51:1-19; Proverbs 10:31-32

NUMBERS 11:1, 11-15
In Numbers 11:1 the people complained and God began to destroy them. But in Numbers 11:11-15 Moses complained and God helped him. Why?

The people complained *to one another*—and only destruction was accomplished. Moses took his complaint *to God,* who can solve any problem.

NUMBERS 11:4, KJV
What was "the mixt multitude"?

This was the rabble who came with the Israelites out of Egypt expecting almost instantaneous fulfillment of the promise of the land. When the fulfillment was delayed, they became pestilent discontents. This leaven worked its way through the whole community of God's children and wrought great evil. They infected the Israelites, who quickly copied their wretched ways.

MARK 14:1, KJV
What is "the feast of Passover and of unleavened bread"?

For the festival of the Passover, all Jewish males over 12 years of age were required to go to Jerusalem. The Passover commemorated the night the Israelites were freed from Egypt (Exod. 12), when God "passed over" homes marked by the blood of a lamb while killing firstborn sons in unmarked homes. The day of Passover was followed by a seven-day festival called the Feast of Unleavened Bread. This, too, recalled the Israelites' quick escape from Egypt when they didn't have time to let their bread rise, so they baked it without yeast. This Jewish holiday found people gathering for a special meal that included lamb, wine, bitter meats, and unleavened bread. Eventually the whole week came to be called Passover because it immediately followed the special Passover holiday.

MARK 14:3
Where is Bethany and why is it important?

Bethany is located on the eastern slope of the Mount of Olives (Jerusalem is on the western side). This town was the home of Jesus' friends Lazarus, Mary, and Martha, who were also present at this dinner (John 11:2). The woman who anointed Jesus' feet was Mary, Lazarus's and Martha's sister (John 12:1-3).

MARCH 9

NUMBERS 12:17, TLB
What is the "hill country of the Negeb" where Moses sent the spies?

This is the promised land, also called the land of Canaan. It was indeed magnificent, as the twelve spies discovered. The Bible often calls it the land flowing with milk and honey. Although the land was relatively small—150 miles long and 60 miles wide—its lush hillsides were covered with fig, date, and nut trees. It was the land God had promised to Abraham, Isaac, and Jacob.

NUMBERS 13:26
Where is Kadesh?

Although Kadesh was only a desert oasis, it was a crossroads in Israel's history. When the spies returned to Kadesh from scouting the new land, the people had to decide either to enter the land or to retreat. They chose to retreat and were condemned to wander 40 years in the desert. It was also at Kadesh that Moses disobeyed God (Num. 20:7-12). For this, he too was denied entrance into the promised land. Aaron and Miriam died there, for they could not enter the new land either. Kadesh was near Canaan's southern borders, but because of the Israelites' lack of faith, they needed more than a lifetime to go from Kadesh to the promised land.

MARK 14:26
What hymn did they sing after the Lord's Last Supper?

The hymn they sang was most likely taken from Psalms 115–118, traditionally sung at the Passover meal. Christ and his disciples surrounded by their enemies were not afraid to fulfill the duty of singing Psalms. Paul and Silas did the same when in prison in Philippi (Acts 16:25).

MARK 14:35-36
Was Jesus trying to get out of his task?

Jesus expressed his true feelings, but he did not deny or rebel against God's will. He reaffirmed his desire to do what God wanted. Jesus' prayer highlights the terrible suffering he had to endure—an agony so much more magnified because he had to take on the sins of the whole world. This "cup" was the agony of alienation from God, his Father, at the cross (Heb. 5:7-9). The sinless Son of God took on our sins and was separated for a while from God so that we could be eternally saved. While praying, Jesus was aware of what doing the Father's will would cost him. He understood the suffering he was about to encounter, and he did not want to have to endure the horrible experience. But Jesus prayed, "Not what I will, but what you will."

MARCH 10

NUMBERS 14:22, TLB
What were the ten times that Israel "refused to trust and obey" God?

God wasn't exaggerating when he said that the Israelites had already failed ten times to trust and obey him. Here is a list of their ten failures: (1) lacking trust at the crossing of the Red Sea (Exod. 14:11-12); (2) complaining over bitter water at Marah (Exod. 15:24); (3) complaining in the Desert of Sin (Exod. 16:3); (4) collecting more than the daily quota of manna (Exod. 16:20); (5) collecting manna on the Sabbath (Exod. 16:27-29); (6) complaining over lack of water at Rephidim (Exod. 17:2-3); (7) engaging in idolatry with a golden calf (Exod. 32:7-10); (8) complaining at Taberah (Num. 11:1-2); (9) more complaining over the lack of delicious food (Num. 11:4); (10) failing to trust God and enter the promised land (Num. 14:1-4).

MARK 14:53ff.
Why didn't Jesus get a fair trial from the Jewish religious leaders?

The Romans controlled Israel, but the Jews were given some authority over religious and minor civil disputes. The Jewish ruling body, the Sanhedrin, was made up of 71 of Israel's religious leaders. It was assumed that these men would be just. Instead they showed great injustice in the trial of Jesus, even to the point of making up lies to use against him (Mark 14:57). This trial by the Sanhedrin had two phases. A small group met at night (John 18:12-24), and then the full Sanhedrin met at daybreak (Luke 22:66-71). They tried Jesus for religious offenses such as calling himself the Son of God, which, according to law, was blasphemy. The trial was fixed: these religious leaders had already decided to kill Jesus (Luke 22:2).

MARK 14:58
What was wrong with what the witnesses said at Jesus' trial?

The accusation that the false witnesses finally agreed to use twisted Jesus' actual words. Jesus did not say, "I will destroy this temple that is made with hands;" he said, "Destroy this temple, and in three days I will raise it up" (John 2:19, NKJV). Jesus was not talking about Herod's temple, but about the death and resurrection of his own body.

MARCH 11

NUMBERS 16:1-3
Why did Korah rebel?

Korah and his associates had seen the advantages of the priesthood in Egypt. Egyptian priests had great wealth and political influence, something Korah wanted for himself. Korah may have assumed that Moses, Aaron, and his sons were trying to make the Israelite priesthood the same kind of political machine, and he wanted to be a part of it. He did not understand that Moses' main ambition was to serve God rather than to control others. Also Korah was of the priestly tribe, but Abiram and Dathan came from the tribe of Reuben. Therefore their rebellion involved the taking up of priestly functions by non-Levites, which was forbidden by God.

NUMBERS 16:37
Why were the rebel's censers holy?

Korah and his followers had offered incense and in so doing had taken fire from the altar, an act which was forbidden. As soon as they had kindled their fire, the fire of God consumed them. But the sacred fire from the altar had made their censer plates holy. God had no respect for the abominable sacrifice of the wicked. Yet he commanded that the censer plates containing the true fire be recovered and beaten into a cover for the altar. This was to remind the Israelites forever that rash actions provoke the wrath of God. God provided this outward memorial to warn all future aspirants seeking to take over what belonged exclusively to the Levitical priesthood.

MARK 15:35
Why did the onlookers at the cross think Jesus was calling for Elijah?

Jesus spoke the words: *Eloi, Eloi, lama sabachthani* in Aramaic. The onlookers misunderstood his first two words (*Eloi, Eloi*) and thought he was calling for the prophet Elijah. Jesus died in the darkness, for the light of God's countenance was withdrawn from his son and from the earth. Jesus was made sin for us (2 Cor. 5:21); he endured the wrath of God and the absence of the Father for the first and last time. Thus he cried out in his suffering and distress, "My God, my God, why hast thou forsaken me" (Mark 15:34, KJV). Jesus did not ask this question in surprise or despair. He was quoting the first line of Psalm 22. The whole psalm is a prophecy expressing the deep agony of the Messiah's death for the world's sin.

MARCH 12

NUMBERS 17:5-8
What was God's purpose in causing Aaron's rod to bud?

The rod of Aaron was placed in the inner room of the tabernacle along with rods for the other eleven tribes. His rod alone budded and blossomed—a sign from God that Aaron and his house were the sole priestly representatives before him. No longer were the Israelites to question Aaron's unique priestly authority. The rod was first kept in the sanctuary as a symbol and ultimately placed in the ark of the covenant (Heb. 9:4).

NUMBERS 18:21, KJV
What was the "tenth in Israel" that was given to Levi?

This was the *tithe* assessed for the Levites. The Levites were the fewest of the tribes in number. Since they received no land and therefore could not plow and sow, they needed support from the other tribes as a reward for their labors. In turn the Levites who were not priests were to tithe their tithe to support the priests (Num. 18:26). Some have said the tithe of the tithe went to the high priest, because no specific provision was made for the one who occupied that office and he would have greater expenses.

MARK 16:4
Did Jesus roll the stone away from his tomb when he was resurrected?

No, the angels rolled away the stone. They did this not so Jesus could get out, but so others could get in and see for themselves that Jesus had indeed risen from the dead, just as he said.

MARK 16:5; LUKE 24:4
Why does Mark's Gospel say that one angel met the women at the tomb, while Luke mentions two angels?

These accounts are not contradictory. Each Gospel writer chose to highlight different details as he explained the same story, just as eyewitnesses to a news story each may highlight a different aspect of that event. Mark probably emphasized only the angel who spoke. The unique emphasis of each Gospel shows that the four accounts were written independently. This should give us confidence that all four are true and reliable.

MARCH 13

NUMBERS 19:9-10
What is the significance of the red heifer's ashes?

When a person touched a dead body, he was considered unclean (i.e., unable to approach God in worship). This ritual purified the unclean person so that once again he could offer sacrifices and worship God. Death was the strongest of defilements because it was the final result of sin. Thus a special sacrifice—a red heifer—was required. It had to be offered by someone who was not unclean. When it had been burned on the altar, its ashes were used to purify water for ceremonial cleansing—not so much literally as symbolically. The unclean person then washed himself, and often his clothes and belongings, with this purified water as an act of becoming clean again.

NUMBERS 20:5-12
Was God's punishment of Moses too harsh?

The people had nagged Moses, slandered him, and rebelled against both him and God. The Lord had told Moses to *speak* to the rock; however, Moses *struck* it, not once, but twice, apparently in anger. God did the miracle; yet Moses was taking credit for it when he said, "we bring you water out of this rock." For this he was forbidden to enter the promised land. Moses was the leader and model for the entire nation. Because of this great responsibility to the people, he could not be let off lightly. By striking the rock, Moses disobeyed God's direct command and dishonored God in the presence of his people.

LUKE 1:11-12
Did Zechariah really see an angel, or was he dreaming?

This was not a dream or a vision. The angel appeared in visible form and spoke audible words to the priest. Angels are spirit beings who live in God's presence and do his will. Only two angels are mentioned by name in Scripture—Michael and Gabriel—but there are many who act as God's messengers. Here, Gabriel (Luke 1:19) delivered a special message to Zechariah.

LUKE 1:13
What is the meaning of the name John?

Two names in the New Testament were prescribed by God, not chosen by human parents. *John* means "the Lord is gracious," and *Jesus* means "Savior." Throughout the Gospels, God acts graciously and gives salvation to his people.

MARCH 14

Numbers 21:1–22:20; Luke 1:26-56; Psalms 57:1-11; Proverbs 11:9-11

Q NUMBERS 21:5
Why did Israel complain so much?

In Psalm 78, we learn the sources of Israel's complaining: (1) their spirits were not faithful to God (Ps. 78:8); (2) they refused to obey God's law (Ps. 78:10); (3) they forgot the miracles God had done for them (Ps. 78:11).

Q NUMBERS 21:8-9, TLB
Was the "bronze snake" in Numbers 21:8-9 the same one Jesus mentioned in John 3?

Yes, but when the bronze snake was hung on the pole, the Israelites didn't know the fuller meaning Jesus Christ would bring to this event (see John 3:14-15). Jesus explained that just as the Israelites were healed of their sickness by looking at the snake on the pole, all believers today can be saved from the sickness of sin by looking to Jesus' death on the cross. It was not the snake that healed the people, but their belief that God could heal them. This belief was demonstrated by their obedience to God's instructions.

Q LUKE 1:31-33
Had anyone ever been named Jesus before?

Yes. *Jesus,* a Greek form of the Hebrew name *Joshua,* was a common name meaning "the Lord saves." Just as Joshua had led Israel into the promised land (see Josh. 1:1-2), so Jesus would lead his people into eternal life. The symbolism of his name was not lost on the people of his day, who took names seriously and saw them as a source of power. In Jesus' name people were healed, demons were banished, and sins were forgiven.

Q LUKE 1:34
Was Mary really a virgin?

The birth of Jesus to a virgin is a miracle that many people find hard to believe. These three facts can aid our faith: (1) Luke was a medical doctor, and he knew perfectly well how babies are made. It would have been just as hard for him to believe in a virgin birth as it is for us, and yet he reports it as fact. (2) Luke was a painstaking researcher who based his Gospel on eyewitness accounts. Tradition holds that he talked with Mary about the events he recorded in the first two chapters. This is Mary's story, not a fictional invention. (3) Christians and Jews worship God as the Creator of the universe. Therefore, they should believe that God has the power to create a child in a virgin's womb.

MARCH 15

PSALM 58
Why does David sound so angry and vengeful in Psalm 58?

This is one of the "imprecatory" (justice) psalms that call upon God to deal with enemies. These psalms sound extremely harsh, but we must remember: (1) David could not understand why he was forced to flee from men who were unjustly seeking to kill him. He was God's anointed king over a nation called to annihilate the evil people of the land. (2) David's call for justice was sincere; it was not a cover for his own personal vengeance. He truly wanted to seek God's perfect ideal for his nation. (3) David did not say that *he* would take revenge, but gave the matter to God. These are merely his suggestions. (4) These psalms use hyperbole (or overstatement). They were meant to motivate others to take a strong stand against sin and evil. Some have conjectured that this Psalm was written by David at a time preceding the effort of Soul to kill him. Saul had recourse to the law and had David condemned in his absence and pronounced a traitor. The leaders of Israel, anxious to gain Saul's favor, agreed to do what Saul wanted. David then wrote this Psalm.

LUKE 1:57
Why is John the Baptist so important?

Jesus said, "Of all men ever born, none shines more brightly than John the Baptist" (Matt. 11:11, TLB), yet little is known about his life. Aside from Scripture, only Josephus, the Jewish historian, says anything about him. Scripture tells us he was the son of Elizabeth and Zechariah. He was six months older than Jesus. He was born in an unnamed town in the hill country of Judah (Luke 1:39). Little is said of his early life. He is important because he was the forerunner who announced the coming of the long-awaited Messiah, and his ministry was prophetic. He preached about the coming kingdom, stressing repentance and confession of sin. He baptized Jesus. Herod imprisoned him A.D. 28) because he preached against Herod's marriage to his brother Philip's wife, Herodias. Herodias and her daughter Salome forced Herod to behead John (Mark 6:14ff.).

LUKE 1:80
Why did John live out in the wilderness?

Prophets used the isolation of the uninhabited desert to enhance their spiritual growth and to focus their message on God. By being in the wilderness, John remained separate from the economic and political powers so that he could aim his message against them. It also showed separation from the hypocritical religious leaders of his day. His message was different from theirs, and his life proved it.

MARCH 16

Numbers 24:1–25:18; Luke 2:1-35; Psalms 59:1-17; Proverbs 11:14

NUMBERS 1:17
Why does Balaam prophesy that "there shall come a star from Jacob"?

The star out of Jacob is often interpreted to be a prophecy of the coming Messiah. It was probably this prophecy that convinced the wise men to travel to Israel to search for the baby Jesus (see Matt. 2:1-2). By using a sorcerer to speak of the coming Christ, God did not make sorcery acceptable; in fact, the Bible condemns it in several places (Exod. 22:18; 2 Chron. 33:6; Rev. 18:23). Rather, God showed his ultimate sovereignty over good and evil.

NUMBERS 25:1, NKJV
Why did Israel "commit harlotry with the women of Moab"?

This combination of sexual sin and idolatry was Balaam's idea (see Num. 31:16; Rev. 2:14). Not until Balaam had inflicted great damage on them did the Israelites realize that he was greedy, used sorcery, and was deeply involved in pagan religious practices. Israel's sin involved the worship of Baal, the most popular god in Canaan, the land Israel was about to enter. Represented by a bull, symbol of strength and fertility, he was the god of the rains and harvest. The Israelites were continually attracted to Baal worship, in which prostitution played a large part, throughout their years in Canaan.

LUKE 2:1
Why was it important who was the Roman emperor at the time of Jesus' birth?

Luke is the only Gospel writer who related the events he recorded to world history. His account was addressed to a predominantly Greek audience that would have been interested in and familiar with the political situation. Palestine was under the rule of the Roman empire; Emperor Caesar Augustus, the first Roman emperor, was in charge. The Roman rulers, considered to be like gods, stood in contrast to the tiny baby in a manger who was truly God in the flesh.

LUKE 2:7
The baby Jesus was laid in a manger. What is a manger?

This mention of the manger is the basis for the traditional belief that Jesus was born in a stable. Stables were often caves with feeding troughs (mangers) carved into the rock walls. Despite popular Christmas card pictures, the surroundings were dark and dirty. This was not the atmosphere the Jews expected as the birthplace of the Messiah King. They thought their promised Messiah would be born in royal surroundings.

MARCH 17

NUMBERS 26:2
Why did God want Moses to take another census?

The people were not to be numbered except by the command of God. Later on King David numbered the people without receiving God's command to do so, and was severely punished. This is the second great census in the book of Numbers. Both were taken to count the number of men able to go to war. The first census (Numbers 1–2) counted the Hebrews who had left Egypt. When the old generation died in the wilderness, another census was needed to count the new generation ready to enter the promised land. The new census revealed that although over 600,000 men (not counting women and children) had died in the wilderness, the new generation had increased by almost the same amount. The census was one of the first major steps in preparing the people to enter the land they had waited so long to possess.

LUKE 2:43-45
How could Jesus' parents have lost their boy?

At age twelve, Jesus was considered almost an adult, and so he didn't spend a lot of time with his parents during the feast. Those who attended these feasts often traveled in caravans for protection from robbers along the Palestine roads. It was customary for the women and children to travel at the front of the caravan, with the men bringing up the rear. A twelve-year-old boy conceivably could have been in either group, and both Mary and Joseph assumed Jesus was with the other one. But when the caravan left Jerusalem, Jesus stayed behind, absorbed in his discussion with the religious leaders.

LUKE 2:46-49
Why was Jesus in the Temple?

This was the Temple School. It was a kind of seminary that was famous throughout Judea as a place of learning. The apostle Paul studied there under Gamaliel, one of its foremost teachers (Acts 22:3). At the time of the Passover, the greatest rabbis of the land would assemble to teach and to discuss great truths. The coming Messiah would no doubt have been a popular discussion topic, for "everyone was expecting the Messiah to come soon" (Luke 3:15). Jesus would have been eager to listen and to ask probing questions. It was not his youth, but the depth of his wisdom, that astounded these teachers.

MARCH 18

Numbers 26:52–28:15; Luke 3:1-22; Psalms 61:1-8; Proverbs 11:16-17

NUMBERS 26:53-54
Why was the land divided "based on the number of names"?

The division of the land was to be based on numbers, not on tribes. Tribes with more members received more land. It was the intention of God to set up an economic system by which each family received land and thus had a productive base for its support. The land was to be held forever by the families to which it was given. It was God's land, tenanted by God's people, with the external title in the name of the family. It belonged to the family by right and was to be passed down to the children and the children's children.

LUKE 3:12
Why is it important that tax collectors came to John the Baptist?

Tax collectors were notorious for their dishonesty. Romans gathered funds for their government by farming out the collection privilege to whoever promised to get the most money from a given area. Tax collectors earned their own living by adding a sizable sum—whatever they could get away with—to the total and keeping this money for themselves. Unless the people revolted and risked Roman retaliation, they had to pay whatever was demanded. Obviously they hated the tax collectors, who were generally dishonest, greedy, and ready to betray their own countrymen for cold cash. John's message demanded at least three specific responses: (1) share what you have with those who need it, (2) whatever your job is, do it well and with fairness, and (3) be content with what you're earning. John had no time to address comforting messages to those who lived careless or selfish lives—he was calling the people to right living.

LUKE 3:15
The people seemed to be very excited about John. Why was this?

There had not been a prophet in Israel for more than four hundred years. It was widely believed that when the Messiah came, prophecy would reappear (Joel 2:28-29; Malachi 3:1; 4:5). When John burst onto the scene, the people were excited. He was obviously a great prophet, and they were sure that the eagerly awaited age of the Messiah had come. Some, in fact, thought John himself was the Messiah. John spoke like the prophets of old, saying that the people must turn from their sin to avoid punishment and turn to God to experience his mercy and approval. This is a message for all times and places, but John spoke it with particular urgency—he was preparing the people for the coming Messiah.

MARCH 19

Numbers 28:16–29:40; Luke 3:23-38; Psalms 62:1-12; Proverbs 11:18-19

NUMBERS 29:1-2, KJV
What is the significance of the "day of blowing the trumpets"?

The Feast of Trumpets demonstrated three important principles of worship: (1) The people gathered together to celebrate and worship. (2) The normal daily routine was suspended, and no hard work was done. (3) The people gave God something of value by sacrificing animals as burnt offerings to him. (4) Spending time away from the normal routine of life was symbolic of giving themselves to God and demonstrating their dedication.

PROVERBS 11:19
Why does the righteous man attain life?

Wisdom makes the hours of the day more profitable and the years more fruitful (9:11). The righteous live life more fully each day. They also attain life because people usually live longer when they live right, with proper diet, exercise, and rest. In addition, they need not fear death because eternal life is God's gift to them (John 11:25). By contrast, evil people not only find eternal death, but also miss out on real life on earth.

LUKE 23-38
What is the difference between the genealogy in Luke and the one in Matthew?

Here Jesus' genealogy is traced back through Mary. The genealogy recorded in Matthew 1:1-17 traces his line through Joseph, his legal but not actual father. Matthew's genealogy goes back to Abraham and shows that Jesus was related to all Jews. Luke's goes back to Adam, showing he is related to all human beings. This is consistent with Luke's picture of Jesus as the Savior of the whole world. From Abraham to David the two lists are practically identical and are based on 1 Chronicles 2, but from David to Joseph they diverge. Matthew's list, which clearly omits some generations, traces the line through David's son Solomon, whereas Luke traces it through Nathan, another of David's sons by Bathsheba. Both trace Jesus' ancestry through Joseph even though both make it clear that Joseph was not Jesus' physical father. Joseph is called the son of Heli in Luke 3:23, in accordance with Jewish legal custom; this means he was the husband of Heli's daughter. Since this is the case this is actually Mary's genealogy that Luke may have received personally from her. It is fitting that Luke, a Greek, would include Mary's genealogy because of the prominence he gives women in his Gospel.

MARCH 20

NUMBERS 31:1
Who were the Midianites?

The Midianites were a nomadic people who descended from Abraham and his second wife, Keturah. The land of Midian lay far to the south of Canaan, but large bands of Midianites roamed many miles from their homeland, searching for grazing areas for their flocks. Such a group was near the promised land when the Israelites arrived. These Midianites were responsible for enticing Israel into Baal worship. When Moses fled from Egypt (Exod. 2), he took refuge in the land of Midian. His wife and father-in-law were Midianites. Despite this alliance, the Israelites and Midianites were always bitter enemies. In Numbers 25:16-18 God commanded Israel to destroy the Midianites for leading them into idolatry. But Israel took the women as captives, rather than killing them, probably because of the tempting enticements of the Midianites' sinful life-style. Their destruction of the sinful culture was a lukewarm effort. When the Israelites later entered the promised land, it was their indifferent attitude to sin that eventually ruined them.

LUKE 4:3
Why was it necessary for Jesus to be tempted?

Temptation is part of the human experience. For Jesus to be fully human, for him to understand us completely, he had to face temptation (Heb. 4:15). Also, Jesus had to undo Adam's work. Adam, though created perfect, gave in to temptation and passed sin on to the whole human race. Jesus, by contrast, resisted Satan. His victory offers salvation to all of Adam's descendants (Rom. 5:12-19).

LUKE 14:18-19
Why didn't Jesus quote the entire passage in Isaiah 61?

Jesus was quoting from Isaiah 61:1-2, stopping in the middle of verse 2, just before "and the day of his wrath to their enemies." He did this because the time of God's blessings is fulfilled in Jesus' first coming, but the time of God's wrath awaits his second coming. His hearers were expecting just the opposite of the Messiah: they thought he would crush their enemies first, and then usher in God's blessings.

LUKE 4:26-28
Why did the people get so angry when Jesus spoke of the widow of Zarephath and Naaman the Syrian?

Jesus' remarks filled the people of Nazareth with rage because he was saying that God sometimes chose to reach Gentiles rather than Jews. Jesus implied that his hearers were as unbelieving as the citizens of the northern kingdom of Israel in the days of Elijah and Elisha, a time notorious for its great wickedness.

MARCH 21

Numbers 32:1–33:39; Luke 4:31–5:11; Psalms 64:1-10; Proverbs 11:22

NUMBERS 32:16
What is a sheepfold?

A sheepfold was a shelter for enclosing and protecting sheep. A simple sheepfold had four roughly built stone walls, high enough to keep wild animals out. Sometimes the top of the wall was lined with thorns to further discourage predators and thieves. The pen's single entrance made it easier for a shepherd to guard his flock. Often several shepherds used a single pen and took turns guarding the entrance. Mingling the animals was no problem since each flock responded readily to its own shepherd's voice. The three tribes who chose to remain east of the Jordan River wanted to build pens to protect their flocks and cities to protect their families, before the men crossed the river to help the rest of the tribes conquer the promised land.

LUKE 4:31
If the religious leaders were so opposed to Jesus, why did they let him teach in the synagogues?

Jesus was taking advantage of the custom of allowing visitors to teach. Itinerant rabbis were always welcome to speak to those gathered each Sabbath in the synagogues. The apostle Paul also profited from this practice (see Acts 13:5; 14:1).

LUKE 4:40, TLB
Why did the people come to Jesus "as the sun went down"?

This was the Sabbath (Luke 4:31), their day of rest. Sabbath lasted from sunset on Friday to sunset on Saturday. The people didn't want to break the law that prohibited travel on the Sabbath, so they waited until the Sabbath hours were over before coming to Jesus. Then, as Luke the physician notes, they came with all kinds of diseases, and Jesus healed each one.

LUKE 5:1-2
What is Lake Gennesaret? Why were they washing their nets?

The Lake of Gennesaret was also known as the Sea of Galilee or the Sea of Tiberias. Fishermen on the Sea of Galilee used nets, often bell-shaped nets with lead weights around the edges. A net would be thrown flat onto the water, and the lead weights would cause it to sink around the fish. Then the fishermen would pull on a cord, drawing the net around the fish. Nets had to be kept in good condition, so they were washed to remove weeds and then mended.

MARCH 22

Numbers 33:40–35:34; Luke 5:12-28; Psalms 65:1-13; Proverbs 11:23

 **NUMBERS 33:50-56**
Why were the Israelites told to destroy the people living in Canaan?

God had several compelling reasons for giving this command: (1) God was stamping out the wickedness of an extremely sinful nation. The Canaanites brought on their own punishment. Idol worship expressed their deepest evil desires. It ultimately led to the worship of Satan and the total rejection of God. (2) God was using Moses and Israel to judge Canaan for its sins in fulfillment of the prophecy in Genesis 9:25. (3) God wanted to remove all trace of pagan beliefs and practices from the land. He did not want his people to mix or compromise with idolatry in any way. The Israelites did not fully understand God's reasons, and they did not carry out his command. This eventually led them to compromise and corruption. In all areas of life, we should obey God's Word without question because we know he is just, even if we cannot fully understand his overall purposes. God warned that if the Israelites did not drive the wicked inhabitants out of the promised land, later these people would become a source of great irritation. That is exactly what happened.

LUKE 5:21
Why did the scribes and Pharisees accuse Jesus of blasphemy?

When Jesus told the paralytic his sins were forgiven, the Jewish leaders accused Jesus of blasphemy—claiming to be God or to do what only God can do. In Jewish law, blasphemy was punishable by death (Lev. 24:16). In labeling Jesus' claim to forgive sins blasphemous, the religious leaders showed they did not understand that Jesus *is* God, and he has God's power to heal both the body and the soul. Forgiveness of sins was a sign that the Messianic age had come (Isa. 40:2; Joel 2:32; Mic. 7:18-19; Zech. 13:1). The scribes and Pharisees asked, "Who can forgive sins, but God alone?" (Luke 5:21, KJV). Jesus had the power on earth to forgive sins and his healings were proof of that power. The scribes and Pharisees asked the right question here. If God alone can forgive sins and Jesus did this, then he must be God. Jesus' claim to be God eventually led to his crucifixion.

MARCH 23

Numbers 36:1–Deuteronomy 1:46; Luke 5:29–6:11; Psalms 66:1-20; Proverbs 11:24-26

DEUTERONOMY 1:1-5
When did the events in Deuteronomy take place?

The 40 years of desert wandering come to an end in this book. The events of Deuteronomy cover only a week or two of the 11th month of the 40th year (1:3). The 12th and last month was spent in mourning for Moses (34:8). Then the Israelites entered the promised land the first month of the 41st year after the exodus (Joshua 4:19).

DEUTERONOMY 1:6
Why does Moses' summary of Israel's forty-year journey begin at Mount Horeb (Sinai) and not in Egypt?

Moses left out the first part of the Exodus because he was not giving an itinerary—he was summarizing the nation's development. In Moses' mind the nation of Israel began at the base of Mount Sinai, not in Egypt, for it was at Mount Sinai that God gave his covenant to the people (Exodus 19–20).

LUKE 6:4, NASB
What is the "consecrated bread"?

Each week, twelve consecrated loaves of bread, representing the twelve tribes of Israel, were placed on a table in the temple. This bread was called the bread of the presence. After its use in the temple, it was to be eaten only by priests. Jesus, accused of Sabbath-breaking, referred to a well-known story about David (1 Sam. 21:1-6). Once, when fleeing from Saul, David and his men ate this consecrated bread. Their need was more important than ceremonial regulations. Jesus was appealing to the same principle: human need was more important than human regulations and rules. By comparing himself and his disciples with David and his companions, Jesus was saying, "If you condemn me, you must also condemn King David."

LUKE 6:5, NASB
What did Jesus mean when he said that he was "Lord of the Sabbath"?

He meant that he had the authority to overrule the Pharisees' traditions and regulations because he had created the Sabbath. The Creator is always greater than the creation.

MARCH 24

Deuteronomy 2:1–3:29; Luke 6:12-38; Psalms 67:1-7; Proverbs 11:27

DEUTERONOMY 2:4
Why were the children of Esau afraid of Israel?

God was concerned for the children of Esau (the Edomites), who was the brother of Jacob. When the Israelites passed through Edom, God advised them to be careful. The Israelites were known as warriors, and the children of Esau—the Edomites—would be understandably nervous as the great crowd passed through their land. God warned the Israelites not to start a fight, to respect the Edomites' territory, and to pay for whatever they used. God wanted the Israelites to deal justly with these neighbors.

DEUTERONOMY 3:25
Why did Moses pray to be allowed to enter the land when God had already told him he could not enter?

God's earlier judgment on Moses was not accompanied by an oath. In other situations Moses had prevailed with God and the circumstances had been reversed. Here, though, God told him to ask no more. But, although he was never allowed to walk on its earth, Moses was allowed to climb the mountain and look into Canaan (Deut. 3:27). Thus God in judgment often remembers mercy.

LUKE 6:13
Why did Jesus name the Twelve "apostles"?

Jesus had many *disciples* (learners), but he chose only twelve *apostles* (messengers). The apostles were his inner circle, to whom he gave special training and sent out with his own authority. These were the men who started the Christian church. In the Gospels these twelve men are usually called the disciples, but in the book of Acts they are called apostles.

LUKE 6:21
Is the hunger about which Jesus speaks in Luke 6:21 the same as the hunger for righteousness in Matthew 5:6?

Some think that Jesus was talking about the same hunger. Others say this is physical hunger, which is in line with Old Testament scriptures that speak of God's concern for the poor. In any case, in a nation where riches were seen as a sign of God's favor, Jesus startled his hearers by pronouncing blessings on the hungry. In doing so, however, he was in line with an ancient tradition. The Old Testament is filled with texts proclaiming God's concern for the poor and needy. See, for example, 1 Samuel 2:5; Psalm 146:7; Isaiah 58:6-7; and Jesus' own mother's prayer in Luke 1:53.

MARCH 25

Deuteronomy 4:1-49; Luke 6:39–7:10; Psalms 68:1-18; Proverbs 11:28

DEUTERONOMY 4:2
What is meant by adding to or subtracting from God's commands?

These laws were the word of God, and they were complete. How could any human being, with limited wisdom and knowledge, edit God's perfect laws? To add to the laws would make them a burden; to subtract from the laws would make them incomplete. Thus the laws were to remain unchanged. To presume to make changes in God's law is to assume a position of authority over God who gave the laws (Matt. 5:17-19; 15:3-9; Rev. 22:18-19). The religious leaders at the time of Christ did exactly this; they elevated their own laws to the same level as God's. Jesus rebuked them for this (Matt. 23:1-4).

DEUTERONOMY 4:40
Was Israel guaranteed prosperity for obeying God's laws?

Yes, but we have to look carefully at what that means. God's laws were designed to make his chosen nation healthy, just, and merciful. When the people followed those laws, they prospered. This does not mean, however, that no sickness, sadness, or misunderstandings existed among them. Rather, it means that as a nation they prospered and that individual's problems were handled as fairly as possible.

LUKE 7:2-10, TLB
Who was this army captain and why did he send Jewish elders to Jesus instead of going himself?

He was a *centurion,* a Roman army officer in charge of one hundred men. Apparently the centurion recognized that the Jews possessed God's message for mankind—it is recorded that he loved the nation and built the synagogue. Thus, in his time of need, it was natural for him to turn to Jesus. He sent Jewish elders to Jesus because he was well aware of the Jewish hatred for Roman soldiers and he may not have wanted to interrupt a Jewish gathering. Matthew 8:5 says the Roman centurion visited Jesus himself, while Luke 7:3 says he sent Jewish elders to present his request to Jesus. For his Jewish audience, Matthew emphasized the man's faith. For his Gentile audience, Luke highlighted the good relationship between the Jewish elders and the Roman centurion. The centurion didn't come to Jesus, and he didn't expect Jesus to come to him. Just as this officer did not need to be present to have his orders carried out, so Jesus didn't need to be present to heal.

MARCH 26

Q **DEUTERONOMY 36:4,** NRSV
What does the term "the LORD alone" mean?

"The LORD alone" is sometimes translated "the LORD is one." Monotheism—belief in only one God—was a distinctive feature of Hebrew religion. Many ancient religions believed in many gods. But the God of Abraham, Isaac, and Jacob is the God of the whole earth, the only true God. This was an important insight for the nation of Israel, because they were about to enter a land filled with people who believed in many gods. Both then and today, there are people who prefer to place their trust in many different "gods." But the day is coming when God will be recognized as the only one. He will be the king over the whole earth (Zech. 14:9).

Q **LUKE 7:11-17**
What is the significance of the resurrection of the widow's son in the village of Nain?

Not only did Jesus save the boy from death but he also saved the widow from a lifetime of suffering. She had lost her husband, and now her only son was dead—her last means of support. The crowd of mourners would go home, and she would be left penniless and alone. The widow was probably past the age of childbearing and would not marry again. Unless a relative came to her aid, her future was bleak. She would be an easy prey for swindlers, and she would likely be reduced to begging for food. In fact, as Luke repeatedly emphasizes, this woman was just the kind of person Jesus had come to help.

Q **LUKE 7:16**
Why did the people think that Jesus was a prophet?

The people thought of Jesus as a prophet because, like the Old Testament prophets, he boldly proclaimed God's message and sometimes raised the dead. Both Elijah and Elisha raised children from the dead (1 Kings 17:17-24; 2 Kings 4:18-37). The people were correct in thinking that Jesus was a prophet, but he was much more—he is God himself.

Q **LUKE 7:31-34**
Who is Jesus talking about in Luke 7:31-34?

This is a parable in which Jesus likens the Pharisees to two groups of children. One group plays a wedding song and expects the second group to dance to their tune. The second group plays a funeral dirge, and the first group will not weep with them. The Pharisees and lawyers rejected John the Baptist because he was an ascetic. They then rejected Jesus because he acted the opposite way. No matter which way God offered them eternal life, they turned it down.

MARCH 27

DEUTERONOMY 7:2
How can a God of love and mercy wipe out everyone, even children?

Although God is loving and merciful, he is also just. These enemy nations were as much a part of God's creation as Israel was, and God does not allow evil to continue unchecked. God had punished Israel by keeping out of the promised land all those who had disobeyed. The command to destroy these nations was both a judgment (Deut. 9:4-6) and a safety measure. On one hand, the people living in the land were being judged for their sin, and Israel was God's instrument of judgment—just as God would one day use other nations to judge Israel for its sin (2 Chron. 36:17; Isa. 10:12). On the other hand, God's command was designed to protect the nation of Israel from being ruined by the idolatry and immorality of its enemies. To think that God is too "nice" to judge sin is faulty thinking.

DEUTERONOMY 8:10
Is Deuteronomy 8:10 the verse that tells us to say grace before eating?

This verse is traditionally cited as the reason we say grace before or after meals. Its purpose, however, was to warn the Israelites not to forget God when their needs and wants were satisfied.

LUKE 7:36-50
If Jesus was eating a meal in Luke 7:36-50, why did the woman kneel behind him to anoint his feet?

Although the woman was not an invited guest, she entered the house anyway and knelt behind Jesus at his feet. In Jesus' day, it was customary to recline while eating. Dinner guests would lie on couches with their heads near the table, propping themselves up on one elbow and stretching their feet out behind them. The woman could easily anoint Jesus' feet without approaching the table.

LUKE 8:2-3
Was it unusual in those days for women to travel with a man like Jesus?

Jesus lifted women up from the agony of degradation and servitude to the joy of fellowship and service. In Jewish culture, women were not supposed to learn from rabbis. By allowing these women to travel with him, Jesus was showing that all people are equal under God. These women supported Jesus' ministry with their own money. They owed a great debt to him because he had driven demons out of some and had healed others.

MARCH 28

DEUTERONOMY 9:6, TLB
If the Israelites were so wicked and stubborn, why did God make such wonderful promises to them?

There are two good reasons: (1) A bargain is a bargain. God and Israel had made a treaty, or covenant (Gen. 15, 17; Exod. 19–20). God promised to be faithful to them and they promised to obey him. The agreement was irrevocable and for all time. Even though the Israelites rarely upheld their end of the bargain, God would always be faithful to his part. (Although he had punished them several times, he had always remained faithful.) (2) God's mercy is unconditional. No matter how many times the people turned from God, he was always there to restore them.

DEUTERONOMY 10:5
Are the tablets of the law still in the ark?

"Where they are to this day" (TLB) refers to the time when this book was written (1407–1406 B.C.). The tablets of the law were still in the ark about five hundred years later when Solomon put it in his newly built temple (1 Kings 8:9). The ark last appears in the Israelites' history during the reign of Josiah, about three hundred years after Solomon (2 Chron. 35:3) and presumably was lost when Jerusalem was destroyed in 587 B.C.

LUKE 8:10
Why didn't the crowds understand Jesus' words?

Perhaps they were looking for a military leader or a political Messiah and could not fit his gentle teaching style into their preconceived idea. Perhaps they were afraid of pressure from religious leaders and did not want to look too deeply into Jesus' words. God told Isaiah that people would hear without understanding and see without perceiving (Isa. 6:9), and that kind of reaction confronted Jesus. The parable of the sower was an accurate picture of the people's reaction to the rest of his parables.

MARCH 29

DEUTERONOMY 10:16
What did Moses mean when he said to circumcise your heart?

The apostle Paul wrote similarly in Romans 2:29: "A man is a Jew if he is one inwardly; and circumcision is circumcision of the heart, by the Spirit, not by the written code." This means that circumcision has value if Jews keep the law. But if they are circumcised and then break the law, their circumcision is of no avail. Therefore the circumcised Jew is no better than the uncircumcised Gentile if all he has is circumcision. True circumcision is of the heart, not of the flesh; it is spiritual and not literal.

LUKE 8:26
Where is the country of the Gadarenes?

The region of the Gadarenes is located southeast of the Sea of Galilee, near the town of Gadara, one of the most important cities of the region. Gadara was a member of the Decapolis. These ten cities with independent governments were largely inhabited by Gentiles, which explains the herd of pigs (Luke 8:33). The Jews did not raise pigs because pigs were considered unclean and thus unfit to eat.

LUKE 8:30
Why was the demon's name "Legion"?

The demon's name was Legion. A legion was the largest unit in the Roman army, having between three thousand and six thousand soldiers and divided into ten cohorts of six centuries each. In the New Testament the word suggests "a great number" meaning the man was possessed by many demons.

LUKE 8:33
Why didn't Jesus just destroy these demons—or send them to the Bottomless Pit?

Because the time for such work had not yet come. He healed many people of the destructive effects of demon-possession, but he did not yet destroy demons. His time for that has not yet come. But it will come. The book of Revelation records the future victory of Jesus over Satan, his demons, and all evil.

MARCH 30

 ### DEUTERONOMY 14:28
Why did God instruct Israel to store the full tithe "within your towns" every third year?

This was an organized system of caring for the poor. God told his people to use their tithe every third year for those who were helpless, hungry, or poor (Deut. 14:29). These regulations were designed to prevent the country from sinking under crushing poverty and oppression. It was everyone's responsibility to care for those less fortunate. Families were to help other family members, and towns were to help members of their community. National laws protected the rights of the poor, but helping the poor was also an active part of religious life.

 ### LUKE 8:45
Why Jesus want to know who had touched him?

It isn't that Jesus didn't know who had touched him; it's that he wanted the woman to step forward and identify herself. Jesus wanted to teach her that his cloak did not contain magical properties, but that her faith in him had healed her. He may also have wanted to teach the crowds a lesson. According to Jewish law, a man who touched a menstruating woman became ceremonially unclean (Lev. 15:19-28). This was true whether her bleeding was normal or, as in this woman's case, the result of illness. To protect themselves from such defilement, Jewish men carefully avoided touching, speaking to, or even looking at women. By contrast, Jesus proclaimed to hundreds of people that this "unclean" woman had touched him—and then he healed her. In Jesus' mind, this suffering woman was not to be overlooked. As God's creation, she deserved attention and respect.

 ### LUKE 9:2
Why did Jesus announce his kingdom by both preaching and healing?

If he had limited himself to preaching, people might have seen his kingdom as spiritual only. On the other hand, if he had healed without preaching, people might not have realized the spiritual importance of his mission. Most of his listeners expected a Messiah who would bring wealth and power to their nation; they preferred material benefits to spiritual discernment. The truth about Jesus is that he is both God and man, both spiritual and physical; and the salvation that he offers is both for the soul and the body.

MARCH 31

DEUTERONOMY 17:6-7
Why did the witnesses throw the first stones?

A person was not put to death on the testimony of only one witness. On the witness of two or three, a person could be condemned and then sentenced to death by stoning. The condemned person was taken outside the city gates, and the witnesses were the first to throw heavy stones down on him or her. Bystanders would then pelt the dying person with stones. This system would "purge the evil" by putting the idolater to death. At the same time, it protected the rights of accused persons two ways. First, by requiring several witnesses, it prevented any angry individual from giving "false testimony." Second, by requiring the accusers to throw the first stones, it made them think twice about accusing unjustly. They were responsible for finishing what they had started.

DEUTERONOMY 17:14-20
Did God want Israel to have a king?

God was not encouraging Israel to appoint a king to rule the nation. He was actually against the idea because he was their King, and the people were to obey and follow him. But God knew that the people would one day demand a king for selfish reasons—they would want to be like the nations around them (1 Sam. 8). If they insisted on having a king, he wanted to make sure they chose the right person. That is why he included these instructions both for the people's benefit as they chose their king and for the king himself as he sought to lead the nation according to God's laws.

LUKE 9:21-22
Why did Jesus tell his disciples not to tell anyone that he was the Christ?

At this point, they didn't fully understand the significance of that confession—nor would anyone else. Everyone still expected the Messiah to come as a conquering king. But even though Jesus was the Messiah, he still had to suffer, be rejected by the leaders, be killed, and rise from the dead. When the disciples saw all this happen to Jesus, they would understand what the Messiah had come to do. This was the turning point in Jesus' instruction to his disciples. From then on he began teaching clearly and specifically what they could expect, so that they would not be surprised when it happened. He explained that he would not *now* be the conquering Messiah because he first had to suffer, die, and rise again. But one day he would return in great glory to set up his eternal kingdom.

APRIL 1

Deuteronomy 18:1–20:20; Luke 9:28-50; Psalms 73:1-28; Proverbs 12:10

DEUTERONOMY 18:15
Who was the prophet God would raise up to be like Moses?

Moses was prophesying about the coming Messiah, Jesus Christ, although most Jews thought that Joshua was this prophet. In the Gospels there is reference to Jesus as "the prophet" recalling this prophecy by Moses (Luke 24:19; John 6:14; 7:52) In Acts 3:20-22, Peter quoted this verse to show that the prophet was Jesus Christ. Peter wanted to show them that their long-awaited Messiah had come. In Acts 7:37, Stephen used this verse to support the same claim. These words of Moses show that the coming of Jesus Christ to earth was not an afterthought, but part of God's original plan.

DEUTERONOMY 18:10, KJV
What was the practice of making one's "son or daughter to pass through the fire"?

The NIV translates this: "Let no one be found among you who sacrifices his son or daughter in the fire." Child sacrifice and occult practices were strictly forbidden by God. These practices were common among pagan religions. Israel's own neighbors actually sacrificed their children to the god Molech (Lev. 20:2-5). Other neighboring religions used supernatural means, such as contacting the spirit world, to foretell the future and gain guidance. Because of these wicked practices, God would drive out the pagan nations (Deut. 18:12). The Israelites were to replace their evil practices with the worship of the one true God.

LUKE 9:33, KJV
Why did Peter want to make "three tabernacles"?

When Peter suggested making three shelters (TLB), he may have been thinking of the Feast of Tabernacles, where shelters were set up to commemorate the exodus, God's deliverance from slavery in Egypt. But Jesus did not take Peter, James, and John to the top of a mountain to remember the past. He wanted to show them who he really was—not just a great prophet, but God's own Son. Moses, representing the law, and Elijah, representing the prophets, appeared with Jesus. Then God's voice singled out Jesus as the long-awaited Messiah who possessed divine authority, who fulfilled and replaced both the Law and the Prophets (Matt. 5:17). Peter wanted to keep Moses and Elijah with them by setting up tents for them. This reveals his misunderstanding of faith. He thought it was built on three cornerstones: the law, the prophets, and Jesus. But Peter grew in his understanding, and eventually he would write of Jesus as "a chosen and precious cornerstone" of the church (1 Pet. 2:6).

APRIL 2

Deuteronomy 21:1–22:30; Luke 9:51–10:12; Psalms 74:1-23; Proverbs 12:11

DEUTERONOMY 22:5
Does Deuteronomy 22:5 mean that women cannot wear pants?

This verse commands men and women not to reverse their sexual roles. It is not a statement about clothing styles. Today role rejections are common—there are men who want to become women and women who want to become men. It's not the clothing style that offends God, but using the style to act out a different sex role. God had a purpose in making us uniquely male and female.

DEUTERONOMY 22:13-30
Why did God include all these laws about sexual sins?

Instructions about sexual behavior would have been vital for three million people on a 40-year camping trip. But they would be equally important when they entered the promised land and settled down. Paul, in Colossians 3:5-8, recognizes the importance of strong rules about sex for believers. Sins involving sex are not innocent dabblings in forbidden pleasures, as is so often portrayed, but powerful destroyers of relationships. They confuse and tear down the climate of respect, trust, and credibility so essential for solid marriages and secure children.

LUKE 9:50; 11:23, KJV
Why did Jesus say "he that is not against us is for us" and later say the opposite: "He that is not with me is against me"?

The explanation is that both statements are true when the context is understood. In Luke 9:50 Jesus refers to those who are for him but who are not openly associated with the disciples. They are not opponents of Jesus but believers who seek to serve him through faith and prayer. In Luke 11:23 Jesus refers to those who are not his followers in any true sense, and thus are against him.

LUKE 10:52
What was a Samaritan?

After Assyria invaded Israel, the northern kingdom, and resettled it with its own people (2 Kings 17:24-41), the mixed race that developed became known as the Samaritans. "Purebred" Jews hated these "half-breeds," and the Samaritans in turn hated the Jews. So many tensions arose between the two peoples that Jewish travelers between Galilee and southern Judea often walked around rather than through Samaritan territory, even though this lengthened their trip considerably. Jesus held no such prejudices, and he sent messengers ahead to get things ready in a Samaritan village. But the village refused to welcome these Jewish travelers.

APRIL 3

DEUTERONOMY 13:17-18, KJV
Why is a word like "whore" used in God's Word?

Prostitution was not overlooked in God's law—it was strictly forbidden. To forbid this practice may seem obvious to us, but it may not have been so obvious to the Israelites. Almost every other religion known to them included prostitution as an integral part of its worship services. Prostitution makes a mockery of God's original idea for sex, treating sex as an isolated physical act rather than an act of commitment to another. Outside of marriage, sex destroys relationships. Within marriage, if approached with the right attitude, it can be a relationship builder.

DEUTERONOMY 24:19-21
Why were God's people instructed to leave some of their harvest in the fields?

This was done so that travelers and the poor could gather it. This second gathering, called gleaning, was a way for them to provide food for themselves. Years later, Ruth obtained food for herself and Naomi by gleaning behind the reapers in Boaz's field, picking up the leftovers (Ruth 2:2). Because this law was being obeyed years after it was written, Ruth, a woman in Christ's lineage, was able to find food.

LUKE 10:18
Why did Jesus say, "I say saw Satan falling from heaven as a flash of lightning"?

Jesus may have been looking ahead to his victory over Satan at the cross. John 12:31-32 indicates that Satan would be judged and driven out at the time of Jesus' death. On the other hand, Jesus may have been warning his disciples against pride. Perhaps he was referring to Isaiah 14:12-17, which begins, "How you have fallen from heaven, O morning star, son of the dawn!" Some interpreters identify this verse with Satan and explain that Satan's pride led to all the evil we see on earth today. To Jesus' disciples, who were thrilled with their power over evil spirits, he may have been giving this stern warning: "Yours is the kind of pride that led to Satan's downfall. Be careful!"

LUKE 10:21
What was Jesus' relationship to the Holy Spirit?

Jesus Christ was conceived by the Holy Spirit (Matt. 1:20), baptized by the Holy Spirit (Matt. 3:16), anointed by the Holy Spirit (Luke 4:18), guided by the Holy Spirit (Luke 4:1), empowered by the Holy Spirit (Luke 4:14), and filled with the Holy Spirit. He lived in union with the Holy Spirit, and dependent upon him.

APRIL 4

Deuteronomy 26:1–27:26; Luke 10:38–11:13; Psalms 76:1-12; Proverbs 12:15-17

DEUTERONOMY 26:19, NRSV
What does it mean that Israel would be set "high above all nations"?

If Israel obeyed God and kept his commandments God would make it "high above all nations," and the Israelites would be a holy people to him. "High above all nations" implies that God would accept the Israelites, their friends would admire them, and their enemies would envy them. As holy unto God, they would be separated unto him, devoted to him, and rightly employed in the divine service.

DEUTERONOMY 27:11-26
Why did Moses instruct the twelve tribes to stand on two mountains and charge the Levites to pronounce twelve curses?

Once Israel has entered the land, the covenant must be publicly renewed and accepted by oral testimony. Six of the tribes were to be stationed on Mount Ebal and the other six on Mount Gerazim. The six on Mount Gerazim were children of Leah and Rachel; the other six were children of the bondwomen. Curses were to be declared as judgments against those things that were prohibited and the Israelites were to shout, "Amen." By this, Israel acknowledged the equity of the curses and promised they would not do what was prohibited. Their assent would make any disobedience their own fault and any judgment that followed would be what they deserved.

PSALM 76:10
How can wrath bring praise to God?

Hostility to God and his people gives God the opportunity to do great deeds. For example, the Pharaoh of Egypt refused to free the Hebrew slaves (Exod. 5:1-2) and thus allowed God to work mighty miracles for his people (Exod. 11:9). God turns the tables on evildoers and brings glory to himself from the foolishness of those who deny him or revolt against him. God's wrath expressed in judgment brings praise from those who have been delivered.

PROVERBS 12:16, KJV
What does "a prudent man covereth shame" mean?

This has also been translated "the prudent ignore an insult" (NRSV). A person who has been insulted by a fool should not pick up the insult, for the insult will do no harm; but anger, resentment, and heat will do what the insult in itself could not do.

APRIL 5

DEUTERONOMY 28:64, TLB
When was Israel scattered "among all nations, from one end of the earth to the other"?

This severe warning was fulfilled when The northern kingdom of Israel was defeated and carried away into captivity by Assyria (722 B.C., see 2 Kings 17:6), and Judah was carried away to Babylonia by Nebuchadnezzar (586 B.C., see 2 Kings 24:14-15; 25:7, 21). A sizable Jewish community remained in Babylon down to Medieval times. Other Jews, voluntarily and as refugees, also settled in Egypt and elsewhere (see Jer. 43:7). In the first century A.D. Philo numbered the Jews in Egypt at a million. There were large colonies in Syria and in at least 71 cities of Asia Minor. Jews were expelled from Rome in 139 B.C.. Another expulsion from Rome is mentioned in Acts 18:2. Later, in A.D. 70, the Romans Titus and Vespasian destroyed Jerusalem forcing many Jews to flee their homeland. This dispersal of the Jews throughout the nations is often called the *Diaspora*. The epistles of James and 1 Peter (see (James 1:1; 1 Pet. 1:1)) are both addressed to the Jewish believers in the Dispersion that is mentioned in Acts 8:1, and the apostle Paul usually began his work in a place by preaching in the synagogue established by the dispersed Jews.

LUKE 11:15-19
What is the meaning of Luke 11:15-19?

There are two common interpretations of these verses: (1) Some of the Pharisees' followers actually cast out demons. If this was so, the Pharisees' accusations were becoming more desperate. To accuse Jesus of being empowered by Beelzebub, the prince of demons (or Satan himself), because Jesus was driving out demons, was also to say that the Pharisees' own followers were doing Satan's work. Jesus turned the religious leaders' accusation against them.

(2) Another possibility is that the Pharisees' followers were *not* driving out demons; and even if they tried, they did not succeed. Jesus first dismissed their claim as absurd: why would the devil drive out his own demons? Then he engaged in a little irony: "by whom do your followers drive them out?" Finally he concluded that his work of driving out demons proves that the kingdom of God had arrived. Though these two interpretations may differ, they arrive at the same conclusion—the kingdom of God had arrived with the coming of Jesus Christ.

APRIL 6

DEUTERONOMY 29:29
Why are there secrets God has not revealed?

There are some secrets God has chosen not to reveal to us, possibly for the following reasons: (1) our finite minds cannot fully understand the infinite aspects of God's nature and the universe (Eccl. 3:11); (2) some things are unnecessary for us to know; and (3) God is infinite and all-knowing, and we do not have the capacity to know everything he does. This verse shows that although God has not told us everything there is to know about obeying him, he has told us enough. Thus disobedience comes from an act of the will, not a lack of knowledge. Through God's Word we know enough about him to be saved by faith and to serve him.

LUKE 11:37-39
Why was washing so important to the Pharisees?

This washing was done not for health reasons, but as a symbol of washing away any contamination from touching anything unclean. Not only did the Pharisees make a public show of their washing, but they also commanded everyone else to follow a practice originally intended only for the priests.

LUKE 11:46
What were the "burdens" that people "could hardly carry"?

These "burdens" were the details the Pharisees had added to God's law. To the commandment, "Remember the Sabbath day by keeping it holy" (Exod. 20:8), for example, they had added instructions regarding how far a person could walk on the Sabbath, which kinds of knots could be tied, and how much weight could be carried. Healing a person was considered unlawful work on the Sabbath, although rescuing a trapped animal was permitted (Luke 14:5). No wonder Jesus condemned their additions to the law.

LUKE 11:52
Why did Jesus criticize the Pharisees so harshly?

The Pharisees (1) washed their hands but not their hearts, (2) remembered to tithe but forgot justice, (3) loved people's praise, (4) made impossible religious demands, and (5) would not accept the truth about Jesus and prevented others from believing it as well. They went wrong by focusing on outward appearances and ignoring the inner condition of their hearts.

APRIL 7

Deuteronomy 31:1–32:27; Luke 12:8-34; Psalms 78:32-55; Proverbs 12:21-23

DEUTERONOMY 31:10-13
Why was the Law read to the people every seven years?

The laws were to be read to the whole assembly so that everyone, including the children, could hear them. Every seven years the entire nation would gather together and listen as a priest read the law to them. There were no books, Bibles, or newsstands to spread God's Word, so the people had to rely on word of mouth and an accurate memory. Memorization was an important part of worship, because if everyone knew the law, ignorance would be no excuse for breaking it.

DEUTERONOMY 31:23
Why did Moses charge Joshua to bring Israel into the Promised Land?

Joshua had been appointed to take over the leadership of Israel and guide the people into the promised land (Moses could not enter the land due to his disobedience—Num. 20:12). Joshua, first mentioned in Exodus 17:9, had been Moses' assistant for many years (Josh. 1:1). One of his key qualifications was his faith. As one of the twelve spies to first enter Canaan, only he and Caleb believed that God could help Israel conquer the land (Num. 13:1–14:30). Moses told Joshua to be strong and courageous twice in this chapter (Deut. 31:7, 23). Indeed, this was a frightening task with three million people to care for, settle disputes for, and lead into battle.

LUKE 12:10
How do I know if I have committed the "unforgivable sin"?

Jesus said that blasphemy against the Holy Spirit is unforgivable. This has worried many sincere Christians, but it does not need to. The unforgivable sin means attributing to Satan the work that the Holy Spirit accomplishes (see Matt. 12:31; Mark 3:28-29). Thus it is deliberate and ongoing rejection of the Holy Spirit's work and even of God himself. Those who have committed this sin have shut themselves off from God so thoroughly that they are unaware of any sin at all. Those who fear having committed it show, by their very concern, that they have not sinned in this way.

APRIL 8

DEUTERONOMY 32:49-50
Did Moses really die on Mount Nebo or was he taken away like Enoch and Elijah?

Moses was the only person who ever spoke with God face to face (Exod. 33:11; Num. 12:8). He was called Israel's greatest prophet. Yet even this great man was not allowed to enter the promised land, because he disobeyed God (Num. 20:12). Unlike Elijah, who was taken from the earth without experiencing death, Moses was to die (Deut. 34:5). At the transfiguration of Jesus, Elijah, who never died, appeared in his earthly body, and Moses, who did die, also appeared in a body. The place of Moses' burial was undoubtedly to remain unknown (Deut. 34:6) so that his grave would not become a focal point of worship and lead to a depreciation of the true worship of God.

LUKE 12:40
How can I be ready for Christ's return?

Christ's return at an unexpected time is not a trap, a trick by which God hopes to catch us off guard. In fact, God is delaying his return so more people will have the opportunity to become believers (see 2 Pet. 3:9). Before Christ's return, we have time to live out our beliefs and to reflect Jesus' love as we relate to others. People who are ready for their Lord's return are (1) not hypocritical, but sincere (Luke 12:1), (2) not fearful, but ready to witness (Luke 12:4-9), (3) not worried, but trusting (Luke 12:25-26), (4) not greedy, but generous (Luke 12:34), (5) not lazy, but diligent (Luke 12:37).

LUKE 12:50
What is the "terrible baptism" in Luke 12:50?

The "baptism" to which Jesus referred was his crucifixion. Jesus was dreading the physical pain, but even worse would be the spiritual pain of complete separation from God that would accompany his death for the sins of the world.

LUKE 12:54-59
Why does Jesus talk about the weather in relation to his second coming?

For most of recorded history, the world's principal occupation was farming. The farmer depended directly on the weather for his livelihood. He needed just the right amounts of sun and rain to make his living, and he grew skilled at interpreting natural signs. Jesus was announcing an earthshaking event that would be much more important than the year's crops—the coming of God's kingdom. Like a rainstorm or a sunny day, there were signs that the kingdom would soon arrive. But Jesus' hearers, though skilled at interpreting weather signs, were intentionally ignoring the signs of the times.

APRIL 9

Deuteronomy 33:1-29; Luke 13:1-21; Psalms 78:65-72; Proverbs 12:25

Q PSALM 78:71-72
Why was David, who was Israel's king, called their shepherd?

Although David had been on the throne when this psalm was written, he is called a shepherd and not a king. Shepherding, a common profession in biblical times, was a highly responsible job. The flocks were completely dependent upon shepherds for guidance, provision, and protection. David had spent his early years as a shepherd (1 Sam. 16:10-11). This was a training ground for the future responsibilities God had in store for him. When he was ready, God took him from caring for sheep to caring for Israel, God's people.

Q LUKE 13:1-5
What are the terrible incidents mentioned in Luke 13:1-5 and what is their significance?

Apparently Pilate's soldiers murdered some Jews in the act of offering blood sacrifices and mixed their blood with that of their offerings. Perhaps Pilate feared an insurrection by these Jews. Those killed by the tower of Siloam may have been working for the Romans on an aqueduct there. The Pharisees, who were opposed to using force to deal with Rome, would have said that the Galileans deserved to die for rebelling. The Zealots, a group of anti-Roman terrorists, would have said the aqueduct workers deserved to die for cooperating. Jesus said that neither the Galileans nor the workers should be blamed for their calamity. And instead of blaming others, everyone should look to his or her own day of judgment. Whether a person is killed in a tragic accident or miraculously survives is not a measure of righteousness. Everyone has to die; that's part of being human. But not everyone needs to remain in death (i.e., perish). Jesus promises that those who believe in him will not perish but have eternal life (John 3:16).

Q LUKE 13:10-17
Why did the leader of the synagogue consider healing work?

The religious leaders saw healing as part of a doctor's profession, and practicing one's profession on the Sabbath was prohibited. The synagogue ruler could not see beyond the law to Jesus' compassion in healing this crippled woman. Jesus shamed him and the other leaders by pointing out their hypocrisy. They would untie their animals and care for them, but they refused to rejoice when a human being was freed from Satan's bondage.

APRIL 10

Deuteronomy 34:1–Joshua 2:24; Luke 13:22–14:6; Psalms 79:1-13; Proverbs 12:26

DEUTERONOMY 1:1-12
If Moses wrote Deuteronomy, how did he write about his own death and burial and the people's mourning?

Some hold that this story of Moses' death was added by a different writer at a later time, possibly Joshua, son of Nun. Others accept it as a form of predictive prophecy penned by Moses himself, who had been informed of the details of his approaching death and who told the story in advance of its actual occurrence. If this chapter was written by someone other than Moses it does not cast doubt on Moses' authorship of chapters 1-33.

LUKE 13:6-9
What is the significance of the fig tree in the parable in Luke 13:6-9?

In the Old Testament, a fruitful tree was often used as a symbol of godly living (see, for example, Ps. 1:3 and Jer. 17:7-8). Jesus pointed out what would happen to the other kind of tree—the kind that took valuable time and space and still produced nothing for the patient gardener. This was one way Jesus warned his listeners that God would not tolerate forever their lack of productivity.

LUKE 13:33-34
Why was Jesus focusing on Jerusalem?

Jerusalem, the city of God, symbolized the entire nation. It was Israel's largest city and the nation's spiritual and political capital, and Jews from around the world visited it frequently. But Jerusalem had a history of rejecting God's prophets (1 Kings 19:10; 2 Chron. 24:19; Jer. 2:30; 26:20-23), and it would reject the Messiah just as it had rejected his forerunners.

LUKE 14:1-6, TLB
Why were the Pharisees watching Jesus "like a hawk"?

Earlier Jesus had been invited to a Pharisee's home for discussion (Luke 7:36). This time a prominent Pharisee invited Jesus to his home specifically to trap him into saying or doing something for which he could be arrested. It may be surprising to see Jesus on the Pharisees' turf after he had denounced them so many times. But he was not afraid to face them, even though he knew that their purpose was to trick him into breaking their laws.

APRIL 11

Joshua 3:1–4:24; Luke 14:7-35; Psalms 80:1-19; Proverbs 12:27-28

JOSHUA 1:1-5
What qualifications did Joshua have to become the leader of Israel?

(1) God appointed him (Num. 27:18-23). (2) He was one of only two living eyewitnesses to the Egyptian plagues and the exodus from Egypt. (3) He was Moses' personal aide for 40 years. (4) Of the twelve spies, only he and Caleb showed complete confidence that God would help them conquer the land.

JOSHUA 2:4-5
Was Rahab justified in lying to save the lives of the spies?

Although the Bible does not speak negatively about her lie, it is clear that lying is sin. In Hebrews 11:31, however, Rahab is commended for her faith in God. Her lie is not mentioned. Several explanations have been offered: (1) God forgave Rahab's lie because of her faith; (2) Rahab was simply deceiving the enemy, a normal and acceptable practice in wartime; (3) because Rahab was not a Jew, she could not be held responsible for keeping the moral standards set forth in God's law; (4) Rahab broke a lesser principle—telling the truth—to uphold a higher principle—protecting God's people.

LUKE 14:16-24
What is the meaning of the parable of the great feast?

In ancient days it was customary to send two invitations to a party—the first to announce the event, the second to tell the guests that everything was ready. The guests in Jesus' story insulted the host by making excuses when he issued the second invitation. In Israel's history, God's first invitation came from Moses and the prophets; the second came from his Son. The religious leaders accepted the first invitation. They believed that God had called them to be his people, but they insulted God by refusing to accept his Son. Thus, as the master in the story sent his servant into the streets to invite the needy to his banquet, so God sent his Son to the whole world of needy people to tell them that God's kingdom had arrived and was ready for them.

EXODUS 4:22
Is the "son" referred to in Psalm 80:15, 17 the Son of God?

This is probably not the Messiah, but Israel, whom God calls elsewhere his "firstborn son". The psalmist is making a plea that God would restore his mercy to Israel, the people he chose to bring his message into the world.

APRIL 12

Joshua 5:1–7:15; Luke 15:1-32; Psalms 81:1-16; Proverbs 13:1

JOSHUA 5:2-3
Why did God want Israel circumcised at this time?

The rite of circumcision marked Israel's position as God's covenant people. When God made the original covenant with Abraham, he required that each male be circumcised as a sign of cutting off the old life and beginning a new life with God (Gen. 17:13). Other cultures at that time used circumcision as a sign of entry into adulthood, but only Israel used it as a sign of following God. The rite had no value unless faith were present, so it was neglected during the wilderness wandering. When Israel was about to enter Canaan, God ordered Joshua to command all males to be circumcised, "rolling away the shame of Egypt" by so doing. A man would only be circumcised once. "Again" here refers to the fact that many of the young men were uncircumcised at this time (see 5:5).

JOSHUA 5:14-15
Who was the angel in Joshua 5:14-15?

This *captain of the host* was no mere angel. His presence was an appearance of Christ in person. Joshua worshipped the captain; his worship was accepted and he was neither rebuked nor instructed otherwise. The captain said the place was holy and Joshua removed his shoes. Just as God used the burning bush to give Moses outward, confirming evidence of the divine presence in his life, so God now gave similar assurance to Joshua as he began a new phase of his life of following the assault on Canaan.

LUKE 15:1-2
Why were the Pharisees and teachers of the law bothered that Jesus associated with tax collectors and sinners?

The religious leaders were always careful to stay "clean" according to Old Testament law. In fact, they went well beyond the law in their avoidance of certain people and situations and in their ritual washings. By contrast, Jesus took their concept of "cleanness" lightly. He risked defilement by touching those who had leprosy and by neglecting to wash in the Pharisees' prescribed manner, and he showed complete disregard for their sanctions against associating with certain classes of people. He came to offer salvation to sinners, to show that God loves them. Jesus didn't worry about the accusations. Instead he continued going to those who needed him, regardless of the effect these rejected people might have on his reputation.

APRIL 13

Joshua 7:16–9:2; Luke 16:1-18; Psalms 82:1-8; Proverbs 13:2-3

JOSHUA 7:24-26
Why did Achan's entire family pay for his sin?

The biblical record does not tell us if they were accomplices to his crime, but in the ancient world, the family was treated as a whole. Achan, as the head of his family, was like a tribal chief. If he prospered, the family prospered with him. If he suffered, so did they. Many Israelites had already died in battle because of Achan's sin. Now he was to be completely cut off from Israel. Achan's entire family was to be stoned along with him so that no trace of the sin would remain in Israel. In our permissive and individualistic culture we have a hard time understanding such a decree, but in ancient cultures it was a common punishment. The punishment fit the crime: Achan had disobeyed God's command to destroy everything in Jericho; thus everything that belonged to Achan had to be destroyed.

JOSHUA 8:2
Why did God allow the Israelites to keep the plunder and livestock in Joshua 8:2?

Israel's laws for handling the spoils of war covered two situations. (1) Cities like Jericho which were under God's *ban* (judgment for idolatry) could not be looted (see Deut. 20:16-18). God's people were to be kept holy and separate from every influence of idolatry. (2) The distribution of plunder from cities not under the ban was a normal part of warfare. It provided the army and the nation with the necessary food, flocks, and weapons needed to sustain itself in wartime. Ai was not under the ban. The conquering army needed the food and equipment. Because soldiers were not paid, the loot was part of their incentive and reward for going to war.

PSALM 82:6
Why does Psalm 82:6 call the rulers and judges of Israel "gods" and "sons of the Most High"?

In Psalm 82 God is speaking to judges and administrators who have been chosen to represent him in teaching and enforcing his holy law. They were called gods because they represented God in executing judgment. John 10:34-36 records Jesus using this passage to defend his claims to be God. His argument was as follows: if God would call mere men "gods," why was it blasphemous for him, the true Son of God, to declare himself equal with God?

APRIL 14

Joshua 9:3–10:43; Luke 16:19–17:10; Psalms 83:1-18; Proverbs 13:4

JOSHUA 10:12
How did the sun stand still?

Of course, in relation to the earth the sun always stands still—it is the earth that travels around the sun. But the terminology used in Joshua should not cause us to doubt the miracle. After all, we are not confused when someone tells us the sun rises or sets. The point is that the day was prolonged, not that God used a particular method to prolong it. Two explanations have been given for how this event occurred: (1) A slowing of the earth's normal rotation gave Joshua more time, as the original Hebrew language seems to indicate. (2) Some unusual refraction of the sun's rays gave additional hours of light. Regardless of God's chosen method, the Bible is clear that the day was prolonged by a miracle and that God's intervention turned the tide of battle for his people.

LUKE 16:19-31, NRSV
Did the rich man go to Hades because he was wealthy?

The Pharisees considered wealth to be a proof of a person's righteousness. Jesus startled them with this story in which a diseased beggar is rewarded and a rich man is punished. The rich man did not go to Hades because of his wealth but because he was selfish with it. He refused to feed Lazarus, take him in, or care for him. The rich man was hardhearted in spite of his great blessings.

LUKE 16:22
What is "Abraham's bosom"?

The phrase "carried by the angels into Abraham's bosom" (KJV) has been translated "carried . . . to be with Abraham in the place of the righteous dead" (TLB). Figuratively speaking, this is paradise.

2 CHRONICLES 20
Was the conspiracy and covenant in Psalm 83:5 an actual event or a product of the psalmist's creativity?

This alliance against God may refer to the gathering of certain kings to fight against Jehoshaphat and the people of Judah. The psalm's author is called Asaph, but this can mean Asaph or one of his descendants. A descendant of Asaph named Jahaziel prophesied victory for Judah in the battle against Jehoshaphat (2 Chron. 20:13-17). The psalmist says the alliance against Judah is really against God. Thus Jahaziel exclaimed, "The battle is not yours, but God's" (2 Chron. 20:15). God is "the Most High over all the earth" (Ps. 83:18), and the enemies of Israel were considered God's enemies.

APRIL 15

Joshua 11:1–12:24; Luke 17:11-37; Psalms 84:1-12; Proverbs 13:5-6

JOSHUA 11:10-13
Why was Hazor burned but not the other cities?

Victorious invaders usually kept captured cities intact, moving into them and making them centers of commerce and defense. For example, Moses predicted in Deuteronomy 6:10-12 that Israel would occupy cities they themselves had not built. Hazor, however, was burned. As a former capital of the land, it symbolized the wicked culture that Israel had come to destroy. Also destruction broke the backbone of the federation and weakened the will of the people to resist.

JOSHUA 11:21, TLB
Are the descendants of Anak in Joshua 11:21 the giants the spies feared in Numbers 13:33?

Yes. The Anakims (KJV) were the tribes of giants the Israelite spies described when they gave their negative report on the promised land (Num. 13–14). This time the people did not let their fear of the giants prevent them from engaging in battle and claiming the land God had promised.

LUKE 17:21
How can the kingdom of God be "within" his people?

Some versions say "the kingdom of God is *among* you"; the word can be translated either way. If Jesus meant a kingdom *within,* he was emphasizing that it would begin with spiritual change in his followers. If he meant a kingdom *among* them, he was saying that he, the King, was in their midst. Perhaps Luke chose a word with both meanings because both possibilities are true.

LUKE 17:37
Why did Jesus give an answer that seems unrelated to the disciples' question?

To answer the disciples' question, Jesus quoted a familiar proverb. One vulture circling overhead does not mean much, but a gathering of vultures means that a dead body is nearby. Likewise, one sign of the end may not be significant, but when many signs occur, the second coming is near.

PSALM 84:6
Is the "Valley of Weeping" an actual place?

Probably not; rather, it is symbolic of a dry valley miraculously turned into fertile land by rains. The pilgrimage to the temple in Jerusalem passed through a barren valley called Baca. Its location is unknown. Because *Baca* can mean "weeping," it may have been a symbolic reference to the times of tearful struggles through which people must pass on their way to meet God.

APRIL 16

 ### NUMBERS 34:13
How did God decide which tribe was given which portion of land)?

The division of the land to the nine and a half tribes was to be done by lot in accordance with God's instructions to Moses. This procedure avoided friction and exempted Joshua from making decisions that might be unpopular and for which he could be blamed. The Scriptures do not tell us precisely how lots were cast, nor do they say whether the practice was approved or disapproved by God. Lots were used in the New Testament as well as the Old Testament and were employed when important decisions were required. Proverbs 16:33 says: "The lot is cast into the lap; but the whole disposing thereof is of the LORD" (KJV). It was supposed that God, who is sovereign, was behind the way the lot fell. There is often an interesting connection between the land a tribe received and the character of the tribe's founder. For example, because of Joseph's godly character (Gen. 49:22-26), the tribes descended from him—Ephraim and Manasseh—were given the richest, most fertile land in all of Canaan. Judah, who offered himself in exchange for his brother Benjamin's safety (Gen. 44:18-34), received the largest portion of land, which eventually became the southern kingdom and the seat of David's dynasty. Reuben, who slept with one of his father's wives (Gen. 49:4), was given desert land, the region described here.

 ### JOSHUA 13:29
What is the "half-tribe of Manasseh"?

The tribe of Manasseh was divided into two half-tribes. This occurred when many people from the tribe wanted to settle east of the Jordan River in an area that was especially suited for their flocks (Numb. 32:33). The rest of the tribe preferred to settle west of the Jordan River in the land of Canaan.

 ### LUKE 18:15-17
Why did the people bring their children to Jesus?

It was customary for a mother to bring her children to a rabbi for a blessing, and that is why these mothers gathered around Jesus. The disciples, however, thought the children were unworthy of the Master's time—less important than whatever else he was doing. But Jesus welcomed them, because little children have the kind of faith and trust needed to enter God's kingdom.

APRIL 17

Joshua 15:1-63; Luke 18:18-43; Psalms 86:1-17; Proverbs 13:9-10

Q **PSALM 86:8,** KJV
When David said, "Among the gods there is none like unto thee, O Lord," was he saying that there are other gods?

Rather, all other so-called gods are false gods. None of them is wise, mighty, and good. Nor do their works support the claims of their adherents that they are true gods. The God of Israel alone does great works (Ps. 86:10).

Q **LUKE 18:31-34**
What did the prophets write about the Son of Man?

Predictions about what would happen to Jesus are found in the Old Testament. Psalm 41:9 speaks of his betrayal: "Yea, mine own familiar friend, in whom I trusted, which did eat of my bread, hath lifted up his heel against me" (KJV). Psalm 22:16-18 says, "The enemy, this gang of evil men, circles me like a pack of dogs; they have pierced my hands and feet. I can count every bone in my body. See these men of evil gloat and stare; they divide my clothes among themselves by a toss of the dice" (TLB). This speaks of Christ's crucifixion. Isaiah 53:4-7 also describes the crucifixion: "Surely he has borne our infirmities and carried our diseases; yet we accounted him stricken, struck down by God, and afflicted. But he was wounded for our transgressions, crushed for our iniquities; upon him was the punishment that made us whole and by his bruises we are healed. . . . and the LORD has laid on him the iniquity of us all. He was oppressed, and he was afflicted, yet he did not open his mouth; like a lamb that is led to the slaughter, and like a sheep that before its shearers is silent, so he did not open his mouth" (NRSV). Psalm 16:10 predicts the resurrection: "Because you will not abandon me to the grave, nor will you let your Holy One see decay." The disciples didn't understand Jesus, apparently because they focused on what he said about his death and ignored what he said about his resurrection. Even though Jesus spoke plainly, they did not grasp the significance of his words until they saw the risen Christ face to face.

Q **LUKE 18:31-34**
How many times did Jesus reveal his death to the disciples?

This was the third time the Lord revealed his death to the disciples. The first was in Caesarea Philippi, before his transfiguration (Matt. 16:21; Luke 9:22). The second was in Galilee, after his transfiguration (Matt. 17:22; Luke 9:44-45). This time he was on the way to Jerusalem. The disciples didn't fully comprehend the purpose of Jesus' death until Pentecost (Acts 2).

APRIL 18

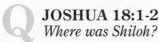

JOSHUA 18:1-2
Where was Shiloh?

With most of the conquest behind them, Israel moved their religious center from Gilgal (Josh. 5:8-9) to Shiloh about twenty miles north of Jerusalem. This was probably the first place where the tabernacle was set up permanently. The Tent of Meeting was part of the tabernacle and was where God lived among his people (Exod. 25:8). Its central location in the land made it easier for the people to attend the special worship services and yearly feasts. The family of Samuel, a great priest and prophet, often traveled to Shiloh, and Samuel was taken there when he was a small boy (1 Sam. 1:3, 22). The tabernacle remained in Shiloh through the period of the judges (about three hundred years). Apparently the city was destroyed by the Philistines when the ark of the covenant was captured (1 Sam. 4–5). Shiloh never lived up to its reputation as Israel's religious center, for later references in the Bible point to the wickedness and idolatry in the city (Ps. 78:56-60; Jer. 7:12-15).

LUKE 19:7-8
Why did the crowd call Zacchaeus a sinner and why did he give his wealth to the poor?

To finance their great world empire, the Romans levied heavy taxes on all nations under their control. The Jews opposed these taxes because they supported a secular government and its pagan gods, but they were still forced to pay. Tax collectors were among the most unpopular people in Israel. Jews by birth, they chose to work for Rome, and were considered traitors. Besides, it was common knowledge that tax collectors were making themselves rich by gouging their fellow Jews.

Zacchaeus was curious and determined to see Jesus and even climbed a tree to do so. Without saying a word to Jesus, he was told that Jesus would stay at his house. For a Jew to enter the house of a tax collector was unheard of. No wonder the people muttered when Jesus went home with the tax collector Zacchaeus. But despite the fact that Zacchaeus was both a cheater and a turncoat, Jesus loved him; and in response, the little tax collector was converted. Judging from the crowd's reaction to him, Zacchaeus must have been a very crooked tax collector. But after he met Jesus, he realized that his life needed straightening out. By giving to the poor and making restitution—with generous interest—to those he had cheated, Zacchaeus demonstrated inward change by outward action.

APRIL 19

JOSHUA 19:49
Why was the land divided with boundaries?

There were several good reasons for establishing these well-set boundaries instead of turning the promised land into a single undivided nation. (1) The boundaries gave each tribe ownership of an area, promoting loyalty and unity that would strengthen each tribe. (2) The boundaries delineated areas of responsibility and privilege, which would help each tribe develop and mature. (3) The boundaries reduced conflicts that might have broken out if everyone had wanted to live in the choicest areas. (4) The boundaries fulfilled the promised inheritance to each tribe that began to be given as early as the days of Jacob (Gen. 48:21-22).

LUKE 19:36-37
Why were the people so happy that Jesus was coming to Jerusalem?

This is the event Christians celebrate on Palm Sunday. The people lined the road, praising God, waving palm branches, and throwing their cloaks in front of the colt as it passed before them. "Long live the King" was the meaning behind their joyful shouts, because they knew that Jesus was intentionally fulfilling the prophecy in Zechariah 9:9: "See, your king comes to you, righteous and having salvation, gentle and riding on a donkey, on a colt, the foal of a donkey." To announce that he was indeed the Messiah, Jesus chose a *time* when all Israel would be gathered at Jerusalem, a *place* where huge crowds could see him, and a *way* of proclaiming his mission that was unmistakable. The people went wild. They were sure their liberation was at hand. But the people who were praising God for giving them a king had the wrong idea about Jesus. They expected him to be a national leader who would restore their nation to its former glory, and thus they were deaf to the words of their prophets and blind to Jesus' real mission. When it became apparent that Jesus was not going to fulfill their hopes, many people would turn against him.

LUKE 19:42-44
Did Jesus' prophecy in Luke 19:42-44 come true?

About forty years after Jesus said these words, they came true. In A.D. 66, the Jews revolted against Roman control. Three years later Titus, son of the Emperor Vespasian, was sent to crush the rebellion. Roman soldiers attacked Jerusalem and broke through the northern wall but still couldn't take the city. Finally they laid siege to it, and in A.D. 70 they were able to enter the severely weakened city and burn it. Six hundred thousand Jews were killed during Titus's onslaught.

APRIL 20

JOSHUA 22:1-12
Why was a second altar built by the Jordan River?

God had specifically commanded that there be only one central place for offering sacrifices. At this time that place was on Mount Ebal. When the tribes of Reuben and Gad and the half-tribe of Manasseh built an altar at the Jordan River, the rest of Israel feared that these tribes were starting their own religion and rebelling against God. But before beginning an all-out war, Phinehas led a delegation to learn the truth, following the principle taught in Deuteronomy 13:12-19. He was prepared to negotiate rather than fight if a battle was not necessary. When he learned that the altar was for a memorial rather than for pagan sacrifice, war was averted and unity restored. The erection of the altar was a tribute to the spiritual sensitivities of those who wanted to perpetuate the name and the worship of the true God.

LUKE 20:9-19
What is the meaning of the parable in Luke 20:9-19?

The characters in this story are easily identified. Even the religious leaders understood it. The owner of the vineyard is God; the vineyard is Israel; the tenants are the religious leaders; the servants are the prophets and priests God sent to Israel; the son is the Messiah, Jesus; and the others are the Gentiles. Jesus' parable indirectly answered the religious leaders' question about his authority; it also showed them that he knew about their plan to kill him. The parable was applied to the Jewish nation for its rejection of God's Messiah. Jesus warned of the dire consequences of this decision—not only were they to be cast out; their inheritance was to be given over to Gentiles, who were offered the kingdom the Jews had rejected.

LUKE 20:17
What was Jesus' purpose in mentioning the "stone which the builders rejected"?

Quoting Psalm 118:22, Jesus showed the unbelieving leaders that even their rejection of the Messiah had been prophesied in Scripture. Ignoring the capstone, or cornerstone, which represents the Messiah, was dangerous. A person could be tripped or crushed (judged and punished). Although Jesus would be rejected by the Jews, he would become the cornerstone of a new "building," the church (Acts 4:11-12). The cornerstone in a building was used as a base to make sure the other stones of the building were straight and level. Likewise, Jesus' life and teaching would be the church's foundation, or base. Jesus' comments were veiled, but the religious leaders had no trouble interpreting them. They immediately wanted to arrest him.

APRIL 21

Q JOSHUA 23:6-13
Why did Joshua give Israel the warnings in Joshua 23:6-13?

Joshua knew the nation's weak spots. Before dying, he called the people together and gave commands to help them where they were most likely to slip: (1) follow all that is written in the Book of the Law of Moses without turning aside; (2) don't associate with the pagan nations or worship their gods; (3) don't intermarry with the pagan nations. These temptations were right in their backyard.

Q LUKE 20:27-38
Why did the Sadducees ask Jesus about the resurrection?

The Sadducees, a group of conservative religious leaders, honored only the Pentateuch—Genesis through Deuteronomy—as Scripture. They also did not believe in a resurrection of the dead because they could find no mention of it in those books. The Sadducees decided to try their hand at tricking Jesus, so they brought him a question that had always stumped the Pharisees. After addressing their question about marriage, Jesus answered their *real* question about resurrection. Basing his answer on the writings of Moses—an authority they respected—he upheld belief in resurrection. Not believing in the resurrection, the Sadducees wanted Jesus to say something they could refute. Even so, Jesus did not ignore or belittle their question. He answered it, and then he went beyond it to the real issue.

Q LUKE 20:41-44
What was the purpose of Jesus' question about the identity of the Messiah?

Here Jesus turned the tables on the Pharisees and Sadducees and asked them a question that went right to the heart of the matter—what they thought about the identity of the Messiah. Jesus' question is this: If David calls his son Lord, how then can he who is Lord be David's son? The true answer is: (1) Christ as God was David's Lord; (2) Christ as man was David's son. In his human nature he was the offspring of David; in his divine nature he was the root of David. The Pharisees knew that the Messiah would be a descendant of David, but they did not understand that he would be more than a human descendant—he was God himself. Jesus quoted from Psalm 110:1 to show that David knew that the Messiah would be both man *and* God. The Pharisees expected only a human ruler to restore Israel's greatness as in the days of David and Solomon, but Jesus wanted to give them a revelation of who he really was.

APRIL 22

Joshua 24:1-33; Luke 21:1-28; Psalms 89:38-52; Proverbs 13:20-23

JOSHUA 24:32
Why did Israel still have the "bones of Joseph"?

Joseph died in Egypt approximately two hundred years before he was buried at last in Canaan. He had carefully left instructions with the Israelites that he was not to be buried in that land but was to be taken away when Israel left Egypt. The coffin containing his mummy was cared for by the Israelites through the long wilderness journey and was now interred in Shechem in the plot of ground purchased by Jacob from the sons of Hamor. His coffin must have been a constant reminder to the Israelites and their offspring of their great ancestor, who believed the promise made to Abraham about Canaan and who desired to be buried in its sacred soil.

LUKE 21:5
Were Jesus and his disciples looking at the original temple?

The temple the disciples were admiring was not Solomon's temple—that had been destroyed by the Babylonians in the seventh century B.C. This temple had been built by Ezra after the return from exile in the sixth century B.C., desecrated by the Seleucids in the second century B.C., reconsecrated by the Maccabees soon afterward, and enormously expanded by Herod the Great over a 46-year period. It was a beautiful, imposing structure with a significant history, but Jesus said that it would be completely destroyed. This happened in A.D. 70 when the Roman army burned Jerusalem.

LUKE 21:24
When are the "times of the Gentiles" when Jerusalem will "be trampled on by the Gentiles"?

This verse has also been translated "and Jerusalem shall be conquered and trampled down by the Gentiles until the period of Gentile triumph ends in God's good time" (TLB). The "times of the Gentiles" began with Babylon's destruction of Jerusalem in 586 B.C. and the exile of the Jewish people. Israel was no longer an independent nation but was under the control of Gentile rulers. In Jesus' day, Israel was governed by the Roman empire, and a Roman general would destroy the city in A.D. 70. Jesus was saying that the domination of God's people by his enemies would continue until God decided to end it. The "times of the Gentiles" refers not just to the repeated destructions of Jerusalem, but also to the continuing and mounting persecution of God's people until the end.

APRIL 23

JUDGES 2:1-5
Did God abandon Israel in Judges 2:1-5?

This event marks a significant change in Israel's relationship with God. At Mount Sinai, God made a sacred and binding agreement with the Israelites called a covenant. God's part was to make Israel a special nation (Gen. 12:1-3), to protect them, and to give them unique blessings for following him. Israel's part was to love God and obey his laws. But because they rejected and disobeyed God, the agreement to protect them was no longer in effect. But God wasn't going to abandon his people. Although God's agreement to help Israel conquer the land was no longer in effect, his promise remained valid to make Israel a nation through whom the whole world would be blessed (fulfilled in the Messiah's coming). God still wanted the Israelites to be a holy people, and he often used oppression to bring them back to him, just as he warned he would (Lev. 26; Deut. 28). The Book of Judges records a number of instances where God allowed his people to be oppressed so that they would repent of their sins and return to him.

LUKE 22:3
If Satan entered into Judas Iscariot, why is Judas considered responsible for betraying Jesus?

Satan's part in the betrayal of Jesus does not remove any of the responsibility from Judas. Disillusioned because Jesus was talking about dying rather than about setting up his kingdom, Judas may have been trying to force Jesus' hand and make him use his power to prove he was the Messiah. Or perhaps Judas, not understanding Jesus' mission, no longer believed that Jesus was God's chosen one. Whatever Judas thought, he had already determined to betray Jesus (John 13:2). In so doing he left himself wide open to Satan (John 13:27). Satan assumed that Jesus' death would end Jesus' mission and thwart God's plan. Like Judas, he did not know that Jesus' death and resurrection were the most important parts of God's plan all along.

LUKE 22:10, NRSV
Why were the disciples to look for a man carrying a jar of water?

Ordinarily women carried pitchers or jars to and from the wells. Men carried water skins. Here a man carries a jar. He stood out in the crowd and was thus easily identifiable by Jesus' disciples. Unless this was a prearranged signal, this event demonstrates Jesus' divine foreknowledge.

APRIL 24

Judges 2:10–3:31; Luke 22:14-34; Psalms 92:1–93:5; Proverbs 14:1-2

JUDGES 2:12-14
Why were idols so bad in God's sight?

To worship an idol violated the first two of the Ten Commandments (Exod. 20:3-6). Bowing to an idol meant that a person did not believe God was the one true God. The Canaanites had gods for almost every season, activity, or place. To them, the Lord was just another god to add to their collection of gods. Israel, by contrast, was to worship only Jehovah (Yahweh). They could not possibly believe that God was the one true God and at the same time bow to an idol. Idol worshipers could not see their god as their creator, because they created him. These idols represent sensual, carnal, and immoral aspects of human nature. God's nature is spiritual and moral. Adding the worship of idols to the worship of God could not be tolerated.

JUDGES 2:17
Why would the people of Israel turn so quickly from their faith in God?

Simply put, the Canaanite religion appeared more attractive to the sensual nature and offered more short-range benefits (sexual permissiveness and increased fertility in childbearing and farming). One of its most attractive features was that people could remain selfish and yet fulfill their religious requirements. They could do almost anything they wished and still be obeying at least one of the many Canaanite gods.

LUKE 22:20, TLB
Why is the wine of the Lord's Supper "the token of God's new agreement to save you—an agreement sealed with the blood I shall pour out to purchase back your souls"?

In Old Testament times, God agreed to forgive people's sins if they sacrificed animals. When this sacrificial system was inaugurated, the agreement between God and man was sealed with the blood of animals (Exod. 24:8). But animal blood did not in itself remove sin and had to be repeated day by day and year after year. Jesus instituted a new covenant. Under this new covenant, Jesus would die in the place of sinners. Unlike the blood of animals, his blood would truly remove the sins of all who put their faith in him. And Jesus' sacrifice would never have to be repeated; it would be good for all eternity. The prophets looked forward to this new covenant that would fulfill the old sacrificial agreement (Jer. 31:31-34), and John the Baptist called Jesus "the Lamb of God, who takes away the sin of the world" (John 1:29).

APRIL 25

Judges 4:1–5:31; Luke 22:35-53; Psalms 94:1-23; Proverbs 14:3-4

Q **JUDGES 4:2-3**
What were Sisera's iron chariots like?

Chariots were the tanks of the ancient world. Made of iron or wood, they were pulled by one or two horses and were the most feared and powerful weapons of the day. Some chariots even had razor sharp knives extending from the wheels designed to mutilate helpless foot soldiers. The Canaanite army had nine hundred iron chariots. Israel was not powerful enough to defeat such an invincible army. Therefore, Jabin and Sisera had no trouble oppressing the people—until a faithful woman named Deborah called upon God.

Q **JUDGES 4:4**
Why did God choose a woman to lead his people?

Deborah is the only judge described as a prophetess. As such, she conveyed to the people the word she received from God's Spirit. In this role she was able to foretell the future with the help of the Spirit. God is not partial to men over women in principle, for the Scriptures are full of incidents in which God chose to employ women in his service. There were prophetesses, deaconesses, and other women who played an important part in the unfolding scheme of redemption. Miriam, Rahab, Lydia, Elizabeth, Mary, and others stand out as illustrations of God's choice of godly women.

Q **LUKE 22:34; MARK 14:30**
Why does Mark say before the rooster crows twice Peter will deny Jesus, when Luke only says "before the rooster crows?" Is this a discrepancy in the Bible?

The various Gospel accounts contain slight differences related to the crowing of the rooster. This does not mean that there is an inconsistency in the Bible. It does indicate that one gospel writer was more detailed than another. Jesus probably said that Peter's third denial would come before the second sounding of the rooster. Still, it is common to simply say that the rooster crowed, as Luke did, even if it has sounded several times. To provide additional information to the account of Peter's denial, as Mark did, is not a contradiction to the somewhat briefer testimony of Luke. Both are valid witnesses. Matthew, Mark, and Luke all include an account of Peter's denial of his Lord. Only the Gospel of Mark provides a count of the times the cock would crow. This may be because Mark's gospel is commonly considered to be Mark's record of Peter's account of the life of Jesus Christ. If this is the case, it is not surprising that Peter would remember in detail the crushing experience of his own denial of Christ and include the number of times the cock crowed.

APRIL 26

Judges 6:1-40; Luke 22:54–23:12; Psalms 95:1–96:13; Proverbs 14:5-6

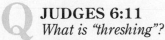 **JUDGES 6:11**
What is "threshing"?

Threshing was the process of separating the grains of wheat from the useless outer shell called chaff. This was done in a large area, often on a hill, where the wind could blow away the lighter chaff as the beaten wheat was tossed into the air. If Gideon had done this, however, he would have been an easy target for the bands of raiders who were overrunning the land. Therefore, he was forced to thresh his wheat in a winepress, a pit that was probably hidden from view and that would not be suspected as a place to find a farmer's crops.

JUDGES 6:37
Was Gideon testing God when he put out the fleece, or was he simply asking God for more encouragement?

If he was testing or simply asking, his motive was right (to obey God and defeat the enemy), but his method was less than ideal. Gideon seems to have known that his requests might displease God (Judg. 6:39), and yet he demanded two miracles (Judg. 6:37, 39). He had witnessed three miracles as proof of his mission (Judg. 6:21, 38, 40). Gideon had all the facts, but still he hesitated. He delayed obeying God because he wanted even more proof. Demanding extra signs was an indication of unbelief.

JUDGES 6:39
After seeing the miracle of the wet fleece, why did Gideon ask for another miracle?

Perhaps he thought the results of the first test could have happened naturally. A thick fleece could retain moisture long after the sun had dried the surrounding ground. "Putting out fleeces" is a poor decision-making method. Those who do this put limitations on God by substituting a "fleece" for the wisdom that comes through Bible study and prayer.

LUKE 22:66-71
What did the Jewish leaders accuse Jesus of doing?

Here, Jesus turned the high priest's question around by saying, "You are right in saying I am." In doing so Jesus identified himself with God by using a familiar title for God found in the Old Testament: "I am" (Exod. 3:14). The high priest recognized Jesus' claim and accused him of blasphemy. For any other human this claim would have been blasphemy, but in this case it was true. Blasphemy, the sin of claiming to be God or of attacking God's authority and majesty in any way, was punishable by death (Lev. 24:10ff.). The Jewish leaders had the evidence they wanted.

APRIL 27

Judges 7:1–8:17; Luke 23:13-43; Psalms 97:1–98:9; Proverbs 14:7-8

JUDGES 7:12-13
What is the meaning of the soldier's dream in Judges 7:12-13?

This soldier dreamed of a huge loaf of barley bread tumbling into camp. Barley grain was only half the value of wheat, and the bread made from it was considered inferior. In the same way, Israel's tiny band of men was considered inferior to the vast forces of Midian and Amalek. But God would make the underdog Israelites seem invincible.

JUDGES 7:15
How could Gideon worship while near an enemy encampment?

Gideon stood just outside the enemy camp "worshiping God." Rituals, motions, and loud praise would have announced his presence to the enemy, so Gideon's worship was a silent attitude of joy, thanksgiving, and praise to God. Worship is not limited to a particular form or building. Jesus said that true worshipers worship the Father in spirit and in truth (John 4:23). True worship begins with a worshipful attitude.

LUKE 23:22, TLB
What does it mean to be "scourged"?

When Pilate said he would *scourge* Jesus he was referring to a punishment that could have killed Jesus. The usual procedure was to bare the upper half of the victim's body and tie his hands to a pillar before whipping him with a three-pronged whip. The number of lashes was determined by the severity of the crime. After being flogged, Jesus also endured other agonies. He was slapped, struck with fists, and mocked. A crown of thorns was placed on his head, and he was beaten with a stick and stripped before being hung on the cross.

LUKE 23:34
Besides his words of forgiveness in Luke 23:34, what did Jesus say on the cross?

There are seven sayings of Jesus uttered from the cross. They were spoken in the following order: (1) the word of forgiveness: "Father, forgive them; for they know not what they do" (Luke 23:34, KJV); (2) the word of salvation: "Today shalt thou be with me in paradise" (Luke 23:43, KJV); (3) the word of affection: "Woman, behold thy son"; "Behold thy mother" (John 19:26-27, KJV); (4) the word of despair: "My God, my God, why hast thou forsaken me?" (Matt. 27:46; Mark 15:34, KJV); (5) the word of physical torment: "I thirst" (John 19:28, KJV); (6) the word of triumph: "It is finished" (John 19:30, KJV); and (7) the word of committal: "Father, into thy hands I commend my spirit" (Luke 23:46, KJV)

APRIL 28

Judges 8:18–9:21; Luke 23:44–24:12; Psalms 99:1-9; Proverbs 14:9-10

JUDGES 8:27
Why did Gideon make the golden ephod?

An ephod was a linen garment worn by priests over their chests. It was considered holy (Exod. 28:5-35; 39:2-26; Lev. 8:7-8). Gideon probably had good motives for making the ephod but these are unknown. It may have been a visible remembrance commemorating the victory. Unfortunately, the people began to worship the ephod as an idol.

JUDGES 9:1
Where is Shechem?

Abimelech was declared ruler of Israel at Shechem, the site of other key Bible events. This city was about twenty-five miles north of Jerusalem near Mount Gerizim. It was one of Abraham's first stops upon arriving in Canaan (Gen. 12:6-7). When Jacob lived there, two of his sons killed all the men in Shechem because the prince's son raped their sister (Gen. 34). Joseph's bones were buried in Shechem (Josh. 24:32); Israel renewed its covenant with God there (Josh. 24); and the kingdom of Israel split apart at this same city (1 Kings 12).

JUDGES 9:7-15
What was the meaning of Jotham's parable?

In Jotham's parable the trees represented Gideon's 70 sons, and the thornbush represented Abimelech. Jotham's point was that if the person chosen as king was a "fruitful tree," then good fruit would come from his reign. But if a "thorn bush" was chosen, it would catch fire and burn. Abimelech, like a thornbush, could offer Israel no real protection or security. Jotham's parable came true when Abimelech destroyed the city of Shechem (Judg. 9:45), burned "the tower of Shechem" (the city of Beth Millo, Judg. 9:46-49), and was finally killed at Thebez.

LUKE 24:1, NRSV
Why did the women bring spices to Jesus' tomb?

The women brought spices to the tomb as we would bring flowers to a grave—as a sign of love and respect (2 Chron. 16:14). They were also used for embalming. Ordinarily a body was embalmed at burial and not a day and a half later, but Jesus died only a few hours before sundown Friday when the Sabbath began. By the time Joseph had received Pilate's permission to take the body and had put it in his tomb, there was no longer time for embalming without breaking the Sabbath. The women went home and kept Sabbath as the law required, from sundown Friday to sundown Saturday, before gathering up their spices and returning to the tomb.

APRIL 29

Judges 9:22–10:18; Luke 24:13-53; Psalms 100:1-5; Proverbs 14:11-12

Q JUDGES 9:53-54
What is a millstone, and how could it kill Abimelech?

In times of battle, women were sometimes asked to join the men at the city wall to drop heavy objects on the soldiers below. A millstone would have been an ideal object for this purpose. It was a round stone about 18 inches in diameter with a hole in the center. Millstones were used to grind grain into flour. The grain was placed between two millstones. The top millstone was turned, crushing the grain. Abimelech's death was especially humiliating: he was killed by a woman, not by fighting; and he was killed by a farm implement instead of a weapon. Abimelech therefore asked his armor bearer to stab him with his sword before he died from the blow of the millstone.

Q JUDGES 10:17-18
Who were the Ammonites?

The power of the Ammonite nation was at its peak during the period of the judges. These people were descendants of Ammon, conceived when Lot's younger daughter slept with her drunken father (Gen. 19:30-38). The land of Ammon was located just east of the Jordan River across from Jerusalem. South of Ammon lay the land of Moab, the nation conceived when Lot's older daughter slept with her father. Moab and Ammon were usually allies. It was a formidable task to defeat these nations.

Q LUKE 24:6-7
Why is the resurrection so important?

(1) Because Christ was raised from the dead, we know that the kingdom of heaven has broken into earth's history. Our world is now headed for redemption, not disaster. (2) Because of the resurrection, we know that death has been conquered, and we too will be raised from the dead to live forever with Christ. (3) The resurrection gives authority to the church's witness in the world. In Acts the apostles' most important message was the proclamation that Jesus Christ had been raised from the dead! (4) The resurrection gives meaning to the church's regular feast, the Lord's Supper. We break bread with our risen Lord, who comes in power to save us. (5) The resurrection helps us find meaning even in great tragedy. No matter what happens to us as we walk with the Lord, the resurrection gives us hope for the future. (6) The resurrection assures us that Christ is alive and ruling his kingdom. He is not legend; he is alive and real. (7) God's power that brought Jesus back from the dead is available to us so that we can live for him in an evil world.

APRIL 30

Judges 11:1–12:5; John 1:1-28; Psalms 101:1-8; Proverbs 14:13-14

JUDGES 11:30-31
Did Jephthah really vow to sacrifice a person in exchange for victory in battle?

Scholars are divided over the issue. Those who say Jephthah was considering human sacrifice use the following arguments: (1) He was from an area where pagan religion and human sacrifice were common. In his eyes, it may not have seemed like a sin. (2) Jephthah may not have had a background in religious law. Perhaps he was ignorant of God's command against human sacrifice. Those who say Jephthah could not have been thinking about human sacrifice point to other evidence: (1) As leader of the people, Jephthah must have been familiar with God's laws; human sacrifice was clearly forbidden (Lev. 18:21; 20:1-5). (2) No legitimate priest would have helped Jephthah carry out his vow if a person was to be the sacrifice. Whatever Jephthah had in mind when he made the vow, did he or did he not sacrifice his daughter? Some think he did, because his vow was to make a burnt offering. Some think he did not, and they offer several reasons: (1) If the girl was to die, she would not have spent her last two months in the hills. (2) God would not have honored a vow based on a wicked practice. (3) Verse 39 says that she never married, not that she died, implying that she was set apart for service to God, not killed.

JOHN 1:14
What does "the Word became flesh" mean?

This is called the "incarnation." When the Son of God was born, God became a man. He was not part man and part God; he was completely human and completely divine (Col. 2:9). The incarnation is the act whereby the second person of the Trinity, the Son of God, took on real human flesh. He was one person with two natures—a perfectly divine nature and a perfectly human (yet sinless) nature. As the God-man he had all the attributes of deity (Col. 1:19; Heb. 1:8-10). As man he had all the attributes of humanity. His two natures are separate, distinct, and without fusion or mixture. Before Christ came, people could know God partially. After Christ came, people could know God fully because he became visible and tangible in Christ. Christ is the perfect expression of God in human form. The two most common errors people make about Jesus are to minimize his humanity or to minimize his divinity. Jesus is both God and man.

MAY 1

Q JUDGES 13:18
Why did the angel keep his name a secret from Manoah?

In those days people believed that if they knew someone's name, they knew his character and how to control him. By not giving his name, the angel was not allowing himself to be controlled by Manoah. He was also saying that his name was a mystery beyond understanding and too wonderful to imagine. Manoah asked the angel for an answer that he wouldn't have understood.

Q JUDGES 13:19
Why did Manoah sacrifice a grain offering to the Lord?

A grain offering was grain, oil, and flour shaped into a cake and burned on the altar along with the *burnt offering* (the young goat). The grain offering, described in Leviticus 2, was offered to God as a sign of honor, respect, and worship. It was an acknowledgment that because the Israelites' food came from God, they owed their lives to him. With the grain offering, Manoah showed his desire to serve God and demonstrated his respect.

Q JUDGES 14:3
Why wouldn't Samson's parents let him marry the woman he chose?

Samson's parents objected to his marrying the Philistine woman for two reasons: (1) It was against God's law (Exod. 34:15-17; Deut. 7:1-4). A stark example of what happened when the Israelites married pagans can be found in Judges 3:5-7. (2) The Philistines were Israel's greatest enemies. Marriage to a hated Philistine would be a disgrace to Samson's family. But Samson's father gave in to Samson's demand and allowed the marriage, even though he had the right to refuse his son.

Q JOHN 1:29
Why did John call Jesus the "Lamb of God"?

Every morning and evening, a lamb was sacrificed in the temple for the sins of the people (Exod. 29:38-42). Isaiah prophesied that the Messiah, God's servant, would be led to the slaughter like a lamb (53:7). To pay the penalty for sin, a life had to be given—and God chose to provide the sacrifice himself. The sins of the world were removed when Jesus died as the perfect sacrifice. This is the way our sins are forgiven (1 Cor. 5:7). The "sin of the world" means everyone's sin, the sin of each individual.

MAY 2

Q JUDGES 15:15
What was the source of Samson's great strength?

Samson's strength did not come from his Nazirite vow, his spurning of strong drink or from his hair. It lay in his relationship to God, of which these other things were only symbols. Samson himself acknowledged that God was the author of his power (Judg. 15:18).

Q JUDGES 16:23-24
Who was Dagon?

Dagon was the chief god of the Philistines, the god of grain and harvest. Many temples were built to Dagon, and the worship there included human sacrifice. The temples were also the local entertainment centers. Just as people today crowd into theaters, Philistine townspeople crowded into the local temple. They sat on the flat temple roof and looked into the courtyard below. What they often saw was the torture and humiliation of prisoners. Since the Philistines had control over the Israelites, they thought their god was stronger. But when the ark of God was placed before Dagon, the idol fell over and broke into pieces (1 Sam. 5:1-7). God's strength goes beyond numbers or physical might.

Q JOHN 2:14, TLB
Why were there "merchants . . . and moneychangers" in the temple?

The temple tax had to be paid in local currency, so foreigners had to have their money changed. But the moneychangers often would charge exorbitant exchange rates. The people also were required to make sacrifices for sins. Because of the long journey, many could not bring their own animals. Some who brought animals would have them rejected for imperfections. So animal merchants would do a flourishing business in the temple courtyard. The price of sacrificial animals was much higher in the temple area than elsewhere. Jesus was angry at the dishonest, greedy practices of the money changers and merchants, and he particularly disliked their presence on the temple grounds. They were making a mockery of God's house of worship.

Q JOHN 2:17, TLB
What is the meaning of the prophecy "Concern for God's House will be my undoing?

This quotation from Psalm 69:9 is also translated "Zeal for your house will consume me" (NRSV). Jesus took the evil acts in the temple as an insult against God and thus did not deal with them halfheartedly. He was consumed with righteous anger against sin and disrespect for God.

MAY 3

Judges 17:1–18:31; John 3:1-21; Psalms 104:1-23; Proverbs 14:20-21

JUDGES 17:7-12
Why did Micah hire the priest?

Apparently the Israelites no longer supported the priests and Levites with their tithes, because so many of the people no longer worshiped God. The young Levite in this story probably left his home in Bethlehem because the money he received was not enough to live on. But Israel's moral decay affected even the priests and Levites. This man accepted money (Judg. 17:10-11), idols (Judg. 18:20), and position (Judg. 17:12) in a way that was inconsistent with God's laws. While Micah revealed the religious downfall of individual Israelites, this priest illustrated the religious downfall of priests and Levites.

JUDGES 18:27
Did the tribe of Dan have the right to kill the citizens of Laish?

No. God had commanded Israel to clean out and destroy certain cities because of their idolatry and wickedness, but Laish did not fall under that judgment. It was not within the assigned boundaries of Dan, and its people were peaceful in contrast to the warlike Canaanites. But the tribe of Dan had no regard for God's law. God's law said to destroy a city for idolatry (Deut. 13:12-15). The Danites themselves were guilty of this sin. This story shows how far some of the tribes had wandered away from God.

JOHN 3:6
Who is the Holy Spirit?

God is three persons in one—the Father, the Son, and the Holy Spirit. God became a man in Jesus so that Jesus could die for our sins. Jesus rose from the dead to offer salvation to all people through spiritual renewal and rebirth. When Jesus ascended into heaven, his physical presence left the earth, but he promised to send the Holy Spirit so that his spiritual presence would still be among mankind (see Luke 24:49). The Holy Spirit first became available to all believers at Pentecost (Acts 2). Whereas in Old Testament days the Holy Spirit empowered specific individuals for specific purposes, now all believers have the power of the Holy Spirit available to them. For more on the Holy Spirit, read John 14:16-28; Romans 8:9; 1 Corinthians 12:13; and 2 Corinthians 1:22.

JOHN 3:8
Why was Jesus talking about the wind in John 3:8?

Jesus explained that we cannot control the work of the Holy Spirit. He works in ways we cannot predict or understand. Just as you did not control your physical birth, so you cannot control your spiritual birth. It is a gift from God through the Holy Spirit (Rom. 8:16; 1 Cor. 2:10-12; 1 Thess. 1:5-6).

MAY 4

JUDGES 19:1–21:45
What is the significance of the tragic story in Judges 19:1–21:45?

When the Israelites' faith in God disintegrated, their unity as a nation also disintegrated. They could have taken complete possession of the land if they had obeyed God and trusted him to keep his promises. But when they forgot him, they lost their purpose, and soon "everyone did as he saw fit" (Judg. 21:25). When they stopped letting God lead them, they became no better than the evil people around them. When they made laws for their own benefit, they set standards far below those of God's.

JUDGES 19:24
Why did the man sacrifice his daughter and his guest's concubine to the mob?

Protecting a guest at any cost ranked at the top of a man's code of honor. But here the hospitality code turned to fanaticism. The rape and abuse of a daughter and companion was preferable to the *possibility* of a conflict between a guest and a neighbor. The two men were selfish (they didn't want to get hurt themselves); they lacked courage (they didn't want to face a conflict even when lives were at stake); and they disobeyed God's law (they allowed deliberate abuse and murder). What drastic consequences can result when social protocol carries more authority than moral convictions!

JUDGES 19:30
How could such an abominable event occur in Israel?

The horrible crime described in this chapter wasn't Israel's worst offense. Even worse was the nation's failure to establish a government based upon God's moral principles, where the law of God was the law of the land. As a result, laws were usually unenforced and crime was ignored. Sexual perversion and lawlessness were a by-product of Israel's disobedience to God. The Israelites weren't willing to speak up until events had gone too far.

JUDGES 20:27-28
Why was the Ark of God in Bethel and not Shiloh?

This is the only place in Judges where the ark of the covenant is mentioned. This probably indicates how seldom the people consulted God. Phinehas, the high priest, was also the high priest under Joshua (Josh. 22:13). The reference to Phinehas as high priest and the location of the tabernacle in Bethel instead of Shiloh probably indicate that the events of this story occurred during the early years of the judges.

MAY 5

Judges 21:1–Ruth 1:22; John 4:4-42; Psalms 105:1-15; Proverbs 14:25

Q RUTH 1:4-5
Should Naomi's sons have married women from Moab?

Friendly relations with the Moabites were discouraged (Deut. 23:3-6) but probably not forbidden, since the Moabites lived outside the promised land. Marrying a Canaanite (and all those living within the borders of the promised land), however, was against God's law (Deut. 7:1-4). Moabites were not allowed to worship at the tabernacle because they had not let the Israelites pass through their land during the exodus from Egypt. As God's chosen nation, Israel should have set the standards of high moral living for the other nations. Ironically it was Ruth, a Moabitess, whom God used as an example of genuine spiritual character. This shows just how bleak life had become in Israel during those days.

Q RUTH 1:11
Why did Naomi speak of "sons, who could become your husbands"?

Naomi's comment here refers to *levirate marriage,* the obligation of a dead man's brother to care for the widow (Deut. 25:5-10). This law kept the widow from poverty and provided a way for the family name of the dead husband to continue. Naomi, however, had no other sons for Ruth or Orpah to marry, so she encouraged them to remain in their homeland and remarry. Orpah agreed, which was her right. But Ruth was willing to give up the possibility of security and children in order to care for Naomi.

Q JOHN 4:6
Why is the well in John 4 called "Jacob's well"?

Jacob's well was on the property originally owned by Jacob (Genesis 33:18, 19). It was not a spring-fed well, but a well into which water seeped from rain and dew, collecting at the bottom. Wells were almost always located outside the city along the main road. Twice each day, morning and evening, women came to draw water. This woman came at noon, however, probably to avoid meeting people who knew her reputation. Jesus gave this woman an extraordinary message about living water that would quench her spiritual thirst forever.

Q JOHN 4:10
What did Jesus mean by "living water"?

In the Old Testament, many verses speak of thirsting after God as one thirsts for water (Ps. 42:1; Isa. 55:1; Jer. 2:13; Zech. 13:1). God is called the fountain of life (Ps. 36:9) and the spring of living water (Jer. 17:13). In saying he would bring living water that could forever quench a person's thirst for God, Jesus was claiming to be the Messiah who could give what the soul desires.

MAY 6

Q RUTH 3:2, TLB
Why was it important that Boaz was Naomi's "close relative"?

Here Naomi was encouraging Ruth to see if Boaz would take the responsibility of being a "kinsman-redeemer" to her (2:20). A kinsman-redeemer was a relative who volunteered to take responsibility for the extended family. When a woman's husband died, the law (Deut. 25:5-10) provided that she could marry a brother of her dead husband. But Naomi had no more sons. In such a case, the nearest relative to the deceased husband could become a kinsman-redeemer and marry the widow. The nearest relative did not have to marry the widow. If he chose not to, the next nearest relative could take his place. If no one chose to help the widow, she would probably live in poverty the rest of her life, because in Israelite culture the inheritance was passed on to the son or nearest male relative, not to the wife. To take the sting out of these inheritance rules, there were laws for kinsman-redeemers.

Q RUTH 3:2
What is a "threshing floor"?

The threshing floor was the place where the grain was separated from the harvested wheat. The wheat stalks were crushed, either by hand or by oxen, and the valuable grain (inner kernels) separated from the worthless chaff (the outside shell). The floor was made from rock or soil and located outside the village, usually on an elevated site where the winds would blow away the lighter chaff when the crushed wheat was thrown into the air (winnowed). Boaz spent the night beside the threshing floor for two reasons: (1) to prevent theft and (2) to wait for his turn to thresh grain. (Threshing was often done at night, because daylight hours were spent harvesting.)

Q RUTH 3:4
Did Naomi want Ruth to seduce Boaz while he was sleeping at the threshing floor?

Naomi's advice seems strange, but she was not suggesting a seductive act. Naomi was only telling Ruth to act in accordance with Israelite custom and law. It was common for a servant to lie at the feet of his master and even share a part of his covering. By observing this custom, Ruth would inform Boaz that he could be her kinsman-redeemer—that he could find someone to marry her or marry her himself. It was family business, nothing romantic. But the story later became beautifully romantic as Ruth and Boaz developed an unselfish love and deep respect for each other.

MAY 7

1 Samuel 1:1–2:21; John 5:1-23; Psalms 105:37-45; Proverbs 14:28-29

Q 1 SAMUEL 1:6
Why would Peninnah taunt Hannah for being barren?

Hannah had been unable to conceive children, and in Old Testament times, a childless woman was considered a failure. Her barrenness was a social embarrassment for her husband. Children were a very important part of the society's economic structure. They were a source of labor for the family, and it was their duty to care for their parents in their old age. If a wife could not bear children she was often obligated, by ancient Middle Eastern custom, to give one of her servant girls to her husband to bear children for her. Although Elkanah could have left Hannah (a husband was permitted to divorce a barren wife), he remained lovingly devoted to her despite social criticism and his rights under civil law.

Q 1 SAMUEL 2:12-17
What were Eli's sons doing wrong in their service as priests?

The law stipulated that the needs of all the Levites were to be met through the people's tithes (Num. 18:20-24; Josh. 13:14, 33). Because Eli's sons were priests, they were to be taken care of this way. But Eli's sons took advantage of their position to satisfy their lust for power, possessions, and control. Their contempt and arrogance toward both people and worship undermined the integrity of the whole priesthood. Eli's sons were taking parts of the sacrifices *before* they were offered to God on the altar. They were also eating meat before the fat was burned off. This was against God's laws (Lev. 3:3-5). In effect, Eli's sons were treating God's offerings with contempt. Offerings were given to show honor and respect to God while seeking forgiveness for sins, but through their irreverence, Eli's sons were actually sinning while making the offerings. To add to their sins, they were also sleeping with the women who served there (1 Sam. 2:22). Eli knew that his sons were evil, but he did little to correct or stop them, even when the integrity of God's sanctuary was threatened. As the high priest, Eli should have responded by executing his sons (Num. 15:22-31). No wonder he chose not to confront the situation. But by ignoring their selfish actions, Eli let his sons ruin their own lives and the lives of many others.

MAY 8

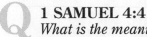

1 SAMUEL 4:4
What is the meaning of "The Lord Almighty, who is enthroned between the cherubim"?

This conveys that God's presence rested on the ark of the covenant between the two golden cherubim (or angels) attached to its lid. The people believed that the ark would bring victory when Hophni and Phinehas carried it into battle. The ark of the covenant contained the Ten Commandments given by God to Moses. The ark was supposed to be kept in the Most Holy Place, a sacred part of the tabernacle that only the high priest could enter once a year. Hophni and Phinehas desecrated the room by unlawfully entering it and removing the ark. The Israelites rightly recognized the great holiness of the ark, but they thought that the ark itself—the wood and metal box—was their source of power. They began to use it as a good luck charm, expecting it to protect them from their enemies. A symbol of God does not guarantee his presence and power. Their attitude toward the ark came perilously close to idol worship. When the ark was captured by their enemies, they thought that Israel's glory was gone (1 Sam. 4:19-22) and that God had deserted them (1 Sam. 7:1-2). God uses his power according to his own wisdom and will. He responds to the faith of those who seek him.

JOHN 5:18
Why did the Jewish leaders not understand who Jesus was?

In this verse Jesus was identifying himself with God, his Father. There could be no doubt as to his claim to be God. Jesus does not leave us the option to believe in God while ignoring God's Son (John 5:23). The Pharisees also called God their Father, but they realized Jesus was claiming a unique relationship with him. In response to Jesus' claim, the Pharisees had two choices: to believe him or to accuse him of blasphemy. They chose the second. The Old Testament mentioned three signs of the coming Messiah. In this chapter, John shows that Jesus has fulfilled all three signs. All power and authority are given to him as the Son of Man (cf. John 5:27 with Dan. 7:13-14). The lame and sick are healed (cf. John 5:20, 26 with Isa. 35:6; Jer.31:8-9). The dead are raised to life (cf. John 5:21, 28 with Deut. 32:39; 1 Sam. 2:6; 2 Kings 5:7). The Jewish leaders should have recognized these signs, but they did not.

1 Samuel 5:1–7:17; John 6:1-21; Psalms 106:13-31; Proverbs 14:32-33

1 SAMUEL 6:2
What was the guilt offering in 1 Samuel 6:3-5 supposed to accomplish?

This was a normal reaction to trouble in the Canaanite religion. The Philistines thought their problems were the result of their gods being angry. They recognized their guilt in taking the ark and now were trying everything they could to placate Israel's God. The diviners probably helped choose the gift they thought would placate Jehovah. But the offering consisted of images of tumors ("emerods," KJV) and rats, not the kind of guilt offering prescribed in God's laws (Lev. 5:14–6:7; 7:1-10).

1 SAMUEL 6:19
Why were people killed for looking into the ark?

The Israelites had made an idol of the ark. They had tried to harness God's power, to use it for their own purposes (victory in battle). But the Lord of the universe cannot be controlled by humans. To protect the Israelites from his power, he had warned them not even to look at the sacred sanctuary objects in the Most Holy Place or they would die (Num. 4:20). Only Levites were allowed to move the ark. Because of Israel's disobedience, God carried out his promised judgment. God could not allow the people to think they could use his power for their own ends. He could not permit them to disregard his warnings and come into his presence lightly. He did not want the cycle of disrespect, disobedience, and defeat to start all over again. God did not kill the men of Beth Shemesh to be cruel. He killed them because overlooking their presumptuous sin would encourage the whole nation of Israel to ignore God.

JOHN 6:1-14
Since the feeding of the multitude is related in the other Gospels, why does John repeat it here?

The feeding of the five thousand is the only miracle recorded in all four Gospels. John probably wrote about this because it provides a necessary backdrop for the following section on Jesus as the bread of life. John 6:11 says that Jesus gave thanks to God for the boy's loaves and fishes. He may have prayed "Blessed art you, O Lord our God, King of the universe, who brings forth bread from the earth," a common Jewish prayer of thanksgiving.

MAY 10

1 SAMUEL 8:4-9
Why did Israel want a king?

There are several reasons Israel wanted a king: (1) Samuel's sons were not fit to lead Israel. (2) The 12 tribes of Israel continually had problems working together because each tribe had its own leader and territory. It was hoped that a king would unite the tribes into one nation and one army. (3) The people wanted to be like the neighboring nations. This is exactly what God didn't want. Having a king would make it easy for them to forget that God was their real leader. It was not wrong for Israel to want a king; God had mentioned the possibility in Deuteronomy 17:14-20. Yet, in reality, the people were rejecting God as their leader. The Israelites wanted laws, an army, and a human monarch in the place of God. They wanted to run the nation through human strength, even though only God's strength could make them flourish in the hostile land of Canaan.

JOHN 6:28-29
How can believing be the "work of God"?

Here Jesus answered a question that still puzzles many sincere seekers for God: What should I do to satisfy God? The religions of the world are mankind's attempts to answer this question. Jesus' reply is brief and simple: we must believe in the One whom God has sent. Satisfying God does not come from what we *do*, but from whom we *believe*.

JOHN 6:35
When I eat bread am I actually eating Jesus?

Bread and Christ are not the same thing. People eat bread to satisfy physical hunger and to sustain physical life. Here *bread* is used figuratively to illustrate that Jesus Christ supplies divine life to the believer just as bread nourishes the physical life. *I am the bread of life* is to be taken no more literally than the words "I am the door," or "I am the vine." Jesus is not physical bread, an actual door, or a grape vine. But just as physical bread must be eaten to receive its nourishing benefits, so the bread of life, Jesus Christ, must be eaten by receiving him through faith (John 6:29). In this way all who come to Jesus as the bread of life will find their spiritual hunger satisfied.

MAY 11

1 SAMUEL 10:1
Why did Samuel pour oil on Saul's head?

When an Israelite king took office he was not only crowned, he was anointed. The coronation was the political act of establishing the king as ruler; the anointing was the religious act of making the king God's representative to the people. A king was always anointed by a priest or prophet. The special anointing oil was a mixture of olive oil, myrrh, and other expensive spices. It was poured over the king's head to symbolize the presence and power of the Holy Spirit of God in his life. This anointing ceremony was to remind the king of his great responsibility to lead his people by God's wisdom and not his own.

1 SAMUEL 11:8
Why is the tribe of Judah mentioned separately from the other 11 tribes of Israel?

There are several reasons for this. Judah was the largest tribe (Num. 1:20-46), and it was the tribe from which most of Israel's kings would come (Gen. 49:8-12). Later, Judah would be one of the few tribes to return to God after a century of captivity under a hostile foreign power. Judah would also be the tribe through which the Messiah would come (Mic. 5:2).

JOHN 6:53
What does it mean to "eat the flesh of the Son of Man"?

Many of Jesus' disciples, especially those beyond the smaller select group, were offended by what Jesus said here because they thought in terms of cannibalism (John 6:60). Here Jesus is not speaking of a literal eating of his flesh. What he says is a figure of speech designed to teach a great spiritual truth in physical terms. The Lord's Supper was not yet instituted, so it does not refer to that either. This is a spiritual eating and drinking of Christ by receiving him through faith. It is neither sacramental nor cannibalistic.

JOHN 6:66
Why did Jesus' words cause many of his followers to desert him?

(1) They may have realized that he wasn't going to be the conquering Messiah-King they expected. (2) He refused to give in to their self-centered requests. (3) He emphasized faith, not deeds. (4) His teachings were difficult to understand, and some of his words were offensive.

MAY 12

1 SAMUEL 12:22, KJV
Why did God make Israel "his people"?

God did not choose them because they deserved it (Deut. 7:7-8), but in order that they might become his channel of blessing to all people through the Messiah (Gen. 12:1-3). Because God chose the people of Israel, he would never abandon them; but because they were his special nation, he would often punish them for their disobedience in order to bring them back to a right relationship with him.

1 SAMUEL 12:23
Is failing to pray for others a sin?

Samuel's words seem to indicate that it is. His actions illustrate two of God's people's responsibilities: (1) they should pray consistently for others (Eph. 6:18), and (2) they should teach others the right way to God (2 Tim. 2:2). Samuel disagreed with the Israelites' demand for a king, but he assured them that he would continue to pray for them and teach them.

JOHN 7:13, KJV
Why were the people afraid of the Jews?

When John speaks of "the Jews" in his Gospel he is often referring to the Jewish leaders, not the Jewish people in general. John himself was a Jew, as were the people in this case who were afraid of "the Jews." These religious leaders had a great deal of power over the common people. Apparently these leaders couldn't do much to Jesus at this time, but they threatened anyone who might publicly support him. Expulsion from the synagogue was one of the reprisals for believing in Jesus (John 9:22-23). To a Jew, this was one of the worst possible social stigmas.

JOHN 7:21-23
Why does Jesus mention circumcision in John 7:21-23?

According to Moses' law, circumcision was to be performed eight days after a baby's birth (Gen. 17:9-14; Lev. 12:3). This rite was carried out on all Jewish males to demonstrate their identity as part of God's covenant people. If the eighth day after birth was a Sabbath, the circumcision would still be performed (even though it was considered work). While the religious leaders allowed certain exceptions to Sabbath laws, they allowed none to Jesus, who was simply showing mercy to those who needed healing.

MAY 13

1 Samuel 13:23–14:52; John 7:30-53; Psalms 109:1-31; Proverbs 15:5-7

Q 1 SAMUEL 14:24-26
Why did Saul pronounce the curse in 1 Samuel 14:24-26?

Saul made an oath without thinking through the implications. The results? (1) His men were too tired to fight; (2) they were so hungry they ate meat that still contained blood which was against one of the oldest and strongest Hebrew food laws (3) Saul almost killed his own son (14:42-44). Saul's impulsive oath sounded heroic, but it had disastrous side effects. Saul made this oath because he was overly anxious to defeat the Philistines and wanted to give his soldiers an incentive to finish the battle quickly. In the Bible, God never asked people to make oaths or vows, but if they did, he expected them to keep them (Leviticus 5:4; Numbers 30).

Q JOHN 7:45
What were the temple police?

Although the Romans ruled Palestine, they gave the Jewish religious leaders authority over minor civil and religious affairs. The religious leaders supervised their own temple guards and gave them power to arrest anyone causing a disturbance or breaking any of their ceremonial laws. Because these leaders had developed hundreds of trivial laws, it was almost impossible for anyone, even the leaders themselves, not to break, neglect, or ignore at least a few of them some of the time. But these temple police couldn't find one reason to arrest Jesus. And as they listened to Jesus to try to find evidence, they couldn't help hearing the wonderful words he said.

Q JOHN 7:50-51
Who was Nicodemus?

Nicodemus was the Pharisee who visited Jesus at night (chapter 3). Apparently Nicodemus had become a secret believer. Since most of the Pharisees hated Jesus and wanted to kill him, Nicodemus risked his reputation and high position when he spoke up for Jesus. He confronted the Pharisees with their failure to keep their own laws. The Pharisees saw themselves losing ground—the temple guards came back impressed by Jesus (7:46), and one of the Pharisees' own, Nicodemus, was defending him. With their hypocritical motives being exposed and their prestige slowly eroding, they began to move to protect themselves. Pride would interfere with their ability to reason, and soon they would become obsessed with getting rid of Jesus just to save face. What was good and right no longer mattered; they began to break their own laws by plotting to murder Jesus.

MAY 14

1 Samuel 15:1–16:23; John 8:1-20; Psalms 110:1-7; Proverbs 15:8-10

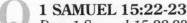

1 SAMUEL 15:22-23
Does 1 Samuel 15:22-23 mean that God does not want sacrifices?

This is the first of numerous places in the Bible where the theme "to obey is better than sacrifice" is stated (Ps. 40:6-8; 51:16-17; Prov. 21:3; Isa. 1:11-17; Jer. 7:21-23; Hos. 6:6; Mic. 6:6-8; Matt. 12:7; Mark 12:33; Heb. 10:8-9). Was Samuel saying that sacrifice is unimportant? No, he was urging Saul to look at his reasons for making the sacrifice rather than at the sacrifice itself. A sacrifice was a ritual transaction between man and God that physically demonstrated a relationship between them. But if the person's heart was not truly repentant or if he did not truly love God, the sacrifice was a hollow ritual. Religious ceremonies or rituals are empty unless they are performed with an attitude of love and obedience. "Being religious" (going to church, serving on a committee, giving to charity) is not enough if we do not act out of devotion and obedience to God.

1 SAMUEL 16:13
Why did David not become king after he was anointed?

David was anointed king, but it was done in secret; he was not publicly anointed until much later (2 Sam. 2:4; 5:3). Saul was still legally the king, but God was preparing David for his future responsibilities. The anointing oil poured over David's head stood for holiness. It was used to set people or objects apart for God's service. Each king and high priest of Israel was anointed with oil. This commissioned him as God's representative to the nation. Although God rejected Saul's kingship by not allowing any of his descendants to sit on Israel's throne, Saul himself remained in his position until his death.

JOHN 8:3-11
Could the Jewish leaders trap Jesus with their question about stoning the woman caught in adultery?

The Jewish leaders had already disregarded the law by arresting the woman without the man. The law required that both parties to adultery be stoned (Lev. 20:10; Deut. 22:22). The leaders were using the woman as a trap so they could trick Jesus. If Jesus said the woman should not be stoned, they would accuse him of violating Moses' law. If he urged them to execute her, they would report him to the Romans, who did not permit the Jews to carry out their own executions (John 18:31).

MAY 15

1 Samuel 17:1–18:4; John 8:21-30; Psalms 111:1-10; Proverbs 15:11

1 SAMUEL 17:8-9
Why did Goliath want to fight against Israel alone?

An army often avoided the high cost of battle by pitting its strongest warrior against the strongest warrior of the enemy. Such a warrior is called the "champion" of his army or nation. This practice avoided great bloodshed because the winner of the fight was considered the winner of the battle. Goliath had the definite advantage against David from a human standpoint. But Goliath didn't realize that in fighting David, he also had to fight God. In the days of the exodus, most of the Israelites had been afraid to enter the promised land because of the giants living there (Num. 13:32-33). King Og of Bashan, for example, needed a bed over 13 feet long (Deut. 3:11). Now Goliath, over nine feet tall, taunted Israel's soldiers and appeared invincible to them. Saul, the tallest of the Israelites, may have been especially worried because he was obviously the best match for Goliath. In God's eyes, however, Goliath was no different than anyone else.

1 SAMUEL 17:55-58
Why didn't Saul know who David was?

Although David had played his harp many times in front of Saul, Saul's question to Abner seems to show he didn't know David very well. There are several explanations to this confusing passage: (1) since David was scheduled to marry Saul's daughter if he was successful (1 Sam. 17:25), Saul wanted to know more about his family. (2) Saul's unstable mental condition (1 Sam. 16:14) may have prevented him from recognizing David. David was still only a part-time staff member at Saul's palace (1 Sam. 17:14-15), and Saul may not have bothered to get to know him or learn much about him.

PSALMS 111:1, TLB
What is the meaning of the word "hallelujah"?

Hallelujah means "praise the Lord." It is uses in the Bible only in songs of praise and appears exclusively in the books of Psalms and Revelation (Rev. 19:1-6, where it appears four times) The word "alleluia" in Revelation is a transliteration from the Hebrew word. Other Hebrew words for praise, *hillel* and *hallel*, appear many times in the Old Testament. The word "hallelujah," the highest form of praise, occurs only about fifteen times in the Old Testament, all in the Psalms.

MAY 16

1 Samuel 18:5–19:24; John 8:31-59; Psalms 112:1-10; Proverbs 15:12-14

1 SAMUEL 18:10; 16:14
What was the evil spirit the Lord sent to Saul?

There are several possibilities: (1) Saul was simply depressed; (2) the Holy Spirit had left Saul and God allowed an evil spirit (a demon) to torment him as judgment for his disobedience (this would demonstrate God's power over the spirit world—1 Kings 22:19-23); (3) a good angel was sent to torment Saul by convicting him of his coming judgment. In any case, Saul was driven to insanity, which led him to attempt to murder David.

1 SAMUEL 19:1-2
Is it ever right to disobey your father, as Jonathan did in 1 Samuel 19:1-2?

It is clearly a principle of Scripture that when a father instructs a son to break God's laws, the son should obey God rather than man. This principle assumes that the son is old enough to be accountable and to see through any deception. A son's role is to be respectful, helpful, and obedient to his father. The fifth commandment says, "Honor your father and mother" (Exod. 20:12). Proverbs 23:22 says, "Listen to your father who begot you, and do not despise your mother when she is old" (NRSV). Ephesians 6:1-2 quotes Exodus 20:12 saying, "Children, obey your parents in the Lord, for this is right. Honor your father and mother" (NRSV). But there is a difference between obeying and honoring. To honor means to show respect and love; to obey means to do as one is told. But this does not mean to follow commands or advice that violate God's laws. Saul commanded Jonathan to murder David which was in violation of the sixth commandment.

JOHN 8:58, TLB
What did Jesus mean when he said "I was in existence before Abraham was ever born"?

This is one of the most powerful statements uttered by Jesus. When he said that he existed before Abraham was born, he undeniably proclaimed his divinity. Other translations say, "Before Abraham was, *I Am*." Not only did Jesus say that he existed before Abraham; he also applied God's holy name (*I Am*—Exod. 3:14) to himself. This claim demands a response. It cannot be ignored. The Jewish leaders tried to stone Jesus for blasphemy because he claimed equality with God. But Jesus *is* God.

MAY 17

1 SAMUEL 21:10
Why did David lie in 1 Samuel 21:2?

David lied to protect himself from Saul. Some excuse this lie because a war was going on, and it is the duty of a good soldier to deceive the enemy. But nowhere is David's lie condoned. In fact, the opposite is true because his lie led to the death of 85 priests (1 Sam. 22:9-19). David's small lie seemed harmless enough, but it led to tragedy. The Bible makes it very clear that lying is wrong (Lev. 19:11). Lying, like every other sin, is serious in God's sight and may lead to all sorts of harmful consequences.

1 SAMUEL 16:13
Why did the Philistines accept their archenemy, David, into their camp?

The Philistines may have been initially happy to accept a defector who was a high military leader. Any enemy of Saul would have been a friend of theirs. They could not have known that David had been anointed Israel's next king. Soon, however, the Philistines became nervous about David's presence. After all, he had slain thousands of their own people (1 Sam. 18:7). David then protected himself by acting insane because it was the custom not to harm mentally unstable people.

JOHN 9:7
Where was the Pool of Siloam?

The pool of Siloam was built in Jerusalem by King Hezekiah when he was threatened with invasion by Assyria. His workers constructed an underground tunnel from a spring outside the city walls to carry water into the city. Thus the people could always get water without fear of being attacked. This was especially important during times of siege (see 2 Kings 20:20; 2 Chron. 32:30). An inscription found in the tunnel tells how the two teams of tunnelers met at midpoint, a remarkable engineering feat. Hezekiah's tunnel begins from an earlier one built by the Jebusites (possibly mentioned in 2 Sam. 5:8).

JOHN 9:14-16
What did Jesus do to break the Sabbath?

The Jewish Sabbath, Saturday, was the weekly holy day of rest. The Pharisees had made a long list of specific do's and don'ts regarding the Sabbath. Kneading the mud and healing the man were considered work and therefore were forbidden. Jesus may have purposely made the mud in order to emphasize his teaching about the Sabbath—that it is right to care for others' needs even if it involves working on a day of rest.

MAY 18

1 SAMUEL 22:2
How did David make an army out of debtors and malcontents?

Those in distress, in debt, or discontented joined David, who himself was an outlaw. These people thought they could improve their lot by helping David become king. David's control over this band of men shows his resourcefulness and ability to lead and motivate others. It takes great leadership skills to build an army out of the kind of men that followed David. This group eventually formed the core of his military leadership and became known as David's "mighty men" (2 Samuel 23:8, NKJV).

1 SAMUEL 22:18
Why would Saul have his own priests killed?

Saul suspected a conspiracy among Jonathan, David, and the priests. His suspicion came from Doeg's report of seeing David talking to Ahimelech, the high priest, and receiving food and a weapon from him (1 Samuel 22:9-10). Saul's action showed his mental and emotional instability and how far he had strayed from God. By destroying everything in Nob, Saul was placing the city under the ban (declaring it to be utterly destroyed) described in Deuteronomy 13:12-17, which was supposed to be used only in cases of idolatry and rebellion against God. But it was Saul, not the priests, who had rebelled against God.

JOHN 10:1
What is the significance of the sheepfold in John 10:1?

At night, sheep were often gathered into a sheep pen (sheepfold) to protect them from thieves, weather, or wild animals. The sheep pens were caves, sheds, or open areas surrounded by walls made of stones or branches. The shepherd often slept in the pen to protect the sheep. Just as a shepherd cares for his sheep, Jesus, the good shepherd, cares for his flock (those who follow him). The prophet Ezekiel, in predicting the coming of the Messiah, called him a shepherd (Ezek. 34:23).

JOHN 10:11
What is the difference between the good shepherd in John 10:11, the great shepherd in Hebrews 13:20, and the chief shepherd in 1 Peter 5:4?

The good shepherd died for his sheep, the great shepherd conforms the sheep to his image, and the chief shepherd is coming again with his reward for the sheep. The good shepherd's work is finished, the great shepherd's work is in the present, and the chief shepherd's work is in the future.

MAY 19

1 SAMUEL 24:5, NRSV
Why was David "stricken to the heart because he had cut off a corner of Saul's cloak"?

David had great respect for Saul, even though Saul was trying to kill him. Although Saul was sinning and rebelling against God, David still respected the position he held as God's anointed king. David knew he would one day be king, and he also knew it was not right to strike down the man God had placed on the throne. If he assassinated Saul he would be setting a precedent for his own opponents to remove him some day.

1 SAMUEL 25:4-8
Why should Nabal have been obligated to feed David's entire army?

Our customs are different from those of the ancient Middle East. First, simple hospitality demanded that travelers—any number of them—be fed. Nabal was very rich and could have easily afforded to meet David's request. Second, David wasn't asking for a handout. He and his men had been protecting Nabal's work force, and part of Nabal's prosperity was due to David's vigilance.

JOHN 10:35
What is the "word of God"?

This verse is a clear statement of the truth of the Bible. If we accept Christ as Lord, we also accept his confirmation of the Bible as God's word. The sixty-six books that make up the Bible are called the canon. The word "canon," meaning "rod" or "rule," speaks of those books that measured up to the standard of acceptability. The books in the canon constitute authoritative books comprising God's revelation. The canon of the Old Testament was well known in Jesus' day and included the thirty-nine books we have in our Bibles. Jesus placed his stamp of approval on the Old Testament scriptures and here called them the *Word of God.* He also said the Word of God *cannot be broken.* The books now in the New Testament were first separate books sent to and used by various churches in Asia Minor, Greece, and Rome. Copies were made and circulated widely. Gradually the twenty-seven books which presently comprise the New Testament were accepted and acknowledged to be God's word. Lists of these canonical letters and Gospels were drawn up, possibly as a safeguard against spurious apocryphal "Gospels" and so-called "apostolic letters" produced by Gnostics and other heretics.

MAY 20

1 SAMUEL 28:3-8
If Saul had banned all mediums and wizards from Israel, why did he turn to one for counsel?

Although he had removed the sin of witchcraft from the land, he did not remove it from his heart. Saul, after God's Spirit left him, in desperation sought help from the medium at En-dor in order to find the will of God. Saul hoped Samuel might help him if only he could speak with him. But God had strictly forbidden the Israelites to have anything to do with black magic, fortune tellers, witches, wizards, or anyone who claimed to bring forth spirits from the dead (Deut. 18:9-14).

1 SAMUEL 28:12
Did Samuel really come back from the dead at the medium's call?

The medium shrieked at the appearance of Samuel—she knew too well that the spirits she usually contacted were either contrived or satanic. Somehow Samuel's appearance revealed to her that she was dealing with a power far greater than she had known. She did not call up Samuel by trickery or by the power of Satan; God brought Samuel back to give Saul a prediction regarding his fate, a message Saul already knew. This in no way justifies efforts to contact the dead or communicate with persons or spirits from the past. God is against all such practices (Gal. 5:19-21).

JOHN 11:35
Why did Jesus weep?

When Jesus saw the weeping and wailing, he too wept openly. Perhaps he empathized with their grief, or perhaps he was troubled at their unbelief. In either case, Jesus showed that he cares enough for us to weep with us in our sorrow. Scripture never says Jesus laughed, although we can imagine that he had a robust sense of humor and that he undoubtedly expressed his pleasure with laughter. But here the Bible records his grief over physical death. In Luke 19:41 Jesus wept over the fate of Jerusalem.

JOHN 11:37-38
Why was the grave of Lazarus in a cave?

Tombs at this time were usually caves carved in the limestone rock of a hillside. A tomb was often large enough for people to walk inside. Several bodies would be placed in one tomb. After burial, a large stone was rolled across the entrance to the tomb.

MAY 21

Q 1 SAMUEL 30:26
Why did David send part of the battle spoils to the tribe of Judah?

(1) David was from the tribe of Judah. (2) David was recognizing that Judah was the largest tribe of Israel and represented the greatest authority. (3) After Saul's death, the tribe of Judah split off from the rest of the tribes (2 Sam. 2:4) because they refused to recognize Saul's son as king. David may have anticipated this split. If so, he was preparing the leaders of Judah to accept him as their king.

Q 1 SAMUEL 30:3-4
Why wouldn't Saul's armor-bearer obey and kill Saul?

Saul's armor-bearer faced a moral dilemma—should he carry out a sinful order from a man he was supposed to obey? He knew he should obey his master, the king, but he also knew murder was wrong. He decided not to kill Saul. The Philistines had a well-earned reputation for torturing their captives. Saul no doubt knew about Samson's fate (Judg. 16:18-31) and did not want to risk physical mutilation or other abuse. When his armor-bearer refused to kill him, he took his own life. Thus Saul faced death the same way he faced life. He took matters into his own hands without thinking of God or asking for his guidance.

Q JOHN 12:3
What is the "pure nard" that composed the perfume Mary used to anoint Jesus' feet?

Pure nard was a fragrant ointment imported from the mountains of India. Thus it was very expensive. The amount Mary used was worth a year's wages. Nard was used to anoint kings. Mary may have been anointing Jesus as her kingly Messiah.

Q JOHN 12:10-11
Why did the chief priests want to kill Lazarus?

The chief priests' blindness and hardness of heart caused them to sink ever deeper into sin. They rejected the Messiah and planned to kill him, and then plotted to murder Lazarus as well. One sin leads to another. From the Jewish leaders' point of view, they could accuse Jesus of blasphemy because he claimed equality with God. But Lazarus had done nothing of the kind. They wanted Lazarus dead simply because he was a living witness to Jesus' power.

MAY 22

2 SAMUEL 1:2-16
Why did David have the messenger that brought the news of Saul's death killed?

This man identified himself as an Amalekite from Saul's camp (2 Sam. 1:2-8). He may have been an Amalekite under Israelite jurisdiction, but more likely he was a battlefield scavenger. Obviously the man was lying both about his identity and about what happened on the battlefield. Because he had Saul's crown with him, something the Philistines wouldn't have left behind, we can infer that he found Saul dead on the battlefield before the Philistines arrived (1 Sam. 31:8). The man lied to gain some personal reward for killing David's rival, but he misread David's character. If David had rewarded him for murdering the king, David would have shared his guilt. Instead, David had the messenger killed.

2 SAMUEL 1:26
What was the nature of David's relationship with Jonathan if Jonathan's love for David was "deeper than the love of women"?

By saying this David was not implying that he had a sexual relationship with Jonathan. Homosexual acts were absolutely forbidden in Israel. Leviticus 18:22 calls homosexuality "detestable," and Leviticus 20:13 decrees the death penalty for those who practice homosexuality. David was simply restating the deep brotherhood and faithful friendship he had with Jonathan.

JOHN 12:31, NRSV
Who is the "ruler of this world" in John 12:31?

This is Satan, an angel who rebelled against God. Satan is real, not symbolic, and is constantly working against God and those who obey him. Satan tempted Eve in the garden and persuaded her to sin; he tempted Jesus in the desert and did not succeed (Matt. 4:1-11). Satan has great power, but people can be delivered from his reign of spiritual darkness because of Christ's victory on the cross. Jesus' resurrection shattered Satan's deathly power (Col. 1:13-14).

JOHN 12:40
Does John 12:40 mean God intentionally prevented these people from believing in him?

Jesus was paraphrasing Isaiah 6:9-10. People in Jesus' time, like those in the time of Isaiah, would not believe despite the evidence (John 12:37). As a result, God hardened their hearts. This means he simply confirmed their own choices. After a lifetime of resisting God, they had become so set in their ways that they wouldn't even try to understand Jesus' message.

MAY 23

2 Samuel 2:12–3:39; John 13:1-30; Psalms 119:1-16; Proverbs 15:29-30

2 SAMUEL 3:2-4
Why did David have so many wives?

Polygamy was a socially acceptable practice for kings at this time, although God specifically warned against it (Deut. 17:14-17). Sadly, the numerous sons born to David's wives caused him great trouble. Rape (2 Sam. 13:14), murder (2 Sam. 13:28), rebellion (2 Sam. 15:13), and greed (1 Kings 1:5-6) all resulted from the jealous rivalries among the half brothers. Solomon, one of David's sons and his successor to the throne, also took many wives who eventually turned him away from God (1 Kings 11:3-4).

2 SAMUEL 3:29
Why did David say such harsh words about Joab?

David was upset over Abner's death for several reasons. (1) He was grieved over the loss of a skilled military officer. (2) He wanted to place the guilt of Abner's murder on Joab, not himself. (3) He was on the verge of becoming king over the entire nation, and utilizing Abner was the key to winning over the northern tribes. Abner's death could have revived the civil war. (4) Joab violated David's agreement to protect Abner. Joab's murderous act ruined David's plans, and David was especially angry that his own commander had committed the crime.

JOHN 13:5
Why did Jesus wash his disciples' feet?

He washed the disciples' feet to (1) show his disciples that he loved them; (2) demonstrate the emptying of himself; (3) teach them about spiritual washing which is much more important than the washing of feet; and (4) provide the disciples with his example so that they might also demonstrate their humility.

EZRA 6:14-15
Who wrote Psalm 119?

This is both the longest psalm and the longest chapter in the Bible. It may have been written by Ezra after the temple was rebuilt as a repetitive meditation on the beauty of God's Word and how it helps us stay pure and grow in faith. Psalm 119 has 22 carefully constructed sections, each corresponding to a different letter in the Hebrew alphabet and each verse beginning with the letter of its section. Almost every verse mentions God's Word. Such repetition was common in the Hebrew culture. People did not have personal copies of the Scriptures to read as we do, so God's people memorized his Word and passed it along orally. The structure of this psalm allowed for easy memorization.

MAY 24

Q ## 2 SAMUEL 5:3-5
Wasn't David already the king? Why was he crowned again?

This was the third time David was anointed king. First he was privately anointed by Samuel (1 Samuel 16:13). Then he was made king over the tribe of Judah (2 Sam. 2:4). Finally he was crowned king over all Israel. As an outlaw, life had looked bleak, but God's promise to make him king over all Israel was now being fulfilled. Although the kingdom would be divided again in less than 75 years, David's dynasty would reign over Judah, the southern kingdom, for over four hundred years.

Q ## 2 SAMUEL 6:16-23
Why did Michal despise David when he danced before the Lord?

Michal was David's first wife, but here she is called daughter of Saul, possibly to show how similar her attitude was to her father's. Her contempt for David probably did not start with David's grand entrance into the city. Perhaps she thought it was undignified to be so concerned with public worship at a time when it was so unimportant in the kingdom. Or maybe she thought it was not fitting for a king to display such emotion. She may have resented David's taking her from Paltiel. Whatever the reason, this contempt she felt toward her husband escalated, and Michal ended up childless for life. Michal was so concerned about David's undignified actions that she did not rejoice in the Ark's return to the city. She emphasized outward appearances while David emphasized the inward condition of his heart before God. He was willing to look foolish in the eyes of some in order to worship God fully and honestly.

Q ## JOHN 13:34
Did God first give the commandment to love one another in John 13:34?

To love others was not a new commandment (see Lev. 19:18), but to love others as much as Christ loved others was revolutionary. Now we are to love others based on Jesus' sacrificial love for us.

Q ## JOHN 14:9
What did Jesus mean when he said "Anyone who has seen me has seen the Father"?

Jesus is the visible, tangible image of the invisible God. He is the complete revelation of what God is like. Jesus explained to Philip, who wanted to see the Father, that to know Jesus is to know God. The search for God, for truth and reality, ends in Christ. (See also Col. 1:15; Heb. 1:1-4.)

MAY 25

2 Samuel 7:1–8:18; John 14:15-31; Psalms 119:33-48; Proverbs 15:33

 **2 SAMUEL 7:5**
Why didn't God want David to build the temple?
God told David that his job was to unify and lead Israel and to destroy its enemies. This huge task would require David to shed a great deal of blood. In 1 Chronicles 28:3, we learn that God did not want his temple built by a warrior. Therefore, David made the plans and collected the materials so that his son Solomon could begin work on the temple as soon as he became king (1 Kings 5–7). David accepted his part in God's plan and did not try to go beyond it. This does not mean that God rejected David. In fact, God was planning to do something even greater in David's life than allowing him the prestige of building the temple. Although God turned down David's request, he promised to continue the house (or dynasty) of David forever. David's earthly dynasty ended four centuries later, but Jesus Christ, a direct descendant of David, was the ultimate fulfillment of this promise (Acts 2:22-36). Christ will reign for eternity—now in his spiritual kingdom and in heaven, and later, on earth, in the new Jerusalem (Luke 1:30-33; Rev. 21).

2 SAMUEL 7:10-11
Why did David slaughter his enemies in 2 Samuel 8:1-5?
Part of God's covenant with David included the promise that the Israelites' enemies would be defeated and would no longer oppress them. God fulfilled this promise by helping David defeat the opposing nations. Several enemies are listed in this chapter: (1) *The Moabites,* descendants of Lot who lived east of the Dead Sea. They posed a constant military and religious threat to Israel (Num. 25:1-3; Judg. 3:12-30; 1 Sam. 14:47). David seemed to have a good relationship with the Moabites at one time. (2) *King Hadadezer of Zobah.* His defeat at David's hands fulfilled God's promise to Abraham that Israel would control the land as far north as the Euphrates River (Gen. 15:18). (3) *The Edomites,* descendants of Esau (Gen. 36:1) who were also archenemies of Israel (see 2 Kings 8:20; Jer. 49:7-22; Ezek. 25:12-14).

MAY 26

2 Samuel 9:1–11:27; John 15:1-27; Psalms 119:49-64; Proverbs 16:1-3

Q 2 SAMUEL 11:1ff.
What is the lesson of David's experience with Bathsheba?

As David looked from the roof of the palace, he saw a beautiful woman bathing, and he was filled with lust. David should have left the roof and fled the temptation. Instead, he entertained the temptation by inquiring about Bathsheba. The results were devastating. In this episode David allowed himself to fall deeper and deeper into sin. (1) David abandoned his purpose by staying home from war (2 Sam. 11:1). (2) He focused on his own desires (2 Sam. 11:3). (3) When temptation came he looked into it instead of turning away from it (2 Sam. 11:4). (4) He sinned deliberately (2 Sam. 11:4). (5) He tried to cover up his sin by deceiving others (2 Sam. 11:6-15). (6) He committed murder to continue the cover-up (2 Sam. 11:15, 17). Eventually David's sin was exposed (2 Sam. 12:9) and punished (2 Sam. 12:10-14). (7) The consequences of David's sin were far-reaching, affecting many others (2 Sam. 11:17; 12:11, 14-15). David could have chosen to stop and turn from evil at any stage along the way. But once sin gets started, it is difficult to stop (James 1:14-15).

Q JOHN 15
Why did Jesus use the grapevine for his allegory in John 15?

The grapevine is a prolific plant; a single vine bears many grapes. In the Old Testament, grapes symbolized Israel's fruitfulness in doing God's work on the earth (Ps. 80:8; Isa. 5:1-7; Ezek. 19:10-14). In the Passover meal, the fruit of the vine symbolized God's goodness to his people. The vine was the emblem of peace and prosperity. It also symbolized the people of God, his *vine* planted in the promised land (Ps. 80:8ff.; Isa. 5:1ff.). Five of Jesus' parables use vine growing images, and here he described himself as the true vine with whom all true believers have an organic relationship.

Q JOHN 15:9-10
Why does Jesus speak of love when talking about the vine?

Love is the relationship of the branches and the vine. In John 15 Jesus speaks of love's four relationships: (1) the Father loves the Son (v. 9); (2) the Father's love is the pattern of Christ's love for his believers (v.); (3) love is the abode of the believers who keep Christ's commandments (vv. 9-10); (4) Christ's commandment is that the believers love one another (v. 17).

MAY 27

2 Samuel 12:1-31; John 16:1-33; Psalms 119:65-80; Proverbs 16:4-5

2 SAMUEL 12:10-14
What were the results of Nathan's prophecy in 2 Samuel 12:10-14?

The predictions in these verses came true. Because David murdered Uriah and stole his wife, (1) murder was a constant threat in his family (2 Sam. 13:26-30; 18:14-15; 1 Kings 2:23-25); (2) his household rebelled against him (2 Sam. 15:13); (3) his wives were given to another in public view (2 Sam. 16:20-23); (4) his first child by Bathsheba died (2 Sam. 12:18). If David had known the painful consequences of his sin, he might not have pursued the pleasures of the moment.

2 SAMUEL 12:14
Why did the child of David and Bathsheba have to die?

This was not a judgment on the child for being conceived out of wedlock, but a judgment on David for his sin. David and Bathsheba deserved to die, but God spared their lives and took the child instead. God still had work for David to do in building the kingdom. Perhaps the child's death was a greater punishment for David than his own death would have been. It is also possible that had the child lived, God's name would have been dishonored among Israel's pagan neighbors. What would they have thought of a God who rewards murder and adultery by giving a king a new heir? A baby's death is tragic, but despising God brings death to entire nations. While God readily forgave David's sin, he did not negate all its consequences.

2 SAMUEL 12:15
Who was Nathan?

Nathan the prophet is first mentioned in 2 Samuel 7:2. God made certain that a prophet was living during the reign of each of the kings of Israel. The prophet's main tasks were to urge the people to follow God and to communicate God's laws and plans to the king. Most of the kings rejected the prophets God sent. Nathan was a prophet of great wisdom, bravery, obedience, and loyalty. He was instrumental at three critical times in David's life. (1) He told David that his son would build the Temple and that David's dynasty would last forever (2 Sam. 7:1-17). (2) He confronted David with his sin of adultery (2 Sam. 12:1-14). (3) He helped David place Solomon on the throne (1 Kings 1:11-53).

MAY 28

2 Samuel 13:1-39; John 17:1-26; Psalms 119:81-96; Proverbs 16:6-7

Q 2 SAMUEL 13:16
Why was sending Tamar away a greater crime than rape and incest?

By throwing her out, Amnon made it look as if Tamar had made a shameful proposition to him, and there were no witnesses on her behalf because he had gotten rid of the servants. His crime destroyed her chances of marriage—because she was no longer a virgin, she could not be given in marriage.

Q 2 SAMUEL 13:21-24
Why didn't David punish Amnon for raping Tamar?

David probably hesitated because (1) he didn't want to cross Amnon, who was his firstborn son (1 Chron. 3:1) and therefore next in line to be king, and (2) David was guilty of a similar sin himself in his adultery with Bathsheba. While David was unsurpassed as a king and military leader, he lacked skill and sensitivity as a husband and father.

Q JOHN 17
What is the purpose of John chapter 17?

This is Jesus' prayer for his disciples who were his family. The ones he had preached to he now prays for. When Jacob was dying he prayed for and blessed his sons, the twelve patriarchs (Gen. 49:1ff.). When Moses was about to die, he prayed for the twelve tribes (Deut. 33:1ff.). Now Jesus prays for the twelve apostles. This prayer was a preface to his redeeming death in which he speaks of the favors and blessing he purchased through his death for his people. It illustrates his intercession within the veil for his people then, now, and through the ages until he comes again.

Q JOHN 17:21
What is the meaning of John 17:21?

This is the heart of Christ's prayer in this chapter. Christ prays that his people would be united with each other in life and experience because they are united with him. This includes fellowship with God through Jesus Christ by the Spirit (1 John 1:3); fellowship with those who are already in glory and fellowship with all believers who are still on earth (Gal. 2:9-10; 1 John 1:7). All believers enjoy organic unity with each other as members of the mystical body of Christ known only to God. The outward expression of this inner unity is shown when the believers gather for the public worship of God, celebrate the Lord's Supper, and practice water baptism.

MAY 29

2 Samuel 14:1–15:22; John 18:1-24; Psalms 119:97-112; Proverbs 16:8-9

2 SAMUEL 15:2
Why did Absalom go to the city gate early every morning?

The city gate was like city hall and a shopping center combined. Because Jerusalem was the nation's capital, both local and national leaders met there daily to transact business and conduct government affairs. The city gate was the perfect spot for this because government and business transactions needed witnesses to be legitimate, and anyone entering or leaving the city had to enter through the gate. Merchants set up their tent-shops near the gate for the same reason. Absalom, therefore, went to the city gate to win the hearts of Israel's leaders as well as those of the common people. Absalom's political strategy was to steal the hearts of the people with his good looks, grand entrances, apparent concern for justice, and friendly embraces. Many were fooled and switched their allegiance.

2 SAMUEL 15:14
Why couldn't David simply crush Absalom's rebellion?

There were several reasons he chose to flee: (1) The rebellion was widespread (2 Sam. 15:10-13) and would not have been easily suppressed; (2) David did not want the city of Jerusalem to be destroyed; (3) David still cared for his son and did not want to hurt him. We know that David expected to return to Jerusalem soon, because he left ten of his wives to take care of the palace (2 Sam. 15:16).

JOHN 18:13
Who were Annas and Caiaphas?

Both Annas and Caiaphas had been high priests. Annas was Israel's high priest from A.D. 6 to 15, when he was deposed by Roman rulers. Caiaphas, Annas's son-in-law, was appointed high priest from A.D. 18 to 36/37. According to Jewish law, the office of high priest was held for life. Many Jews therefore still considered Annas the high priest. Annas retained much authority among the Jews but Caiaphas made the final decisions. Caiaphas and Annas cared more about their political ambitions than about their responsibility to lead the people to God. Though religious leaders, they had become evil. They should have been sensitive to God's revelation, known that Jesus was the Messiah about whom the Scriptures spoke, and pointed the people to him. In their evil aspirations they wanted to eliminate all opposition. Instead of honestly evaluating Jesus' claims based on their knowledge of Scripture, they sought to further their own selfish ambitions and were even willing to kill God's Son to do it.

MAY 30

2 SAMUEL 16:21-23
Who was Ahithophel, and why did he tell Absalom to sleep with his father's wives?

Ahithophel was an adviser to Absalom. Most rulers had advisers to help them make decisions about governmental and political matters. They probably arranged the king's marriages, as well, because these were usually politically motivated unions. But God made Ahithophel's advice seem foolish, just as David had prayed (2 Sam. 15:31). This incident fulfilled Nathan's prediction that because of David's sin, another man would sleep with his wives (2 Sam. 12:11-12). To sleep with any of the king's wives or concubines was to make a claim to the throne. Ahithophel suggested that Absalom defile his father's concubines for all Israel to *hear* about it. But wicked Absalom went farther than that; he wanted all Israel to see, as well as hear of his defilement.

JOHN 18:28
Why did Jesus' accusers stay outside of Pilate's palace?

By Jewish law, entering the house of a Gentile would cause a Jewish person to be ceremonially defiled. As a result, he could not take part in worship at the temple or celebrate the feasts until he was restored to a state of "cleanness." Afraid of being defiled, these men stayed outside the house where they had taken Jesus for trial. They kept the ceremonial requirements of their religion while harboring murder and treachery in their hearts.

JOHN 18:31ff.
Did Pilate want to release Jesus?

Pilate made four attempts to deal with Jesus: (1) he tried to put the responsibility on the chief priests (John 18:31); (2) he tried to use a local custom so he could release Jesus (John 18:39); (3) he tried to compromise, having Jesus flogged rather than handing him over to die (John 19:1-3); and (4) he tried a direct appeal to the sympathy of the accusers (John 19:15).

JOHN 19:18
What is "crucifixion"?

This was a Roman form of execution. The condemned man was forced to carry his cross along a main road to the execution site, as a warning to the people. Types of crosses and methods of crucifixion varied. Jesus was nailed to his cross; some people were tied with ropes. Death came by suffocation because the weight of the body made breathing difficult as the victim lost strength. Crucifixion was a hideously slow and painful death.

MAY 31

2 Samuel 17:1-29; John 19:23-42; Psalms 119:129-152; Proverbs 16:12-13

JOHN 19:30
Why did Jesus say, "It is finished"?

Until this time, a complicated system of sacrifices had atoned for sins. Sin separates people from God, and only through the sacrifice of an animal, a substitute, could people be forgiven and become clean before God. But people sin continually, so frequent sacrifices were required. Jesus, however, became the final and ultimate sacrifice for sin. The word *finished* is the same as "paid in full." Jesus came to *finish* God's work of salvation (John 4:34; 17:4), to pay the full penalty for our sins. With his death, the complex sacrificial system ended because Jesus took all sin upon himself. Now we can freely approach God because of what Jesus did for us. Those who believe in Jesus' death and resurrection can live eternally with God and escape the penalty that comes from sin.

JOHN 19:31-35
Why didn't the soldiers break Jesus' legs?

The Roman soldiers would break victims' legs to hasten the death process. When a person hung on a cross, death came by suffocation, but the victim could push against the cross with his legs to hold up his body and keep breathing. With broken legs, he would suffocate almost immediately. These Romans were experienced soldiers. They knew from many previous crucifixions whether a man was dead or alive. There was no question that Jesus was dead when they checked him, so they decided not to break his legs as they had done to the other victims. Piercing his side and seeing the sudden flow of blood and water was further proof of his death. Some people say Jesus didn't really die, that he only passed out—and that's how he came back to life. But we have the witness of an impartial party, the Roman soldiers, that Jesus died on the cross (see Mark 15:44-45).

JOHN 19:38-42
Who were Joseph of Arimathea and Nicodemus?

Joseph of Arimathea and Nicodemus were secret followers of Jesus. They were afraid to make this allegiance known because of their positions in the Jewish community. Joseph was a leader and honored member of the Jewish council. Nicodemus, also a member of the council, had come to Jesus by night (John 3:1) and later tried to defend him before the other religious leaders (John 7:50-52). Joseph and Nicodemus risked their reputations to provide for Jesus' burial.

JUNE 1

2 SAMUEL 18:33
Why was David so upset over the death of his rebel son?

(1) David realized that he, in part, was responsible for Absalom's death. Nathan, the prophet, had said that because David had killed Uriah, his own sons would rebel against him. (2) David was angry at Joab and his officers for killing Absalom against his wishes. (3) David truly loved his son, even though Absalom did nothing to deserve his love. It would have been kinder and more loving to deal with Absalom and his runaway ego when he was younger. But just as God bestows undeserved grace upon us, David was gracious to Absalom. However, the death of Absalom brought David to the depths of despair. The king here displays his humanness and his weaknesses. David showed a preference for a graceless son who, although he was witty and handsome, had been abandoned by God and man. Instead of weeping, he should have been rejoicing that the divine providence of God had worked the will of God. David was more concerned about the death of Absalom than he was about the nation, the army that won the battle, or the deaths of those who perished to save David and his kingship. This threatened Israel more than Absalom had done by his revolution.

JOHN 20:11
Was Mary Magdalene the first person to see Jesus in resurrection?

Yes. The order of Christ's resurrection appearances seems to be as follows: (1) to Mary Magdalene and the other women (Matt. 28:9; Mark 16:9-10; John 20:11-18); (2) to the disciples on the road to Emmaus (Mark 16:12; Luke 24:13-15); (3) to Peter (Luke 24:34; 1 Cor. 15:5); (4) to the ten disciples in the upper room (20:19); (5) to the eleven in the upper room with Thomas present (Mark 16:14; Luke 24:36; John 20:26); (6) to the disciples at the Sea of Tiberias (21:26); (7) to the eleven on a mountain in Galilee (Matt. 28:16-20); (8) to five hundred of the brethren (1 Cor. 15:6); (9) to James (1 Cor. 15:7); (10) to all of the apostles (1 Cor. 15:7); (11) to those present when he ascended into heaven (Mark 16:19; Luke 24:50-51; Acts 1:3-12); (12) to Paul on the road to Damascus (Acts 9:3-6).

JUNE 2

2 SAMUEL 19:11-13
Why was the tribe of Judah hesitant to bring David back as king?

Apparently the elders of Judah had consented to Absalom's rebellion. It is not surprising that leaders who had backed Absalom would hesitate before inviting David back. David's appointment of Amasa was a shrewd political move. First, Amasa had been commander of Absalom's army; by making Amasa his commander, David would secure the allegiance of the rebel army. Second, by replacing Joab as commander in chief, David punished him for his previous crimes (2 Sam. 3:26-29). Third, Amasa had a great deal of influence over the leaders of Judah (2 Sam. 19:14). All of these moves would help to unite the kingdom.

PSALM 120
Psalm 119 is so long, why is Psalm 120 so short?

Psalms 120–134 are called "Pilgrim Psalms" or "Songs of Ascent." These fifteen psalms are the shortest of all the Psalms. Two of them have only three verses. They were sung by those who journeyed (and thus "ascended") to the temple for the annual feasts. Each psalm is a "step" along the journey. Psalm 120 begins the journey in a distant land in hostile surroundings; Psalm 122 pictures the pilgrims arriving in Jerusalem; and the rest of the psalms move toward the temple, mentioning various characteristics of God. They were written by different people but may have been sung together like verses in a hymn with a musical pause at the end of each.

JOHN 21:15, KJV
What did Jesus mean by his question "Lovest thou me more than these"?

There have been differing understandings about this question. Some think it means: "Do you love me more than you love these other disciples?" Others, that it means: "Do you love me more than these other disciples love me?" And still others: "Do you love me more than your boats, nets, and fishes?" Two different Greek words are used for "love." The first two times the word *agapao,* which means devoted love, is used. When Peter refuses to use the same word, Jesus turns to the word *phileo,* which indicates the love of friendship. Peter accepts this word and admits that he loves Jesus this way. Peter was humbler now than earlier in his life and was making no claim to superior love (see John 13:36-37).

JUNE 3

2 Samuel 20:14–22:20; Acts 1:1-26; Psalms 121:1-8; Proverbs 16:18

 2 SAMUEL 20:23
Who was Benaiah?

Benaiah was the captain of David's bodyguard and a famous member of that special group of mighty men called "the Thirty" (2 Sam. 23:24). He remained loyal to David during Absalom's rebellion. Later he helped establish Solomon as king (1 Kings 1:32-40; 2:28-34) and eventually replaced Joab as commander of Israel's army (1 Kings 2:35).

 2 SAMUEL 21:1-14
Why were Saul's sons killed for the murders their father committed?

Although the Bible does not record Saul's act of vengeance against the Gibeonites, it was apparently a serious crime making him guilty of their blood. In many Near Eastern cultures, including Israel's, an entire family was held guilty for the crime of the father because the family was considered an indissoluble unit. Saul broke the vow that the Israelites made to the Gibeonites (Joshua 9:16-20). This was a serious offense against God's law (Num. 30:1-2). Either David was following the custom of treating the family as a unit, or Saul's sons were guilty of helping Saul kill the Gibeonites.

 ACTS 1:5
When were the disciples baptized in the Holy Spirit?

At Pentecost (Acts 2:1-4) the Holy Spirit was made available to all who believed in Jesus. We receive the Holy Spirit (are baptized with him) when we receive Jesus Christ. The baptism of the Holy Spirit must be understood in the light of his total work in a Christian's life. (1) The Spirit marks the beginning of the Christian experience. We cannot belong to Christ without his Spirit (Rom. 8:9); we cannot be united to Christ without his Spirit (1 Cor. 6:17); we cannot be adopted as his children without his Spirit (Rom. 8:14-17; Gal. 4:6-7); we cannot be in the body of Christ except by baptism in the Spirit (1 Cor. 12:13). (2) The Spirit is the power of our new lives. He begins a lifelong process of change as we become more like Christ (Gal. 3:3; Phil. 1:6). When we receive Christ by faith, we begin an immediate personal relationship with God. The Holy Spirit works in us to help us become like Christ. (3) The Spirit unites the Christian community in Christ (Eph. 2:19-22). The Holy Spirit can be experienced by all, and he works through all (1 Cor. 12:11; Eph. 4:4).

JUNE 4

2 Samuel 22:21–23:23; Acts 2:1-47; Psalms 122:1-9; Proverbs 16:19-20

2 SAMUEL 22:22-24
In 2 Samuel 22:22-24 was David saying that he had never sinned?

No, David was well aware of his sins. Psalm 51 shows David's tremendous anguish over his sin against Uriah and Bathsheba. But David understood God's faithfulness and was writing this hymn from God's perspective. He knew that God had made him clean again—"whiter than snow" (Ps. 51:7) and with a "pure heart" (Ps. 51:10).

2 SAMUEL 23:3
Who is the one who "shall come . . . who rules in the fear of God?

In the style of a prophet, David spoke of a just and righteous ruler. This will be fulfilled in Jesus Christ when he returns to rule in perfect justice and peace. For similar prophecies see Isaiah 11:1-10; Jeremiah 23:5-6; 33:15-18; Zechariah 9:9-10. For the fulfillment of some of these prophecies see Matthew 4:14-16; Luke 24:25-27, 44-49; John 5:45-47; 8:28-29.

2 SAMUEL 23:16
Why did David pour out the water his soldiers had risked their lives to get?

David poured out the water as an offering to God because he was so moved by the sacrifice it represented. When Hebrews offered sacrifices, they never consumed the blood. It represented life, and they poured it out before God. David would not drink this water which represented the lives of his soldiers. Instead, he offered it to God.

LUKE 3:16
What were the tongues of fire in Acts 2:3?

This was a fulfillment of John the Baptist's words about the Holy Spirit's baptizing with fire, and of the prophet Joel's words about the outpouring of the Holy Spirit (Joel 2:28-29). Why tongues of fire? Tongues symbolize speech and the communication of the gospel. Fire symbolizes God's purifying presence, which burns away the undesirable elements of our lives and sets our hearts aflame to ignite the lives of others. On Mount Sinai, God confirmed the validity of the Old Testament law with fire from heaven (Exod. 19:16-18). At Pentecost, God confirmed the validity of the Holy Spirit's ministry by sending fire. At Mount Sinai, fire had come down on one place; at Pentecost, fire came down on many believers, symbolizing that God's presence is now available to all who believe in him.

JUNE 5

2 Samuel 23:24–24:25; Acts 3:1-26; Psalms 123:1-4; Proverbs 16:21-23

2 SAMUEL 24:1-3, TLB
What was wrong with taking a census?

A census was commanded in Numbers to prepare an army for conquering the promised land (Num. 1:2; 26:2). A census amounted to a draft or conscription for the army. The land was now at peace, so there was no need to enlist troops. Israel had extended its borders and become a recognized power. David's sin was pride and ambition in counting the people so that he could glory in the size of his nation and army, its power and defenses. By doing this, he put his faith in the size of his army rather than in God's ability to protect them regardless of their number. Even Joab knew a census was wrong, but David did not heed his advice.

2 SAMUEL 24:12-14
Why did God punish David and Israel?

Both David and the Israelites were guilty of sin (2 Sam. 24:1). David's sin was pride, but the Bible does not say why God was angry with the people of Israel. Perhaps it was due to their support of the rebellions of Absalom (2 Sam. 15–18) and Sheba (2 Sam. 20), or perhaps they put their trust in military security and financial prosperity rather than God, as David did. God dealt with the whole nation through David, who exemplified the national sin of pride. God gave David three choices. Each was a form of punishment God had told the people they could expect if they disobeyed his laws (disease—Deut. 28:20-22; famine—28:23-24; war—28:25-26). David wisely chose the form of punishment that came most directly from God. He knew how brutal and harsh men in war could be, and he also knew God's great mercy.

2 SAMUEL 24:18
Why did God choose Araunah's threshing floor for David's altar?

Many believe that this threshing floor where David built the altar is the location where Abraham nearly sacrificed his son Isaac (Gen. 22:1-18). Araunah, a Jebusite (called Ornan in 1 Chron. 21:15ff.) not only sold David his threshing floor, but also his oxen for the burnt offering and their yokes for the fire. He gave up his entire livelihood at this fateful moment in Israel's history. After David's death, Solomon built the temple on this spot (2 Chron. 3:1).

JUNE 6

Q 1 KINGS 1:5
Why did Adonijah make himself king of Israel?

Adonijah was David's fourth son and the logical choice to succeed him as king. David's first son, Amnon, had been killed by Absalom for having raped his sister (2 Sam. 13:20-33). His second son, Daniel, is mentioned only in the genealogy of 1 Chronicles 3:1 and had probably died by this time. David's third son, Absalom, died in an earlier rebellion (2 Sam. 18:1-18). Although many people expected Adonijah to be the next king (2 Sam. 2:13-25), David (and God) had other plans (2 Sam. 1:29-30). Adonijah decided to seize the throne without David's knowledge. He knew that Solomon, not he, was David's first choice to be the next king (2 Sam. 1:17). This was why he did not invite Solomon and David's loyal advisers when he declared himself king (2 Sam. 1:9-10). But his deceptive plans to gain the throne were unsuccessful.

Q ACTS 4:5
Who were the rulers, elders, and teachers of the law?

These men made up the Jewish council—the same council that had condemned Jesus to death (Luke 22:66). It had 70 members plus the current high priest, who presided over the group. The Sadducees held a majority in this ruling group. These were the wealthy, intellectual, and powerful men of Jerusalem. Jesus' followers stood before this council just as he had.

Q ACTS 4:32-35, KJV
Since the early church had "all things in common," was it similar to communism?

This passage does not support the notion that communism was practiced in the early church. The early church was able to share possessions and property as a result of the unity brought by the Holy Spirit working in and through the believers' lives. This way of living is different from communism because (1) the sharing was voluntary; (2) it didn't involve *all* private property, but only as much as was needed; (3) it was not a membership requirement in order to be a part of the church. The donations were simply expressions of Christian love and concern. The spiritual unity and generosity of these early believers attracted others to them. This organizational structure is not a biblical command, but it offers vital principles for us to follow. Scripture teaches the inalienable right to private property.

JUNE 7

1 Kings 2:1–3:3; Acts 5:1-42; Psalms 125:1-5; Proverbs 16:25

Q 1 KINGS 3:1
Why did Solomon marry a daughter of the Egyptian Pharaoh?

Marriage between royal families was a common practice in the ancient Near East because it secured peace. Although Solomon's marital alliances built friendships with surrounding nations, they were also the beginning of his downfall. These relationships became inroads for pagan ideas and practices. Solomon's foreign wives brought their gods to Jerusalem and eventually lured him into idolatry (1 Kings 11:1-6).

Q 1 KINGS 3:2-3, KJV
What were the "high places"?

God's laws said that the Israelites could make sacrifices only in specified places (Deut. 12:13-14). This was to prevent the people from instituting their own methods of worship and allowing pagan practices to creep into their worship. But many Israelites, including Solomon, made sacrifices in the surrounding hills. These sacrifices were made at the *high places*. Solomon loved God, but this act was sinful. It took the offerings out of the watchful care of priests and ministers loyal to God and opened the way for false teaching to be tied to these sacrifices. God appeared to Solomon to grant him wisdom, but at night, not during the sacrifice. God honored his prayer but did not condone the sacrifice.

Q ACTS 5:1-10
What was the sin of Ananias and Sapphira?

The sin Ananias and Sapphira committed was not stinginess or holding back part of the money—it was their choice whether or not to sell the land and how much to give. Their sin was lying to God and God's people—saying they gave the whole amount but holding back some for themselves and trying to make themselves appear more generous than they really were. This act was judged harshly because dishonesty, greed, and covetousness are destructive in a church, preventing the Holy Spirit from working effectively.

Q ACTS 5:34
Who was Gamaliel?

Gamaliel was an unexpected ally for the apostles, although he probably did not support their teachings. He was a distinguished member of the council and a teacher. While Gamaliel may have saved the apostles' lives, his real intentions probably were to prevent a division in the council and to avoid arousing the Romans. His advice to the council gave the apostles some breathing room to continue their work. The council decided to wait, hoping that this would all fade away harmlessly. They couldn't have been more wrong. Ironically, Paul, later one of the greatest apostles, was one of Gamaliel's students (Acts 22:3).

JUNE 8

1 Kings 3:4–4:34; Acts 6:1-15; Psalms 126:1-6; Proverbs 16:26-27

Q 1 KINGS 3:12
In what way did God answer Solomon's prayer for wisdom?

Solomon asked for wisdom ("discernment"), not wealth, but God gave him riches and long life as well. God made him wiser than anyone else had ever been. In Proverbs 1:1-9, we read Solomon's definition of wisdom: "to trust and reverence the Lord." No other human being has had the wisdom of Solomon, yet many have remained more faithful to the Lord throughout their lives. Solomon is remembered for his wisdom, but not for his faithfulness to God. Solomon's settlement of the dispute between the two prostitutes in 1 Kings 3:13-18 was a classic example of his wisdom. This wise ruling was verification that God had answered Solomon's prayer and given him a discerning heart. Throughout most of his reign, Solomon applied his wisdom well because he sought God. The fruits of this wisdom were peace, security, and prosperity for the nation. Solomon's era is often looked upon as the ideal of what any nation can become when united in trust and obedience to God. The book of Proverbs records many of the three thousand wise proverbs mentioned in 1 Kings 4:32.

Q ACTS 6:1
What was the church's problem in Acts 6:1?

In the early church there were Hebraic Jews (native Jewish Christians who spoke Aramaic, a Semitic language) and Hellenized Jews, (Greek-speaking Christians, Jews from other lands who were converted at Pentecost). The Greek-speaking Christians complained that their widows were being unfairly treated. This favoritism was probably not intentional, but was more likely caused by the language barrier. To correct the situation, the apostles put seven respected Greek-speaking men in charge of the food distribution program. This solved the problem and allowed the apostles to keep their focus on teaching and preaching the Good News about Jesus.

Q ACTS 6:14
What were the charges against Stephen?

When Stephen was brought before the Sanhedrin (the council of religious leaders), the accusation against him was the same that the religious leaders had used against Jesus (Matt. 26:59-61). The group falsely accused Stephen of wanting to change Moses' customs, because they knew that the Sadducees, who controlled the council, believed *only* in Moses' laws.

JUNE 9

1 Kings 5:1–6:38; Acts 7:1-29; Psalms 127:1-5; Proverbs 16:28-30

1 KINGS 5:6-8
Why didn't Solomon use wood from Israel for building the temple?

Solomon asked Hiram to send cedar and cypress wood for the Temple because he knew these were precious woods considered the best for building; they were close-grained, very hard, and rot-resistant. They were also beautiful and had a fragrant scent. Hiram, who as David's friend had built his house (2 Sam. 5:11), had the logs tied into rafts and floated down the seacoast from Tyre to a port in Israel, from which they were carried overland to Jerusalem.

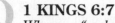
1 KINGS 6:7
Why was "no hammer, chisel or any other iron tool" heard at the site of the building of the Temple?

In honor of God, the temple in Jerusalem was built without the sound of a hammer or any other tool at the building site. This meant that the stone had to be "dressed" (cut and shaped) miles away at the quarry. The people's honor and respect for God extended to every aspect of constructing this house of worship.

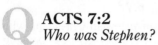
ACTS 7:2
Who was Stephen?

Stephen was named among the managers of food distribution in the early church (Acts 6:1-6). Long before violent persecution broke out against Christians, there was already social ostracism. Jews who accepted Jesus as Messiah were usually cut off from their families. As a result, the believers depended on each other for support. The sharing of homes, food, and resources was both a practical and necessary mark of the early church. Eventually, the number of believers made it necessary to organize the sharing. People were being overlooked. There were complaints. Those chosen to help manage were chosen for their integrity and sensitivity to God. Stephen appears to be the leader of these men. Besides being a good administrator, he was also a powerful speaker. When confronted in the Temple by various antagonistic groups, Stephen's logic in responding was convincing. This is clear from the defense he made before the Court. He presented a summary of the Jews' own history and made powerful applications that stung his listeners. During his defense Stephen must have known he was speaking his own death sentence. Members of the Court could not stand to have their evil motives exposed. They stoned him to death while he prayed for their forgiveness. His death had a lasting impact on young Saul (Paul) of Tarsus, who would move from being a violent persecutor of Christians to being one of the greatest champions of the gospel the church had known.

JUNE 10

1 Kings 7:1-51; Acts 7:30-50; Psalms 128:1-6; Proverbs 16:31-33

1 KINGS 6:38; 7:1
Why did it take Solomon longer to build his house than to build God's temple?

The temple was finished in less than eight years but we should not suppose that Solomon's own dwelling was more ornate than the temple because it took six years longer than the temple to build. Rather, he was less anxious to build his house than the temple. Greater effort and therefore less time was spent on God's house than on his own.

EXODUS 30:17-21
What is the "molten sea" mentioned in 1 Kings 7:23?

This "sea" was an enormous tank. Designed and used for the priests' ceremonial washings, it was placed in the temple court near the altar of burnt offering. There the priests washed themselves before offering sacrifices or entering the temple. It was filled with water by the Gibeonites or Nethinim, who supplied all the water for the house of God and contained "two thousand baths" (KJV). This was approximately twelve thousand gallons.

1 KINGS 7:51
What happened to the tabernacle after the temple was finished, and why did the Israelites change from one to the other?

As a tent, the tabernacle was a portable place of worship designed for the people as they were traveling toward the promised land. The temple was a permanent place to worship God after the Israelites were at peace in their land. To bring the ark of the Lord's covenant to the temple signified God's actual presence there. When the ark was brought into the newly constructed temple, the need for the tent no longer existed. Though nothing is said about what happened to the tabernacle after the temple was built, it must have been destroyed.

ACTS 7:38, KJV
What is the "church in the wilderness"?

Stephen used the Greek word *ekklesia* (translated "church") to describe the congregation or people of God in the desert. This word means "called out ones" and was used by the first-century Christians to describe their own community or "assembly." Stephen's point was that the giving of the law through Moses to the Jews was the sign of the covenant. By obedience, then, would they continue to be God's covenant people. But because they disobeyed (7:39), they broke the covenant and forfeited their right to be the chosen people.

JUNE 11

1 Kings 8:1-66; Acts 7:51–8:13; Psalms 129:1-8; Proverbs 17:1

Q 1 KINGS 8:10-11
What was the cloud that "filled the house of the LORD"?

This was probably the same *pillar of cloud* that led the children of Israel in the wilderness. The cloud signified both the presence and the blessing of God in the temple. The glory of Solomon's temple was not its size, beauty, or cost. Its glory came from the divine presence which came after the ark was carried into the holy place by the priests. Once the ark was in place and the priests were departing from the temple, the glory of God filled the building. It was the cloud of the presence. From that time forward, only the high priest would enter the holy of holies once a year to make atonement for the sins of the people.

Q 1 KINGS 8:41-43
Did the nations ever come to worship at Solomon's temple?

God chose Israel to be a blessing to the whole world (Gen. 12:1-3). This blessing found its fulfillment in Jesus—a descendant of Abraham and David (Gal. 3:8-9) —who became the Messiah for all people, Jews and non-Jews. When the Israelites first entered the promised land, they were ordered to clear out several wicked nations; thus we read in the Old Testament of many wars. But we should not conclude that war was Israel's first duty. After subduing the evil people, Israel was to become a light to the surrounding nations. Sadly, Israel's own sin and spiritual blindness prevented them from reaching out to the rest of the world with God's love. Jesus came to do what the nation of Israel failed to do.

Q ACTS 7:58
Who was the young man who witnessed the martyrdom of Stephen?

This was Saul who is also called Paul (see Acts 13:9), the great missionary who wrote many of the letters in the New Testament. Saul was his Hebrew name; Paul, his Greek name, was used as he began his ministry to the Gentiles. When Luke introduces him, Paul was hating and persecuting Jesus' followers. This is a great contrast to the Paul about whom Luke will write for most of the rest of the book of Acts—a devoted follower of Christ and a gifted gospel preacher. Paul was uniquely qualified to talk to the Jews about Jesus because he had once persecuted those who believed in Jesus, and he understood how the opposition felt.

JUNE 12

1 KINGS 10:5, NRSV
Why does 1 Kings 10:5 say "there was no more spirit" in the Queen of Sheba?

The Queen of Sheba came to see she had heard about Solomon was true. Contests using riddles or proverbs were often used to test wisdom. The queen may have used some of these as she questioned Solomon (1 Kings 10:1, 3). When she realized the extent of his riches and wisdom, *there was no more spirit in her* or "she was overwhelmed" (NIV) and no longer questioned his power or wisdom, becoming an admirer instead. Her experience was repeated by many kings and dignitaries who paid honor to Solomon (1 Kings 4:34).

1 KINGS 10:14-29
How did Solomon acquire such great riches?

When Solomon asked for wisdom, God promised him riches and honor as well (1 Kings 3:13). These verses show just how extensive his wealth became as a result of God's promise. Israel was no longer a second-rate nation, but at the height of its power and wealth. Solomon's riches became legendary. Great men came from many nations to listen to Israel's powerful king. Jesus would later refer to "Solomon in all his splendor" (Matt. 6:29).

ACTS 8:14
Why were Peter and John sent to Samaria?

Peter and John were sent to Samaria to find out whether or not the Samaritans were truly becoming believers. The Jewish Christians were still unsure whether non-Jews and half-Jews could receive the Holy Spirit. It wasn't until Peter's experience with Cornelius (Acts 10) that the apostles became fully convinced that the Holy Spirit was for all people. It was John who had asked Jesus if they should call fire down from heaven to burn up a Samaritan village that refused to welcome them (Luke 9:51-55). Here he and Peter went to the Samaritans to pray with them.

ACTS 8:27
What is an "Ethiopian eunuch"?

Ethiopia was located in Africa south of Egypt. The eunuch was obviously very dedicated to God because he had traveled such a long distance to worship in Jerusalem. The Jews had contact with Ethiopia (known as Cush) in ancient days (Ps. 68:31; Jer. 38:7), so this man may have been a Gentile convert to Judaism. Because he was in charge of the treasury of Ethiopia, this man's conversion brought Christianity into the power structures of another government. This is the beginning of the witness "to the ends of the earth" (Acts 1:8).

JUNE 13

1 KINGS 11:5-8
Who were the gods that Solomon worshiped and built temples for?

Ashtoreth was a goddess that symbolized reproductive power—a mistress of the god Baal. Molech was the national god of the Ammonites, called "detestable" because its worship rites included child sacrifice. Chemosh was the Moabites' national god. The Israelites were warned against worshiping all other gods in general and Molech in particular (Exod. 20:1-6; Lev. 18:21; 20:1-5).

1 KINGS 3:1
If Solomon was so wise, why did he turn from God?

While Solomon applied his wisdom to political affairs, he did not always apply it to his spiritual life. He knew the right way to live, but he did not always have the will to do it. Solomon's many wives turned his heart away from God, which eventually led to his downfall. His wisdom failed him at this point. Solomon didn't turn away from God all at once or in a brief moment. His spiritual coldness started with a minor departure from God's laws. Over the years, that little sin grew until it resulted in Solomon's downfall.

ACTS 9:3
Where was Damascus?

Damascus, a key commercial city, was 175 miles northeast of Jerusalem in the Roman province of Syria. Several trade routes linked Damascus to other cities throughout the Roman world. Saul may have thought that by stamping out Christianity in Damascus, he could prevent its spread to other areas.

ACTS 9:23
Did Saul go directly back to Jerusalem?

In Galatians 1:17-18, Paul left Damascus and traveled to Arabia, the desert region just southeast of Damascus, where he lived for three years. It is unclear whether his three-year stay occurred between Acts 9:22 and 9:23, or between Acts 9:25 and 9:26. Some commentators say that "many days" could mean a long period of time. They suggest that when Paul returned to Damascus, the governor under Aretas ordered his arrest (2 Cor. 11:32) in an effort to keep peace with influential Jews. The other possibility is that Paul's night escape occurred during his first stay in Damascus, just after his conversion, when the Pharisees were upset over his defection from their ranks. He would have fled to Arabia to spend time alone with God and to let the Jewish religious leaders cool down. Regardless of which theory is correct, there was a period of at least three years between Paul's conversion (Acts 9:3-6) and his trip to Jerusalem (Acts 9:26).

JUNE 14

1 Kings 12:20–13:34; Acts 9:26-43; Psalms 132:1-18; Proverbs 17:6

1 KINGS 12:20
Were there two nations when Jeroboam returned from Egypt?

Yes, this marks the beginning of the division of the kingdom that lasted for centuries. The prophet Ahijah predicted the division of the kingdom of Israel (1 Kings 11:29-39). Ten of Israel's 12 tribes followed Jeroboam and called their new nation Israel (the northern kingdom). The other two tribes remained loyal to Rehoboam and called their nation Judah (the southern kingdom). These were Judah, the largest tribe, and Benjamin, the smallest. They were often mentioned as one tribe because they shared the same border. The kingdom did not split overnight. It was already dividing as early as the days of the judges because of tribal jealousies, especially between Ephraim, the most influential tribe of the north, and Judah, the chief tribe of the south.

ACTS 9:36
Where is Joppa?

The important harbor city of Joppa sat 125 feet above sea level overlooking the Mediterranean Sea. Joppa was the town into which the cedars of Lebanon had been floated to be shipped to Jerusalem and used in the temple construction (2 Chron. 2:16; Ezra 3:7). The prophet Jonah left the port of Joppa on his ill-fated trip (Jonah 1:3). In Joppa, Peter stayed at the home of Simon, a tanner (Acts 9:43). Tanners made animal hides into leather. It is significant that Peter was at Simon's house, because tanning involved contact with dead animals, and Jewish law considered it an "unclean" job. Peter was already beginning to break down his prejudice against people who were not of his kind.

PSALM 132:12
When did God make the promise mentioned in Psalm 132:12?

The promise that David's sons would sit on Israel's throne forever is found in 2 Samuel 7:8-29. This promise had two parts: (1) David's descendants would perpetually rule over Israel as long as they followed God, and (2) David's royal line would never end. The first part was conditional; as long as the kings obeyed God ("keep my covenant and the statutes I teach them"), their dynasty continued. The second part of the promise was unconditional. It was fulfilled in Jesus Christ, a descendant of David, who reigns forever.

JUNE 15

1 Kings 14:1–15:24; Acts 10:1–23a; Psalms 133:1-3; Proverbs 17:7-8

Q 1 KINGS 14:19
What is the "book of the annals of the kings of Israel"?

Three books are mentioned in 1 and 2 Kings—the book of the annals of the kings of Israel (1 Kings 14:19), the book of the annals of the kings of Judah (1 Kings 14:29), and the book of the annals of Solomon (1 Kings 11:41). These historical records of Israel and Judah were the main sources of material God directed the author to use to write 1 and 2 Kings. No copies of these books have been found.

Q 1 KINGS 14:25
If Solomon's kingdom was so rich and powerful how could Egypt attack it?

When Rehoboam came to power, he inherited a mighty kingdom. Everything he could ever want was given to him. But he did not recognize why he had so much or how it had been obtained. To teach Rehoboam a lesson, God allowed Shishak of Egypt to invade Judah and Israel. Egypt was no longer the world power it had once been, and Shishak, possibly resenting Solomon's enormous success, was determined to change that. Shishak's army was not strong enough to destroy Judah and Israel, but he weakened them so much that they were never the same again. Just five years after Solomon died, the temple and palace were ransacked. When the people became spiritually corrupt and immoral (1 Kings 14:24), it was just a short time until they lost everything. Wealth, idol worship, and immorality had become more important to them than God.

Q ACTS 10:12
What was the meaning of the vision Peter saw in Acts 10:12?

According to Jewish law, certain foods were forbidden to be eaten (see Lev. 11). The food laws made it difficult for Jews to eat with Gentiles without risking defilement. In fact, the Gentiles themselves were often seen as "unclean." Peter's vision meant that he should not look upon the Gentiles as inferior people whom God would not redeem. Before having the vision, Peter would have thought that a Gentile Roman officer could not accept Christ. Afterward, he understood that it was his responsibility to go with the messengers into a Gentile home and tell Cornelius the Good News of salvation in Jesus Christ.

Q PSALM 133:2
What is the "precious ointment" mentioned in Psalm 133:2?

Expensive oil was used by Moses to anoint Aaron as the first high priest of Israel (Exod. 29:7) and to dedicate all the priests to God's service. Brotherly unity, like the anointing oil, shows that we are dedicated to serving God wholeheartedly.

JUNE 16

1 Kings 15:25–17:24; Acts 10:23b–48; Psalms 134:1-3; Proverbs 17:9-11

Q ### 1 KINGS 17:1
Who was Elijah?

Elijah was the first in a long line of important prophets God sent to Israel and Judah. Israel, the northern kingdom, had no faithful kings throughout its history. Each king was wicked, actually leading the people in worshiping pagan gods. There were few priests left from the tribe of Levi (most had gone to Judah), and the priests appointed by Israel's kings were corrupt and ineffective. With no king or priests to bring God's Word to the people, God called prophets to try to rescue Israel from its moral and spiritual decline. For the next three hundred years these men and women would play vital roles in both nations, encouraging the people and leaders to turn back to God.

Q ### 1 KINGS 17:1
Why did Elijah say there would be no more rain?

Those who worshiped Baal believed he was the god who brought the rains and bountiful harvests. So when Elijah walked into the presence of this Baal-worshiping king and told him there would be no rain for several years, Ahab was shocked. Ahab had built a strong military defense, but it would be no help against drought. He had many priests of Baal, but they could not bring rain. Elijah bravely confronted the man who led his people into evil, and he told of a power far greater than any pagan god—the Lord God of Israel. When rebellion and heresy were at an all-time high in Israel, God responded not only with words but with action.

Q ### ACTS 10:34
What did Peter mean when he said, "God does not show favoritism"?

Perhaps the greatest barrier to the spread of the gospel in the first century was the Jewish-Gentile conflict. Most of the early believers were Jewish, and to them it was scandalous even to think of associating with Gentiles. But God told Peter to take the gospel to a Roman, and Peter obeyed despite his background and personal feelings. (Later Peter struggled with this again—see Gal. 2:11-14.) God was making it clear that the Good News of Christ is for everyone!

JUNE 17

1 Kings 18:1-46; Acts 11:1-30; Psalms 135:1-21; Proverbs 17:12-13

Q ACTS 11:1
Why was it so significant that Gentiles were being converted?

A Gentile was anyone who was not a Jew; the Jewish believers are sometimes referred to as "the circumcised believers" (11:2). Most Jewish believers thought that God offered salvation only to the Jews because God had given his law to them (Exod. 19-20). A group in Jerusalem believed that Gentiles could be saved, but only if they followed all the Jewish laws and traditions—in essence, if they became Jews. Both were mistaken. God chose the Jews and taught them his laws so they could bring the message of salvation to *all* people. This is what had happened in Cornelius's house (Acts 10) fulfilling Old Testament prophecy: see Genesis 12:3; Psalm 22:27; Isaiah 42:4; 49:6; 56:3-7; 60:1-3; Jeremiah 16:19-21; Zechariah 2:11; Malachi 1:11; Romans 15:9-12.

Q ACTS 11:19-22
Why is Antioch so prominent in the record of Acts?

It was in Antioch that Christianity was launched on its worldwide mission and where the believers aggressively preached to the Gentiles (non-Jews who did not worship God). Philip had preached in Samaria, but the Samaritans were part Jewish (Acts 8:5); Peter preached to Cornelius, but he already worshiped God (Acts 10:2). Believers who were scattered after the outbreak of persecution in Jerusalem spread the gospel to other Jews in the lands they fled to (Acts 11:19). At this time, the believers began actively sharing the Good News with Gentiles. With the exception of Jerusalem, Antioch of Syria played a more important role in the early church than any other city. After Rome and Alexandria, Antioch was the largest city in the Roman world. In Antioch, the first Gentile church was founded, and there the believers were first called Christians (Acts 11:26). Paul used the city as his home base during his missionary journeys. Antioch was the center of worship for several pagan cults that promoted much sexual immorality and other forms of evil common to pagan religions. It was also a vital commercial center—the gateway to the eastern world. Antioch was a key city both to Rome and to the early church. The young church at Antioch was a curious mixture of Jews (who spoke Greek or Aramaic) and Gentiles. It is significant that this is the first place where the believers were called Christians (or "Christ-ones," Acts 11:26), because all they had in common was Christ—not race, culture, or even language.

JUNE 18

1 Kings 19:1-21; Acts 12:1-23; Psalms 136:1-26; Proverbs 17:14-15

 2 KINGS 9–10
Why did Elijah anoint the three particular people in 1 Kings 19:15-16?

God asked Elijah to anoint three different people. The first was Hazael, as king of Aram. Elijah was told to anoint an enemy king because God was going to use Aram as his instrument to punish Israel for its sin. Aram brought Israel's *external* punishment. Israel's *internal* punishment came from Jehu, the next man Elijah was to anoint. As king of Israel, Jehu would destroy those who worshiped the false god Baal. The third person Elijah was told to anoint was Elisha, the prophet who would succeed him. Elisha's job was to work in Israel, the northern kingdom, to help point the people back to God. At this time, the southern kingdom was ruled by Jehoshaphat, a king devoted to God.

1 KINGS 19:19
What is the significance of Elijah's coat?

The coat, or cloak (mantle, KJV) was the most important article of clothing a person could own. It was used as protection against the weather, as bedding, as a place to sit, and as luggage. It could be given as a pledge for a debt or torn into pieces to show grief. Elijah put his cloak on Elisha's shoulders to show that he would become Elijah's successor. Later, when the transfer of authority was complete, Elijah left his cloak for Elisha (2 Kings 2:11-14).

1 KINGS 19:21
Why did Elisha kill his oxen and have a feast in 1 Kings 19:21?

Elisha was plowing when the call of God came to him to take over Elijah's mantle (coat) and become God's prophet (1 Kings 19:19). He was the last in line of twelve farmers plowing with yoked oxen. By killing his yoke of oxen, Elisha made a strong commitment to follow Elijah. Without them, he could not return to his life as a wealthy farmer. This meal was more than a feast among farmers. It was an offering of thanks to the Lord who chose Elisha to be his prophet.

 PSALM 136
Why is the phrase, "His love endures forever," repeated throughout Psalm 136?

This psalm may have been a responsive reading, with the congregation saying these words in unison after each sentence. The repetition made this important lesson sink in. "Lovingkindness" is a translation of a Hebrew word that envelops the aspects of love, kindness, mercy, and faithfulness.

JUNE 19

1 KINGS 20:1
Why did God allow Syria to attack Israel?

With two evil and two good kings up to this point, the southern kingdom, Judah, wavered between godly and ungodly living. But the northern kingdom, Israel, had eight evil kings in succession. To punish both kingdoms for living their own way instead of following God, God allowed other nations to gain strength and become their enemies. Three main enemies threatened Israel and Judah during the next two centuries—Aram, Assyria, and Babylon. Aram, the first to rise to power, presented an immediate threat to Ahab and Israel.

ACTS 12:25
Who was John Mark?

John Mark was Barnabas's cousin (Col. 4:10). His mother, Mary, often opened her home to the apostles (Acts 12:12), so John Mark was exposed to the great men and teachings of the early church. John Mark joined Paul and Barnabas on their first missionary journey, but he left them in the middle of the trip.

ACTS 13:13
Why did John Mark leave the apostles?

No reason is given why John Mark left Paul and Barnabas. Some suggestions are: (1) he was homesick; (2) he resented the change in leadership from Barnabas (his cousin) to Paul; (3) he became ill (an illness that may have affected all of them—see Gal. 4:13); (4) he was unable to withstand the rigors and dangers of the missionary journey; (5) he may have planned to go only that far but had not communicated this to Paul and Barnabas. Paul implicitly accused John Mark of lacking courage and commitment, refusing to take him along on another journey (see Acts 15:37-38). It is clear from Paul's later letters, however, that he grew to respect Mark (Col. 4:10), and that he needed Mark in his work (2 Tim. 4:11).

ACTS 14:14
What happened in a synagogue service?

First the *Shema* was recited (this is Deut. 6:4, which Jews repeated several times daily). Certain prayers were spoken; then there was a reading from the law (the books of Genesis through Deuteronomy), a reading from the Prophets intending to illustrate the law, and a sermon. A different person was chosen to lead the service each week. Since it was customary for the synagogue leader to invite visiting rabbis to speak, Paul and Barnabas usually had an open door when they first went to a synagogue. But as soon as they spoke about Jesus as Messiah, the door would slam shut. They were usually not invited back by the religious leaders, and sometimes they were thrown out of town!

1 Kings 22:1-53; Acts 13:16-41; Psalms 138:1-8; Proverbs 17:17-18

1 KINGS 22:20-22
Does God allow angels to entice people to do evil?

To understand evil one must first understand God. (1) God himself is good (Ps. 11:7). (2) God created a good world that fell because of man's sin (Rom. 5:12). (3) Someday God will recreate the world and it will be good again (Rev. 21:1). (4) God is stronger than evil (Matt. 13:41-43; Rev. 19:11-21). (5) God allows evil, and thus he has control over it. God did not create evil, and he offers help to those who wish to overcome it (Matt. 11:28-30). (6) God uses everything—both good and evil—for his good purposes (Gen. 50:20; Rom. 8:28). The Bible shows us a God who hates all evil and will one day do away with it completely and forever (Rev. 20:10-15).

ACTS 4:37
Who was Barnabas?

Acts 4:37 records that Barnabas was among the first to sell possessions to help the Christians in Jerusalem. When Greeks began to be added to the church in Antioch the church at Jerusalem sent Barnabas to Antioch to help the new converts. Acts 11:23-24 records that "When he arrived and saw the wonderful things God was doing, he was filled with excitement and joy, and encouraged the believers to stay close to the Lord, whatever the cost. Barnabas was a kindly person, full of the Holy Spirit and strong in faith. As a result large numbers of people were added to the Lord" (TLB). Later, when Paul arrived in Jerusalem following his conversion, the local Christians were reluctant to welcome him. Only Barnabas proved willing to risk his life to meet with Paul and then convince the others that their former enemy was now a believer in Jesus. It was Barnabas who encouraged Mark to go with him and Paul to Antioch. Mark joined them on their first missionary journey, but during the trip returned home. Barnabas wanted to invite Mark to join them for another journey, but Paul would not agree. As a result, the partners went separate ways, Barnabas with Mark and Paul with Silas. Barnabas' patient encouragement was confirmed by Mark's eventual effective ministry. Paul and Mark were later reunited in missionary efforts.

JUNE 21

2 KINGS 2:9
Why did Elisha say, "Let me inherit a double portion of your spirit"?

Elisha asked for a double portion of Elijah's spirit (prophetic ministry). Deuteronomy 21:17 helps explain Elisha's request. According to custom, the firstborn son received a double portion of the father's inheritance. He was asking to be Elijah's heir, or successor, the one who would continue Elijah's work as leader of the prophets. But the decision to grant Elisha's request was up to God. Elijah only told him how he would know if his request had been granted.

2 KINGS 2:11-18
Did Elijah die?

Elijah was taken to heaven without dying. He is the second person mentioned in Scripture to do so. Enoch was the first (Gen. 5:21-24). The other prophets may not have seen God take Elijah, or they may have had a difficult time believing what they saw. In either case, they wanted to search for Elijah (2 Kings 2:16-18). Finding no physical trace of him would confirm what had happened and strengthen their faith. The only other person taken to heaven in bodily form was Jesus after his resurrection from the dead (Acts 1:9).

ACTS 13:46
Why was it necessary for the gospel to go first to the Jews?

God planned that through the Jewish nation *all* the world would come to know God (Gen. 12:3). The Messiah was first promised to the Jews, so the gospel of Christ was first preached to them. Paul, a Jew himself, loved his people (Rom. 9:1-5) and wanted to give them every opportunity to join him in proclaiming God's salvation. Unfortunately, many Jews did not recognize Jesus as Messiah, and they did not understand that God was offering salvation to anyone, Jew or Gentile, who comes to him through faith in Christ.

PSALM 139:19-22
Why was David filled with so much hatred?

David's hatred for his enemies came from his zeal for God. David regarded his enemies as God's enemies, so his hatred was a desire for God's righteous justice and not for personal vengeance. David asked God to search his heart and mind and point out any wrong motives that may have been behind his strong words.

JUNE 22

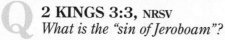

2 KINGS 3:3, NRSV
What is the "sin of Jeroboam"?

The sins of Israel's kings are often compared to "the sins of Jeroboam" (NIV), the first ruler of the northern kingdom of Israel. His great sin was to divide God's people and institute idol worship throughout his kingdom, causing people to turn away from God (1 Kings 12:25-33). By ignoring God and allowing idol worship, Joram clung to Jeroboam's sins.

2 KINGS 3:4
Why was Israel so often attacked by neighboring nations?

Israel and Judah held some of the most fertile land and strategic positions in the ancient Near East. It is no wonder that neighboring nations like Moab envied them and constantly attempted to seize the land. Moab lay just southeast of Israel. The country had been under Israel's control for some time due to Ahab's strong military leadership. When Ahab died, Mesha, the Moabite king, took the opportunity to rebel. While Israel's next king, Ahaziah, did nothing about the revolt, his successor, Joram, decided to take action. He joined forces with Jehoshaphat, king of Judah, and went to fight the Moabites. Together, Israel and Judah brought the Moabites to the brink of surrender. But when they saw the Moabite king sacrifice his own son and successor (2 Kings 3:27), they withdrew even though they had won the battle. Moab fought many other battles with both Israel and Judah. Some of them, in fact, were recorded by Mesha (c. 840 B.C.), who carved his exploits on a plaque called the Moabite Stone (discovered in 1868).

ACTS 14:11-12
Why did the People in Lystra think Paul and Barnabas were Roman gods?

Zeus and Hermes (also known as "Jupiter and Mercury," TLB) were two popular gods in the Roman world. People from Lystra claimed that these gods had once visited their city. According to legend, no one offered them hospitality except an old couple, so Zeus and Hermes killed the rest of the people and rewarded the old couple. When the citizens of Lystra saw the miracles of Paul and Barnabas, they assumed that the gods were revisiting them. Remembering the story of what had happened to the previous citizens, they immediately honored Paul and Barnabas and showered them with gifts.

JUNE 23

2 Kings 4:18–5:27; Acts 15:1-35; Psalms 141:1-10; Proverbs 17:23

Q 2 KINGS 5:9-15
Why didn't Naaman want to wash in the Jordan River?

Naaman, a great hero, was used to getting respect, and he was outraged when Elisha treated him like an ordinary person. A proud man, he expected royal treatment. To wash in a great river would be one thing, but the Jordan was small and dirty. To wash in the Jordan, Naaman thought, was beneath a man of his position. But Naaman had to humble himself and obey Elisha's commands in order to be healed.

Q ACTS 15:1ff.
What was the purpose of the council at Jerusalem?

The delegates to the council at Jerusalem came from the churches in Jerusalem and Antioch. The conversion of Gentiles was raising an urgent question for the early church—do the Gentiles have to adhere to the laws of Moses and other Jewish traditions to be saved? One group of Jewish Christians insisted that following the law, including submitting to the rite of circumcision, was necessary for salvation. The Gentiles, however, did not think they needed to become Jewish in order to become Christians. So Paul and Barnabas discussed this problem with the leaders of the church. The council upheld the convictions expressed by Paul and Barnabas that following the Jewish laws, including being circumcised, was not essential for salvation. The question of whether the Gentile believers should obey the law of Moses to be saved was an important one. The controversy intensified largely due to the success of the new Gentile churches. The conservatives in the Jerusalem church were led by converted Pharisees (Acts 15:5) who preferred a legalistic religion to one based on faith alone. If the conservatives had won, the Gentiles would have been required to be circumcised and converted to Judaism. This would have seriously confined Christianity to simply being another sect within Judaism. James' judgment in Act 15:20-21 was that Gentile believers did not have to be circumcised, but they should stay away from food polluted by idols, from sexual immorality (a common part of idol worship), and from eating meat of strangled animals and from consuming blood (reflecting the biblical teaching that the life is in the blood—Lev. 17:14). If Gentile Christians would abstain from these practices, they would please God and get along better with their Jewish brothers and sisters in Christ. This compromise helped the church grow unhindered by the cultural differences of Jews and Gentiles.

JUNE 24

2 Kings 6:1–7:20; Acts 15:36–16:15; Psalms 142:1-7; Proverbs 17:24-25

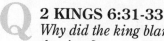

2 KINGS 6:31-33
Why did the king blame Elisha for the famine and troubles of the siege?

Here are some possible reasons: (1) Some commentators say that Elisha must have told the king to trust God for deliverance. The king did this and even wore sackcloth (2 Kings 6:30), but at this point the situation seemed hopeless. Apparently the king thought Elisha had given him bad advice and not even God could help them. (2) For years there was conflict between the kings of Israel and the prophets of God. The prophets often predicted doom because of the kings' evil, so the kings saw them as troublemakers. Thus Israel's king was striking out in frustration at Elisha. (3) The king may have remembered when Elijah helped bring an end to a famine (1 Kings 18:41-46). Knowing Elisha was a man of God, perhaps the king thought he could do any miracle he wanted and was angry that he had not come to Israel's rescue.

ACTS 16:1-3
Who was Timothy and why did he have to be circumcised?

Timothy is the first second-generation Christian mentioned in the New Testament. His mother, Eunice, and grandmother, Lois (2 Tim. 1:5), had become believers and had faithfully influenced him for the Lord. Although Timothy's father apparently was not a Christian, the faithfulness of his mother and grandmother prevailed. Timothy and his mother, Eunice, were from Lystra. Eunice had probably heard Paul's preaching when he was there during his first missionary journey (Acts 14:6-18). Timothy was the son of a Jewish mother and Greek father—to the Jews, a half-breed like a Samaritan. So Paul asked Timothy to be circumcised to remove some of the stigma he may have had with Jewish believers. Timothy was not required to be circumcised (the Jerusalem council had decided that—chapter 15), but he voluntarily did this to overcome any barriers to his witness for Christ.

ACTS 16:12
Where was Philippi?

This was the key city in the region of Macedonia (northern Greece and Albania today). Paul founded a church during this visit (A.D. 50-51). Later, Paul wrote a letter to the church, the book of Philippians, probably from a prison in Rome (A.D. 61). The letter was personal and tender, showing Paul's deep love for and friendship with the believers there.

JUNE 25

2 Kings 8:1–9:13; Acts 16:16-40; Psalms 143:1-12; Proverbs 17:26

Q 2 KINGS 9:1-10
Why did the young prophet run for his life in 2 Kings 9:1-10?

Elijah had prophesied that many people would be killed when Jehu became king (1 Kings 19:16-17). Thus Elisha advised the young prophet to leave the area as soon as he delivered his message. Jehu's actions seem harsh, as he hunted down relatives and friends of Ahab (2 Chron. 22:8-9), but unchecked Baal worship was destroying the nation. If Israel was to survive, the followers of Baal had to be eliminated. Jehu fulfilled the need of the hour—justice.

Q ACTS 16:16-19
Why did a demon announce the truth about Paul, and why did this annoy Paul?

This girl's fortune-telling ability came from evil spirits. Fortune-telling was a common practice in Greek and Roman culture. This young slave girl had an evil spirit, and she made her master rich by interpreting signs and telling people their fortunes. The master was exploiting her unfortunate condition for personal gain. What the slave girl said was true, although the source of her knowledge was a demon. If Paul accepted the demon's words, he would appear to be linking the gospel with demon-related activities. This would damage his message about Christ.

Q ACTS 16:24
What were the "stocks" that held Paul and Silas in the jail?

Paul and Silas were stripped, beaten, and placed in stocks in the inner cell. Stocks were made of two boards joined with iron clamps, leaving holes just big enough for the ankles. The prisoner's legs were placed across the lower board, and then the upper board was closed over them. Sometimes both wrists and ankles were placed in stocks.

Q ACTS 16:37-38
Why were the police officers afraid when they heard that Paul and Silas were Roman citizens?

Roman citizenship carried with it certain privileges. These Philippian authorities were alarmed because it was illegal to whip a Roman citizen. In addition, every citizen had the right to a fair trial—which Paul and Silas had not been given. Paul refused to take his freedom and run. He wanted to teach the rulers in Philippi a lesson and to protect the other believers from the treatment he and Silas had received. The word would spread that Paul and Silas had been found innocent and freed by the leaders, showing that believers should not be persecuted—especially if they were Roman citizens.

JUNE 26

2 Kings 9:14–10:31; Acts 17:1-34; Psalms 144:1-15; Proverbs 17:27-28

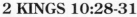 2 KINGS 10:28-31
Why did Jehu destroy the idols of Baal but not the golden calves in Bethel and Dan?

Jehu's motives may have been more political than spiritual. (1) If Jehu had destroyed the golden calves, his people would have traveled to the temple in Jerusalem, in the rival southern kingdom, and worshiped there (which is why Jeroboam set them up in the first place; see 1 Kings 12:25-33). (2) Baal worship was associated with the dynasty of Ahab, so it was politically advantageous to destroy Baal. The golden calves, on the other hand, had a longer history in the northern kingdom and were valued by all political factions. (3) Baal worship was anti-God, but the golden calves were thought by many to be visible representations of God himself, even though God's law stated clearly that such worship was idolatrous (Exod. 20:3-6).

ACTS 17:7
Did Paul teach that Jesus came to replace Caesar?

No, but the Jewish leaders had no other charge that would be heard by the city government. The Romans did not care about theological disagreements between the Jews and these preachers. Treason, however, was a serious offense in the Roman empire. Although Paul and Silas were not advocating rebellion against Roman law, their loyalty to another king sounded suspicious.

ACTS 17:18
Who were the Epicureans and Stoics?

The Epicureans and Stoics were the dominant philosophers in Greek culture. The Epicureans believed that seeking happiness or pleasure was the primary goal of life. By contrast, the Stoics placed thinking above feeling and tried to live in harmony with nature and reason, suppressing their desire for pleasure. Paul's teaching cut across both teachings and appeared to them to be novel.

ACTS 17:19, KJV
What was the "Areopagus"?

This was "the hill of Ares"—the Greek god of war corresponding to the Roman god, Mars; it was a little hill northwest of the Acropolis in Athens on which the Council of the Areopagus originally met and from which it took its name. In New Testament times it met in the Royal Porch in the Athens market place. It is probably here that Paul spoke. This was an ancient institution and despite considerable reduction in its powers it still retained great prestige and had special jurisdiction in religious matters. Paul's speech to the Council concluded with the resurrection of Jesus; on hearing that, the Council dismissed him as unworthy of consideration.

JUNE 27

2 KINGS 12:4-5
Why did the temple need repair?

The temple needed repair because it had been damaged and neglected by previous evil leaders, especially Athaliah (2 Chron. 24:7). The temple was to be a holy place, set apart for worship of God. Thanks to Joash's fund-raising program, it could be restored. The dirt and filth that had collected inside over the years were cleaned out; joints were remortared; pagan idols and other traces of idol worship were removed; and the gold and bronze were polished. The neglected condition of the temple reveals how far the people had strayed from God.

2 KINGS 12:20
Why did Joash's officers kill him?

The reasons for the officials' plot against Joash are listed in 2 Chronicles 24:17-26. Joash had begun to worship idols, had killed the prophet Zechariah, and had been conquered by the Arameans. When Joash turned away from God, his life began to unravel. The officials didn't kill Joash because he turned from God; they killed him because his kingdom was out of control. In the end he became an evil man and was killed by evil people.

ACTS 18:1
Where was Corinth?

Corinth was the political and commercial center of Greece, surpassing Athens in importance. It had a reputation for great wickedness and immorality. A temple to Aphrodite—goddess of love and war—had been built on the large hill behind the city. In this popular religion, people worshiped the goddess by giving money to the temple and taking part in sexual acts with male and female temple prostitutes. Paul found Corinth a challenge and a great ministry opportunity. Later, he would write a series of letters to the Corinthians dealing in part with the problems of immorality. First and Second Corinthians are two of those letters.

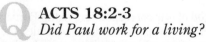
ACTS 18:2-3
Did Paul work for a living?

Yes, each Jewish boy learned a trade and tried to earn his living with it. Paul and Aquila had been trained in tent making, cutting and sewing the woven cloth of goats' hair into tents. Tents were used to house soldiers, and so these tents may have been sold to the Roman army. As a tent maker, Paul was able to go wherever God led him, carrying his livelihood with him. The word "tent maker" in Greek was also used to describe a leather worker.

JUNE 28

2 Kings 13:1–14:29; Acts 18:23–19:12; Psalms 146:1-10; Proverbs 18:2-3

 ACTS 18:25-28
Who was Apollos?

Apollos was from Alexandria in Egypt, the second most important city in the Roman empire, and the home of a great university. He was a scholar, orator, and debater; and after his knowledge about Christ was made more complete, God greatly used these gifts to strengthen and encourage the church. Reason is a powerful tool in the right hands and in the right situation. Apollos used the gift of reason to convince many in Greece of the truth of the gospel. Apollos had heard only what John the Baptist had said about Jesus (see Luke 3:1-18), so his message was not the complete story. John focused on repentance from sin, the first step. But the whole message is to repent from sin and then believe in Christ. Apollos did not know about Jesus' life, crucifixion, and resurrection. Nor did he know about the coming of the Holy Spirit. Priscilla and Aquila explained the way of salvation to him.

 ACTS 19:1-2
What does it mean to "receive the Spirit"?

In the book of Acts, believers received the Holy Spirit in a variety of ways. Usually the Holy Spirit would fill a person as soon as he or she professed faith in Christ. Here that filling happened later because these disciples' knowledge was incomplete. God was confirming to these believers, who did not initially know about the Holy Spirit, that they were a part of the church. The Holy Spirit's filling endorsed them as believers. Pentecost was the formal outpouring of the Holy Spirit on the church. The other outpourings in the book of Acts were God's way of uniting new believers to the church.

ACTS 19:3-4
What was "John's baptism"?

John's baptism was a sign of repentance from sin only, not a sign of new life in Christ. Like Apollos (Acts 18:24-26), these Ephesian believers needed further instruction on the message and ministry of Jesus Christ. They believed in Jesus as the Messiah, but they did not understand the significance of his death and resurrection or the work of the Holy Spirit.

JUNE 29

2 Kings 15:1–16:20; Acts 19:13-41; Psalms 147:1-20; Proverbs 18:4-5

 ## 2 KINGS 16:10-18
Why did King Ahaz install a new altar in the temple?

Ahaz went to Damascus to express gratitude and loyalty to Tiglath-Pileser. Because the Assyrians had captured Damascus, the capital of Aram (732 B.C.), Ahaz was afraid of a southern sweep. But he was relying more on money than on God to keep the powerful king out of his land, and his plan failed. Although Tiglath-Pileser did not conquer Judah, he caused much trouble, and Ahaz regretted asking for his help (2 Chron. 28:20-21). Ahaz copied pagan religious customs, changed the temple services, and used the temple altar for his personal benefit. In so doing, he demonstrated a callous disregard for God's commands. Ahaz replaced the altar of burnt offering with a replica of the pagan altar he had seen in Damascus. (The original bronze altar was not thrown out, but was kept for use in divination. The basins were where the sacrifices were washed. The Sea was a huge reservoir of water for temple use.) This was extremely serious because God had given specific directions on how the altar should look and be used (Exod. 27:1-8). Building this new altar was like installing an idol. But because Judah was Assyria's vassal, Ahaz was eager to please the Assyrian king. Sadly, Ahaz allowed the king of Assyria to replace God as Judah's leader. Ahaz had become a weak king with a weak and compromising high priest. Judah's religious system was in shambles. It was now built on pagan customs, and its chief aim was only to please those in power.

ACTS 19:26ff.
Why did Demetrius stir up the people against Paul?

When Paul preached in Ephesus, Demetrius and his fellow craftsmen did not quarrel with his doctrine. Their anger boiled because his preaching threatened their profits. They made silver statues of the Ephesian goddess Artemis. The craftsmen knew that if people started believing in God and discarding the idols, their livelihood would suffer. Demetrius' strategy for stirring up a riot was to appeal to his fellow workmen's love of money and then to encourage them to hide their greed behind the mask of patriotism and religious loyalty.

JUNE 30

2 Kings 17:1–18:12; Acts 20:1-38; Psalms 148:1-14; Proverbs 18:6-7

2 KINGS 17:23, NRSV
Was the exile recorded in 2 Kings 17:5-6 the dispersal of the Jews that God had threatened?

Yes, "the Lord removed Israel out of his sight, as he had foretold through all his servants the prophets". This was the third and final invasion of Assyria into Israel. (The first two invasions are recorded in 2 Kings 15:19 and 15:29.) The first wave was merely a warning to Israel—to avoid further attack, pay money, and not rebel. The people should have learned their lesson and returned to God. When they didn't, God allowed Assyria to invade again, this time carrying off some captives from the northern border. But the people still did not realize that they had caused their own troubles. Thus Assyria invaded for the third and final time, destroying Israel completely, carrying away most of the people, and resettling the land with foreigners. God was doing what he had said he would do in Deuteronomy 28:36-37. He had given Israel ample warning; the people knew what would come, but they still ignored God. Israel was now no better than the pagan nations it had destroyed in the days of Joshua. The nation had turned sour and rejected its original purpose—to honor God and be a light to the world.

ACTS 20:16
Why was Paul in a hurry to get to Jerusalem?

Paul had missed attending the Passover in Jerusalem, so he was especially interested in arriving on time for Pentecost, which was 50 days after Passover. He was carrying with him gifts for the Jerusalem believers from churches in Asia and Greece (see Rom. 15:25-26; 1 Cor. 16:1ff.; 2 Cor. 8–9). The Jerusalem church was experiencing difficult times. Paul may have been anxious to deliver this gift to the believers at Pentecost because it was a day of celebration and thanksgiving to God for his provision.

ACTS 20:28
What is "the flock" in Acts 20:28?

The flock is the church. The church is given several names in the New Testament, names descriptive of its function, position, and relation to Christ its head: (1) his body (Eph. 1:22-23; Col. 1:24); (2) the flock of God (1 Pet. 5:2); (3) God's farm, God's building (1 Cor. 3:9); (4) God's temple (2 Cor. 6:16); and (5) the bride at the marriage supper of the Lamb (Rev. 21:9).

JULY 1

2 Kings 18:13–19:37; Acts 21:1-16; Psalms 149:1-9; Proverbs 18:8

2 KINGS 18:13
When did Assyria conquer Judah?

This occurred in 701 B.C., four years after Sennacherib had become Assyria's king. Sennacherib was the son of Sargon II, the king who had deported Israel's people into captivity. To keep Assyria from attacking, Judah paid tribute annually. But when Sennacherib became king, Hezekiah stopped paying this money, hoping Assyria would ignore him. When Sennacherib's army retaliated, Hezekiah realized his mistake and paid the tribute money (2 Kings 18:14), but Sennacherib attacked anyway (2 Kings 18:19ff.). Although Sennacherib attacked Judah, he was not as war-hungry as the previous Assyrian kings, preferring to spend most of his time building and beautifying his capital city, Nineveh. With fewer invasions, Judah was able to grow stronger as a nation.

ISAIAH 6:1
Is the "Isaiah" mentioned in 2 Kings 19:2 the same prophet who wrote the book of Isaiah?

Yes. Isaiah the prophet had been working for God since the days of Uzziah—forty years. Although Assyria was a world power, it could not conquer Judah as long as Isaiah counseled the kings. Isaiah prophesied during the reigns of Uzziah (Azariah), Jotham, Ahaz, and Hezekiah. Ahaz ignored Isaiah, but Hezekiah listened to his advice.

ACTS 21:8
Who was Philip?

This Philip was chosen to be a deacon in Acts 6:5. He was also an evangelist along with Stephen who was martyred. After Stephen's death Philip had great success preaching in Samaria. He was responsible for the conversion of the Ethiopian eunuch (Acts 8:26ff.). When Paul stayed at his home, Philip was settled in Caesarea. He had four daughters who prophesied. Philip introduced Christianity to northeast Africa through the Ethiopian eunuch. In this way he was the first to overcome Jewish prejudice and to expand the boundaries of the church interracially via the admission of Gentiles to the faith.

ACTS 21:9
Were women allowed to prophesy in the early church?

Obviously the Holy Spirit gave the gift of prophecy to both men and women. Women who prophesied in Old Testament times included Miriam (Exod. 15:20), Deborah (Judg. 4:4), Huldah (2 Kings 22:14), Noadiah (Neh. 6:14), and Isaiah's wife (Isa. 8:3). In New Testament times women also prophesied (see Luke 2:36-38; Acts 2:17; 1 Cor. 11:5).

JULY 2

2 Kings 20:1–22:2; Acts 21:17-36; Psalms 150:1-6; Proverbs 18:9-10

2 KINGS 20:11
What is the "stairway of Ahaz" and why did the shadow go back on it ten steps?

Some translations call this the "dial of Ahaz." Egyptian sundials were made in the form of miniature staircases so that the shadow moved up and down the steps. Hezekiah's long day has been the subject of much discussion. The account simply states that the sundial of Ahaz went ten degrees backward. If it had been merely an optical illusion rather than an actual lengthening of the day, Hezekiah would hardly have been impressed that it was a real sign from God. He expected something more than an illusion. We must conclude that a miracle was performed here, and that it occurred without disorder or harm to the celestial system.

ACTS 21:21-27
Was Paul going against his own teaching by participating in a Jewish ceremony?

The Jerusalem council (Acts 15) had settled the issue of circumcision of Gentile believers, but evidently there was a rumor that Paul had gone beyond their decision by forbidding Jewish traditions. This was not true, so Paul willingly submitted to Jewish custom to show that he was not working against the council's decision and that he was still Jewish in his life-style. In this case Paul submitted himself to Jewish custom to keep peace in the Jerusalem church. Although Paul was a man of strong convictions, he was willing to compromise on non-essential points, becoming all things to all people so that he might save some (1 Cor. 9:19-23). There are two ways to think of the Jewish laws. Paul rejected one way and accepted the other. (1) Paul rejected the idea that the Old Testament laws bring salvation to those who keep them. Salvation is freely given by God's gracious act. We receive salvation through faith. The laws are of no value for salvation except to show us our sin. (2) Paul accepted the view that the Old Testament laws prepare us for and teach us about the coming of Jesus Christ. Christ fulfilled the law and released us from its burden of guilt. Paul was simply keeping the laws as custom to avoid offending those he wished to reach with the gospel (see Rom. 3:21-31; 7:4-6; 13:9-10).

JULY 3

2 KINGS 22:8
What was the scroll that the high priest found in the temple?

This scroll may have been the entire Pentateuch (Genesis–Deuteronomy) or just the book of Deuteronomy. Because of the long line of evil kings, the record of God's laws had been lost. Josiah, who was about 26 years old at this time, wanted religious reform throughout the nation. When God's Word was found, drastic changes had to be made to bring the kingdom in line with God's commands.

2 KINGS 23:13, KJV
What is the "mount of corruption"?

The Mount of Olives is here called the mount of corruption because it had become a favorite spot to build pagan shrines. Solomon built a pagan shrine and other kings built places of idol worship there. But God-fearing kings such as Hezekiah and Josiah destroyed these pagan worship centers.

ACTS 21:37-40
Paul spoke Greek in Acts 21:37-39 and Hebrew (or Aramaic) in Acts 21:40ff. What language did he normally speak?

There were four main languages used in the world of the New Testament; Paul probably spoke all four. *Hebrew* was the language of the Jewish religion and Jewish Bible. *Aramaic* was the common language of Palestine, the Jewish homeland. *Greek* was the language spoken in Paul's native city of Tarsus and was the common language of the Roman Empire. *Latin* was the language used in the Roman legal system. The inscription on Jesus' cross was written in Hebrew (or Aramaic), Latin, and Greek so everyone passing by could read it (John 19:19-20). By speaking in Greek to the Roman commander, Paul showed that he was a cultured, educated man and not just a common rebel starting riots in the streets. The language caught the commander's attention and gave Paul protection and the opportunity to give his defense. Paul wrote his epistles to the churches in Greek. Paul spoke in Hebrew (or Aramaic) to the Jewish mob gathered in the street. He spoke this language not only to communicate to his listeners, but also to show that he was a devout Jew, had respect for the Jewish laws and customs, and was learned in Hebrew. Jesus Christ spoke in Aramaic and it is certain that Paul did also since this language was necessary for everyday life in Palestine. It is also likely that Paul, a highly educated man, was fluent in Latin.

JULY 4

 ACTS 22:25
Why was it important to the Roman commander that Paul was a Roman citizen?

By law, a Roman citizen could not be punished until he had been proven guilty of a crime. Paul was born a Roman citizen, whereas the commander had purchased his citizenship. Buying citizenship was a common practice and a good source of income for the Roman government. Bought citizenship was considered inferior to citizenship by birth.

 ACTS 23:2-5
Why was Paul slapped, and why did Paul speak back to the high priest as he did?

Josephus, a respected first-century historian, described Ananias the high priest as profane, greedy, and hot-tempered. Paul's outburst came as a result of the illegal command that Ananias had given. Ananias had violated Jewish law by assuming that Paul was guilty without a trial and ordering his punishment (see Deut. 19:15). Paul didn't recognize Ananias as the high priest.

 ACTS 23:6-7
Why did the council divide when Paul spoke of the resurrection of the dead?

The Sadducees and Pharisees were two groups of religious leaders, but with strikingly different beliefs. The Pharisees believed in a bodily resurrection, but the Sadducees did not. The Sadducees adhered only to Genesis through Deuteronomy, which contain no explicit teaching on resurrection. Paul's words moved the debate away from himself and toward their festering controversy about the resurrection. The Jewish council was split.

PSALM 2
Who is the King referred to in Psalm 2?

This is Christ. Several psalms are called *Messianic* because of their prophetic descriptions of Jesus the Messiah's life, death, resurrection, and future reign. David, who may have been the author of this psalm, was a shepherd, soldier, and king. We can see he was also a prophet (Acts 2:29-30) for this psalm describes the rebellion of the nations and the coming of Christ to establish his eternal reign. This psalm is often mentioned in the New Testament (see Acts 4:25-26; 13:33; Heb. 1:5-6; 5:5; Rev. 2:26-27; 12:5; 19:15). Psalm 2:6 pictures Christ as the ascended one who will reign over a reconstituted Zion in the future. The incarnation of Jesus Christ is seen in verse 7: "Thou art my Son" (KJV, see Matt. 3:17).

JULY 5

1 CHRONICLES 1:1ff.
What is the purpose of the genealogies in 1 Chronicles?

This long list of names was compiled after the people of Judah, the southern kingdom, were taken captive to Babylon. As the exiles looked forward to the day when they would return to their homeland, one of their biggest fears was that the records of their heritage would be lost. The Jews placed great importance upon their heritage because each person wanted to be able to prove that he was a descendant of Abraham, the father of the Jewish people. Only then could he enjoy the benefits of the special blessings God promised to Abraham and his descendants. This list reconstructed the family tree for both Judah, the southern kingdom, and Israel, the northern kingdom, before their captivities and served as proof for those who claimed to be Abraham's descendants. There is more to this long genealogy than meets the eye. It holds importance for us today because it supports the Old Testament promise that Jesus the Messiah would be a descendant of Abraham and David. This promise is recorded in Genesis 12:1-3 and 2 Samuel 7:12-13.

ACTS 23:26
Who was Felix?

Felix was the Roman governor or procurator of Judea from A.D. 52 to 59. This was the same position Pontius Pilate had held. While the Jews were given much freedom to govern themselves, the governor ran the army, kept the peace, and gathered the taxes. Felix was hated by the Jews; their rioting and charges against him resulted in his being recalled to Rome. His appointment had come from Claudius Caesar through Felix's friendship with Pallas, who had the ear of Claudius. Felix's governorship was later confirmed by Nero. Before returning to Rome, Felix tried to win Jewish favor by leaving Paul in jail (Acts 24:27).

ACTS 23:26
How did Luke know what was written in the letter from Claudius Lysias?

In his concern for historical accuracy, Luke used many sources to make sure that his writings were correct (see Luke 1:1-4). This letter was probably read aloud in court when Paul came before Felix to answer the Jews' accusations. Also, because Paul was a Roman citizen, a copy may have been given to him as a courtesy.

JULY 6

ACTS 24:1-9
What were the charges against Paul?

Ananias, the high priest; Tertullus, the lawyer; and several Jewish leaders traveled 60 miles to Caesarea, the Roman center of government, to bring their false accusations against Paul. Their murder plot had failed (Acts 23:12-15), but they persisted in trying to kill him. This attempt at murder was both premeditated and persistent. Tertullus was a special orator called to present the religious leaders' case before the Roman governor. He made three accusations against Paul: (1) he was a troublemaker, stirring up riots among the Jews around the world; (2) he was the ringleader of an unrecognized religious sect, which was against Roman law; and (3) he had tried to desecrate the temple. The religious leaders hoped that these accusations would persuade Felix to execute Paul in order to keep the peace in Palestine. While the charge that Paul was a troublemaker was insulting to Paul, it was too vague to be a substantial legal charge. The Nazarene sect referred to the Christians—named here after Jesus' hometown of Nazareth. Tertullus and the religious leaders seemed to have a strong argument against Paul, but Paul refuted their accusations point by point. Paul was also able to present the gospel message through his defense. Paul's accusers were unable to present specific evidence to support their general accusations. For example, Paul was accused of starting trouble among the Jews in the province of Asia (24:18-19), but the Jews in the province of Asia (western Turkey) were not present to confirm this.

PSALM 4:2
Why did God's people worship idols?

Idol worship was a recurring problem for Israel throughout its history. The Israelites had entered a land filled with idols and had not destroyed them as God had commanded; therefore, idols continued to be a temptation for them (Judg. 2:1-3). Worshiping idols of wood and stone mocked God, the Creator of wood and stone.

PSALM 4:5
What does the psalmist mean by "right sacrifices"?

Worship in David's day included animal sacrifices by the priests in the tabernacle. The animal's blood "covered" (was the remedy for) the sins of the one who offered the animal. There were specific rules for offering sacrifices, but more important to God than ceremony was the offerer's *right* attitude of submission and obedience (1 Sam. 15:22-23).

JULY 7

1 CHRONICLES 4:10
Who was Jabez?

This is the only mention of Jabez in the Bible. It is significant that he is remembered for prayer rather than a heroic act. In his prayer, he asked God to (1) bless him, (2) help him in his work, (3) be with him in all he did, and (4) keep him from evil and disaster. Jabez acknowledged God as the true center of his work. God granted what he asked.

1 CHRONICLES 5:1
Why is Reuben's sin recorded in a genealogy?

The purpose of this epitaph was not to smear Reuben's name, but to show that painful memories aren't the only results of sin. The real consequences of sin are ruined lives. As the oldest son, Reuben was the rightful heir to both a double portion of his father's estate and the leadership of Abraham's descendants, who had grown into a large tribe. But his sin stripped away his rights and privileges and ruined his family.

ACTS 25:10-11
Why did Paul appeal to Caesar?

Paul knew that he was innocent of the charges against him and could appeal to Caesar's judgment. He knew his rights as a Roman citizen and as an innocent person. The Jews wanted him returned to Jerusalem for trial. If this happened Paul's life would be in jeopardy. Paul had met his responsibilities as a Roman, and so he took the opportunity to claim Rome's protection. Every Roman citizen had the right to appeal to Caesar and be tried by the highest courts in the empire. Festus saw Paul's appeal as a way to send him out of the country and thus pacify the Jews. Paul wanted to go to Rome to preach the gospel (Rom. 1:10), and he knew that his appeal would give him the opportunity. To go to Rome as a prisoner was better than not to go there at all.

ACTS 25:13
Who was Agrippa?

This was Herod Agrippa II, son of Herod Agrippa I, and a descendant of Herod the Great. He had power over the temple, controlled the temple treasury, and could appoint and remove the high priest. Bernice was the sister of Herod Agrippa II. She married her uncle, Herod Chalcis, became a mistress to her brother Agrippa II, and then became mistress to the emperor Vespasian's son, Titus. Here Agrippa and Bernice were making an official visit to Festus.

JULY 8

1 Chronicles 5:18–6:81; Acts 26:1-32; Psalms 6:1-10; Proverbs 18:20-21

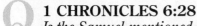

1 CHRONICLES 6:28
Is the Samuel mentioned in 1 Chronicles 6:28 the same man whose story is told in the book of 1 Samuel?

Yes. When Samuel became God's leader and spokesman, Israel was on the brink of collapse. The last few chapters of the book of Judges give a vivid picture of the moral decay and the resulting decline of the nation. But with God's help, Samuel brought the nation from ruin to revival. He unified the people by showing them that God was their common leader and that any nation that focused on him would find and fulfill its true purpose.

1 CHRONICLES 6:57-58
What were the "cities of refuge" given to the sons of Aaron?

God had told the tribes to designate specific cities to be cities of refuge (Num. 35). These cities were to provide refuge for a person who accidentally killed someone. Of the 48 cities given to the Levites, six were cities of refuge. These six cities were probably put under the Levites' supervision because they would be the most impartial judges. Such cities were needed because the ancient customs of justice called for revenge in the event of the death of a relative or loved one (2 Sam. 14:7). The Levites would hold a preliminary hearing outside the gates while the accused person was kept in the city until the time of his trial. If the killing was judged accidental, the person would stay in the city until the death of the high priest. At that time, he would be allowed to go free, and he could start a new life without worrying about avengers. If it was not accidental, the person would be delivered to the slain person's avengers. This system of justice shows how God's law and his mercy go hand in hand.

ACTS 26:26
Why would Agrippa have known about Jesus?

Paul was appealing to the *facts*—people were still alive who had heard Jesus and seen his miracles; the empty tomb could still be seen; and the Christian message was turning the world upside down (Acts 17:6). The history of Jesus' life and the early church are facts that are still open for us to examine.

JULY 9

 MATTHEW 19:8-9
Why didn't God condemn Shaharaim's polygamy and divorces in 1 Chronicles 8:8-10?

These verses list Shaharaim's children by Hodesh after he had divorced his first two wives, Hushim and Baara. Divorce and polygamy are sometimes recorded in the Old Testament without critical comments. This does not mean that God takes divorce lightly. Malachi 2:15-16 says, "Do not break faith with the wife of your youth. 'I hate divorce,' says the LORD God of Israel.'" Jesus explained that although divorce was allowed, it was not God's will: "Moses permitted you to divorce your wives because your hearts were hard. But it was not this way from the beginning".

 ACTS 27:2
Who traveled with Paul to Rome?

Use of the pronoun *we* indicates that Luke, the author of the Gospel of Luke and Acts, accompanied Paul on this journey. Aristarchus, a Thessalonican, is the man who was dragged into the theater at the beginning of the riot in Ephesus (Acts 19:29), and accompanied Paul to Jerusalem (Acts 20:4). He was Paul's "fellow laborer" in Philemon 24 and was his "fellow prisoner" in Colossians 4:10. Julius, the Roman centurion, was assigned to guard Paul. Julius developed a respect for Paul, gave him a certain amount of freedom (Acts 27:3), and later spared his life (Acts 27:43).

 ACTS 27:9
What kind of weather prevented the ship from sailing?

Ships in ancient times had no compasses and navigated by the stars. Overcast weather made sailing almost impossible and very dangerous. Sailing was doubtful in September and impossible by November. This event occurred in October (A.D. 59). Despite Paul's warning (Acts 27:10), the pilot and the owner of the ship didn't want to spend the winter in Lasea, and so took a chance and set sail. At first the weather was favorable, then the deadly *Euroclydon* (KJV) or "northeaster" arose (Acts 27:14).

JULY 10

1 Chronicles 9:1–10:14; Acts 27:21-44; Psalms 8:1-9; Proverbs 18:23-24

 1 CHRONICLES 9
Why is the list of the returnees from Babylon listed before the earlier history of Israel?

Chronologically, this chapter could be placed at the end of 2 Chronicles because it records the names of the exiles who returned from the Babylonian captivity. The writer included it here to show his concern for their need, as a nation, to return to what made them great in the first place—obedience to God. The chronology of chapters 1–9 covers Israelite history from creation to the exile in Babylon (586 B.C.). At chapter 10 the narrative goes back to the beginning of Israel's kingdom period, picking up with Israel's first king, Saul. 1 Chronicles begins with Saul's death; his entire reign is covered in 1 Samuel.

 1 CHRONICLES 10:10
Who was the god "Dagon"?

Dagon was the most important god of the Philistines. He was believed to bring rain and provide rich harvests. The Philistines built temples to him when they settled in the grain-producing land of Canaan. In times of drought, people begged Dagon for pity, even to the point of sacrificing their children in his temples. In times of plenty, the temples were used for perverted forms of entertainment, such as the humiliation of captives (see Judg. 16:23-30). But Dagon, like the other pagan gods, was powerless against the one true God (1 Sam. 5:1-7).

 ACTS 27:28
What does Acts 27:28 mean when it says "they took soundings and found twenty fathoms"?

Soundings were made by throwing a weighted, marked line into the water. When the lead hit the bottom, sailors could tell the depth of the water from the marks on the rope. A fathom is six feet.

 ACTS 27:42
Why would the soldiers want to kill their prisoners?

The soldiers would pay with their own lives if any of their prisoners escaped. Their instinctive reaction was to kill the prisoners so they wouldn't get away. Julius, the centurion, was impressed with Paul and wanted to save his life. Julius was the highest ranking official and therefore he could make this decision. This act preserved Paul for his later ministry in Rome and fulfilled Paul's prediction that all the people on the ship would be saved (Acts 27:22).

JULY 11

 1 CHRONICLES 12:18
How did the Holy Spirit work in Old Testament times?

When there was an important job to be done, God chose a person to do it, and the Spirit gave that person the needed power and ability. The Spirit gave Bezalel artistic ability (Exod. 31:1-5), Jephthah military prowess (Judg. 11:29), David power to rule (1 Sam. 16:13), and Zechariah an authoritative word of prophecy (2 Chron. 24:20). Here the Holy Spirit came upon David's warriors. The Spirit came upon individuals in order to accomplish specific goals. Beginning at Pentecost, however, the Spirit came upon all believers, not only to empower them to do God's will, but also to dwell in them day by day (Acts 2:14-21).

 ACTS 28:30
What happened to Paul after he got to Rome?

While Paul was under house arrest, he did more than speak to the Jews. He wrote letters, commonly called his Prison Letters, to the Ephesians, Colossians, and Philippians. He also wrote personal letters, such as the one to Philemon. Timothy often visited him (Phil. 1:1; Col. 1:1; Philem. 1), as did Tychicus (Eph. 6:21), Epaphroditus (Phil. 4:18), and Mark (Col. 4:10). Paul witnessed to the whole Roman guard (Phil. 1:13) and was involved with the Roman believers. Tradition says that Paul was released after two years of house arrest in Rome and then set off on a fourth missionary journey. Some reasons for this tradition are as follows: (1) Luke does not give us an account of his trial before Caesar, and Luke was a detailed chronicler; (2) the prosecution had two years to bring the case to trial, and time may have run out; (3) in his letter to the Philippians, written during his imprisonment in Rome, Paul implied that he would soon be released and would do further traveling; (4) Paul mentions several places where he intended to take the gospel, but he never visited those places in his first three journeys; and (5) early Christian literature talks plainly about other travels by Paul. It may be that during Paul's time of freedom, he continued to travel extensively, even going to Spain (see Rom. 15:24, 28) and back to the churches in Greece. The books of 1 Timothy and Titus were written during this time. Later, Paul was imprisoned again, probably in Rome, where he wrote his last letter (2 Timothy).

JULY 12

1 Chronicles 12:19–14:17; Romans 1:1-17; Psalms 9:13-20; Proverbs 19:4-5

 1 CHRONICLES 13:10
Why did Uzza die?

As the ark was being brought back to Israel on an ox cart, the oxen stumbled. Uzza, trying to steady the ark with his hand, was killed instantly for touching it. The mistake was not in David's desire to move the ark, but in his method for its return. David either ignored or was unaware of the specific instructions in God's law about how the ark was to be moved. According to Numbers 4:5-15, the ark was to be moved only by the Levites, who were to carry it using the carrying poles—they were *never* to touch the ark itself. To touch it was a capital offense under Hebrew law (Num. 4:15). God's action was directed against both David and Uzza. David placed the ark on a cart, following the Philistines' example (1 Sam. 6:7-8) rather than God's commands. Uzza, though sincere in his desire to protect the ark, had to face the consequences of the sin of touching it. Also, Uzza may not have been a Levite. As David sought to bring Israel back into a relationship with God, God had to remind the nation dramatically that enthusiasm must be accompanied by obedience to his laws. The next time David tried to bring the ark to Jerusalem, he was careful to handle it correctly.

 ROMANS 1:1
How did Christianity spread to Rome?

Paul wrote this letter to the church in Rome. Neither he nor the other church leaders, James and Peter, had yet been to Rome. Most likely, the Roman church had been established by believers who had been at Jerusalem for Pentecost (Acts 2:10) and/or travelers who had heard the Good News in other places and had brought it back to Rome (for example, Priscilla and Aquila—Acts 18:2; Rom. 16:3-5). Paul wrote the letter to the Romans during his ministry in Corinth (at the end of his third missionary journey just before returning to Jerusalem; Acts 20:3; Rom. 15:25) to encourage the believers and to express his desire to visit them someday (within three years he would). The Roman church had no New Testament because the Gospels were not yet being circulated in their final written form. Thus, this letter may well have been the first piece of Christian literature the Roman believers had seen. Written to both Jewish and Gentile Christians, the letter to the Romans is a systematic presentation of the Christian faith.

JULY 13

1 CHRONICLES 16:15-18
When did God make the covenant mentioned in 1 Chronicles 16:15-18?

This covenant was given to Abraham (Gen. 15:18-21), and then passed on to Isaac (Gen. 26:24-25) and Jacob (Gen. 28:13-15). God promised to give the land of Canaan (present-day Israel) to their descendants. He also promised that the Messiah would come from their line.

ROMANS 1:18-20
Why is "the wrath of God revealed from heaven" against someone who has never heard about Christ?

Paul says that God has revealed himself plainly in the creation to *all* people. And yet people reject even this basic knowledge of God. Also, everyone has an inner sense of what God requires, but they choose not to live up to it. Put another way, people's moral standards are always better than their behavior. If people suppress God's truth in order to live their own way, they have no excuse. They know the truth, and they will have to endure the consequences of ignoring it.

ROMANS 1:20
What kind of God does nature reveal?

Nature shows us a God of might, intelligence, and intricate detail; a God of order and beauty; a God who controls powerful forces. That is *general* revelation. Through *special* revelation (the Bible and the coming of Jesus), we learn about God's love and forgiveness, and the promise of eternal life. God has graciously given us both sources that we might more completely believe in him.

ROMANS 1:21-24
How could intelligent people turn to idolatry?

Idolatry begins when people reject what they know about God. Instead of looking to him as the Creator and sustainer of life, they see themselves as the center of the universe. They soon invent "gods" that are convenient projections of their own selfish plans and decrees. These gods may be wooden figures, but they may also be goals or things we pursue such as money, power, or comfort. They may even be misrepresentations of God himself—making God in our image, instead of the reverse. The common denominator is this—idolaters worship the things God made rather than God himself.

JULY 14

1 CHRONICLES 16:39
If the Ark was in Jerusalem and the Tabernacle was in Gibeon, where did Israel worship?

David brought the ark to Jerusalem although the tabernacle was still at Gibeon. His plan was to reunite the tabernacle and ark in a new temple at Jerusalem which would then become Israel's only worship center. The temple, however, was not built until Solomon's time. In the meantime, Israel had two worship centers and two high priests (1 Chron. 15:11), one at Gibeon and one at Jerusalem.

1 CHRONICLES 17:3-14
Why didn't God want David to build his temple?

God did not want a warrior to build his temple (1 Chron. 28:3; cf. 1 Kings 5:3), and David had shed much blood in unifying the nation. So the honor of building the temple would go to David's son Solomon. David would pass on to Solomon a peaceful and united kingdom, ready to begin work on a beautiful temple.

ROMANS 2:12-14
What is the law?

The law of God is the revealed expression of the will of God. The Ten Commandments constitute the moral law (Exod. 20:2-17; Deut. 5:6-21). The judicial and ceremonial laws of the Old Testament were given with a specific people in mind—the Jews—and for a specific period in their history. The moral law is timeless, for it concerns itself with the permanent relations of man with respect to marriage, sex, property, and family obedience.

ROMANS 2:15
What is the conscience?

God gave Adam a conscience that was uncorrupted before he sinned. After his sin it was depraved and corrupted, but not totally erased. Conscience serves as a witness to truth (Prov. 20:27), but moral choice tells whether it has been obeyed (Josh. 24:15). A man's own conscience accuses him of sin (Gen. 42:21; 2 Sam. 24:10; Matt. 27:3), and it will condemn him when the books are opened. Every mouth will be silenced, and God's judgments will be seen to be true and just (Rev. 20:12-15). The believer who is walking in the Spirit will repent of and confess any known sin. In this way it is possible to have a blameless conscience that is void of offense (Rom. 9:1; 14:22; cf. Acts 24:16). Conscience is educated and perfected by faith through the redeeming sacrifice of Jesus Christ.

JULY 15

1 CHRONICLES 21:1
The Bible says Satan incited David to take a census. Can Satan force people to do wrong?

No, Satan only *tempted* David with the idea, but David *decided to act* on the temptation. Ever since the Garden of Eden, Satan has been tempting people to sin. David's census was not against God's law, but his reason for the census was wrong—pride in his mighty army while forgetting that his real strength came from God. Even Joab, not known for his high moral ideals, recognized the census as sin.

1 CHRONICLES 21:14
Why did seventy thousand innocent people die for David's sin?

Our society places great emphasis upon the individual. In ancient times, however, the family leaders, tribal leaders, and kings represented the people they led, and all expected to share in their successes as well as in their failures and punishments. David deserved punishment for his sin, but his death could have resulted in political chaos and invasion by enemy armies, leaving hundreds of thousands dead. Instead, God graciously spared David's life. He also put a stop to the plague so that most of the people of Jerusalem were spared.

ROMANS 3:2
What were the advantages of being a Jew?

The Jewish nation had many advantages. (1) They were entrusted with God's laws ("the very words of God"—Exod. 19-20; Deut. 4:8). (2) They were the race through whom the Messiah came to earth (Isa. 11:1-10; Matt. 1:1-17). (3) They were the beneficiaries of covenants with God himself (Gen. 17:1-16; Exod. 19:3-6). But these privileges did not make them better than anyone else (see Rom. 3:9). In fact, because of them the Jews were even more responsible to live up to God's requirements.

PSALM 11:1
Didn't David ever run away from his enemies?

David was forced to flee for safety several times. Being God's anointed king did not make him immune to injustice and hatred from others. This psalm may have been written when he was being hunted by Saul (1 Samuel 18–31) or during the days of Absalom's rebellion (2 Samuel 15–18). In both instances, David fled, but not as if all was lost. He knew God was in control. While David wisely avoided trouble, he did not fearfully run away from his troubles.

JULY 16

1 Chronicles 22:1–23:32; Romans 3:9-31; Psalms 12:1-8; Proverbs 19:13-14

1 CHRONICLES 23:28-32
What was the difference between priests and Levites?

Priests and Levites had different jobs in and around the temple. Priests were authorized to perform the sacrifices. Levites were set apart to help the priests. They did the work of elders, deacons, custodians, assistants, musicians, moving men, and repairmen. Both priests and Levites came from the tribe of Levi, but priests also had to be descendants of Aaron, Israel's first high priest (Exod. 28:1-3). Priests and Levites were supported by Israel's tithes and by revenues from certain cities that had been given to them.

ROMANS 3:25
What happened to people who lived before Christ came and died for sin? If God condemned them, was he being unfair? If he saved them, was Christ's sacrifice unnecessary?

Paul shows that God forgave all human sin at the cross of Jesus. Old Testament believers looked forward in faith to Christ's coming and were saved, even though they did not know Jesus' name or the details of his earthly life. New Testament believers look back in faith to their crucified Savior.

ROMANS 3:28
Why does God save us by faith alone?

(1) Faith eliminates the pride of human effort, because faith is not a deed that we do. (2) Faith exalts what God has done, not what people do. (3) Faith admits that we can't keep the law or measure up to God's standards—we need help. (4) Faith is based on our relationship with God, not our performance for God.

ROMANS 3:31
What is the meaning of Romans 3:31?

There were some misunderstandings between the Jewish and Gentile Christians in Rome. Worried Jewish Christians were asking Paul, "Does faith wipe out everything Judaism stands for? Does it cancel our Scriptures, put an end to our customs, declare that God is no longer working through us?" (This is essentially the question used to open chapter 3.) "Absolutely not!" says Paul. When we understand the way of salvation through faith, we understand the Jewish religion better. We know why Abraham was chosen, why the law was given, why God worked patiently with Israel for centuries. Faith does not wipe out the Old Testament. Rather, it makes God's dealings with the Jewish people understandable. In chapter 4, Paul will expand on this theme (see also Rom. 5:20-21; 8:3-4; 13:9-10; Gal. 3:24-29; and 1 Tim. 1:8 for more on this concept).

JULY 17

1 CHRONICLES 25:1
Why would people prophesy to musical accompaniment?

There is more to prophesying than predicting the future. Prophecy also involves singing God's praises and preaching God's messages (1 Cor. 14:1ff). Prophets could be musicians, farmers (Amos 1:1), wives (2 Kings 22:14), or leaders (Deut. 34:10)—anyone who boldly and accurately spoke out for God and tried to bring people back to worshiping him. From a large group of musicians David chose those who showed an unusual ability to tell about God and to encourage others in song.

1 CHRONICLES 26:1, TLB
What was the function of the temple guards?

There were four thousand temple guards (gatekeepers, 23:4-5, NIV). They were all Levites and did many other jobs as well. Some of their duties included (1) checking out the equipment and utensils used each day and making sure they were returned, (2) storing, ordering, and maintaining the food supplies for the priests and sacrifices, (3) caring for the furniture, (4) mixing the incense that was burned daily, (5) accounting for the gifts brought.

ROMANS 4:10-12
Why is circumcision important to the Jews? Was this why God called Abraham righteous?

Circumcision was a sign to others and a personal seal or certification for the Jews that they were God's special people. Circumcision of all Jewish boys set the Jewish people apart from the nations who worshiped other gods; thus it was a very important ceremony. God gave the blessing and the command for this ceremony to Abraham (Gen. 17:9-14). Rituals did not earn any reward for Abraham; he had been blessed long before the circumcision ceremony was introduced. Abraham found favor with God by faith alone, before he was circumcised. Genesis 12:1-4 tells of God's call to Abraham when he was 75 years old; the circumcision ceremony was introduced when he was 99 (Gen. 17:1-14). Ceremonies and rituals serve as reminders of our faith, and they instruct new and younger believers. But we should not think that they give us any special merit before God. They are outward signs and seals that demonstrate inward belief and trust. The focus of our faith should be on Christ and his saving actions, not on our own actions.

JULY 18

1 CHRONICLES 26:29
Did the Levites serve in functions outside the temple?

Some of the Levites were employed in the affairs of government, with no responsibilities at the temple. They were ministers of justice in the civil realm, caring for God's tithes, the king's tax money, and the affairs of the nation. They served the nation in secular matters and also in religious matters having to do with such things as idolatry and the like.

1 CHRONICLES 27:1, KJV
What are the "courses" mentioned in 1 Chronicles 27:1?

This word is sometimes translated "divisions" (NRSV, NIV) and can mean "administrative units" (TLB). King David maintained a standing army and had control over the military operations of the nation. The military was divided into courses, as were the priests, each course served one month at a time. This rotation of service made their support less burdensome. The whole number of those under arms totaled 288,000. There were various divisions among the soldiers similar to those of armies in our day. The captains might be considered as being equivalent to the generals in our armies today.

ROMANS 4:17
What does "the father of many nations" mean?

The promise (or covenant) God gave Abraham stated that Abraham would be the father of many nations (Gen. 17:2-4) and that the entire world would be blessed through him (Gen. 12:3). This promise was fulfilled in Jesus Christ. Jesus was from Abraham's line, and the whole world was blessed through him. Paul points out that the promise to Abraham to be the father of many nations extended beyond Israel to all nations of the world.

ROMANS 4:18, NKJV
What does it mean that Abraham "contrary to hope, in hope believed"?

An interpretation of this verse is: "Abraham believed God even though such a promise just couldn't come to pass" (TLB). Abraham believed God in hope or even against hope. Sense, reason, and experience told him that the promise of a son by Sarah could not happen, but in spite of this he believed. When no ground for hope appeared he cherished the believing expectation. He believed in hope, which arose from his belief in God's all sufficiency and that he would and could do what he had promised. He staggered not at the promise of God through unbelief.

JULY 19

1 CHRONICLES 28:5
Since Solomon was not David's oldest son why did he succeed David as the King?

The kingdom of Israel belonged to God, not to David or anyone else. Israel's king, then, was God's deputy, commissioned to carry out God's will for the nation. Thus God could choose the person he wanted as king without following customary lines of succession. David was not Saul's heir, and Solomon was not David's oldest son, but this did not matter, because God appointed them.

1 CHRONICLES 29:29
Who were Samuel the seer, Nathan the prophet and Gad the seer?

These were God's prophets during David's reign. *The book of Samuel the seer* evidently refers to the two books of Samuel. The chronicler was selective in what he reported and did not include some of the materials contained in the book of Samuel. In Chronicles there is no treatment of the plots and counterplots for the kingship at the time of David's death. The writer assumed that the reader would be familiar with the book of Samuel.

ROMANS 5:13-14
What is the cause of death?

Paul has shown that keeping the law does not bring salvation. Now he adds that breaking Moses' law is not what brings death. Death is the result of Adam's sin and of the sins we all commit, even if they don't resemble Adam's. Paul reminds his readers that for thousands of years the law had not yet been explicitly given, and yet people died. The law was added, he explains in Romans 5:20, to help people see their sinfulness, to show them the seriousness of their offenses, and to drive them to God for mercy and pardon. This was true in Moses' day, and it is still true today. Sin is a deep discrepancy between who we are and who we were created to be. The law points out our sin and places the responsibility for it squarely on our shoulders. But the law offers no remedy. When we are convicted of sin, we must turn to Jesus Christ for healing.

JULY 20

 2 CHRONICLES 2:17-18
What had been David's part in the construction of the temple?
David had wanted to build a temple for God (2 Samuel 7). God denied his request because David had been a warrior, but God said that David's son Solomon would build the temple. God allowed David to make the plans and preparations for the temple (1 Chron. 23–26; 28:11-13). David bought the land (2 Sam. 24:18-25; 1 Chron. 22:1), gathered most of the construction materials (1 Chron. 22:14-16), and received the plans from God (1 Chron. 28:11-12). It was Solomon's responsibility to make the plans a reality. His job was made easier by his father's exhaustive preparations.

 ROMANS 6:1
If God loves to forgive, why not give him more to forgive? If forgiveness is guaranteed, do we have the freedom to sin as much as we want?
Paul's forceful answer is *By no means!* Such an attitude—deciding ahead of time to take advantage of God—shows that a person does not understand the seriousness of sin. God's forgiveness does not make sin less serious; his Son's death for sin shows us the dreadful seriousness of sin. Jesus paid with his life so we could be forgiven. The availability of God's mercy must not become an excuse for careless living and moral laxness.

ROMANS 6:6
How can I be free from the power of sin?
The power and penalty of sin died with Christ on the cross. Our "old self," our sinful nature, died once and for all, so we are freed from its power. The "body of sin" is not the human body per se, but our rebellious sin-loving nature inherited from Adam. Though our body willingly cooperates with our sinful nature, we must not regard the body as evil. It is the sin in us that is evil. And it is this power of sin at work in our body that is defeated. Paul has already stated that through faith in Christ we stand acquitted, "not guilty," before God. Here Paul emphasizes that we need no longer live under sin's power. God does not take us out of the world or make us robots—we will still feel like sinning, and sometimes we will sin. The difference is that before we were saved we were slaves to our sinful nature, but now we can choose to live for Christ (see Gal. 2:20).

JULY 21

2 Chronicles 4:1–6:11; Romans 7:1-13; Psalms 17:1-15; Proverbs 19:22-23

Q 2 CHRONICLES 4:6
Why was everything in the temple built on such a grand scale?

The great size and numbers were necessary to accommodate the huge crowds that would visit for the feasts, such as the Passover (2 Chron. 30:13). The numerous daily sacrifices required many priests and much equipment.

Q 2 CHRONICLES 5:9
If the books of 1 and 2 Chronicles were written after the temple was destroyed, why does 2 Chronicles 5:9 say that the poles of the ark "are there to this day" (NKJV)?

Under God's inspiration, some books of the Bible were compiled and edited from other sources. Because 1 and 2 Chronicles cover many centuries, they were compiled from several sources by a single person. The phrase "they are still there today" (see also 1 Kings 8:8) was taken from material written before Judah's exile in 586 B.C. Although 1 and 2 Chronicles were compiled after the exile and after Solomon's temple was destroyed, the writer thought it best to leave this phrase in the narrative.

Q 2 CHRONICLES 5:1ff.
Why is there so much emphasis on the temple in the Old Testament?

(1) It was a symbol of religious authority. The temple was God's way of centralizing worship at Jerusalem in order to insure that correct belief would be kept intact through many generations. (2) It was a symbol of God's holiness. The temple's beautiful atmosphere inspired respect and awe for God; it was the setting for many of the great visions of the prophets. (3) It was a symbol of God's covenant with Israel. The temple kept the people focused upon God's law (the tablets of the Ten Commandments were kept in the temple) rather than on the kings' exploits. It was a place where God was especially present to his people. (4) It was a symbol of forgiveness. The temple's design, furniture, and customs were great object lessons for all the people, reminding them of the seriousness of sin, the penalty that sin incurred, and their need of forgiveness. (5) It prepared the people for the Messiah. In the New Testament, Christ said he came to fulfill the law, not destroy it. Hebrews 8:1-2 and 9:11-12 use temple customs to explain what Christ did when he died for us. (6) It was a testimony to human effort and creativity. Inspired by the beauty of God's character, people devoted themselves to high achievements in engineering, science, and art in order to praise him. (7) It was a place of prayer. In the temple, people could spend time in prayer to God.

JULY 22

2 CHRONICLES 6:24
Why would Solomon assume that drought would come as a result of sin?

Sin is not necessarily the direct cause of natural disasters today, but this was a special case. God had made a specific agreement with the Israelites that drought could be a consequence of their sins (Deut. 28:20-24).

2 CHRONICLES 7:1-2
Why did "fire flash down from heaven"?

God sent fire from heaven to consume the offering and to begin the fire that was to burn continuously under the altar of burnt offering (see Lev. 6:8-13). This perpetual fire symbolized God's presence. God also sent fire when inaugurating the tabernacle (Lev. 9:22-24). This was the real dedication of the temple because only God's purifying power can make something holy.

PSALM 18:10
What is a "cherub"?

A cherub is a mighty angel. One of the functions of the cherubim was to serve as guardians. These angels guarded the entrances to both the tree of life (Gen. 3:24) and the Most Holy Place (Exod. 26:31-33). Two cherubim of hammered gold were part of the ark of the covenant (Exod. 25:18-22). The living creatures carrying God's throne in Ezekiel 1 may have been cherubim.

ROMANS 7:15
Why does Paul say that he does what he hates?

This is more than the cry of one desperate man—it describes the experience of any Christian struggling against sin or trying to please God by keeping rules and laws without the Spirit's help. In Romans 7 Paul shares three lessons that he learned in trying to deal with his old sinful desires. (1) Knowledge is not the answer (7:9). Paul felt fine as long as he did not understand what the law demanded. When he learned the truth, he knew he was doomed. (2) Self-determination (struggling in one's own strength) doesn't succeed (7:15). Paul found himself sinning in ways that weren't even attractive to him. (3) Becoming a Christian does not stamp out all sin and temptation from a person's life (7:22-25). Being born again takes a moment of faith, but becoming like Christ is a lifelong process.

JULY 23

2 Chronicles 8:11–10:19; Romans 8:9-21; Psalms 18:16-36; Proverbs 19:26

2 CHRONICLES 8:11
Why did Solomon marry Pharaoh's daughter if he knew she couldn't live in David's palace?

Solomon married Pharaoh's daughter to secure a military alliance with Egypt. He did not let the woman live in David's palace, however, where the ark of God had once been kept. This implies that Solomon knew his pagan marriage would not please God. Solomon married many other foreign women, and this was contrary to God's law (Deut. 7:3-4). These women worshiped false gods and were certain to contaminate Israel with their beliefs and practices. Although Solomon carefully followed God's instructions for building the temple and offering sacrifices (2 Chron. 8:13), he paid no attention to what God said about marrying pagan women. His sin in marrying a foreign wife began his slide away from God (1 Kings 11:1-11).

2 CHRONICLES 10:1
Why was Rehoboam's coronation in Shechem?

The crowning of an Israelite king would normally have taken place in Jerusalem, the capital city. But Rehoboam saw that there was the possibility of trouble in the north; so to maintain his hold on the country, he chose Shechem, a city about 35 miles north of Jerusalem. Shechem was an ancient site for making covenants (Josh. 24:1).

ROMANS 8:15, NRSV
What is the "spirit of adoption"?

Paul uses adoption or "sonship" to illustrate the believer's new relationship with God. In Roman culture, the adopted person lost all rights in his old family and gained all the rights of a legitimate child in his new family. He became a full heir to his new father's estate. Likewise, when a person becomes a Christian, he or she gains all the privileges and responsibilities of a child in God's family. One of these outstanding privileges is receiving the Spirit of God's Son (see Gal. 4:5-6).

ROMANS 8:19
What does the creation have to do with the revealing of the sons of God?

Sin has caused all creation to fall from the perfect state in which God created it. So the world is subject to frustration and is in bondage to decay, so that it cannot fulfill its intended purpose. One day all creation will be liberated and transformed. Until that time it waits in eager expectation for the resurrection and glorification of God's children.

JULY 24

2 CHRONICLES 11:13-14
Why were the priests and Levites mentioned in 2 Chronicles 11:13-14 not living in Jerusalem where the Temple was located?

Before the nation split, the center of worship was in Jerusalem, and people flocked there for the three great annual religious festivals. During the rest of the year, other worship services and rituals were conducted in the tribal territories by priests and Levites who lived throughout the land. They offered sacrifices, taught God's laws, and encouraged the people to continue to follow God and avoid pagan influences. After the nation split, Jeroboam, the new king of Israel, saw these priests and Levites as threats to his new government because they retained loyalty to Jerusalem, now the capital of Judah. So he appointed his own priests, effectively banning the Levites from their duties and forcing them to move to the southern kingdom. Jeroboam's pagan priests encouraged idol worship. With the absence of spiritual leaders, the new northern kingdom was in danger of abandoning God.

2 CHRONICLES 13:1ff.
Since 1 Kings 15:3 says Abijah committed many sins, why does the Chronicles' account only record positive comments about him?

For the most part Abijah was a wicked king. The writer of Chronicles chose to highlight the little good he did in order to show that he was still under God's covenant promise to David. Because of Abijah's fiery speech to Jeroboam (2 Chronicles 13:4-12), he was spared the immediate consequences of his sin.

ROMANS 8:24-25
If I have already believed and am saved, why does Romans 8:24-25 say we were saved in hope?

In Romans, Paul presents the idea that salvation is past, present, and future. It is past because we *were* saved the moment we believed in Jesus Christ as Savior (Rom. 3:21-26; 5:1-11; 6:1-11, 22-23); our new life (eternal life) begins at that moment. And it is present because we *are being* saved. But at the same time, we have not fully received all the benefits and blessings of salvation that will be ours when Christ's new kingdom is completely established. That's our future salvation. While we can be confident of our salvation, we still look ahead with hope and trust toward that complete change of body and personality that lies beyond this life, when we will be like Christ (1 John 3:2).

JULY 25

2 CHRONICLES 16:12
Does 2 Chronicles 16:12 indicate that I should not go doctors when I am sick?

The criticism of Asa's visit to the physicians was not a general indictment of medicine. Asa's problem was that he completely ignored God's help. The medicine practiced at this time was a mixture of superstition and folk remedies. We should certainly avoid any pseudo-medical treatment derived from occult sources. Asa's experience should also encourage us to follow the New Testament practice of receiving prayer for our sickness (James 5:14) as we seek responsible medical help.

ROMANS 9:12-14
Was it right for God to choose Jacob, the younger, to be over Esau?

In Malachi 1:2-3, the statement "Jacob I loved, but Esau I hated" refers to the nations of Israel and Edom rather than to the individual brothers. God chose Jacob to continue the family line of the faithful because he knew his heart was for God. But he did not exclude Esau from knowing and loving him. Keep in mind the kind of God we worship: he is sovereign; he is not arbitrary; in all things he works for our good; he is trustworthy; he will save all who believe in him. When we understand these qualities of God, we know that his choices are good even if we don't understand all his reasons.

ROMANS 9:17
What is the meaning of Romans 9:17?

Paul quotes from Exodus 9:16, where God foretold how Pharaoh would be used to declare God's power. Paul uses this argument to show that salvation was God's proper work, not man's. God's judgment on Pharaoh's sin was to harden his heart, to confirm his disobedience, so that the consequences of his rebellion would be his own punishment.

ROMANS 9:21
In Romans 9:21 is Paul saying that some people are better than others?

With this illustration, Paul is not saying that some of us are worth more than others, but simply that the Creator has control over the created object. The created object, therefore, has no right to demand anything from its Creator—its very existence depends on him.

JULY 26

Q 2 CHRONICLES 18:1ff.
Why did Jehoshaphat have his son marry Ahab's daughter?

Although Jehoshaphat was deeply committed to God, he arranged for his son to marry Athaliah, the daughter of wicked King Ahab of Israel, and then made a military alliance with him. Jehoshaphat's popularity and power made him attractive to the cunning and opportunistic Ahab. This alliance had three devastating consequences: (1) Jehoshaphat incurred God's wrath (2 Chron. 19:2); (2) when Jehoshaphat died and Athaliah became queen, she seized the throne and almost destroyed all of David's descendants (2 Chron. 22:10-12); (3) Athaliah brought the evil practices of Israel into Judah, which eventually led to the nation's downfall.

Q 2 CHRONICLES 18:3-5
Why did Ahab have heathen prophets?

Evil kings did not like God's prophets bringing messages of doom (2 Chron. 18:17; Jeremiah 5:13). Many, therefore, hired prophets who told them only what they wanted to hear (Isaiah 30:10-11; Jeremiah 14:13-16; 23:16, 21, 30-36). These men were false prophets because they extolled the greatness of the king and predicted victory regardless of the real situation.

Q ROMANS 10:1
What will happen to the Jewish people who believe in God but not in Christ? Since they believe in the same God, won't they be saved?

If that were true, Paul would not have worked so hard and sacrificed so much to teach them about Christ. Because Jesus is the most complete revelation of God, we cannot fully know God apart from Christ; and because God appointed Jesus to bring God and man together, we cannot come to God by another path. The Jews, like everyone else, can find salvation only through Jesus Christ (John 14:6; Acts 4:12).

Q ROMANS 10:3-4
Why did God give the law when he knew people couldn't keep it?

According to Paul, one reason the law was given was to show people how guilty they are (Gal. 3:19). The law was a shadow of Christ—that is, the sacrificial system educated the people so that when the true sacrifice came, they would be able to understand his work (Heb. 10:1-4). The system of ceremonial laws was to last until the coming of Christ. The law points to Christ, the reason for all those animal sacrifices.

JULY 27

2 CHRONICLES 20:3
What was the purpose of fasting?

When the nation was faced with disaster, Jehoshaphat called upon the people to get serious with God by going without food (fasting) for a designated time. By separating themselves from the daily routine of food preparation and eating, they could devote that extra time to considering their sin and praying to God for help. Hunger pangs would reinforce their feelings of penitence and remind them of their weakness and their dependence upon God.

ROMANS 11:8-10
Where in the Old Testament are the verses Paul is quoting in Romans 11:8-10?

These verses describe the punishment for hardened hearts predicted by the prophet Isaiah (Isa. 6:9-13). If people refuse to hear God's Good News, they eventually will be unable to understand it. Paul saw this happening in the Jewish congregations he visited on his missionary journeys. (Verse 8 is based on Deut. 29:4 and Isa. 29:10. Verses 9 and 10 are from Ps. 69:22-23.)

ROMANS 11:11ff.
Did Paul expect the Jews to believe the gospel and become a part of the church?

Paul had a vision of a church where all Jews and Gentiles would be united in their love of God and in obedience to Christ. While respecting God's law, this ideal church would look to Christ alone for salvation. A person's ethnic background and social status would be irrelevant (see Gal. 3:28)—what mattered would be his or her faith in Christ. But Paul's vision has not yet been realized. Many Jewish people rejected the gospel. They depended on their heritage for salvation, and they did not have the heart of obedience that was so important to the Old Testament prophets and to Paul. Once Gentiles became dominant in many of the Christian churches, they began rejecting Jews and even persecuting them. Unfortunately, this practice has recurred through the centuries. True Christians should not persecute others. Both Gentiles and Jews have done so much to damage the cause of the God they claim to serve that Paul's vision often seems impossible to fulfill. Yet God chose the Jews, just as he chose the Gentiles, and he is still working to unite Jew and Gentile in a new Israel, a new Jerusalem, ruled by his Son (see Eph. 2:11-22).

JULY 28

2 CHRONICLES 21:7
What happened to God's promise that a descendant of David would always sit on the throne after the nation was destroyed and carried away (2 Chronicles 21:7; see also 2 Sam. 7:8-16)?

There were two parts to God's promise: (1) In the physical sense, as long as there was an actual throne in Judah, a descendant of David would sit upon it. But this part of the promise depended on the obedience of these kings. When they disobeyed, God was not bound to continue David's temporal line. (2) In the spiritual sense, this promise was completely fulfilled in the coming of Jesus the Messiah, a descendant of David, who would sit on the throne of David forever.

2 CHRONICLES 22:10
Who was Athaliah?

She was the daughter of Ahab and Jezebel and is said to have been a wicked woman (2 Chron. 24:7). Athaliah married Jehoram of Judah, who later inherited his father's throne. This marriage accomplished an alliance between the northern and southern kingdoms. Jehoram died after a reign of eight years, leaving Athaliah as queen. She destroyed the royal family and began to reign about 842 B.C. (2 Kings 11:1ff.). She gained the distinction of being the only woman in history to gain the throne of David. Six years of Athaliah were enough for the people of Judah. An ecclesiastical-political plot was formed which resulted in the death of Athaliah. Then Joash, who had been hidden in the temple, became king at seven years of age.

MATTHEW 27:46
Did Jesus quote Psalm 22:1 while he was hanging on the cross?

Yes. This verse includes one of the seven last sayings of Jesus on the cross. Jesus, the Messiah, quoted this verse while hanging on the cross carrying our burden of sin. It was not a cry of doubt, but an urgent appeal to God. The whole Psalm graphically portrays the suffering of the Messiah and adds a second prophecy fulfilled at the crucifixion, namely, that the soldiers would gamble over the Savior's seamless robe (Ps. 22:18; Matt. 27:35; Luke 23:34; John 19:23). David gave an amazingly accurate description of the suffering the Messiah would endure hundreds of years later. David was obviously enduring some great trial, but through his suffering he, like the Messiah to come, gained victory.

JULY 29

2 CHRONICLES 24:22
Did God answer Zechariah's prayer in 2 Chronicles 24:22 and avenge his death?

Yes, a small band of Syrians were God's instrument for judgment. They made themselves masters of Jerusalem. They plundered the city, killed the princes, and sent the spoil to the king of Damascus. Zechariah was also remembered hundreds of years later by Jesus Christ, who said to the Jews of his day, "You will become guilty of all the blood of murdered godly men from righteous Abel to Zechariah (son of Barachiah), slain by you in the Temple between the altar and the sanctuary" (Matt. 23:35, TLB).

2 CHRONICLES 25:18
What is the meaning of the parable in 2 Chronicles 25:18?

In this parable, Judah is the thistle and Israel's army is the cedar. Ahaziah was proud after defeating Edom. He wanted to defeat Israel, but Jehoash warned him not to attack. Ahaziah had more ambition than ability, and he paid for it when he was soundly defeated.

ROMANS 12:11
What is the meaning of Romans 12:11?

A literal translation of the Greek text would read, "In zeal not slothful, Spirit burning, the Lord serving." The NRSV says, "Do not lag in zeal, be ardent in spirit, serve the Lord." The Living Bible says, "Never be lazy in your work but serve the Lord enthusiastically." In the NIV this verse is rendered, "Never be lacking in zeal, but keep your spiritual fervor, serving the Lord." Spirit-filled believers enthusiastically serve the Lord.

ROMANS 12:20, KJV
What does it mean to "heap burning coals" on someone's head?

This may refer to an Egyptian tradition of carrying a pan of burning charcoal on one's head as a public act of repentance. By referring to this proverb, Paul was saying that we should treat our enemies with kindness so that they will become ashamed and turn from their sins. The best way to get rid of enemies is to turn them into friends.

PROVERBS 20:10, KJV
What is the meaning of "divers weights, and divers measures"?

These are inaccurate weights and measures used in business transactions. This verse has also been translated, "The Lord despises every kind of cheating" (TLB).

JULY 30

ROMANS 13:1ff.
Are there times when we should not submit to the government?

Christians understand Romans 13 in different ways. All Christians agree that we are to live at peace with the state as long as the state allows us to live by our religious convictions. For hundreds of years, however, there have been at least three interpretations of how we are to do this. (1) Some Christians believe that the state is so corrupt that Christians should have as little to do with it as possible. Although they should be good citizens as long as they can do so without compromising their beliefs, they should not work for the government, vote in elections, or serve in the military. (2) Others believe that God has given the state authority in certain areas and the church authority in others. Christians can be loyal to both and can work for either. They should not, however, confuse the two. In this view, church and state are concerned with two totally different spheres—the spiritual and the physical—and thus complement each other but do not work together. (3) Still others believe that Christians have a responsibility to make the state better. They can do this politically, by electing Christian or other high-principled leaders. They can also do this morally, by serving as an influence for good in society. In this view, church and state ideally work together for the good of all. None of these views advocate rebelling against or refusing to obey the government's laws or regulations unless those laws clearly require you to violate the moral standards revealed by God.

PSALM 23:1
Why did David call the Lord his "shepherd"?

In describing the Lord as a shepherd, David wrote out of his own experience because he had spent his early years caring for sheep (1 Sam. 16:10-11). Sheep are completely dependent on the shepherd for provision, guidance, and protection. The New Testament calls Jesus the good shepherd (John 10:11); the great Shepherd (Heb. 13:20); and the Chief Shepherd (1 Pet. 5:4). As the Lord is the good shepherd, so we are his sheep—not frightened, passive animals, but obedient followers, wise enough to follow one who will lead us in the right places and in right ways. This psalm does not focus on the animal-like qualities of sheep, but on the qualities of those who follow.

JULY 31

2 Chronicles 29:1-36; Romans 14:1-23; Psalms 24:1-10; Proverbs 20:12

2 CHRONICLES 29:22
Why did the priests sprinkle blood on the altar?

The blood sprinkled on the altar represented the innocence of the sacrificed animal taking the place of the guilt of the person making the offering. The animal died so the sinner could live. This ritual looked forward to the day when Jesus Christ, God's perfect Son, would sacrifice his innocent life on the cross in order that the sinful and guilty human race might be spared the punishment it deserves (Heb. 10:1-14).

ROMANS 14:2
How would Christians end up eating meat that had been offered to idols?

The ancient system of sacrifice was at the center of the religious, social, and domestic life of the Roman world. After a sacrifice was presented to a god in a pagan temple, only part of it was burned. The remainder was often sent to the market to be sold. Thus a Christian might easily—even unknowingly—buy such meat in the marketplace or eat it at the home of a friend.

ROMANS 14:14
Why didn't Paul think it was wrong to eat meat offered to idols?

At the Jerusalem council (Acts 15), the Jewish church in Jerusalem asked the Gentile church in Antioch not to eat meat that had been sacrificed to idols. Paul was at the Jerusalem council, and he accepted this request not because he felt that eating such meat was wrong in itself, but because this practice would deeply offend many Jewish believers. Paul did not think the issue was worth dividing the church over; his desire was to promote unity.

PSALM 24:9-10
Why are there questions and answers in Psalm 24?

This psalm, often set to music, was probably used in corporate worship. It may have been re-enacted many times at the temple. The people outside would call out to the temple gates to open up and let the King of glory in. From inside, the priests or another group would ask, "Who is this King of glory?" Outside, the people would respond in unison, "The LORD strong and mighty, the LORD mighty in battle," proclaiming his great power and strength. This would have been an important lesson for children who were participating. The exchange was then repeated, and the temple gates would swing open, symbolizing the people's desire to have God's presence among them.

AUGUST 1

Q 2 CHRONICLES 31:1ff.
What was the importance of Hezekiah's rule in Judah?

King Hezekiah was one of the few kings of Judah who was constantly aware of God's acts in the past and his interest in the events of every day. He was the fifteenth king of Judah, the southern kingdom; his father was Ahaz and his mother was Abi. The prophets active during his reign were Isaiah, Hosea, and Micah. The Bible describes Hezekiah as a king who had a close relationship with God. Judah was filled with visual reminders of their lack of trust in God, and Hezekiah boldly cleaned house. Altars, idols, and pagan temples were destroyed. Even the bronze serpent Moses had made in the desert was not spared because it had ceased to point the people to God and had also become an idol. The temple in Jerusalem, whose doors had been nailed shut by Hezekiah's own father, was cleaned out and reopened. The Passover was re-instituted as a national holiday, and there was revival in Judah. Hezekiah had a natural inclination to respond to present problems but his life shows little evidence of concern about the future. He took few actions to preserve the effects of his sweeping reforms. His successful efforts made him proud. His unwise display of wealth to the Babylonian delegation got Judah included on Babylon's "Nations to Conquer" list. When Isaiah informed Hezekiah of the foolishness of his act, the king's answer displayed his persistent lack of fore-sight—he was thankful that any evil consequences would be delayed until after he died. And the lives of three kings who followed him—Manasseh, Amon, and Josiah—were deeply affected by both Hezekiah's accomplishments *and* his weaknesses. A key passage that describes Hezekiah is 2 Kings 18:5-6: "He trusted very strongly in the Lord God of Israel. In fact, none of the kings before or after him were as close to God as he was. For he followed the Lord in everything, and carefully obeyed all of God's commands to Moses" (TLB). Hezekiah's story is told in 2 Kings 16:20–20:21; 2 Chronicles 28:27–32:33; Isaiah 36:1–39:8. He is also mentioned in Proverbs 25:1; Isaiah 1:1; Jeremiah 15:4; 26:18-19; Hosea 1:1; Micah 1:1.

AUGUST 2

2 Chronicles 32:1–33:13; Romans 15:23–16:7; Psalms 25:16-22; Proverbs 20:16-18

2 CHRONICLES 32:3-4
Why would Hezekiah plug the springs that gave Jerusalem its water?

Cities had to be built near reliable water sources. Natural springs were some of Jerusalem's major sources of water. In a brilliant military move, Hezekiah plugged the springs outside the city and channeled the water through an underground tunnel (2 Chron. 32:30); therefore, Jerusalem would have water even through a long siege. The tunnel has been discovered along with an inscription describing how it was built: two groups of workers started digging underground, one in Jerusalem and one at the Gihon Spring, meeting in the middle.

ROMANS 15:23-24
Where was Paul when he wrote Romans? Did he go to Spain?

Paul was referring to the completion of his work in Corinth, the city from which he most likely wrote this letter. Most of Paul's three-month stay in Achaia (see Acts 20:3) was probably spent in Corinth. He believed that he had accomplished what God wanted him to do there, and he was looking forward to taking the gospel to new lands west of Rome. When Paul eventually went to Rome, however, it was as a prisoner (see Acts 28). Tradition says that Paul was released for a time, and that he used this opportunity to go to Spain to preach the Good News. This journey is not mentioned in the book of Acts.

ROMANS 16:1
Who was Phoebe?

Phoebe was known as a servant (the Greek word used here is often translated "deacon") and a helper. Apparently she was a wealthy person who helped support Paul's ministry. Phoebe was highly regarded in the church, and she may have delivered this letter from Corinth to Rome. This provides evidence that women had important roles in the early church.

ROMANS 16:3
Who were Priscilla and Aquila?

Priscilla and Aquila were a married couple who had become Paul's close friends. They, along with all other Jews, had been expelled from Rome by the emperor (Acts 18:2-3) and had moved to Corinth. There they met Paul and invited him to live with them and share their work as tentmakers. They were Christians before they met Paul, and probably told him much about the Roman church. They helped believers in Ephesus (Acts 18:18-28), in Rome when they were allowed to return, and again at Ephesus (2 Tim. 4:19).

AUGUST 3

2 Chronicles 33:14–34:33; Romans 16:8-27; Psalms 26:1-12; Proverbs 20:19

2 CHRONICLES 34:3
Wasn't Josiah too young to be a king?

In Josiah's day, boys were considered men at age 12. By 16, Josiah understood the responsibility of his office. Even at this young age, he showed greater wisdom than many of the older kings who came before him because he had decided to seek the Lord God and his wisdom. Josiah's great-grandfather was Hezekiah and they were alike in many ways. Both had close, personal relationships with God. Both were passionate reformers and bright lights of obedience to God among kings with darkened consciences. At a young age, Josiah already understood that there was spiritual sickness in his land and he was outstanding in his efforts to bring revival to the people.

ROMANS 16:26, KJV
What does Paul mean by "the scriptures of the prophets"?

Paul refers, no doubt, to some of his own writings, in which the mystery which was kept secret for many ages has been revealed. Apparently he knew of other New Testament prophetic writings that were in existence at the time of this writing. The Holy Spirit saw to it that what God wanted known to men was put into written form, even as the Old Testament had been put down in writing for its own preservation and for the prevention of errors creeping into the life of Israel and the church.

ROMANS 16:13, KJV
Was Rufus Paul's brother, since Paul greets "his mother and mine" in the same verse?

No, Rufus' mother had cared for Paul. *The Living Bible* renders this verse, ". . . his dear mother who has been such a mother to me." Rufus is mentioned in the Gospel of Mark (15:21) as the son of Simon of Cyrene who was forced to carry Jesus' cross. Mark presumably refers to Rufus because Rufus was known in Rome when Mark's gospel was published there.

PSALM 26:12, KJV
What is the meaning of the phrase "My foot standeth in an even place"?

This verse can also be translated, "My feet stand on level ground." The Living Bible says that David was praising "the Lord for keeping [him] from slipping and falling." David was not saying that God always prevents us from slipping or falling into sin (although he often does). Instead, David was saying that as long as he trusted in God, he could stand on the firm foundation of God's Word and have a godly perspective on life.

AUGUST 4

2 CHRONICLES 35:20-25
When was Josiah killed?

This event occurred in 609 B.C. Nineveh, the Assyrian capital, had been destroyed three years earlier by the Babylonians. The defeated Assyrians regrouped at Haran and Carchemish, but Babylon sent its army to destroy them once and for all. Pharaoh Neco, who wanted to make Egypt a world power, was worried about Babylon's growing strength, so he marched his army north through Judah to help the Assyrians at Carchemish. But King Josiah of Judah tried to prevent Neco from passing through his land on his way to Carchemish. Josiah was killed, and Judah became subject to Egypt. Neco went on to Carchemish and held off the Babylonians for four years, but in 605 he was soundly defeated, and Babylon moved into the spotlight as the dominant world power.

1 CORINTHIANS 7:1
When did Paul write 1 Corinthians?

Paul wrote this letter to the church in Corinth while he was visiting Ephesus during his third missionary journey (A.D. 55, Acts 19:1–20:1). Corinth and Ephesus faced each other across the Aegean Sea. Paul knew the Corinthian church well because he had spent 18 months in Corinth during his second missionary journey (Acts 18:1-18). While in Ephesus, he had heard about problems in Corinth (1 Cor. 1:11). About the same time, a delegation from the Corinthian church had visited Paul to ask his advice about their conflicts (1 Cor. 16:17). Paul's purpose for writing was to correct those problems and to answer questions church members had asked in a previous letter.

1 CORINTHIANS 1:12ff.
Why was it a problem for the Corinthians to follow different teachers?

In this large and diverse Corinthian church, the believers favored different preachers. Because there was as yet no written New Testament, the believers depended heavily on preaching and teaching for spiritual insight into the meaning of the Old Testament. Some followed Paul, who had founded their church; some who had heard Peter (Cephas) in Jerusalem followed him; while others listened only to Apollos, an eloquent and popular preacher who had had a dynamic ministry in Corinth (Acts 18:24; 19:1). Although these three preachers were united in their message, their personalities attracted different people. At this time the church was in danger of dividing. By mentioning Jesus Christ ten times in the first ten verses, Paul makes it clear whom all preachers and teachers should emphasize.

AUGUST 5

Ezra 1:1–2:70; 1 Corinthians 1:18–2:5; Psalms 27:7-14; Proverbs 20:22-23

 **EZRA 1:1**
What is the historical setting of the Book of Ezra?

The Book of Ezra opens in 538 B.C., 48 years after Nebuchadnezzar destroyed Jerusalem, defeated the southern kingdom of Judah, and carried the Jews away to Babylon as captives. Nebuchadnezzar died in 562, and because his successors were not strong, Babylon was overthrown by Persia in 539, just prior to the events recorded in this book. Both the Babylonians and the Persians had a relaxed policy toward their captives, allowing them to own land and homes and to take ordinary jobs. Many Jews such as Daniel, Mordecai, and Esther rose to prominent positions within the nation. King Cyrus of Persia went a step further: he allowed many groups of exiles, including the Jews, to return to their homelands. By doing this, he hoped to win their loyalty and thus provide buffer zones around the borders of his empire. For the Jews this was a day of hope, a new beginning. Cyrus, king of Persia (559–530 B.C.), had already begun his rise to power in the Near East by unifying the Medes and Persians into a strong empire. As he conquered cities, he treated the inhabitants with mercy. Although not a servant of Yahweh, Cyrus was used by God to return the Jews to their homeland. Cyrus may have been shown the prophecy of Isaiah 44:28–45:6, written over a century earlier, which predicted that Cyrus himself would help the Jews return to Jerusalem. Daniel, a prominent government official (Dan. 5:29; 6:28), would have been familiar with the prophecy.

1 CORINTHIANS 1:23
Why did the Jews and Greeks reject Paul's preaching of Christ?

The Jews and the Greeks rejected Jesus for different reasons. The Jews required a sign and Jesus brought none. The Messiah was to be a great temporal prince and Jesus was not that. Because he did not come according to their ideas, they hated him and rejected him. The Greeks looked at Christ from the perspective of the wisdom of the world. They laughed at the idea of a crucified Savior and mocked unlearned and uneducated disciples who proclaimed Jesus as Lord. This sort of Savior neither suited their taste nor satisfied their vanity, so they rejected Jesus too. Paul preached a Jesus who was a stumbling-block to the Jews and foolishness to the Greeks (or Gentiles).

AUGUST 6

Ezra 3:1–4:24; 1 Corinthians 2:6–3:4; Psalms 28:1-9; Proverbs 20:24-25

EZRA 3:8
Why was the temple begun first, even before the city wall?

The temple was used for spiritual purposes; the wall, for military and political purposes. God had always been the nation's protector, and the Jews knew that the strongest stone wall would not protect them if God was not with them. They knew that putting their spiritual lives in order was a far higher priority than assuring the national defense.

EZRA 3:12
Why were people weeping when the temple's foundation was laid?

Fifty years after its destruction, the temple was being rebuilt (536 B.C.). Some of the older people remembered Solomon's temple, and they wept because the new temple would not be as glorious as the first one. Because the new temple was built on the foundation of Solomon's temple, the two structures were not that different in size. But the old temple was far more elaborate and ornate, and was surrounded by many buildings and a vast courtyard. Both temples were constructed of imported cedar wood, but Solomon's was decorated with vast amounts of gold and precious stones. Solomon's temple took over seven years to build; Zerubbabel's took about four years. Solomon's temple was at the hub of a thriving city; Zerubbabel's was surrounded by ruins. No wonder the people wept.

EZRA 4:6-23
Why did Ezra write so much about those who opposed him?

In these verses, Ezra summarizes the entire story of the opposition to building the temple, the walls, and other important buildings in Jerusalem. Chronologically, 4:6 fits between chapters 6 and 7; 4:7-23 refers to the events between Ezra 7 and Nehemiah 1. Ezra grouped them here to highlight the persistent opposition to God's people over the years and God's ability to overcome it.

1 CORINTHIANS 3:1-3
Why did Paul call the Christians at Corinth babies?

Paul called the Corinthians infants in the Christian life because they were not yet spiritually healthy and mature. The proof was that they quarreled like children, allowing divisions to distract them. Immature Christians are "worldly," controlled by their own desires; mature believers are in tune with God's desires.

AUGUST 7

Ezra 5:1–6:22; 1 Corinthians 3:5-23; Psalms 29:1-11; Proverbs 20:26-27

EZRA 5:13
Was Cyrus king of Persia or king of Babylon (Ezra 5:13)?

Because Persia had just conquered Babylon, Cyrus was king of both nations. Babylon is more important to this story because it was the location of the Hebrews' 70-year captivity. The Babylon mentioned in Ezra 5:17 may refer to the city of Babylon, which was the capital of the nation of Babylon.

1 CORINTHIANS 3:22, TLB
Paul says that both life and death are our servants. How can this be?

While nonbelievers are victims of life, swept along by its current and wondering if there is meaning to it, believers can use life well because they understand its true purpose. Nonbelievers can only fear death. For believers, however, death holds no terrors because Christ has conquered all fears (see 1 John 4:18). Through him, they will live eternally in God's presence.

PROVERBS 20:27
Is my spirit the same as my conscience?

The conscience is one function of the human spirit. The spirit God placed in each human being gives light to gauge the rightness of every thought and motive and gives the ability to make prudent decisions. John 3:6 says that the human spirit is reborn by the Holy Spirit. Through this regenerated spirit it is possible for humanity to attain the purposes for which they were created by God.

EZRA 6:16
What happened to the temple built during Ezra's time?

Ezra contains the last mention of the temple in the Old Testament. This second temple built by the returned remnant from Babylon never attained the glory of Solomon's temple nor was the kingship restored after the captivity. Nowhere do the Scriptures state specifically that the glory of God filled the second temple as he did the first. In this account nothing is said about a high priest nor is there any mention of an ark of the covenant. The two tables of the law, which were apparently destroyed when Solomon's temple was burned, were not in the new temple. The second temple was enlarged and beautified by Herod the Great and his successors. It was destroyed in A.D. 70 when the Roman armies sacked Jerusalem. The site of the temple at Ornan's threshing floor on Mount Moriah is now occupied by The Dome of the Rock, a Moslem mosque and holy place.

AUGUST 8

Ezra 7:1–8:20; 1 Corinthians 4:1-21; Psalms 30:1-12; Proverbs 20:28-30

EZRA 7:6
When did Ezra return to Jerusalem?

There is a gap of almost 60 years between the events of chapters six and seven. The story in the Book of Esther occurred during this time, in the reign of Xerxes, who ruled from 486–465 B.C. Artaxerxes, his son, became king in 465, and Ezra returned to Jerusalem in 458, eighty years after the first exiles returned to Jerusalem (Ezra 2:1). This was his first trip to Jerusalem, and it took four months. The temple was completed in 516 B.C. and had been standing for about 58 years. Up to this point in the narrative, Ezra had remained in Babylon, probably compiling a record of the events that had taken place. Why did he have to ask the king if he could return? Ezra wanted to lead many Jews back to Jerusalem, and he needed a decree from the king stating that any Jew who wanted to return could do so. This decree would be like a passport in case they ran into opposition along the way.

1 CORINTHIANS 4:15
Why did Paul call himself the Corinthians' father?

This verse contrasts a child's guardian (NRSV, NIV) with the child's father. In Paul's day, a guardian was a slave who was assigned as a special tutor and caretaker of a child. Paul was portraying his special affection for the Corinthians (greater than a slave) and his special role (more than a caretaker). In an attempt to unify the church, Paul appealed to his relationship with them. By *father,* he meant he was the church's founder. Because he started the church, he could be trusted to have its best interests at heart. Paul's tough words were motivated by love—like the love a good father has for his children (see also 1 Thess. 2:11).

1 CORINTHIANS 4:16, KJV
If Paul didn't want the Corinthians to divide over their favorite teacher why did he tell them to follow him?

Paul was telling the Corinthians to imitate him like a father. He was able to make this statement because he walked close to Christ, spent time in Christ's Word and in prayer, and was aware of Christ's presence in his life at all times. Christ was Paul's example; therefore, Paul's life could be an example to other Christians. Paul wasn't expecting others to imitate everything he did, but they should imitate those aspects of his beliefs and conduct that were modeling Christ's way of living.

AUGUST 9

Ezra 8:21–9:15; 1 Corinthians 5:1-13; Psalms 31:1-8; Proverbs 21:1-2

Q EZRA 8:21
How far did Ezra travel to get from Babylon to Jerusalem?

Ezra and the people traveled approximately nine hundred miles on foot. The trip took them through dangerous and difficult territory and lasted about four months. They prayed that God would give them a safe journey.

Q EZRA 9:1-3
What was wrong with the Jewish men marrying non-Jewish women?

Since the time of the judges, Israelite men had married pagan women and then adopted their religious practices (Judg. 3:5-7). Even Israel's great King Solomon was guilty of this sin (1 Kings 11:1-8). Although this practice was forbidden in God's law (Exod. 34:11-16; Deut. 7:1-4), it happened in Ezra's day, and again only a generation after him (Neh. 13:23-27). Opposition to mixed marriage was not racial prejudice because Jews and non-Jews of this area were of the same Semitic background. The reasons were strictly spiritual. A person who married a pagan was inclined to adopt that person's pagan beliefs and practices.

Q 1 CORINTHIANS 5:5, NRSV
Why should the church "hand this man over to Satan"?

This means to exclude him from the fellowship of believers. Without the spiritual support of Christians, this man would be left alone with his sin and Satan, and perhaps this emptiness would drive him to repentance. "That the sinful nature may be destroyed" implies the hope that the experience would bring him to God to destroy his sinful nature through repentance. *Sinful nature* could mean his body or flesh. This alternative translation would imply that Satan would afflict him physically and thus bring him to God. Putting someone out of the church should be a last resort in disciplinary action.

Q 1 CORINTHIANS 5:6
Why does Paul write about yeast and dough?

Paul was writing to those who wanted to ignore the church problem explained above. They didn't realize that allowing public sin to exist in the church affects all its members. Paul did not expect anyone to be sinless—all believers struggle with sin daily. Instead, he was speaking against those who deliberately sin, feel no guilt, and refuse to repent. This kind of sin cannot be tolerated in the church because it affects others. Yeast makes bread dough rise. A little bit affects the whole batch. Blatant sins, left uncorrected, confuse and divide the congregation.

AUGUST 10

Ezra 10:1-44; 1 Corinthians 6:1-20; Psalms 31:9-18; Proverbs 21:3

EZRA 10:3
Why were the men commanded to send away their wives and children?

Although the measure was extreme, intermarriage to pagans was strictly forbidden (Deut. 7:3-4), and even the priests and Levites had intermarried. Although a severe solution, it involved only 113 of the approximately 29,000 families. Ezra's strong act, though very difficult for some, was necessary to preserve Israel as a nation committed to God. Some of the exiles of the northern kingdom of Israel had lost both their spiritual and physical identity through intermarriage. Their pagan spouses had caused the people to worship idols. Ezra did not want this to happen to the exiles of the southern kingdom of Judah.

1 CORINTHIANS 6:12-13
Does 1 Corinthians 6:12-13 mean that I should deny the needs of my body in order to be spiritual?

Many of the world's religions teach that the soul or spirit is important but the body is not; and Christianity has sometimes been influenced by these ideas. In truth, however, Christianity takes very seriously the realm of the physical. We worship a God who created a physical world and pronounced it good. He promises us a new earth where real people have transformed physical lives—not a pink cloud where disembodied souls listen to harp music. At the heart of Christianity is the story of God himself taking on flesh and blood and coming to live with us, offering both physical healing and spiritual restoration. We humans, like Adam, are a combination of dust and spirit. Just as our spirits affect our bodies, so our physical bodies affect our spirits. We cannot commit sin with our bodies without damaging our souls because our bodies and souls are inseparably joined. In the new earth we will have resurrection bodies that are not corrupted by sin. Then we will enjoy the fullness of our salvation.

1 CORINTHIANS 6
Why does Paul speak so much about fornication and prostitution in 1 Corinthians 6?

This teaching about sexual immorality and prostitutes was especially important for the Corinthian church because the temple of the love-goddess Aphrodite was in Corinth. This temple employed more than a thousand prostitutes as priestesses, and sex was part of the worship ritual. Paul clearly stated that Christians are to have no part in sexual immorality, even if it is acceptable and popular in our culture.

AUGUST 11

Nehemiah 1:1–3:14; 1 Corinthians 7:1-24; Psalms 31:19-24; Proverbs 21:4

NEHEMIAH 1:3
Why were the walls of Jerusalem so important to Nehemiah?

Walls mean little in most present-day cities, but in Nehemiah's day they were essential. They offered safety from raids and symbolized strength and peace. Nehemiah also mourned for his people, the Jews, who had been stifled by a previous edict that kept them from rebuilding their walls (Ezra 4:6-23).

NEHEMIAH 1:2-4
Why did Nehemiah weep about Jerusalem?

Nehemiah was concerned about Jerusalem because it was the Jews' holy city. As Judah's capital city, it represented Jewish national identity, and it was blessed with God's special presence in the temple. Jewish history centered around the city from the time of Abraham's gifts to Melchizedek, king of Salem (Gen. 14:17-20), to the days when Solomon built the glorious temple (1 Kings 7:51) and throughout the history of the kings. Nehemiah loved his homeland even though he had lived his whole life in Babylon. He wanted to return to Jerusalem to reunite the Jews and to remove the shame of Jerusalem's broken-down walls. This would bring glory to God and restore the reality and power of God's presence among his people.

1 CORINTHIANS 7:1-24
Was there a special situation in the church in Corinth that caused Paul to write so much about marriage?

Christians in Corinth were surrounded by sexual temptation. The city had a reputation even among pagans for sexual immorality and religious prostitution. It was to this kind of society that Paul delivered these instructions on sex and marriage. The Corinthians needed special, specific instructions because of their culture's immoral standards. For more on Paul's teaching about marriage, see Ephesians 5. The Corinthian church was in turmoil because of the immorality of the culture around them. Some Greeks, in rejecting immorality, rejected sex and marriage altogether. The Corinthian Christians wondered if this was what they should do also, so they asked Paul several questions: "Because sex is perverted, shouldn't we also abstain in marriage?" "If my spouse is unsaved, should I seek a divorce?" "Should unmarried people and widows remain unmarried?" Paul answered many of these questions by saying, "For now, stay put. Be content in the situation where God has placed you. If you're married, don't seek to be single. If you're single, don't seek to be married. Live God's way, one day at a time, and he will show you what to do."

AUGUST 12

 ## NEHEMIAH 4:1-2
What was a "Samaritan"?

The word Samaritan is used for the first time in the Bible in the Book of Nehemiah. Almost three hundred years before Nehemiah's time, the northern kingdom of Israel was conquered, and most of the people were carried away captive (722 B.C.). Sargon of Assyria repopulated Israel with captives from other lands. These captives eventually intermarried with the few Israelites who remained in the land to form a mixed race of people who became known as Samaritans. The Jews who returned to Jerusalem and the southern region of Judea during the days of Ezra and Nehemiah would have nothing to do with Samaritans, whom they considered to be racially impure. Relations between both groups grew progressively worse—four hundred years later, the Jews and Samaritans hated each other (John 4:9).

1 CORINTHIANS 7:36-38
Is Paul speaking of the bridegroom or the father of the bride?

The bridegroom is much more suitable to the context, for Paul is encouraging appropriate behavior on the part of a man toward his fiancé. This interpretation is reflected in the NIV.

AUGUST 13

Nehemiah 5:14–7:60; 1 Corinthians 8:1-13; Psalms 33:1-11; Proverbs 21:8-10

NEHEMIAH 7:3
Why were the city gates so important to Nehemiah?

Jerusalem was a large city, and because many roads converged there, it required many gates. The wall on each side of these heavy wooden gates was taller and thicker so soldiers could stand guard to defend the gates against attack. Sometimes two stone towers guarded the gate. In times of peace, the city gates were hubs of activity—city council was held there, and shopkeepers set up their wares at the entrance. City gates were usually opened at sunrise, enabling merchants to enter and set up their tent-stores. Nehemiah didn't want Jerusalem to be caught unprepared by an enemy attack, so he ordered the gates closed until well after sunrise when the people were sure to be awake and alert.

NEHEMIAH 7:5ff.
Why did Nehemiah value the genealogies?

Genealogies were greatly valued because it was vitally important for a Jew to be able to prove that he or she was a descendant of Abraham and was, therefore, one of God's people (Gen. 12:1-3; 15; Exod. 19:5-6; Deut. 11:22-28). A lost genealogy put one's status as a Jew at risk. Because this genealogy is almost identical to Ezra's (Ezra 2), most likely Ezra's list was stored in the temple archives and was the one Nehemiah found.

1 CORINTHIANS 8:1ff.
Why does Paul talk about "food sacrificed to idols"?

Paul was answering one of the questions the Corinthians had about whether or not Christians should eat meat that had been offered to idols in the heathen temples. The problem arose because when large religious celebrations or state sacrifices were held, thousands of animals would be offered, and the greater part of the meat would be sold to the butcher shops to be bought by the public. Thus the Christian was constantly exposed to the possibility of buying or eating this meat, which had been forbidden by Jewish law (Num. 25:2; Ps. 106:28). The apostles had also banned it in their decree from Jerusalem (Acts 15:20, 29; 21:25), but Paul does not refer here to that decision. Rather, he bases his instructions on his own apostolic authority.

AUGUST 14

Nehemiah 7:61–9:21; 1 Corinthians 9:1-18; Psalms 33:12-22; Proverbs 21:11-12

NEHEMIAH 8:1
Was Ezra living during the time of Nehemiah?

Ezra and Nehemiah were contemporaries (Neh. 8:9), although Ezra was probably much older. This is the first mention of Ezra in this book. He had arrived in Jerusalem from Babylon 13 years before Nehemiah (458 B.C., see Ezra 7:6-9). Nehemiah, as governor, was the political leader; and Ezra, as priest and scribe, was the religious leader. A scribe in these days was a combination lawyer, notary public, scholar, and consultant. Scribes were among the most educated people, so they were teachers. No doubt the Jews would have liked to set up the kingdom again as in the days of David, but this would have signaled rebellion against the king of Persia to whom they were subject. The best alternative was to divide the leadership between Nehemiah, the governor, and Ezra, the official religious leader. It is significant that Nehemiah was a layman, not a member of the religious establishment or a prophet. He was motivated by his relationship with God, and he devoted his life to doing God's will in a secular world.

1 CORINTHIANS 9:7
What does 1 Corinthians 9:7 have to do with Paul's apostleship?

Paul is reduced to defending the right of the ministry to receive wages for their services. A soldier of war cannot be expected to support himself when he serves in the army. Those who are benefited by his services are to support him. A shepherd has a right to milk his flock to live, and whoever tends a vineyard has a right to eat of its fruit. In verse 9, Paul uses Moses' words, "Thou shalt not muzzle the mouth of the ox that treadeth out the corn" (Deut. 25:4, KJV). If God cares enough for animals to let them feed from their labors, does he not also care for preachers, intending that their listeners should support them?

PSALM 33:18-19
Is Psalm 33:18-19 a guarantee that all believers will be delivered from death and starvation?

No, thousands of Christians have been beaten to death, whipped, fed to lions, or executed because of their faith in Jesus Christ (Rom. 8:35-36; Heb. 11:32-40). God can (and often miraculously does) deliver his followers from pain and death, though sometimes, for purposes known only to him, he chooses not to. When faced with these harsh realities, we must focus on the wise judgments of God. The writer was pleading for God's watchful care and protection.

AUGUST 15

Nehemiah 9:22–10:39;1 Corinthians 9:19–10:13; Psalms 34:1-10; Proverbs 21:13

NEHEMIAH 9:38
What were the terms of the covenant mentioned in Nehemiah 9:38ff.)?

This binding agreement or covenant between the people and God had six provisions. They agreed to: (1) not marry non-Jewish neighbors (10:30), (2) observe the Sabbath (10:31), (3) observe every seventh year as a sabbath year (10:31), (4) pay a temple tax (10:32-33), (5) supply wood for the burnt offerings in the temple (10:34), and (6) give dues to the temple (10:35-38). After years of decadence and exile, the people once again took seriously their responsibility to follow God and keep his laws wholeheartedly.

1 CORINTHIANS 9:27
Did Paul think he could lose his salvation?

When Paul says he might be disqualified (NIV), he does not mean that he could lose his salvation, but rather that he could lose his apostolic privilege of telling others about Christ and that his preaching would be disapproved.

1 CORINTHIANS 10:7-10
Where are the events of 1 Corinthians 10:7-10 recorded in the Old Testament?

The incident referred to in 10:7 is when the Israelites made a golden calf and worshiped it in the desert (Exod. 32). The incident in 10:8 is recorded in Numbers 25:1-9 when the Israelites worshiped Baal of Peor and engaged in sexual immorality with Moabite women. The reference in 10:9 is to the Israelites' complaint about their food (Num. 21:5-6). They put the Lord to the test by seeing how far they could go. In 10:10, Paul refers to when the people complained against Moses and Aaron and the resulting plague (Num. 14:2, 36). The destroying angel is referred to in Exodus 12:23.

1 CORINTHIANS 10:11
Did Paul think the world would end in his lifetime?

No one, including Paul and Jesus, knew when the end of the world would come. In Mark 13:32 Jesus said, "No one, not even the angels in heaven, nor I myself, knows the day or hour when these things will happen; only the Father knows" (TLB). For all practical purposes, however, we have been living in the last days since Christ's ascension. We are to be ready for Christ's return at any moment.

AUGUST 16

NEHEMIAH 11:1-2
Why did people have to be selected and volunteer to live in Jerusalem?

The exiles who returned were few in number compared to Jerusalem's population in the days of the kings. And because the walls had been rebuilt on their original foundations, the city seemed sparsely populated. Nehemiah asked one-tenth of the people from the outlying areas to move inside the city walls to keep large areas of the city from being vacant. Apparently these people did not want to move into the city. Only a few people volunteered, and Nehemiah cast lots to determine who among the remaining people would have to move. Many of them may not have wanted to live in the city because (1) non-Jews attached a stigma to Jerusalem residents, often excluding them from trade because of their religious beliefs; (2) moving into the city meant rebuilding their homes and reestablishing their businesses, a major investment of time and money; (3) living in Jerusalem required stricter obedience to God's Word because of greater social pressure and proximity to the temple.

1 CORINTHIANS 10:16-21
Why was the food offered to idols such a problem to the believers in Corinth?

The idea of unity and fellowship with God through eating a sacrifice was strong in Judaism and Christianity as well as in paganism. In Old Testament days, when a Jew offered a sacrifice, he ate a part of that sacrifice as a way of restoring his unity with God, against whom he had sinned (Deut. 12:17-18). Similarly, Christians participate in Christ's once-for-all sacrifice when they eat the bread and drink the wine symbolizing his body and blood. Recent converts from paganism could not help being affected if they knowingly ate with pagans in their feast the meat offered to idols.

PSALM 34:19-20
Is the righteous man referred to in Psalm 34:19-20 Christ?

Yes, verse 20 says, "He protects all his bones, not one of them will be broken" (NIV). This is a prophecy about Christ when he was crucified. Although it was the Roman custom to break the legs of the victim to speed death, not one of Jesus' bones was broken (John 19:32-37). In addition to the prophetic meaning, David was pleading for God's protection in times of crisis.

AUGUST 17

Nehemiah 12:27–13:31; 1 Corinthians 11:3-16; Psalms 35:1-16; Proverbs 21:17-18

 **1 CORINTHIANS 11:3-11**
Aren't Paul's ideas about submission old-fashioned?

In the phrase, "the head of the woman is man," *head* is not used to indicate control or supremacy, but rather, "the source of." Because man was created first, the woman derives her existence from man, as man does from Christ and Christ from God. Evidently Paul was correcting some excesses in worship that the emancipated Corinthian women were engaging in. Submission is a key element in the smooth functioning of any business, government, or family. God ordained submission in certain relationships to prevent chaos. It is essential to understand that submission is not surrender, withdrawal, or apathy. It does not mean inferiority, because God created all people in his image and because all have equal value. Submission is mutual commitment and cooperation. Thus God calls for submission among *equals*. He did not make the man superior; he made a way for the man and woman to work together. Jesus Christ, although equal with God the Father, submitted to him to carry out the plan for salvation. Likewise, although equal to man under God, the wife should submit to her husband for the sake of their marriage and family. Submission between equals is submission by choice, not by force. We serve God in these relationships by willingly submitting to others in our church, to our spouses, and to our government leaders. God created men and women with unique and complementary characteristics. One sex is not better than the other. We must not let the issue of authority and submission become a wedge to destroy oneness in marriage. Instead, we should use our unique gifts to strengthen our marriages and to glorify God.

1 CORINTHIANS 11:14-15
What does head covering or the length of my hair have to do with my worship of God?

In talking about head coverings and length of hair, Paul is saying that believers should look and behave in ways that are honorable within their own culture. In many cultures long hair on men is considered appropriate and masculine. In Corinth, it was thought to be a sign of male prostitution in the pagan temples. And women with short hair were labeled prostitutes. Paul was saying that in the Corinthian culture, Christian women should keep their hair long. If short hair on women was a sign of prostitution, then a Christian woman with short hair would find it even more difficult to be a believable witness for Jesus Christ.

AUGUST 18

Esther 1:1–3:15; 1 Corinthians 11:17-34; Psalms 35:17-28; Proverbs 21:19-20

 ## ESTHER 1:1-3:15
What is the historical setting for the Book of Esther?

Esther's story begins in 483 B.C., 103 years after Nebuchadnezzar had taken the Jews into captivity (2 Kings 25), 54 years after Zerubbabel led the first group of exiles back to Jerusalem (Ezra 1–2), and 25 years before Ezra led the second group to Jerusalem (Ezra 7). Esther lived in the kingdom of Persia, the dominant kingdom in the Middle East after Babylon's fall in 539 B.C. Esther's parents must have been among those exiles who chose not to return to Jerusalem, even though Cyrus, the Persian king, had issued a decree allowing them to do so. The Jewish exiles had great freedom in Persia, and many remained because they had established themselves there or were fearful of the dangerous journey back to their homeland.

 ## 1 CORINTHIANS 11:20-34
What does the Lord's Supper mean?

The early church remembered that Jesus instituted the Lord's Supper on the night of the Passover meal (Luke 22:13-20). Just as Passover celebrated deliverance from slavery in Egypt, so the Lord's Supper celebrates deliverance from sin by Christ's death. Christians pose several different possibilities for what Christ meant when he said, "This is my body." (1) Some believe that the wine and bread actually become Christ's physical blood and body. (2) Others believe that the bread and wine remain unchanged, but Christ is spiritually present with the bread and wine. (3) Still others believe that the bread and wine symbolize Christ's body and blood. Christians generally agree, however, that participating in the Lord's Supper is an important event in Christian worship and that Christ's presence, however we understand it, strengthens us spiritually.

1 CORINTHIANS 11:25
What is the new covenant?

In the old covenant, people could approach God only through the priests and the sacrificial system. Jesus' death on the cross ushered in the new covenant or agreement between God and us. Now all people can personally approach God and communicate with him. The people of Israel entered into the old agreement after their exodus from Egypt (Exod. 19–20). It was designed to point to the day when Jesus Christ would come. The new covenant completes, rather than replaces, the old covenant, fulfilling everything the old covenant looked forward to (see Jer. 31:31-34). Eating the bread and drinking the cup shows that we are remembering Christ's death for us and renewing our commitment to serve him.

AUGUST 19

Esther 4:1–7:10; 1 Corinthians 12:1-26; Psalms 36:1-12; Proverbs 21:21-22

ESTHER 4:14, NKJV

Esther 4:14 says "relief and deliverance will arise for the Jews from another place." Did Mordecai mean that God would help the Jews?

In the ancient manuscripts God is not specifically mentioned in the Book of Esther, but it is obvious that Mordecai expected God to deliver his people. Though God is not mentioned directly, Esther and Mordecai believed in God's care. Because they acted at the right time, God used them to save his people.

PSALM 36:9, TLB

Is God a fountain?

This vivid image—"fountain of life"—is a poetic metaphor for God. It gives a sense of fresh, cleansing water that gives life to the spiritually thirsty. This same picture is used in Jeremiah 2:13, where God is called the "spring of living water." Jesus spoke of himself as living water that could quench thirst forever and give eternal life (John 4:14).

1 CORINTHIANS 12:1, TLB

What are the "special abilities" mentioned in 1 Corinthians 12:1?

The spiritual gifts given to each person by the Holy Spirit are special abilities that are to be used to minister to the needs of the body of believers. This chapter is not an exhaustive list of spiritual gifts; see Romans 12; Ephesians 4; 1 Peter 4:10-11 for more examples. There are many gifts, people have different gifts, some people have more than one gift, and one gift is not superior to another. All spiritual gifts come from the Holy Spirit, and their purpose is to build up Christ's body, the church.

1 CORINTHIANS 12:13, NRSV

What is the meaning of the phrase "we were all baptized into one body"?

The church is composed of many types of people backgrounds gifts. It is easy for these differences to divide people, as was the case in Corinth. But despite the differences, all believers have one thing in common—the Holy Spirit. On this essential reality the church finds unity. 1 Corinthians 12:13 means that all believers are baptized by one Holy Spirit into one body of believers, the church. We don't lose our individual identities, but we have an overriding oneness in Christ. When a person becomes a Christian, the Holy Spirit takes up residence, and he or she is born into God's family. "We were all given the one Spirit to drink" means that the same Holy Spirit completely fills our innermost beings.

AUGUST 20

Esther 8:1–10:3; 1 Corinthians 12:27–13:13; Psalms 37:1-11; Proverbs 21:23-24

ESTHER 10:3
Is there any official record, outside of the Bible, of Mordecai's position in Persia?

No archaeological records of Mordecai's being second-in-command have been discovered, but during this time there is a strange gap in ancient Persian records. The records indicate that another man held that position in 465 B.C., about seven years after Mordecai was first appointed. One tablet has been discovered naming Mardukaya as an official in the early years of Xerxes's reign; some believe this was Mordecai.

1 CORINTHIANS 12:30, NRSV
What is the gift called "various kinds of tongues"?

The New Testament refers to the gift of tongues several times. At Pentecost one of the miracles that attested to the advent of the Spirit was the gift of tongues. The Holy Spirit gave them this gift, and the languages they spoke were known languages of the various peoples who had come from afar to Jerusalem for Pentecost. In 1 Corinthians 12:20 the gift of tongues (expanded on in chapter 14) appears to be ecstatic utterances rather than known languages. Such tongues-speaking benefits the person who has the gift. Paul states that the use of tongues in the church must conform to certain requirements: (1) not more than two or three shall speak (1 Cor. 14:27); (2) they must speak in order, one at a time (1 Cor. 14:27); (3) women should be silent (1 Cor. 14:34). The private, devotional use of tongues is an individual matter. Not all tongues-speaking is genuine. Some do not believe that speaking in tongues belongs to this present age. Tongues-speaking, however, cannot be ruled out as a matter of principle during this present age. Paul classifies tongues as a lesser gift (1 Cor. 14:5). Speaking in tongues is not needed as a sign of regeneration or of sanctification.

1 CORINTHIANS 13:1, KJV
What is the meaning of "charity"?

The word is translated as *love* elsewhere in the New Testament. Beginning with this verse Paul compares love with such gifts as tongues, prophecy, understanding of mysteries, knowledge, faith, and giving of one's goods to feed the poor; and Paul concludes that where love is lacking, none of these gifts will benefit a man or woman.

AUGUST 21

Job 1:1–3:26; 1 Corinthians 14:1-17; Psalms 37:12-29; Proverbs 21:25-26

JOB 1:6-13
Who is Satan and why is he so evil?

Satan, originally an angel of God, became corrupt through his own pride. He has been evil since his rebellion against God (1 John 3:8). Satan considers God as his enemy. He tries to hinder God's work in people, but he is limited by God's power and can do only what he is permitted (Luke 22:31-32; 1 Tim. 1:19-20; 2 Tim. 2:23-26). Satan is called the enemy because he actively looks for people to attack with temptation (1 Pet. 5:8-9) and because he wants to make people hate God. He does this through lies and deception (Gen. 3:1-6). Job, a blameless and upright man who had been greatly blessed, was a perfect target for Satan. Any person who is committed to God should expect Satan's attacks. Satan, who hates God, also hates God's people. From this conversation, we learn a great deal about Satan. (1) He is accountable to God. All angelic beings, good and evil, are compelled to present themselves before God (Job 1:6). God knew that Satan was intent on attacking Job. (2) Satan can be at only one place at a time (Job 1:6-7). His demons aid him in his work; but as a created being, he is limited. (3) Satan cannot see into our minds or foretell the future (Job 1:9-11). If he could, he would have known that Job would not break under pressure. (4) Because Satan can do nothing without God's permission (Job 1:12), God's people can overcome his attacks through God's power. (5) God puts limitations on what Satan can do (Job 1:12; 2:6). Satan's response to the Lord's question (Job 1:7) tells us that Satan is real and active on earth. Knowing this about Satan should cause us to remain close to the One who is greater than Satan—God himself. Some people suggest that this dialogue was made up by the author of this book. Could this conversation between God and Satan really have happened? Other Bible passages tell us that Satan does indeed have access to God (see Rev. 12:10). He even went into God's presence to make accusations against Joshua the high priest (Zech. 3:1-2). If this conversation didn't take place, then the reasons for Job's suffering become meaningless and the Book of Job is reduced to fiction rather than fact.

AUGUST 22

Job 4:1–7:21; 1 Corinthians 14:18-40; Psalms 37:30-40; Proverbs 21:27

JOB 6:29-30
Was Job saying that he had never sinned?

Job referred to his own integrity, not because he was sinless, but because he had a right relationship with God. He was not guilty of the sins his friends accused him of (see chapter 31 for his summary of the life he had led). Another rendering of this verse could read, "My righteousness still stands." *Righteousness* is not the same as *sinlessness* (Rom. 3:23). No one but Jesus Christ has ever been sinless—free from all wrong thoughts and actions. Even Job needed to make some changes in his attitude toward God, as we will see by the end of the book. Nevertheless, Job was righteous (Job 1:8). He carefully obeyed God to the best of his ability in all aspects of his life.

1 CORINTHIANS 14:34-35
Does 1 Corinthians 14:34-35 mean that women should not speak in church services today?

It is clear from 1 Corinthians 11:5 that women prayed and prophesied in public worship. It is also clear in chapters 12–14 that women are given spiritual gifts and are encouraged to exercise them in the body of Christ. Women have much to contribute and can participate in worship services. In the Corinthian culture, women were not allowed to confront men in public. Apparently some of the women who had become Christians thought that their Christian freedom gave them the right to question the men in public worship. This was causing division in the church. In addition, women of that day did not receive formal religious education as did the men. Women may have been raising questions in the worship services that could have been answered at home without disrupting the services. Paul was asking the women not to flaunt their Christian freedom during worship. The purpose of Paul's words was to promote unity, not to teach about women's role in the church.

1 CORINTHIANS 14:2
What is Paul's view on speaking in tongues?

Paul makes several points about speaking in tongues: (1) it is a spiritual gift from God (1 Cor. 14:2); (2) it is a desirable gift even though it isn't a requirement of faith (1 Cor. 12:28-31); (3) it is less important than prophecy and teaching (1 Cor. 14:4). Although Paul himself spoke in tongues, he stresses prophecy (preaching) because it benefits the whole church, while speaking in tongues primarily benefits the speaker. Public worship must be understandable and edifying to the whole church.

AUGUST 23

Job 8:1–11:20; 1 Corinthians 15:1-28; Psalms 38:1-22; Proverbs 21:28-29

1 CORINTHIANS 15:9-10, NRSV
Did Paul have to work harder than the other apostles because he was the "least of the apostles"?

As a zealous Pharisee, Paul had been an enemy of the Christian church—even to the point of capturing and persecuting believers (see Acts 9:1-3). Thus he felt unworthy to be called an apostle of Christ. Though undoubtedly the most influential of the apostles, Paul was deeply humble. He knew that he had worked hard and accomplished much, but only because God had poured kindness and grace upon him. Paul wrote of working harder than the other apostles. This was not an arrogant boast because he knew that his power came from God and that it really didn't matter who worked hardest. Because of his prominent position as a Pharisee, Paul's conversion made him the object of even greater persecution than the other apostles; thus he had to work harder to preach the same message.

1 CORINTHIANS 15:12-28
Why didn't the Corinthian Christians believe there would be a resurrection?

Most Greeks did not believe that people's bodies would be resurrected after death. They saw the afterlife as something that happened only to the soul. According to Greek philosophers, the soul was the real person, imprisoned in a physical body, and at death the soul was released. There was no immortality for the body, but the soul entered an eternal state. Christianity, by contrast, affirms that the body and soul will be united after resurrection. The church at Corinth was in the heart of Greek culture. Thus many believers had a difficult time believing in a bodily resurrection. Paul wrote this part of his letter to clear up this confusion about the resurrection.

1 CORINTHIANS 15:19
Why does Paul say believers should be pitied if there were only earthly value to Christianity?

In Paul's day, Christianity often brought a person persecution, ostracism from family, and, in many cases, poverty. There were few tangible benefits from being a Christian in that society. It was certainly not a step up the social or career ladder. Even more important, however, is the fact that if Christ had not been resurrected from death, Christians could not be forgiven for their sins and would have no hope of eternal life.

AUGUST 24

Job 12:1–15:35; 1 Corinthians 15:29-58; Psalms 39:1-13; Proverbs 21:30-31

 ### 1 CORINTHIANS 15:29
Were people baptized for the dead?

Some believers may have been baptized on behalf of others who had died unbaptized. Nothing more is known about this practice, but it obviously affirms a belief in resurrection. Paul is not promoting baptism for the dead; he is illustrating his argument that the resurrection is a reality. This verse is unclear in its meaning to us today. It must have been quite clear to the Corinthians. Some have used this verse to support the view that we can undergo water baptism for relatives long since dead and by surrogate baptism they will obtain the forgiveness of sins and inherit eternal life. This notion supposes that those who are saved in this manner do not exercise personal faith and this contradicts every scripture that speaks of justification by faith alone. It is possible that this verse refers to the baptism of new believers who came to the faith through the death-bed witnessing of deceased believers. In this way their baptism would be "for the sake of the dead" believer through whom they had heard the gospel.

 ### 1 CORINTHIANS 15:35-58
What kind of body does 1 Corinthians 15 describe?

Paul compares the resurrection of our bodies with the growth in a garden. Seeds placed in the ground don't grow unless they "die" first. The plant that grows is very different-looking from the seed because God gives it a new "body." There are different kinds of bodies—people, animals, fish, birds. Even the angels in heaven have bodies that are different in beauty and glory. Our resurrected bodies will be very different in some ways, but not completely, from our earthly bodies. Our present bodies are perishable and prone to decay. Our resurrection bodies will be transformed. These spiritual bodies will not be limited by the laws of nature. This does not necessarily mean we'll be superpeople, but our bodies will be different from and more capable than our present earthly bodies. Our spiritual bodies will not be weak, will never get sick, and will never die. The Bible does not reveal everything that our resurrected bodies will be able to do, but we know they will be perfect, without sickness or disease (see Phil. 3:21).

AUGUST 25

Q JOB 19:25-27
Was Job referring to the resurrection in Job 19:25-27?

Job's ringing affirmation of confidence: "I know that my Redeemer lives" (NIV) seems to refer to resurrection. In ancient Israel a *redeemer* was a family member who bought a slave's way to freedom or who took care of a widow (see the note in Ruth 3:1). What tremendous faith Job had, especially in light of the fact that he was unaware of the conference between God and Satan. Job thought that God had brought all these disasters upon him! Faced with death and decay, Job still expected to see God—and he expected to do so in his body. When the book of Job was written, Israel did not have a well-developed doctrine of the resurrection. Although Job struggled with the idea that God was presently against him, he firmly believed that in the end God would be on his side. This belief was so strong that Job became one of the first to talk about the resurrection of the body. The doctrine of the resurrection appears in undeveloped form in the Old Testament. It awaits fuller explanation in the New Testament. (Among the Old Testament references to the resurrection are Ps. 16:10; 49:15; Isa. 26:19; Dan. 12:2; and Hos. 13:14.) In Jesus' day the Jews looked for the resurrection of the body (John 11:24; Heb. 6:1-2). It was denied by the Sadducees, the theological liberals of the day, whereas it was basic to Pharisaic teaching (Acts 23:6-8). Jesus believed and taught the resurrection of the body (Matt. 22:29-32; Luke 14:14; John 5:28-29). The early apostles preached it constantly and consistently (Acts 4:2; 17:18; 24:15). The central theme of the Christian hope is the resurrection of the dead. This doctrine has its foundation in the resurrection of Jesus, a historical event. Some Bible translations of Job 19:26 say, "Then even without my flesh I shall see God." This does not fit well with 19:27, where Job says that he will see God with his own eyes. Most translators today agree that the better translation is "in my flesh I shall see God." In Job's situation, it seemed unlikely that he would, in his flesh, see God. This is the point of Job's faith! He was confident that God's justice would triumph, even if it would take a miracle like resurrection to accomplish this.

AUGUST 26

Job 20:1–22:30; 2 Corinthians 1:1-11; Psalms 40:11-17; Proverbs 22:2-4

 ## 2 CORINTHIANS 1:1-11
Why did Paul write 2 Corinthians?

Paul visited Corinth on his second missionary journey and founded a church there (Acts 18:1ff). He later wrote several letters to the believers in Corinth, two of which are included in the Bible. Paul's first letter to the Corinthians is lost (1 Cor. 5:9-11), his second letter to them is our book of 1 Corinthians, his third letter is lost (see 2 Cor. 2:6-9; 7:12), and his fourth letter is our book of 2 Corinthians. Second Corinthians was written less than a year after 1 Corinthians. Paul wrote 1 Corinthians to deal with divisions in the church. When his advice was not taken and their problems weren't solved, Paul visited Corinth a second time. That visit was painful both for Paul and for the church (2 Cor. 2:1). He then planned a third visit, but delayed it and wrote 2 Corinthians instead (A.D. 56). After writing 2 Corinthians, Paul visited Corinth once more (Acts 20:2-3). 2 Corinthians is not a theological treatise, nor does it have the systematic and ordered appearance characteristic of 1 Corinthians. In this letter, the apostle runs the gamut of human emotions: despair, joy, ecstatic elation, sarcasm, and even threats mark the progress of the epistle. One sees in it the deep currents of a pastor's sense of rejection by his beloved children whom he has brought to Christ, followed by a sense of relief and joy when the crisis is over and the dissidents have been reconciled to him. Even though the letter is after the fact, Paul makes a passionate and detailed response to the attacks leveled against his apostolic commission and authority. Later in the letter, he defends his authority in relation to his person.

 ## 2 CORINTHIANS 1:2
What kind of city was Corinth?

The Romans had made Corinth the capital of Achaia (the southern half of present-day Greece). The city was a flourishing trade center because of its seaport. With the thousands of merchants and sailors who disembarked there each year, it had developed a reputation as one of the most immoral cities in the ancient world; its many pagan temples encouraged the practice of sexual immorality along with idol worship. In fact, the Greek word "to Corinthianize" came to mean "to practice sexual immorality." A Christian church in the city would face many pressures and conflicts.

AUGUST 27

Job 23:1–27:23; 2 Corinthians 1:12–2:11; Psalms 41:1-13; Proverbs 22:5-6

JOB 23:9
When Job was seeking for God did he think God lived in one particular place?

This verse can also be translated, "When I look to the left or right (north or south), I can't find God." Job was not saying that God lives in any one place, but that he appeared to be avoiding him. In Job 23:10, however, he expressed confidence that God knew every detail about his situation and would come to his rescue.

JOB 25:6
Does God consider humanity as worms?

It is important to understand that Bildad, not God, was calling man a worm. Human beings are created in God's image (Gen. 1:26-27). Psalm 8:5 says that man is "a little lower than the heavenly beings." Bildad may have simply been using a poetic description to contrast our worth to the worth and power of God.

2 CORINTHIANS 1:17
Why was it a problem for Paul to change his plans?

Paul's change of plans caused some of his accusers to say that he couldn't be trusted, hoping to undermine his authority. Paul said that he was not the type of person to say "yes" when he meant "no." Paul explained that it was not indecision but concern for their feelings that forced him to change his plans. The reason for his trip—to bring joy (2 Cor. 1:24)—could not be accomplished with the present crisis. Paul didn't want to visit them only to rebuke them severely (2 Cor. 1:23). Just as the Corinthians could trust God to keep his promises, they could trust Paul as God's representative to keep his. He would still visit them, but at a better time.

PSALM 41:9, TLB
Who was David's "best friend"?

"Best friend" can also be translated "close friend." It is not known to whom David was referring here, but this verse is viewed in the New Testament as a prophecy of Christ's betrayal (John 13:18). Judas, one of Jesus' twelve disciples, had spent three years learning from Jesus, traveling and eating with him (Mark 3:14-19), handling the finances for the group. Eventually Judas, who was not Jesus' closest friend but knew Jesus extremely well, betrayed him (Matt. 26:14-16, 20-25).

AUGUST 28

Job 28:1–30:31; 2 Corinthians 2:12-17; Psalms 42:1-11; Proverbs 22:7

Q JOB 28:28
What does it mean to fear the Lord?

"The fear of the Lord" is a key theme in the wisdom literature of the Bible (Job through the Song of Songs). It means to have respect and reverence for God and to be in awe of his majesty and power. This is the starting point to finding real wisdom (see Prov. 1:7-9).

Q 2 CORINTHIANS 2:13
Who was Titus?

Titus was a Greek convert whom Paul greatly loved and trusted (the book of Titus is a letter that Paul wrote to him). Titus was one of the men responsible for collecting the money for the poverty-stricken Jerusalem church (2 Cor. 8:6). Paul may also have sent Titus with the sorrowful letter. On his way to Macedonia, Paul was supposed to meet Titus in Troas. When Paul didn't find him there, he was worried for Titus's safety and left Troas to search for him in Macedonia. There Paul found him (2 Cor. 7:6), and the good news that Paul received (2 Cor. 7:8-16) led to this letter. Paul would send Titus back to Corinth with this letter (2 Cor. 8:16-17).

Q 2 CORINTHIANS 2:16, NKJV
Why does Paul say that he and the apostles are "the aroma of death to death" and "the aroma of life to life"?

In a Roman triumphal procession, the Roman general would display his treasures and captives amidst a cloud of incense burned for the gods. To the victors, the aroma was sweet; to the captives in the parade, who would be put to death after the procession, it was the smell of death. When Christians preach the gospel, it is good news to some and repulsive news to others. Believers recognize the life-giving fragrance of the message. To nonbelievers, however, it smells foul, like death—their own.

Q PSALM 42:1-11
Who was the author of Psalm 42?

Psalms 42–49 were written by the sons of Korah. Korah was a Levite who led a rebellion against Moses (Num. 16:1-35). He was killed, but his descendants remained faithful to God and continued to serve God in the temple. David appointed men from the clan of Korah to serve as choir leaders (1 Chron. 6:31-38), and they continued to be temple musicians for hundreds of years (2 Chron. 20:18-19).

AUGUST 29

2 CORINTHIANS 3:13-18
Why did Moses wear a veil on his face?

When Moses came down Mount Sinai with the Ten Commandments, his face glowed from being in God's presence (Exod. 34:29-35). Moses had to put on a veil to keep the people from being terrified by the brightness of his face. Paul adds that this veil kept them from seeing the radiance fade away. Moses and his veil illustrate the fading of the old system and the veiling of the people's minds and understanding by their pride, hardness of heart, and refusal to repent. The veil kept them from understanding the references to Christ in the Scriptures. When anyone becomes a Christian, Christ removes the veil (2 Cor. 3:16), giving eternal life and freedom from trying to be saved by keeping laws. And without the veil, we can be like mirrors reflecting God's glory.

2 CORINTHIANS 3:17
Is the Lord Jesus the Spirit?

When the Lord Jesus rose from the dead, he became a life-giving Spirit (1 Cor. 15:45). This does not mean that Jesus does not now have a body or that he became the Holy Spirit; it means that he entered into a new spiritual existence when he was glorified. As such, he can live in heaven and in the hearts of the believers at the same time. Admittedly, this is a mystery; but those who know that Christ lives within them appreciate the reality of his presence.

2 CORINTHIANS 3:18, KJV
What is the meaning of the term "from glory to glory"?

This phrase has also been translated "with ever-increasing glory" (NIV). The glory that the Spirit imparts to the believer is more excellent and lasts longer than the glory that Moses experienced. By gazing at Christ with unveiled minds, we can be more like him. In the gospel, we see the truth about Christ, and it transforms us morally as we understand and apply it. Through learning about Christ's life, we can understand how wonderful God is and what he is really like. As our knowledge deepens, the Holy Spirit helps us to change. Becoming Christlike is a progressive experience (see Rom. 8:29; Gal. 4:19; Phil. 3:21; 1 John 3:2).

AUGUST 30

JOB 36:26
Was Elihu saying that we cannot know God?

Elihu meant that finite man cannot comprehend an infinite God and can only know what God chooses to reveal. One theme in the poetic literature of the Bible is that God is incomprehensible; we cannot know him completely. We can have some knowledge about him, for the Bible is full of details about who God is, how we can know him, and how we can have an eternal relationship with him. But we can never know enough to answer all of life's questions (Eccles. 3:11), to predict our own future, or to manipulate God for our own ends. Life always creates more questions than we have answers, and we must constantly go to God for fresh insights into life's dilemmas.

PSALM 44:1-88
What event in history prompted the writing of Psalm 44?

This psalm may have been sung at an occasion like the one in 2 Chronicles 20:18-19, where the faithful Jehoshaphat was surrounded by enemies and the Levites sang to the Lord before the battle. However, this is a psalm for all seasons and for all people. It makes little difference whether the Spirit wrote this looking to the Babylonian captivity, the suffering of the Jews under Antiochus Epiphanes, or the future sufferings of the early church. God's people suffer in all ages and should raise their prayers to a faithful God for deliverance on the basis of God's steadfast, unchanging love.

PSALM 44:2, TLB
When did God drive the "heathen nations from the land"?

Driving out the nations refers to the conquest of Canaan (the promised land) described in the Book of Joshua. God gave the land to Israel—they were supposed to enter and drive out anyone who was wicked and opposed to God. Israel was told to settle the land and to be a witness to the world of God's power and love. Surrounded by enemies, the psalmist remembered what God had done for his people and took heart. It was God who planted Israel in Canaan. He gave his people victory over the inhabitants of the land. However great the victories were, they could not be attributed to the Israelites but to their God.

AUGUST 31

Job 37:1–39:30; 2 Corinthians 4:13–5:10; Psalms 44:9-26; Proverbs 22:13

JOB 38:1ff.
What was God's answer to Job?

Out of a whirlwind, or mighty storm, God spoke. Surprisingly, he didn't answer any of Job's questions; Job's questions were not at the heart of the issue. Instead, God used Job's ignorance of the earth's natural order to reveal his ignorance of God's moral order. If Job did not understand the workings of God's physical creation, how could he possibly understand God's mind and character? There is no standard or criterion higher than God himself by which to judge. God himself is the standard. Our only option is to submit to his authority and rest in his care. In Job 28:22-35 God stated that he has all the forces of nature at his command and can unleash or restrain them at will. No one completely understands such common occurrences as rain or snow, and no one can command them—only God who created them has that power. God's point was that if Job could not explain such common events in nature, how could he possibly explain or question God? And if nature is not ordered the way we might have thought, God's moral purposes may not be what we imagine either.

2 CORINTHIANS 5:1-10
If Paul was so spiritual why was he concerned about his body?

Paul contrasts our earthly bodies ("earthly tent") and our future resurrection bodies ("a building from God, an eternal house in heaven, not built by human hands"). Paul clearly states that our present bodies make us groan, but when we die we will not be spirits without bodies ("be found naked"). We will have new bodies that will be perfect for our everlasting life. Paul wrote as he did because the church at Corinth was in the heart of Greek culture, and many believers had difficulty with the concept of bodily resurrection. Greeks did not believe in a bodily resurrection. Most saw the afterlife as something that happened only to the soul, with the real person imprisoned in a physical body. They believed that at death the soul is released—there is no immortality for the body, and the soul enters an eternal state. But the Bible teaches that the body and soul are inseparable. Paul describes our resurrected bodies in more detail in 1 Corinthians 15:46-58. We will still have personalities and recognizable characteristics in our resurrected bodies, but through Christ's work, our bodies will be better than we can imagine. The Bible does not tell us everything about our resurrected bodies, but we know they will be perfect, without sickness, disease, or pain (see Phil. 3:21; Rev. 21:4).

SEPTEMBER 1

Job 40:1–42:17; 2 Corinthians 5:11-21; Psalms 45:1-17; Proverbs 22:14

JOB 40:15
What was a "behemoth"?

The behemoth was a large land animal, possibly the hippopotamus. It can be said that these are the mightiest of all God's animals. Nothing can withstand them. But God in his goodness did not make the hippopotamus carnivorous, because then many lives would be lost to feed them. They are aquatic and eat vegetation so other animals do not fear them, rather they play about the hippopotamus knowing there is no danger.

2 CORINTHIANS 5:14
Is the "love" in 2 Corinthians 5:14 Paul's love for Christ or Christ's love for him?

Paul is not saying that it is *his* love towards Christ that directs him, although that is quite true; here he speaks of Christ's love toward him and his fellow-workers. That love, which motivated Christ to die on the cross, is the love that moves them and causes them to endure all things.

2 CORINTHIANS 5:17, KJV
Is the "new creature" in 2 Corinthians 5:17 the same as the "new creation"?

For humanity, the *new creature* means he has become "a brand new person" (TLB) in Jesus Christ by regeneration or the new birth (Eph. 2:10); for the universe, the "new creation" means a new heaven and a new earth in eternity (2 Pet. 3:13; Isa. 65:17; Rom. 8:20-21).

2 CORINTHIANS 5:18
What is reconciliation?

Reconciliation occurred (1) through the death of God's Son (Rom. 5:10; Col. 1:22) and through his blood on the cross (Eph. 2:16; Col. 1:20). Here and in Romans 5 Paul uses reconciliation and justification as synonymous. Reconciliation is God's work, not man's; it is secured by faith, which grants to the recipient peace with God and immediate access to God (Eph. 2:16-18).

HEBREWS 1:8-9
Who is the king and who is the bride in Psalm 45?

This is called a "Messianic" psalm because it prophetically describes the Messiah's future relationship to the church, his body of believers. Verse 2 expresses God's abundant blessing on his Messiah; verses 6-8 find their true fulfillment in Christ. The church is described as the bride of Christ in Revelation 19:7-8; 21:9; 22:17.

SEPTEMBER 2

Ecclesiastes 1:1–3:22; 2 Corinthians 6:1-13; Psalms 46:1-11; Proverbs 22:15

Q ECCLESIASTES 1:1-11
Why did Solomon write so skeptically and pessimistically?

Solomon, one person in the Bible who had everything (wisdom, power, riches, honor, reputation, God's favor), here discussed the ultimate emptiness of all that this world has to offer. Near the end of his life, Solomon looked back over everything he had done, and most of it seemed meaningless. A common belief was that only good people prospered and that only the wicked suffered, but that hadn't proven true in his experience. Solomon wrote this book after he had tried everything and achieved much, only to find that nothing apart from God made him happy. He wanted his readers to avoid these same senseless pursuits.

Q 2 CORINTHIANS 6:1
How could the Corinthian believers toss aside God's message?

Confused by the false teachers who taught a different message, perhaps they were doubting Paul and his words. "To toss aside this message" can also be translated "to receive God's grace in vain." The people heard God's message, but did not let it affect what they said and did.

Q PSALM 46:4
There is no river in Jerusalem. Why does Psalm 46:4 say there is a river in the city of God?

Many great cities have rivers flowing through them, sustaining people's lives by making agriculture possible and facilitating trade with other cities. Jerusalem had no river, but it had God who, like a river, sustained the people's lives. As long as God lived among the people, the city was invincible. But when the people abandoned him, God no longer protected them, and Jerusalem fell to the Babylonian army.

Q PROVERBS 22:15, NRSV
What is the "rod of discipline"?

Young children often do foolish and dangerous things simply because they don't understand the consequences. Wisdom and common sense are not transferred by just being a good example. The wisdom a child learns must be taught consciously. "The rod of discipline" stands for all forms of discipline or training. Just as God trains and corrects us to make us better, so parents must discipline their children to make them learn the difference between right and wrong.

SEPTEMBER 3

Ecclesiastes 4:1–6:12; 2 Corinthians 6:14–7:7; Psalms 47:1-9; Proverbs 22:16

 ECCLESIASTES 4:1ff.
If Solomon believed in God, why did he speak of what is wrong in God's creation?

In Ecclesiastes Solomon reflects realistically on several apparent contradictions in God's control of the world: (1) there is wickedness where there should be justice (3:16-17); (2) people created in God's image die just like the animals (3:18-21); (3) no one comforts the oppressed (4:1-3); (4) many people are motivated by envy (4:4-6); (5) people are lonely (4:7-12); (6) recognition for accomplishments is temporary (4:13-16). It is easy to use such contradictions as excuses not to believe in God. But Solomon used them to show how we can honestly look at life's problems and still keep our faith. This life is not all there is, yet even in this life we should not pass judgment on God, because we don't know everything.

 2 CORINTHIANS 6:14, NRSV
What does it mean to not be mismatched with unbelievers?

Paul urges believers not to form binding relationships with nonbelievers because this might weaken their Christian commitment, integrity, or standards. It would be a mismatch. Earlier, Paul had explained that this did not mean isolating oneself from nonbelievers (see 1 Cor. 5:9-10). Paul even tells Christians to stay with their nonbelieving spouses (1 Cor. 7:12-13). Paul wants believers to be active in their witness for Christ to nonbelievers, but they should not lock themselves into personal or business relationships that could cause them to compromise the faith. Believers should avoid situations that could force them to divide their loyalties.

 PSALM 47:9
Who are the "princes of the people" in Psalm 47:9?

This has been translated "The Gentile rulers of the world" (TLB). These are the leaders of the nations who were not Jewish and did not worship Yahweh as the only God. Gentiles could come to believe in God (Acts 13:26) because God wants all people to come to him (Rom. 16:25-26; Gal. 3:14).

 PSALM 47:9
Who was the "God of Abraham"?

Abraham was the father of the Israelite nation. The one true God was sometimes called the "God of Abraham" (Exod. 3:6; 1 Kings 18:36). In a spiritual sense, God's promises to Abraham apply to all who believe in God, Jew or Gentile (Rom. 4:11-12; Gal. 3:7-9). Thus the God of Abraham is our God too.

SEPTEMBER 4

Ecclesiastes 7:1–9:18; 2 Corinthians 7:8-16; Psalms 48:1-14; Proverbs 22:17-19

Q ECCLESIASTES 7:27-28
Did Solomon think women were not capable of being upright?

No, because in the book of Proverbs he personified wisdom as a responsible woman. The point of Solomon's statement is not that women are unwise, but that hardly anyone, man or woman, is upright before God. In his search, Solomon found that goodness and wisdom were almost as scarce among men as among women, even though men were given a religious education program in his culture and women were not. In effect, the verse is saying, "I have found only one in a thousand people who is wise in God's eyes. No. I have found even fewer than that!"

Q ECCLESIASTES 9:5, 10
Why does Solomon say that the "dead know nothing"?

When Solomon says the dead know nothing, he is not contrasting life with afterlife, but life with death. After you die, you can't change what you have done. Resurrection to a new life after death was a vague concept for Old Testament believers. It was only made clear after Jesus rose from the dead.

Q PSALM 48:2
Why is Mount Zion called "the city of the Great King"?

Because the temple was located in Jerusalem, the city was seen as the center of God's presence in the world. The Bible pictures Jerusalem as the place where believers will gather in the "last days" (Isa. 2:2ff.), and as the spiritual home of all believers where God will live among them (Rev. 21:2-3).

Q PSALM 48:8
Will the city of Jerusalem exist forever?

Jerusalem has been destroyed several times since this psalm was written, the phrase, "God makes her secure forever" may refer prophetically to the new Jerusalem where God will judge all nations and live with all believers (Rev. 21).

Q PSALM 48:11
Why was Judah called to rejoice in Psalm 48:11?

The people of Judah were from Israel's largest tribe, which settled in the southern part of Canaan where Jerusalem was located (Josh. 15:1-12). David was from Judah, and he made Jerusalem his capital and the center of the nation's worship. Jesus was also a member of the tribe of Judah. The psalmist was saying that the day would come when God would bring justice to the land, and God's people would get the respect they deserved.

SEPTEMBER 5

Ecclesiastes 10:1–12:14; 2 Corinthians 8:1-15; Psalms 49:1-20; Proverbs 22:20-21

 2 CORINTHIANS 8:9
Was Jesus a poor man?

There is no evidence that Jesus was any poorer than most first-century Palestinians; rather, Jesus became poor by giving up his rights as God and becoming human. In his incarnation God voluntarily became man—the wholly human person, Jesus of Nazareth. As a man, Jesus was subject to place, time, and other human limitations. He did not give up his eternal power when he became human, but he did set aside his glory and his rights (see Phil. 2:5-7). In response to the Father's will, he limited his power and knowledge. Christ became "poor" when he became human, because he set aside so much. Yet by doing so, he made us "rich" because we received salvation and eternal life. What made Jesus' humanity unique was his freedom from sin. In his full humanity, we can see everything about God's character that can be conveyed in human terms. The incarnation is explained further in these Bible passages: John 1:1-14; Romans 1:2-5; Philippians 2:6-11; 1 Timothy 3:16; Hebrews 2:14; 1 John 1:1-3.

 2 CORINTHIANS 8:12
How do I decide how much to give to the Lord's work? What about differences in the financial resources Christians have?

In 2 Corinthians Paul gives the Corinthian church several principles to follow: (1) each person should follow through on previous promises (8:10-11; 9:3); (2) each person should give as much as he or she is able (8:12; 9:6); (3) each person must make up his or her own mind how much to give (9:7); and (4) each person should give in proportion to what God has given him or her (9:10). Sacrificial giving must be responsible. Paul wants believers to give generously, but not to the extent that those who depend on the givers (their families, for example) must go without having their basic needs met. The attitude with which we give is more important than the amount we give. We don't have to be embarrassed if we can give only a small gift. God is concerned about *how* we give from the resources we have (see Mark 12:41-44). According to this standard, the giving of the Macedonian churches was difficult to match.

SEPTEMBER 6

Song of Songs 1:1–4:16; 2 Corinthians 8:16-24; Psalms 50:1-23; Proverbs 22:22-23

 SONG OF SOLOMON 1:1ff.
What is the meaning of the Song of Solomon?

Some say that this is an allegory of God's love for Israel and/or the church. Others say it is a literal story about married love. But in reality, it is both—an historical story with two layers of meaning. On one level we learn about love, marriage, and sex; and on the other level, we see God's overwhelming love for his people. This book tells how Solomon, who frequently visited the various parts of his kingdom, one day visited some royal vineyards in the north. His royal entourage came by surprise upon a beautiful peasant woman tending the vines. Embarrassed, she ran from them. But Solomon could not forget her. Later, disguised as a shepherd, he returned to the vineyards and won her love. Then, he revealed his true identity and asked her to return to Jerusalem with him. Solomon and his beloved are being married in the palace as this book begins. The Song of Songs is a series of seven poems, not necessarily in chronological order. It reflects upon the first meeting of Solomon and the peasant woman, their engagement, their wedding, their wedding night, and the growth of their marriage after the wedding. There are three characters or groups of characters in this book: the girl (the "beloved"), Solomon (the "lover"), and "friends." The girl who caught Solomon's attention may have been from Shunem, a farming community about sixty miles north of Jerusalem. Her tanned skin indicates that she probably worked outside in the vineyards (Song 1:6)—thus she may not have been from the upper class. The friends include either members of Solomon's harem or workers in the palace, as well as the girl's brothers (as in Song 8:8-9).

 SONG OF SOLOMON 1:14
Where was Engedi?

Engedi was an oasis hidden at the base of rugged limestone cliffs west of the Dead Sea. It was known for its fruitful palm trees and fragrant balsam oil. The terrain surrounding Engedi was some of the most desolate in Palestine, and it had an extremely hot desert climate. The henna blossoms in Engedi would have appeared all the more beautiful because of their stark surroundings; thus Solomon was complimenting his beloved's beauty and comparing her favorably with the women she feared.

SEPTEMBER 7

Song of Songs 5:1–8:14; 2 Corinthians 9:1-15; Psalms 51:1-19; Proverbs 22:24-25

SONG OF SOLOMON 8:6-7
What is the meaning of Song of Solomon 8:6-7?

In this final description of their love, the girl includes some of its significant characteristics (see also 1 Cor. 13). Love is as strong as death; it cannot be killed by time or disaster; and it cannot be bought for any price because it is freely given. Love is priceless, and even the richest king cannot buy it. The love between Solomon and his bride did not diminish in intensity after their wedding night. The lovers relied on each other and kept no secrets from each other. Devotion and commitment were the keys to their relationship, just as they are in our relationships to our spouses and to God. The faithfulness of our marital love should reflect God's perfect faithfulness to us. Paul shows how marriage represents Christ's relationship to his church (Eph. 5:22-33), and John pictures the second coming as a great marriage feast for Christ and his bride, his faithful followers (Rev. 19:7-8; 21:1-2). Many theologians have thought that Song of Songs is an allegory showing Christ's love for his church. It makes even better sense to say that it is a love poem about a real human love relationship, and that all loving, committed marriages reflect God's love.

2 CORINTHIANS 9:15, KJV
What is the "unspeakable gift" mentioned in 2 Corinthians 9:15?

Some interpreters suppose that Paul here means the gift of grace given to the Corinthians, which made them able and willing to help the poor saints. Rather it appears to denote Jesus Christ as God's gift, a gift so great that it defies anyone's ability to express it with words.

PSALM 51:7, TLB
What is the "cleansing blood" in Psalm 51:7?

The "cleansing blood" refers to a ceremony where blood from a sacrificed animal was sprinkled on the priests to prepare them to serve God (Exod. 29:19-21). Other translations say "Purge me with hyssop." Hyssop branches were used by the Israelites in Egypt to place the blood of a lamb on the door frames of their homes. This would keep them safe from death (Exod. 12:22). This act demonstrated the Israelites' faith and secured their release from slavery in Egypt. This verse calls for cleansing from sin and readiness to serve the Lord.

SEPTEMBER 8

Isaiah 1:1–2:22; 2 Corinthians 10:1-18; Psalms 52:1-9; Proverbs 22:26-27

 ## ISAIAH 1:1ff.
Who was Isaiah and why did he write the book of Isaiah?

Isaiah was a prophet during the time when the original nation of Israel had been divided into two kingdoms—Israel in the north, and Judah in the south. The northern kingdom had sinned greatly against God, and the southern kingdom was headed in the same direction—perverting justice, oppressing the poor, turning from God to idols, and looking for military aid from pagan nations rather than from God. Isaiah came primarily as a prophet to Judah, but his message was also for the northern kingdom. Sometimes "Israel" refers to both kingdoms. Isaiah lived to see the destruction and captivity of the northern kingdom in 722 B.C.; thus, his ministry began as one of warning. In Isaiah 1:2-4 "Israel" means the southern kingdom, Judah. The people of Judah were sinning greatly and refused to know and understand God. God brought charges against them through Isaiah in this book because they had rebelled and had forsaken the Lord. By these acts, they had broken their moral and spiritual covenant with God (see Deut. 28). By breaking their agreement, they were bringing God's punishment upon themselves. First God gave them prosperity, but they didn't serve him. Then God sent them warnings through Isaiah, but they refused to listen. Finally, he would bring the fire of his judgment (see Isa. 1:7). As long as the people of Judah continued to sin, they cut themselves off from God's help and isolated themselves.

 ## PSALM 52
Was David speaking to a particular individual in Psalm 52?

Yes, this Psalm has to do with the murders committed by Doeg the Edomite. He slew eighty-five priests, including Ahimelech. David later executed Doeg for his treachery. Saul, of course, was behind the slaying of the priests and shared Doeg's guilt. David pictures the acts of the wicked and the judgment that falls upon them, and he offers praise for the righteous. (See 1 Sam. 22 for the details of the executions.)

 ## PSALM 52:8, TLB
What is the significance of a "sheltered olive tree"?

With God by his side, David compared himself to an olive tree flourishing in the house of God (NIV). Not only is an olive tree one of the longest-living trees, but a flourishing or sheltered tree has even greater longevity. David was contrasting God's eternal protection of his faithful servants with the sudden destruction of the wicked (Ps. 52:5-7).

SEPTEMBER 9

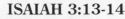

ISAIAH 3:13-14
Why is justice so important in the Bible?

(1) Justice is part of God's nature; it is the way he runs the universe. (2) It is a natural desire in every person. Even as sinners, we all want justice for ourselves. (3) When government and church leaders are unjust, the poor and powerless suffer. Thus they are hindered from worshiping God. (4) God holds the poor in high regard. They are the ones most likely to turn to him for help and comfort. Injustice, then, attacks God's children. When we do nothing to help the oppressed, we are in fact joining with the oppressor. Because we follow a just God, we must uphold justice.

ISAIAH 3:14-15
Does Isaiah 3:16-26 mean that women should not wear jewelry?

The women of Judah had placed their emphasis on clothing and jewelry rather than on God. They dressed to be noticed, to gain approval, and to be fashionable. Yet they ignored the real purpose for their lives. Instead of being concerned about the oppression around them, they were self-serving and self-centered. People who abuse their possessions will end up with nothing. These verses are not an indictment against clothing and jewelry, but a judgment on those who use them lavishly while remaining blind to the needs of others.

2 CORINTHIANS 11:6, KJV
In 2 Corinthians 11:6 Paul said he was "rude in speech". Is this true?

Paul, a brilliant thinker, was not a trained, spellbinding speaker. Although his ministry was effective (see Acts 17), he had not been trained in the Greek schools of oratory and speechmaking, as many of the false teachers probably had been. Paul believed in a simple presentation of the gospel (see 1 Cor. 1:17), and some people thought this showed simple-mindedness. Thus Paul's speaking performance was often used against him by false teachers.

PSALM 53:1
Why do people say there is no God?

Echoing the message of Psalm 14, this psalm proclaims the foolishness of atheism (see also Rom. 3:10). People may say there is no God in order to cover their sin, to have an excuse to continue in sin, and/or to ignore the Judge in order to avoid the judgment. A "fool" does not necessarily lack intelligence; many atheists and unbelievers are highly educated. Fools are people who reject God, the only one who can save them.

SEPTEMBER 10

Isaiah 6:1–7:25; 2 Corinthians 11:16-33; Psalms 54:1-7; Proverbs 23:1-3

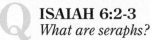 **ISAIAH 6:2-3**
What are seraphs?

Seraphs were a type of angel created by God. Their name is derived from the word for "burn," perhaps indicating their purity as God's ministers. This is the only place in the Bible where seraphs are mentioned. Here they function as God's agents in commissioning Isaiah. Isaiah could understand them when they spoke to him and when they praised God. Because they hovered around God's throne, they may have been heavenly attendants. They were awe-inspiring and powerful creatures—their singing shook the temple!

ISAIAH 7:14
Does Isaiah 7:14 refer to Mary, Jesus' mother?

Virgin is translated from a Hebrew word used for an unmarried woman old enough to be married, one who is sexually mature (see Gen. 24:43; Exod. 2:8; Ps. 68:25; Prov. 30:19; Song 1:3; 6:8). Some have compared this young woman to Isaiah's young wife and newborn son (Isa. 8:1-4). This is not likely because she had a child, Shear-Jashub, and her second child was not named Immanuel. Some believe that Isaiah's first wife may have died, and so this is his second wife. It is more likely that this prophecy had a double fulfillment: (1) a young woman from the house of Ahaz who was not married would marry and have a son. Before three years passed (one year for pregnancy and two for the child to be old enough to talk), the two invading kings would be destroyed; (2) Matthew 1:23 quotes Isaiah 7:14 to show a further fulfillment of this prophecy in that a virgin named Mary conceived and bore a son, Immanuel, Jesus the Christ.

2 CORINTHIANS 11:23-29
Why did Paul write about his sufferings and trials?

Paul was angry that the false teachers had impressed and deceived the Corinthians (11:13-15). Therefore, he had to reestablish his credibility and authority by listing the trials he had endured in his service for Christ. Some of these trials are recorded in the book of Acts (Acts 14:19; 16:22-24). Because Paul wrote this letter during his third missionary journey (Acts 18:23–21:17), his trials weren't over. He would experience yet further difficulties and humiliations for the cause of Christ (see Acts 21:30-33; 22:24-30). Paul was sacrificing his life for the gospel, something the false teachers would never do.

SEPTEMBER 11

 MATTHEW 4:15-16
What is the "great light" mentioned in Isaiah 9:1-7?

In a time of great darkness, God promised to send a light who would shine on everyone living in the shadow of death. He is both "Wonderful Counselor" and "Mighty God." This message of hope was fulfilled in the birth of Christ and the establishment of his eternal kingdom. He came to deliver all people from their slavery to sin. This child who would become their deliverer is the Messiah, Jesus. Matthew quotes these verses in describing Christ's ministry. The territories of Zebulun and Naphtali represent the northern kingdom as a whole. These were also the territories where Jesus grew up and often ministered; this is why they would see "a great light." The apostle John also referred to Jesus as the "light" (John 1:9), and Jesus referred to himself as "the light of the world" (John 8:12).

 2 CORINTHIANS 12:2
What is "heaven"?

The word *heaven*, used more than 275 times in the New Testament, has a variety of meanings. It is spoken of as God's dwelling place (1 Kings 8:30; Matt. 6:9), as God's throne (Isa. 66:1; Acts 7:49), and as God's creation (Rev. 10:6). As the Mediator, Christ entered into heaven (Acts 3:21-22; Heb. 6:19-20; 9:11, 24). All the holy angels are in heaven (Matt. 18:10; 24:36). Believers are to lay up treasure in heaven (Matt. 6:20; Luke 12:33), and heaven holds the priceless gift of eternal life which the saints will inherit in the resurrection (1 Pet. 1:4).

2 CORINTHIANS 12:7-8
What was Paul's "thorn in the flesh"?

We don't know what Paul's thorn in the flesh was, because he doesn't tell us. Some have suggested that it was malaria, epilepsy, or a disease of the eyes (see Gal. 4:13-15). Whatever the case, it was a chronic and debilitating problem, which at times kept him from working. This thorn was a hindrance to his ministry, and he prayed for its removal; but God refused. Paul was a very self-sufficient person, so this thorn must have been difficult for him. It kept Paul humble, reminded him of his need for constant contact with God, and benefited those around him as they saw God at work in his life.

SEPTEMBER 12

 ## ISAIAH 10:12, 17
Did God destroy Assyria as Isaiah said he would?

The predicted punishment of the Assyrians soon took place. In 701 B.C., 185,000 Assyrian soldiers were slain by the angel of the Lord (Isa. 37:36-37). Later, the Assyrian empire fell to Babylon, never to rise again as a world power. This downfall came in 612 B.C. when Nineveh, the capital city, was destroyed. Assyria had been God's instrument of judgment against Israel, but it too would be judged for its wickedness.

 ## ISAIAH 10:20-21; 11:11
What was the "remnant"?

Those who remained faithful to God despite the horrors of the invasion are called the remnant. The key to being a part of the remnant was *faith*. Being a descendant of Abraham, living in the promised land, having trusted God at one time—none of these were good enough. When will this remnant of God's people be returned to their land? Old Testament prophecy is often applied both to the near future and the distant future. Judah would soon be exiled to Babylon, and a remnant would return to Jerusalem in 537 B.C. at Cyrus's decree. In the ages to come, however, God's people would be dispersed throughout the world. These cities represent the four corners of the known world—Hamath in the north, Egypt in the south, Assyria and Babylonia in the east, the islands of the sea in the west. Ultimately God's people will be regathered when Christ comes to reign over the earth.

 ## 2 CORINTHIANS 12:12
Why does Paul mention the "signs of an apostle"?

God gave the apostles outward, confirming, extraordinary indicators to show they were what they said they were. These signs were to keep people from ever saying they were uninformed about the apostles. By observing these signs people would know that the apostles were speaking the truth. These "signs and wonders and mighty deeds" (KJV) were sufficient and beyond question, so that those who refused to heed their words and the works that gave credence to their words would have no defense in the day of judgment.

PSALM 56
Why did David write Psalm 56?

This was probably written on the same occasion as Psalm 34, when David fled from Saul to Philistine territory. He had to pretend insanity before Achish when some servants grew suspicious of him.

SEPTEMBER 13

Isaiah 12:1–14:32; 2 Corinthians 13:1-14; Psalms 57:1-11; Proverbs 23:9-11

 ISAIAH 12:1ff.
Is the book of Isaiah only about God's judgment?

No, but the first twenty-seven chapters are primarily about judgment. Chapters 1–12 speak of judgment against the southern kingdom and, to a lesser extent, against the northern kingdom. Chapters 13–23 are about the judgment on other nations. Chapters 24–27 are often called "Isaiah's Apocalypse." They discuss God's judgment on the entire world for its sin. These chapters describe the last days when God will judge the whole world. At that time he will finally and permanently remove evil. Chapter 13 is an oracle or message from God concerning Babylon. Long before Babylon became a world power and threatened Judah, Isaiah spoke of its destruction. Babylon was the rallying point of rebellion against God after the flood (Gen. 11). Revelation 17 and 18 use Babylon as a symbol of God's enemies. At the time of this oracle, Babylon was still part of the Assyrian empire. Isaiah communicated a message of challenge and hope to God's people, telling them not to rely on other nations but to rely on God alone. And he let them know that their greatest enemies would receive from God the punishment they deserve.

 2 CORINTHIANS 13:14
Is 2 Corinthians 13:14 talking about God as a Trinity?

Paul concludes this epistle with his Trinitarian, apostolic benediction, in which he pronounces the grace of Christ, the love of the Father, and the communion of the Holy Spirit. The word "Trinity" does not appear in Scripture. However, Christianity has always been Trinitarian. This doctrine asserts that God is one in essence, eternally subsisting in three persons, the Father, the Son, and the Holy Spirit. In Matthew 3:16-17, at the baptism of Jesus, the Holy Spirit appears as a dove, and the Father's voice is heard; also in Matthew 28:19 the Trinitarian baptismal formula is given (into the name of the Father and of the Son and of the Holy Spirit). Other biblical evidences for the Trinity can be found in Romans 8:9; 1 Corinthians 12:3-6; Ephesians 4:4-6; 1 Peter 1:2; Jude 20-21; Revelation 1:4-5. All three persons of the Trinity share the same divine attributes. Each has a unique office or work to do. God the Father sent Jesus the Son; God the Son died on Calvary's cross. The Father and Son sent the Holy Spirit, who seals and indwells every believer. Salvation is the work of the Trinity (the Father, the Son, and the Holy Spirit), according to Titus 3:4-6 and 2 Thessalonians 2:13-14.

SEPTEMBER 14

ISAIAH 17:8
What were Asherah poles?

These were images of Asherah, a Canaanite goddess who was the female consort of Baal. Queen Jezebel may have brought the worship of Asherah into the northern kingdom. The cult encouraged immoral sexual practices and attracted many people. The Bible warns against worshiping Asherah poles (Exod. 34:13; Deut. 12:3; 16:21), and Manasseh was condemned for putting up an Asherah pole in the temple (2 Kings 21:7).

ISAIAH 18
When did Isaiah give the prophecy in chapter 18?

This prophecy was probably given in the days of Hezekiah (2 Kings 19–20). The "land of whirring wings" refers to locusts, and probably pictures the armies of Cush. The king of Cush had heard that Assyria's great army was marching south toward them. He sent messengers up the Nile River asking the surrounding nations to form an alliance. Judah was also asked, but Isaiah told the messengers to return home because Judah needed only God's help to repel the Assyrians. Isaiah prophesied that Assyria would be destroyed at the proper time (Isa. 37:21-38).

GALATIANS 1:1-24
What is the background of the book of Galatians?

Paul and Barnabas had just completed their first missionary journey (Acts 13:2–14:28). They had visited Iconium, Lystra, and Derbe, cities in the Roman province of Galatia (present-day Turkey). Upon returning to Antioch, Paul was accused by some Jewish Christians of diluting Christianity to make it more appealing to Gentiles. These Jewish Christians disagreed with Paul's statements that Gentiles did not have to follow many of the religious laws that the Jews had obeyed for centuries. Some of Paul's accusers had even followed him to those Galatian cities and had told the Gentile converts they had to be circumcised and follow all the Jewish laws and customs in order to be saved. According to these men, Gentiles had to first become Jews in order to become Christians. In response to this threat, Paul wrote this letter to the Galatian churches. In it, he explains that following the Old Testament laws or the Jewish laws will not bring salvation. A person is saved by grace through faith. Paul wrote this letter about A.D. 49, shortly before the meeting of the Jerusalem council, which settled the law versus grace controversy (Acts 15).

SEPTEMBER 15

Isaiah 19:1–21:17; Galatians 2:1-16; Psalms 59:1-17; Proverbs 23:13-14

ISAIAH 21:10
What were "threshing" and "winnowing"?

These were two steps in ancient Israel's farming process. The heads of wheat (often used to symbolize Israel) were first trampled to break open the seeds and expose the valued grain inside (this is "threshing"). The seeds were then thrown into the air, and the worthless chaff blew away while the grain fell back to the ground (this is "winnowing"). Israel would experience this same kind of process—the worthless, sinful, rebellious people would be taken away, but God would keep the good "grain" to replenish Israel.

GALATIANS 2:3-5
What does Titus' lack of circumcision have to do with the truth of the gospel?

When Paul took Titus, a Greek Christian, to Jerusalem, the Judaizers (false brothers) said that Titus should be circumcised. Paul adamantly refused to give in to their demands. The apostles agreed that circumcision was an unnecessary rite for Gentile converts. Several years later, Paul circumcised Timothy, another Greek Christian (Acts 16:3). Unlike Titus, however, Timothy was half-Jewish. Paul did not deny Jews the right to be circumcised; he was simply saying that Gentiles should not be asked to become Jews before becoming Christians.

GALATIANS 2:11ff.
What was the problem when Paul opposed Peter in Antioch?

The Judaizers accused Paul of watering down the gospel to make it easier for Gentiles to accept, while Paul accused the Judaizers of nullifying the truth of the gospel by adding conditions to it. The basis of salvation was the issue—is salvation through Christ alone, or does it come through Christ *and* adherence to the law? The argument came to a climax when Peter, Paul, the Judaizers, and some Gentile Christians all gathered together in Antioch to share a meal. Peter moved away from the Gentiles because he did not want to offend James and the Jewish Christians. James had a very prominent position and presided over the Jerusalem council (Acts 15). But Paul charged that Peter's action violated the gospel. By joining the Judaizers, Peter implicitly was supporting their claim that Christ was not sufficient for salvation. Although Peter was a leader of the church, he was acting like a hypocrite. He knew better, yet he was driven by fear of what James and the others would think. Proverbs 29:25 says, "Fear of man will prove to be a snare." Paul knew that he had to confront Peter before his actions damaged the church. So, Paul publicly opposed Peter.

SEPTEMBER 16

ISAIAH 23:1
Where was Tyre?

Isaiah's prophecies against other nations began in the east with Babylon (chapter 13) and ended in the west with Tyre, a city on the seacoast of Phoenicia near the modern city of Tel Aviv. Tyre was one of the most famous cities of the ancient world. A major trading center with a large seaport, Tyre was wealthy and evil. Tyre was rebuked by Jeremiah (Jer. 25:22, 27; 47:4), Ezekiel (Ezek. 26–28), Joel (Joel 3:4-8), Amos (Amos 1:9-10), and Zechariah (Zech. 9:3-4). This is another warning against political alliances with unstable neighbors.

ISAIAH 23:15
What is the significance of the seventy years mentioned in Isaiah 23:15?

Some scholars believe this is a literal seventy years; some say it is symbolic of a long period of time. If it is literal, this may have occurred between 700–630 B.C. during the Assyrian captivity of Israel, or it may have been during the seventy-year captivity of the Jews in Babylon (605–536 B.C.). During the seventy years, the Jews would forget about Tyre. But when they returned from captivity, they would once again trade with Tyre.

GALATIANS 3:6-9
Why does Paul mention Abraham in his argument to the Galatians?

The main argument of the Judaizers was that Gentiles had to become Jews in order to become Christians. Paul exposed the flaw in this argument by showing that real children of Abraham are those who have faith, not those who keep the law. Abraham himself was saved by his faith (Gen. 15:6). All believers in every age and from every nation share Abraham's blessing. This is a comforting promise to us, a great heritage for us, and a solid foundation for living.

PSALM 60:1-3
What is the subject of Psalm 60?

This psalm gives us information about David's reign not found in the books of 1 and 2 Samuel or 1 and 2 Chronicles. Although the setting of the psalm is found in 2 Samuel 8, that passage makes no reference to the fact that David's forces had met stiff resistance and apparently even a temporary defeat (Ps. 60:9-10). David mentioned the enemy nations that surrounded Israel (Ps. 60:8). Moab lay directly to the east, Edom to the south, and Philistia to the west. At the time this psalm was written, David was fighting Syria to the north. Although he was surrounded by enemies, David believed that God would help him triumph.

SEPTEMBER 17

Isaiah 25:1–28:13; Galatians 3:10-22; Psalms 61:1-8; Proverbs 23:17-18

 ISAIAH 26:19
Is Isaiah speaking of the resurrection in Isaiah 25:19?

Some people say there is no life after death. Others believe that there is, but it is not physical life. But here Isaiah tells us that our bodies shall rise again. According to 1 Corinthians 15:50-53, all the dead believers will arise with new imperishable bodies—bodies like the one Jesus had when he was resurrected (see Phil. 3:21). Isaiah 26:19 is not the only Old Testament verse to speak about the resurrection; see also Job 19:26; Psalm 16:10; Daniel 12:2, 13.

 GALATIANS 3:10-11
Why does Paul quote the Old Testament in his argument with the Judaizers?

Paul quoted Deuteronomy 27:26 to prove that, contrary to what the Judaizers claimed, the law cannot justify and save—it can only condemn. Breaking even one commandment brings a person under condemnation. And because everyone has broken the commandments, everyone stands condemned. The law can do nothing to reverse the condemnation (Rom. 3:20-24). But Christ took the curse of the law upon himself when he hung on the cross. He did this so we wouldn't have to bear our own punishment. The only condition is that we accept Christ's death on our behalf as the means to be saved (Col. 1:20-23). Then Paul points to Habakkuk's declaration (Hab. 2:4) that by trusting God—believing in his provision for our sins and living each day in his power—we can break the hold of the Law's curse.

 GALATIANS 3:18-19
What is the purpose of the law?

The law has two functions. On the positive side, it reveals the nature and will of God and shows people how to live. On the negative side, it points out people's sins and shows them that it is impossible to please God by trying to obey all his laws completely. God's promise to Abraham dealt with Abraham's faith; the law focuses on actions. The covenant with Abraham shows that faith is the only way to be saved; the law shows how to obey God in grateful response. Faith does not annul the law; but the more we know God, the more we see how sinful we are. Then we are driven to depend on our faith in Christ alone for our salvation.

SEPTEMBER 18

Isaiah 28:14–30:11; Galatians 3:23–4:31; Psalms 62:1-12; Proverbs 23:19-21

GALATIANS 3:27
Why does Galatians 3:27 say "you . . . have clothed yourselves with Christ"?

In Roman society, a youth coming of age laid aside the robe of childhood and put on a new toga. This represented his move into adult citizenship with full rights and responsibilities. Paul combined this cultural understanding with the concept of baptism. By becoming Christians and being baptized, the Galatian believers were becoming spiritually grown up and ready to take on the privileges and responsibilities of the more mature. Paul was saying that they had laid aside the old clothes of the law, and were putting on Christ's new robe of righteousness (see 2 Cor. 5:21; Eph. 4:23-24).

GALATIANS 4:3-7
In what way were we slaves?

Paul uses the illustration of slavery to show that before Christ came and died for sins, people were in bondage to the law. The "basic principles of the world" are the elementary stages of religious practice, whether in the Jewish or pagan religion. Thinking they could be saved by it, they became enslaved to trying—and failing—to keep it. But we who were once slaves are now God's very own children who have an intimate relationship with him. Because of Christ, there is no reason to be afraid of God. We can come boldly into his presence, knowing that he will welcome us as his family members.

GALATIANS 4:4-5
Why is it important that Jesus was "born of a woman, born under law"?

Jesus was born of a woman—he was human. He was born as a Jew—he was subject to God's law and fulfilled it perfectly. Thus Jesus was the perfect sacrifice because, although he was fully human, he never sinned. His death bought freedom for us who were enslaved to sin so that we could be adopted into God's family.

GALATIANS 4:21ff.
Why does Paul talk about Abraham's two wives?

Paul contrasted those who are enslaved to the law (Hagar, the slave woman) with those who are free from the law (Sarah, the free woman). Hagar's abuse of Sarah (Genesis 16:4) was like the persecution that the Gentile Christians were getting from the Judaizers who insisted on keeping the law in order to be saved. Eventually Sarah triumphed because God kept his promise to give her a son, just as those who worship Christ in faith will also triumph.

SEPTEMBER 19

ISAIAH 31:1
Why was it wrong for Judah to look to other nations for military help?

(1) They were trusting in human beings instead of God. Judah sought protection from those who had far less power than God. Both Egypt and Judah would fall as a result of their arrogance. (2) They were serving their own interests instead of God's, and thus they did not even consult him. They violated God's stipulation in Deuteronomy 17:16. (3) They did not want to pay the price of looking to God and repenting of their sinful ways.

GALATIANS 5:1
Galatians 5:1 says, "For freedom Christ has set us free" (NRSV). What does this mean?

Christ died to set us free from sin and from a long list of laws and regulations. Christ came to set us free—not free to do whatever we want because that would lead us back into slavery to our selfish desires. Rather, thanks to Christ, we are now free and able to do what was impossible before—to live unselfishly. Those who appeal to their freedom so that they can have their own way or indulge their own desires are falling back into sin. But it is also wrong to put a burden of law-keeping on Christians. We must stand against those who would enslave us with rules, methods, or special conditions for being saved or growing in Christ.

GALATIANS 5:2
Why does Galatians 5:2 say "Christ will be of no value to you at all"?

Trying to be saved by keeping the law and being saved by grace are two entirely different approaches. This verse means that Christ's provision for our salvation will not help us if we are trying to save ourselves. Obeying the law does not make it any easier for God to save us. All we can do is accept his gracious gift through faith. Our deeds of service and love should flow out of our gratitude for what Christ did. Those deeds must never be used to try to earn God's love or favor.

PSALM 63:1-11
Why did David write Psalm 63?

Psalms 61, 62, and 63 were probably written when David was seeking refuge during Absalom's rebellion (2 Sam. 15–18). Hiding from his enemies in the barren Desert of Judah, David was intensely lonely. He longed for a friend he could trust to ease his loneliness. No wonder he cried out, "O God, . . . my soul thirsts for you, . . . in a dry and weary land."

SEPTEMBER 20

Isaiah 33:13–36:22; Galatians 5:13-26; Psalms 64:1-10; Proverbs 23:23

ISAIAH 35
Isaiah 35 is much different than the foregoing chapters. Why?

In chapters 1–34, Isaiah has delivered a message of judgment on all nations, including Israel and Judah, for rejecting God. Although there have been glimpses of relief and restoration for the remnant of faithful believers, the climate of wrath, fury, judgment, and destruction has prevailed. Now Isaiah breaks through with a vision of beauty and encouragement. God is just as thorough in his mercy as he is severe in his judgment. God's complete moral perfection is revealed by his hatred of all sin, and this leads to judgment. This same moral perfection is revealed in his love for all he has created. This leads to mercy for those who have sinned but who have sincerely loved and obeyed him. This chapter is a beautiful picture of the final kingdom in which God will establish his justice and destroy all evil. This is the world the redeemed can anticipate after the judgment when creation itself will rejoice in God. Chapter 34 spoke of great distress when God will judge all people for their actions. Chapter 35 pictures the days when life will be peaceful at last and everything will be made right. Carmel and Sharon were regions of thick vegetation and fertile soil. They were symbols of productivity and plenty. The "Way of Holiness," in verses 8-10 is the way that righteous pilgrims will take from the desert of suffering to Zion (Jerusalem). It is found only by following God. Only the redeemed will travel God's highway; they will be protected from wicked travelers and harmful animals.

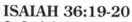

ISAIAH 36:19-20
In Isaiah 36:19-20 Sennacherib told the people of Jerusalem that the gods of the other cities he had conquered had not been able to save their people, so how could the God of Jerusalem save them?

The Lord was supposedly the God of Samaria (the northern kingdom), and it fell. But the Lord was the God of Samaria in name only, because the people were not worshiping him. That is why prophets foretold the fall of Samaria. But for the Lord's own sake and for the sake of David, the Lord would rescue them from the Assyrian army (Isa. 37:35).

Isaiah 37:1–38:22; Galatians 6:1-18; Psalms 65:1-13; Proverbs 23:24

ISAIAH 37:3
What is the meaning of Isaiah 37:3?

Judah is compared to a woman trying to give birth to a child but is too weak to deliver. When the situation seemed hopeless, Hezekiah didn't give up. Instead, he asked the prophet Isaiah to pray that God would help his people.

ISAIAH 37:29
What does it mean to have a "hook in your nose"?

This was a common torture the Assyrians used on their captives. They were often led away with hooks in their noses or bits in their mouths as signs of humiliation.

GALATIANS 6:11
Why does Paul say "I have written to you with my own hand"?

Up to this point, Paul had probably dictated the letter to a scribe. Here he takes the pen into his own hand to write his final, personal greetings. Paul did this in other letters as well, to add emphasis to his words and to validate that the letter was genuine.

GALATIANS 6:13
Were some of Paul's opponents not keeping the law themselves?

Some of the Judaizers were emphasizing circumcision as proof of holiness—but ignoring the other Jewish laws. People often choose a certain principle or prohibition and make it the measure of faith. Some may abhor drunkenness but ignore gluttony. Others may despise promiscuity but tolerate prejudice. The Bible in its entirety is our rule of faith and practice. We cannot pick and choose the mandates we will follow. The Judaizers gloried in the law and circumcision. In verse 14 Paul gloried in the cross of Christ. He desired to glory in nothing else. The cross was the ground of his hope. It was the doctrine he intended to preach, whatever the cost and however much he had to suffer.

PSALM 65:4
Who were the people who were blessed to live in the courts of God's house?

Access to God, the joy of living in the temple courts, was a great honor. God had chosen a special group of Israelites, the tribe of Levi, to serve as priests in the tabernacle (Num. 3:5-51). They were the only ones who could enter the sacred rooms where God's presence resided. Because of Jesus' death on the cross, all believers today have personal access to God's presence everywhere and at any time.

SEPTEMBER 22

Isaiah 39:1–41:16; Ephesians 1:1-23; Psalms 66:1-20; Proverbs 23:25-28

 ISAIAH 40:1
After so many chapters of judgment why does God tell Isaiah to comfort his people?

Judah still had a hundred years of trouble before Jerusalem would fall, then seventy years of exile. So God tells Isaiah to speak tenderly and to comfort Jerusalem. The book of Isaiah makes a dramatic shift at this point. The following chapters discuss the majesty of God, who is coming to rule the earth and judge all people. God will reunite Israel and Judah and restore them to glory. Instead of warning the people of impending judgment, Isaiah here comforts them.

 ISAIAH 40:11
What is the meaning of Isaiah 40:11?

God is often pictured as a shepherd, gently caring for and guiding his flock. He is powerful (Isa. 40:10), yet careful and gentle. He is called a shepherd (Psalm 23); the good shepherd (John 10:11, 14); the great Shepherd (Hebrews 13:20); and the Chief Shepherd (1 Peter 5:4). Note that the shepherd is caring for the most defenseless members of his society: children and those caring for them. This reinforces the prophetic theme that the truly powerful nation is not the one with a strong military, but rather the one that relies on God's caring strength.

 **EPHESIANS 1:1**
What is the background and purpose of the book of Ephesians?

Ephesus, a commercial, political, and religious center for all of Asia Minor, was one of the five major cities in the Roman empire, along with Rome, Corinth, Antioch, and Alexandria. The temple to the Greek goddess Artemis was located there. Paul had been a Christian for nearly 30 years. He had taken three missionary trips and established churches all around the Mediterranean Sea. When he wrote Ephesians, Paul was under house arrest in Rome (see Acts 28:16ff.). During his third missionary journey, he stayed there for almost three years (Acts 19). Paul later met again with the elders of the Ephesian church at Miletus (Acts 20:16-38). Paul wrote this letter to the Ephesian believers and all other believers to give them in-depth teaching about how to nurture and maintain the unity of the church. He wanted to put this important information in written form because he was in prison for preaching the gospel and could not visit the churches himself. The words "in Ephesus" are not present in some early manuscripts. Therefore, this was very likely a circular letter—it was first sent to Ephesus and then circulated to neighboring local churches. The encyclical nature of the epistle is affirmed by the fact that Paul mentions no particular problems or local situations, and he offers no personal greetings.

SEPTEMBER 23

Isaiah 41:17–43:13; Ephesians 2:1-22; Psalms 67:1-7; Proverbs 23:29-35

 ISAIAH 42:1-17
Who is the servant in Isaiah 42:1-17?

Sometimes called the Servant Song, this portion is about the Servant-Messiah, not the servant Cyrus (described in chapter 41). Israel and the Messiah are both often called *servant.* Israel, as God's servant, was to help bring the world to a knowledge of God. The Messiah, Jesus, would fulfill this task and show God himself to the world. Verses 1-4 are quoted in Matthew 12:18-21 with reference to Christ. The chosen servant reveals a character of gentleness, encouragement, justice, and truth.

 EPHESIANS 2:2
Who is "The ruler of the kingdom of the air"?

This was understood by Paul's readers to mean Satan. They believed that Satan and the evil spiritual forces inhabited the region between earth and sky. Satan is thus pictured as ruling an evil spiritual kingdom—the demons and those who are against Christ. *Satan* means "the accuser." He is also called the devil (Eph. 4:27). In the resurrection, Christ was victorious over Satan and his power. Therefore, Jesus Christ is the permanent ruler of the whole world; Satan is only the temporary ruler of the part of the world that chooses to follow him.

 EPHESIANS 2:14
What is the "middle wall of partition"?

This is the barrier people build between themselves. Christ has destroyed this wall so we can have real unity with people who are not like us. This is true reconciliation. Because of Christ's death, we are all one (Eph. 2:14); our hostility against each other has been put to death (Eph. 2:16); we can all have access to the Father by the Holy Spirit (Eph. 2:18); we are no longer foreigners or aliens to God (Eph. 2:19); and we are all being built into a holy temple with Christ as our chief cornerstone (Eph. 2:20-21).

 EPHESIANS 2:17-18, NRSV
Who are "those who were far off" and "those who were near"?

The Jews were near to God because they already knew of him through the Scriptures and worshiped him in their religious ceremonies. The Gentiles were far away because they knew little or nothing about God. Because neither group could be saved by good deeds, knowledge, or sincerity, both needed to hear about the salvation available through Jesus Christ. Both Jews and Gentiles are now free to come to God through Christ.

SEPTEMBER 24

Isaiah 43:14–45:10; Ephesians 3:1-21; Psalms 68:1-18; Proverbs 24:1-2

 ISAIAH 44:28
Was the prophecy in Isaiah 44:28 ever fulfilled)?

Isaiah, who prophesied from about 740–681 B.C., called Cyrus by name almost 150 years before he ruled (559–530 B.C.)! Later historians said that Cyrus read this prophecy and was so moved that he carried it out. Isaiah also predicted that Jerusalem would fall more than a hundred years before it happened (586 B.C.) and that the temple would be rebuilt about two hundred years before it happened.

 ISAIAH 45:1
Since Cyrus was a gentile king why was he called "God's anointed"?

This is the only place in the Bible where a Gentile ruler is said to be "anointed." God is the power over all powers, and he anoints whom he chooses for his special tasks. Cyrus's kingdom spread across two thousand miles (the largest of any empire then known), including the territories of both the Assyrian and the Babylonian empires. Why did God anoint Cyrus? Because God had a special task for him to do for Israel. Cyrus would allow God's city, Jerusalem, to be rebuilt, and he would set the exiles free without expecting anything in return. Few kings of Israel or Judah had done as much for God's people as Cyrus would.

 EPHESIANS 3:1
Why did Paul say he was a "prisoner for Christ Jesus"?

Paul was under house arrest in Rome for preaching about Christ. The religious leaders in Jerusalem, who felt threatened by Christ's teachings and didn't believe he was the Messiah, pressured the Romans to arrest Paul and bring him to trial for treason and for causing rebellion among the Jews. Paul had appealed for his case to be heard by the emperor, and he was awaiting trial (see Acts 28:16-31). Even though he was under arrest, Paul maintained his firm belief that God was in control of all that happened to him.

 EPHESIANS 3:13, TLB
Why should Paul's suffering make the Ephesians feel honored?

If Paul had not preached the gospel, he would not be in jail—but then the Ephesians would not have heard the Good News and been converted either. Just as a mother endures the pain of childbirth in order to bring new life into the world, Paul endured the pain of persecution in order to bring new believers to Christ.

SEPTEMBER 25

Isaiah 45:11–48:11; Ephesians 4:1-16; Psalms 68:19-35; Proverbs 24:3-4

ISAIAH 46:1-4
What difference does it make if Babylon's gods were carried in carts?

Cyrus would carry out God's judgment against Babylon. Bel was the chief deity of the Babylonians; Nebo was the god of science and learning. These "gods," however, needed animals and people to carry them around and could not even save themselves from being taken into captivity. They had no power at all. In contrast to gods who must be hauled around by people, our God created us and cares for us. His love is so enduring that he will care for us throughout our lifetime and even through death.

ISAIAH 47
What is the background of the prophecy against Babylon in Isaiah 47?

Here Isaiah predicted the fall of Babylon more than 150 years before it happened. At this time, Babylon had not yet emerged as the mightiest force on earth, the proud empire that would destroy Judah and Jerusalem. But the Babylonians, Judah's captors, would become captives themselves in 539 B.C. God, not Babylon, has the ultimate power. He used Babylon to punish his sinful people; he would use Medo-Persia to destroy Babylon and free his people.

EPHESIANS 4:6, NRSV
Why does Ephesians 4:6 say that God is "above all and through all and in all"?

God is *above all*—this shows his overruling care (transcendence). He is *through all and in all*—this shows his active presence in the world and in the lives of believers (immanence). Any view of God that violates either his transcendence or his immanence does not paint a true picture of God.

EPHESIANS 4:8, KJV
What does Ephesians 4:8 mean that "he led captivity captive"?

In Psalm 68:18, God is pictured as a conqueror marching to the gates and taking tribute from the fallen city. Paul uses that picture to teach that Christ in his crucifixion and resurrection was victorious over Satan. When Christ ascended to heaven, he gave gifts to the church, some of which Paul discusses in Ephesians 4:11-13.

SEPTEMBER 26

ISAIAH 48:14-15
Who is "The LORD's chosen ally"?

This refers to Cyrus—and this must have shocked the readers of Isaiah in that time. How could the Lord choose a pagan king, an enemy? But it was Cyrus whom God would use to free his people from their captivity in Babylon. Cyrus's mission was to set Israel free by conquering Babylon, then to decree that all Jews could return to their homeland. Who but a prophet of God could tell such an inconceivable but true story almost two hundred years before it happened?

ISAIAH 49:1-7
Who is the "servant" in Isaiah 49:1-7?

This is a prophetic reference to Jesus Christ. Before the servant, the Messiah, was born, God had chosen him to bring the light of the gospel (the message of salvation) to the world (see Acts 13:47). Christ offered salvation to all nations, and his apostles began the missionary movement to take this gospel to the ends of the earth. Missionary work today continues Jesus' great commission (Matt. 28:18-20), taking the light of the gospel to all nations.

ISAIAH 50:7, KJV
Why does Isaiah 50:7 say "I set my face like a flint"?

This verse is echoed in Luke 9:51 when Jesus "steadfastly set his face to go to Jerusalem" (KJV). Jesus went about his work as redeemer with constancy and resolution. He was not to be discouraged nor would he fail to accomplish what he had set out to do.

PSALM 69:8
Is Psalm 69 quoted in the New Testament?

This is one of the psalms most quoted in the New Testament. It is often applied to the ministry and suffering of Jesus. Verse 4, like John 15:25, speaks of Jesus' many enemies. The experience of being scorned by his brothers is expressed in John 7:5. Verse 9 portrays David's zeal for God; Christ showed great zeal when he threw the money changers out of the temple (John 2:14-17). Paul quoted part of Psalm 69:9 in Romans 15:3. Christ's great suffering is portrayed in Psalm 69:20-21 (Matt. 27:48; Mark 15:23; Luke 23:36; John 19:28-30). Verses 22 through 28 are quoted in Romans 11:9-10; and Peter applied Psalm 69:25 to Judas (Acts 1:20).

SEPTEMBER 27

ISAIAH 53:4-5
How could an Old Testament person understand the idea of Christ dying for our sins (our transgressions and iniquities)—actually bearing the punishment that we deserved?

The sacrifices suggested this idea, but it is one thing to kill a lamb, and something quite different to think of God's chosen servant as that Lamb. But God was pulling aside the curtain of time to let the people of Isaiah's day look ahead to the suffering of the future Messiah and the resulting forgiveness made available to all mankind.

EPHESIANS 5:21-30
Why did Paul tell wives to submit and husbands to love?

Perhaps Christian women, newly freed in Christ, found submission difficult; perhaps Christian men, used to the Roman custom of giving unlimited power to the head of the family, were not used to treating their wives with respect and love. Of course both husbands and wives should submit to each other (Eph. 5:21), just as both should love each other. In Paul's day, women, children, and slaves were to submit to the head of the family—slaves would submit until they were freed, male children until they grew up, and women and girls their whole lives. Paul emphasized the equality of all believers in Christ (Gal. 3:28), but he did not suggest overthrowing Roman society to achieve it. Instead, he counseled all believers to submit to one another by choice. This kind of mutual submission preserves order and harmony in the family while it increases love and respect among family members. Submitting to another person is an often misunderstood concept. It does not mean the other person dominates your life and you become a "doormat." Christ—at whose name "every knee should bow, in heaven and on earth and under the earth" (Phil. 2:10)—submitted his will to the Father, and we honor Christ by following his example. When we submit to God, we become more willing to obey his command to submit to others, that is, to subordinate our rights to theirs. In a marriage relationship, both husband and wife are called to submit. For the wife, this means willingly following her husband's leadership in Christ. For the husband, it means putting aside his own interests in order to care for his wife. In Ephesians 5 Paul devotes twice as many words to telling husbands to love their wives as to telling wives to submit to their husbands. How should a man love his wife? (1) He should be willing to sacrifice everything for her. (2) He should make her well-being of primary importance. (3) He should care for her as he cares for his own body. No wife needs to fear submitting to a man who treats her in this way.

SEPTEMBER 28

Isaiah 54:1–57:13; Ephesians 6:1-24; Psalms 70:1-5; Proverbs 24:8

ISAIAH 54:1
Is God calling Israel a childless woman in Isaiah 54:1?

Yes, to be childless at that time was a woman's great shame, a disgrace. Families depended on children for survival, especially when the parents became elderly. Israel (Zion) was unfruitful, like a childless woman, but God would permit her to have many children and would change her mourning into singing.

ISAIAH 55:3
What are the "sure mercies of David"?

This is God's covenant with David, promising a permanent homeland for the Israelites, no threat from pagan nations, and no wars (2 Sam. 7:10-11). But Israel did not fulfill its part of the covenant by obeying God and staying away from idols. Even so, God was ready to renew his covenant again. He is a forgiving God!

ISAIAH 56:7
Was the temple in Jerusalem used as a "house of prayer for all people"?

Prayer was a regular part of the temple service (2 Chron. 8:14; Luke 1:8-9), but when Jesus came to the Temple he quoted this verse in a negative way: "It is written in the Scriptures, 'my temple is to be a place of prayer for all nations,' but you have turned it into a den of robbers" (Mark 11:17, TLB).

ISAIAH 57:7-8
How could the whole nation of Israel commit adultery?

Marriage is an exclusive relationship where a man and a woman become one. Adultery breaks this beautiful bond of unity. When the people turned from God and gave their love to idols, God said they were committing adultery—breaking their exclusive commitment to God.

EPHESIANS 6:5
Why does the New Testament deal with slavery?

Slaves played a significant part in Roman society. There were several million of them in the Roman empire at this time. Because many slaves and owners had become Christians, the early church had to deal straightforwardly with the question of master/slave relations. Paul's statement neither condemns nor condones slavery. Instead, it tells masters and slaves how to live together in Christian households. In Paul's day, women, children, and slaves had few rights. In the church, however, they had freedoms that society denied them. Paul tells husbands, parents, and masters to be caring.

SEPTEMBER 29

Isaiah 57:14–59:21; Philippians 1:1-26; Psalms 71:1-24; Proverbs 24:9-10

PHILIPPIANS 1:1
What is the background and purpose of the book of Philippians?

This is a personal letter to the Philippians, not intended for general circulation to all the churches as was the letter to the Ephesians. Paul wanted to thank the believers for helping him when he had a need. He also wanted to tell them why he could be full of joy despite his imprisonment and upcoming trial. In this uplifting letter, Paul counseled the Philippians about humility and unity and warned them about potential problems. The Roman colony of Philippi was located in northern Greece (called Macedonia in Paul's day). Philip II of Macedon (the father of Alexander the Great) took the town from ancient Thrace in about 357 B.C., enlarged and strengthened it, and gave it his name. This thriving commercial center sat at the crossroads between Europe and Asia. In about A.D. 50, Paul, Silas, Timothy, and Luke crossed the Aegean Sea from Asia Minor and landed at Philippi (Acts 16:11-40). The church in Philippi consisted mostly of Gentile (non-Jewish) believers. Because they were not familiar with the Old Testament, Paul did not specifically quote any Old Testament passages in this letter.

PHILIPPIANS 1:13
How did Paul end up in chains in a Roman prison?

While he was visiting Jerusalem, some Jews had him arrested for preaching the gospel, but he appealed to Caesar to hear his case (Acts 21:15–25:12). He was then escorted by soldiers to Rome, where he was placed under house arrest while awaiting trial—not a trial for breaking civil law, but for proclaiming the Good News of Christ. At that time, the Roman authorities did not consider this to be a serious charge. A few years later, however, Rome would take a different view of Christianity and make every effort to stamp it out of existence. Paul's house arrest allowed him some degree of freedom. He could have visitors, continue to preach, and write letters such as this one. A brief record of Paul's time in Rome is found in Acts 28:11-31. The "whole palace guard" refers to the Praetorian Guard, the elite troops housed in the emperor's palace. This was not Paul's final imprisonment in Rome. But he didn't know that. Awaiting trial, he knew he could either be released or executed. However, he trusted Christ to work it out for his deliverance. Paul's prayer was that when he stood trial, he would speak courageously for Christ and not be timid or ashamed (Phil. 1:19-21).

SEPTEMBER 30

Isaiah 60:1–62:5; Philippians 1:27–2:18; Psalms 72:1-20; Proverbs 24:11-12

ISAIAH 61:1-2
Was Isaiah 61:1-2 quoted by Jesus Christ?

Jesus quoted these words in Luke 4:18-19 when he began his public ministry. As he read to the people in the synagogue, he stopped in the middle of Isaiah 61:2 after the words, "to proclaim the year of the LORD's favor." Rolling up the scroll, he said, "Today this scripture is fulfilled in your hearing" (Luke 4:21). The next phrase in Isaiah 61:2, "and the day of vengeance of our God," will come true when Jesus returns to earth again. We are now under God's favor; his wrath is yet to come.

ISAIAH 61:10
Who is speaking in Isaiah 61:10?

"Me" could refer to the Messiah, the person anointed with the Spirit of the Lord (Isa. 61:1), or to Zion (Isa. 62:1), which symbolizes God's people. The imagery of the bridegroom is often used in Scripture to depict the Messiah (see Matt. 9:15), while the imagery of the bride is used to depict God's people (see Rev. 19:6-8). We too can be clothed with the righteousness of Christ when we believe in him (2 Cor. 5:21).

PHILIPPIANS 2:5-11
Philippians 2:5-11 is poetic. Was Paul quoting from another source?

These verses are probably from a hymn sung by the early Christian church. The passage holds many parallels to the prophecy of the suffering servant in Isaiah 53. As a hymn, it was not meant to be a complete statement about the nature and work of Christ. Several key characteristics of Jesus Christ, however, are praised in this passage: (1) Christ has always existed with God; (2) Christ is equal to God because he *is* God (John 1:1ff.; Col. 1:15-19); (3) though Christ is God, he became a man in order to fulfill God's plan of salvation for all people; (4) Christ did not just have the appearance of being a man—he actually became human to identify with our sins; (5) Christ voluntarily laid aside his divine rights and privileges out of love for his Father; (6) Christ died on the cross for our sins so we wouldn't have to face eternal death; (7) God glorified Christ because of his obedience; (8) God raised Christ to his original position at the Father's right hand, where he will reign forever as our Lord and Judge.

OCTOBER 1

 ISAIAH 63:1-4
What was Edom, and who was the one wearing red garments coming out of Edom?

The nation of Edom was a constant enemy of Israel despite its common ancestry in Isaac (Gen. 25:23). Edom rejoiced at any trouble Israel faced. The imagery in this passage is of a watchman on the wall of Jerusalem, seeing Edom approaching; he fears that the Edomite king in his crimson garment is leading an attack. But it turns out to be the Lord, in blood-stained clothes, who has trampled and destroyed Edom. Bozrah is a city in Edom. (For other prophecies against Edom, see Amos 1:11-12; Obad. 1:10-11; Mal. 1:2-4.)

ISAIAH 64:6
Does Isaiah 64:6 mean that no one is acceptable to God?

This passage doesn't mean that God will reject us if we come to him in faith, nor that he despises our efforts to please him. It means that if we come to him demanding acceptance on the basis of our "good" conduct, God will point out that our righteousness is nothing compared to his infinite righteousness. This message is primarily for the unrepentant person, not the true follower of God.

PHILIPPIANS 2:25
Who was Epaphroditus?

Epaphroditus delivered money from the Philippians to Paul; then he returned with this thank-you letter to Philippi. Epaphroditus may have been an elder in Philippi (Phil. 2:25-30; 4:18) who, while staying with Paul, became ill (Phil. 2:27, 30). After recovering, he returned home. He is mentioned only in Philippians.

 PHILIPPIANS 3:2, KJV
Who are the "dogs", the "evil workers," and the "concision" mentioned in Philippians 3:2?

These "dogs" and "men who do evil" (NIV) were very likely *Judaizers*—Jewish Christians who wrongly believed that it was essential for Gentiles to follow all the Old Testament Jewish laws, especially the rite of circumcision, in order to receive salvation. Many Judaizers were motivated by spiritual pride. Because they had invested so much time and effort in keeping their laws, they couldn't accept the fact that all their efforts couldn't bring them a step closer to salvation. Paul criticized the Judaizers because they looked at Christianity backwards— thinking that what they *did* (*circumcision*—cutting the flesh) made them believers rather than the free gift of grace given by Christ. What believers do is a *result* of faith, not a *prerequisite* to faith. This had been confirmed by the early church leaders at the Jerusalem council several years earlier (Acts 15).

OCTOBER 2

ISAIAH 66:1
In Isaiah 66:1 is God asking that a temple be built for him?

No, it means that even the beautiful temple in Jerusalem was woefully inadequate for a God who is present everywhere. God cannot be confined to any human structure (see 2 Chron. 6:18; Acts 7:49-50). Chapter 66 is a fitting climax to the book Isaiah. It promises that God will lift up the humble, judge all people, destroy the wicked, bring all believers together, and establish a new heaven and a new earth.

ISAIAH 66:2
Why does God speak of those who are "contrite in spirit" in Isaiah 66:2, and then mention people who "have chosen their own ways in verse 3?

These key verses summarize Isaiah's message. He contrasted two ways of living: that of humble persons who have a profound reverence for God's messages and their application to life, and that of those who choose their own way. The sacrifices of the arrogant were only external compliance. In their hearts they were murderers, perverts, and idolaters. God shows mercy to the humble, but he curses the proud and self-sufficient (see Luke 1:51-53).

PHILIPPIANS 3:4-6
Is Paul boasting about his achievements in Philippians 3:4-6?

No, he is actually doing the opposite, showing that human achievements, no matter how impressive, cannot earn a person salvation and eternal life with God. Paul had impressive credentials: upbringing, nationality, family background, inheritance, orthodoxy, activity, and morality (see 2 Cor. 11; Gal. 1:13-24, for more of his credentials). However, his conversion to faith in Christ (Acts 9) wasn't based on what he had done, but on God's grace. Paul did not depend on his deeds to please God because even the most impressive credentials fall short of God's holy standards.

PHILIPPIANS 3:6
Why did Paul, a devout Jewish leader, persecute the church?

Agreeing with the leaders of the religious establishment, Paul thought that Christianity was heretical and blasphemous. Because Jesus did not meet his expectations of what the Messiah would be like, Paul assumed that Jesus' claims were false—and therefore wicked. In addition, he saw Christianity as a political menace because it threatened to disrupt the fragile harmony between the Jews and the Roman government.

OCTOBER 3

JEREMIAH 1:1
What is the historical background of Jeremiah?

After King Solomon's death, the united kingdom of Israel had split into rival northern and southern kingdoms. The northern kingdom was called Israel; the southern, Judah. Jeremiah was from Anathoth, four miles north of Jerusalem in the southern kingdom. He lived and prophesied during the reigns of the last five kings of Judah. This was a chaotic time politically, morally, and spiritually. As Babylon, Egypt, and Assyria battled for world supremacy, Judah found itself caught in the middle of the triangle. Although Jeremiah prophesied for 40 years, he never saw his people heed his words and turn from their sins.

JEREMIAH 1:11-14
What is the significance of Jeremiah's visions in 1:11-14?

The vision of the branch of an almond tree revealed the beginning of God's judgment, because the almond tree is among the first to blossom in the spring. God saw the sins of Judah and the nations, and he would carry out swift and certain judgment. The boiling pot tilting away from the north and spilling over Judah pictured Babylon delivering God's scalding judgment against Jeremiah's people.

JEREMIAH 2:23-24
Why is Israel called "a restive young camel" and "a wild ass"?

The people are compared to animals who search for mates in mating season. Unrestrained, they rush for power, money, alliances with foreign powers, and other gods. The idols did not seek the people; the people sought the idols and then ran wildly after them. Then they became so comfortable in their sin that they could not think of giving it up. Their only shame was in getting caught. If we desire something so much that we'll do anything to get it, this is a sign that we are addicted to it and out of tune with God.

PHILIPPIANS 4:18
What kind of sacrifice is Paul referring to in Philippians 4:18?

Paul was not referring to a sin offering but to a thank offering, "a fragrant offering, an acceptable sacrifice, pleasing to God" (Lev. 7:12-15 contains the instructions for thank offerings). Although the Greek and Roman Christians were not Jews, and they had not offered sacrifices according to the Old Testament laws, they were well acquainted with the pagan rituals of offering sacrifices.

OCTOBER 4

Jeremiah 2:31–4:18; Colossians 1:1-20; Psalms 76:1-12; Proverbs 24:21-22

JEREMIAH 3:1, TLB
What law is Jeremiah 3:1 referring to?

This law, found in Deuteronomy 24:1-4, says that a divorced woman who remarries can never be reunited with her first husband. Judah "divorced" God and "married" other gods. God had every right to permanently disown his wayward people, but in his mercy he was willing to take them back again.

COLOSSIANS 1:1
Where was Colosse?

The city of Colosse was one hundred miles east of Ephesus on the Lycus River. It was not as influential as the nearby city of Laodicea, but as a trading center it was a crossroads for ideas and religions. Colosse had a large Jewish population—many Jews had fled there when they were forced out of Jerusalem under the persecutions of Antiochus III and IV, almost two hundred years before Christ. The church in Colosse had been founded by Epaphras (Col. 1:7), one of Paul's converts. Paul had not yet visited this church. His purpose in writing was to refute heretical teachings about Christ that had been causing confusion among the Christians there.

COLOSSIANS 1:15-16
What is the meaning of Colossians 1:15-16?

This is one of the strongest statements about the divine nature of Christ found anywhere in the Bible. Jesus is not only equal to God (Phil. 2:6), he *is* God (John 1:1, 18; 10:30, 38; 20:28); as the image of the invisible God, he is the exact representation of God. He not only reflects God, but he reveals God to us (John 1:18; 14:9); as the firstborn over all creation, he has all the priority and authority of the firstborn prince in a king's household. He came from heaven, not from the dust of the earth (1 Cor. 15:47), and he is Lord of all (Rom. 9:5; 10:11-13; Rev. 1:5; 17:14). He is completely holy (Heb. 7:26-28; 1 Pet. 1:19; 2:22; 1 John 3:5), and he has authority to judge the world (Rom. 2:16; 2 Cor. 5:10; 2 Tim. 4:1). Therefore, Christ is supreme over all creation, including the spirit world. We, like the Colossian believers, must believe in the deity of Jesus Christ (that Jesus is God) or our Christian faith is hollow, misdirected, and meaningless. This is a central truth of Christianity.

OCTOBER 5

JEREMIAH 5:15
What nation is mentioned in Jeremiah 5:15?

This was Babylon, indeed an ancient nation. The old Babylonian empire had lasted from about 1900 B.C. to 1550 B.C., and earlier kingdoms had been on her soil as early as 3000 B.C. Babylon in Jeremiah's day would shortly rebel against Assyrian domination, form its own army, conquer Assyria, and become the next dominant world power.

COLOSSIANS 2:1
Where was Laodicea?

Laodicea was located a few miles northwest of Colosse. Like the church at Colosse, the Laodicean church was probably founded by one of Paul's converts while Paul was staying in Ephesus (Acts 19:10). The city was a wealthy center of trade and commerce, but later Christ would criticize the believers at Laodicea for their lukewarm condition (Rev. 3:14-22). The fact that Paul wanted this letter to be passed on to the Laodicean church (Col. 4:16) indicates that false teaching may have spread there as well. Paul was counting on ties of love to bring the churches together to stand against this heresy and to encourage each other to remain true to God's plan of salvation in Christ.

COLOSSIANS 2:4
What were the "persuasive words" that were deceiving the Colossians?

The problem that Paul was combating in the Colossian church was similar to *Gnosticism* (from the Greek word *gnosis,* meaning "knowledge"). This heresy (a teaching contrary to Biblical doctrine) undermined Christianity in several basic ways: (1) It insisted that important secret knowledge was hidden from most believers; Paul, however, said that Christ provides all the knowledge we need. (2) It taught that the body was evil; Paul countered that God himself lived in a body—that is, he was embodied in Jesus Christ. (3) It contended that Christ only seemed to be human, but was not; Paul insisted that Jesus is fully human and fully God. Gnosticism became fashionable in the second century. Even in Paul's day, these ideas sounded attractive to many, and exposure to such teachings could easily seduce a church that didn't know Christian doctrine well.

OCTOBER 6

Jeremiah 6:15–8:7; Colossians 2:8-23; Psalms 78:1-31; Proverbs 24:26

 JEREMIAH 7:18
Who was the "Queen of Heaven"?

This was a name for Ishtar, the Mesopotamian goddess of love and fertility. After the fall of Jerusalem, the refugees from Judah who fled to Egypt continued to worship her (Jer. 44:17). A papyrus dating from the fifth century B.C., found at Hermopolis in Egypt, mentions the Queen of Heaven among the gods honored by the Jewish community living there.

 COLOSSIANS 2:8
Was Paul against philosophy?

Paul writes against any philosophy of life based only on human ideas and experiences. Paul himself was a gifted philosopher, so he is not condemning philosophy. He is condemning teaching that credits humanity, not Christ, with being the answer to life's problems. That approach becomes a false religion.

 COLOSSIANS 2:18
Why did people worship angels?

The false teachers were claiming that God was far away and could be approached only through levels of angels. They taught that people had to worship angels in order to reach God. This is unscriptural; the Bible teaches that angels are God's servants, and it forbids worshiping them (Exod. 20:3-4; Rev. 22:8-9).

 COLOSSIANS 2:18
What is an "unspiritual mind"?

The expression "unspiritual mind" referred to the false teachers' denial of the body's significance instead declaring it evil, but their desire for attention from others showed that, in reality, they were obsessed with the physical realm.

PSALM 78:9-10
When did the soldiers of Ephraim run away in battle?

Ephraim was the most prominent tribe of Israel from the days of Moses to Saul's time. The tabernacle was set up in its territory. There is no other biblical record of Ephraim's soldiers turning back from battle, so this is probably a metaphor referring to Ephraim's failure to provide strong leadership during those years. When David became king, the tribe of Judah gained prominence. Because of David's faith and obedience, God chose Jerusalem in Judah to be the place for the new temple and rejected Ephraim (Ps. 78:67). This caused tension between the two tribes. This psalm may have been written because of that tension in order to demonstrate once again why God chose Judah.

OCTOBER 7

JEREMIAH 9:25-26
Did other nations besides Israel practice circumcision?

Circumcision went back to the time of Abraham. For the people of Israel it was a symbol of their covenant relationship to God (Gen. 17:9-14). Circumcision was also practiced by pagan nations, but not as the sign of a covenant with God. By Jeremiah's time, the Israelites had forgotten the spiritual significance of circumcision even though they continued to do the physical ritual.

COLOSSIANS 3:12, KJV
How can I "clothe" myself with everything mentioned in Colossians 3:12?

In Colossians 3:12-17 Paul offers a strategy to help us live for God day by day by putting on the new man (Col. 3:10): (1) imitate Christ's compassionate, forgiving attitude (Col. 3:12-13); (2) let love guide your life (Col. 3:14); (3) let the peace of Christ rule in your heart (Col. 3:15); (4) always be thankful (Col. 3:15, 17); (5) keep God's Word in you at all times (Col. 3:16); (6) Do everything in the name of Jesus Christ (Col. 3:17). All the virtues that Paul encourages us to develop are perfectly bound together by love (Col. 3:14). As we clothe ourselves with these virtues, the last garment we are to put on is love which holds all of the others in place. To pursue any list of virtues without love will lead to distortion, fragmentation, and stagnation (1 Cor. 13:3).

COLOSSIANS 3:15, NRSV
How can the "peace of Christ rule" in my heart?

The word *rule* was used in athletics with reference to umpiring. Paul tells us to let Christ's peace be umpire or referee in our hearts. Our hearts are the center of conflict because there our feelings and desires clash—our fears and hopes, distrust and trust, jealousy and love. How can we deal with these constant conflicts and live as God wants? Paul explains that we must decide between conflicting elements by using the rule of peace—which choice will promote peace in our souls?

COLOSSIANS 3:16, KJV
How can we teach and admonish "in songs and hymns and spiritual songs"?

Although the early Christians had access to the Old Testament and freely used it, they did not yet have the New Testament or any other Christian books to study. Their stories and teachings about Christ were memorized and passed on from person to person. Sometimes the teachings were set to music, and so music became an important part of Christian worship and education.

OCTOBER 8

Jeremiah 10:1–11:23; Colossians 3:18–4:18; Psalms 78:56-72; Proverbs 24:28-29

JEREMIAH 11:14
Why didn't God want Jeremiah to pray for the people?

At first glance this command is shocking—God tells Jeremiah not to pray, and says he won't listen to the people if they pray. A time comes when God must dispense justice. If the people were unrepentant and continued in their sin, neither their prayers nor Jeremiah's would prevent God's judgment. Their only hope was repentance—sorrow for sin, turning from it, and turning to God.

JEREMIAH 11:18-23
Why did people want to kill Jeremiah?

To Jeremiah's surprise, the people of Anathoth, his hometown, were plotting to kill him. They wanted to silence Jeremiah's message for several reasons: (1) economic—his condemnation of idol worship would hurt the business of the idol-makers; (2) religious—the message of doom and gloom made the people feel depressed and guilty; (3) political—he openly rebuked their hypocritical politics; and (4) personal—the people hated him for showing them that they were wrong. Jeremiah had two options: run and hide, or call on God. Jeremiah called, and God answered.

COLOSSIANS 3:22–4:1
Does Paul condone slavery?

Paul does not condemn or condone slavery, but explains that Christ transcends all divisions between people. Slaves are told to work hard as though their master were Christ himself (Col. 3:22-25); but masters should be just and fair (Col. 4:1). Perhaps Paul was thinking specifically of Onesimus and Philemon—the slave and master whose conflict lay behind the letter to Philemon (see the book of Philemon). Philemon was a slave owner in the Colossian church, and Onesimus had been his slave (Col. 4:9).

COLOSSIANS 4:10
Who were Aristarchus and Mark?

Aristarchus was a Thessalonian who accompanied Paul on his third missionary journey. He was with Paul in the riot at Ephesus (Acts 19:29) with Tychicus and Paul in Greece (Acts 20:4), and he went to Rome with Paul (Acts 27:2). Mark started out with Paul and Barnabas on their first missionary journey (Acts 12:25), but he left in the middle of the trip for unknown reasons (Acts 13:13). Barnabas and Mark were relatives, and when Paul refused to take Mark on another journey, Barnabas and Mark journeyed together to preach the Good News (Acts 15:37-41). Mark also worked with Peter (Acts 12:12-13; 1 Pet. 5:13). Later, Mark and Paul were reconciled (Philem. 24). Mark wrote the Gospel of Mark.

OCTOBER 9

Jeremiah 12:1–14:10; 1 Thessalonians 1:1–2:9; Psalms 79:1-13; Proverbs 24:30-34

JEREMIAH 13:18
Who are the king and queen mother in Jeremiah 13:18?

The king was Jehoiachin, and the queen mother was Nehushta. The king's father, Jehoiakim, had surrendered to Nebuchadnezzar but later rebelled. During Jehoiachin's reign, Nebuchadnezzar's armies besieged Jerusalem, and both Jehoiachin and Nehushta surrendered. Jehoiachin was sent to Babylon and imprisoned (2 Kings 24:8-17). Jeremiah's prophecy came true.

1 THESSALONIANS 1:1
What is the background of the book of 1 Thessalonians?

Thessalonica was the capital and largest city (about 200,000 population) of the Roman province of Macedonia. The most important Roman highway—extending from Rome all the way to the Orient—went through Thessalonica. This highway, along with the city's thriving seaport, made Thessalonica one of the wealthiest and most flourishing trade centers in the Roman empire. Recognized as a free city, Thessalonica was allowed self-rule and was exempted from most of the restrictions placed by Rome on other cities in the empire. However, with its international flavor came many pagan religions and cultural influences that challenged the faith of the young Christians there. Paul and his companions probably arrived in Thessalonica in the early summer of A.D. 50. They planted the Christian church in that city, but had to leave in a hurry because their lives were threatened (Acts 17:1-10). At the first opportunity, probably when he stopped at Corinth, Paul sent Timothy back to Thessalonica to see how the new believers were doing. Timothy returned to Paul with good news: the Christians in Thessalonica were remaining firm in the faith and were unified. But the Thessalonians did have some questions about their new faith. Paul had not had time to answer all their questions during his brief visit, and in the meantime, other questions had arisen. So Paul wrote this letter to answer questions and to commend their faithfulness to Christ.

1 THESSALONIANS 2:3
Why did Paul have to say that his words were "not of deceit, nor of uncleanness, nor in guile"?

This pointed statement may be a response to accusations from the Jewish leaders who had stirred up the crowds (Acts 17:5). Paul did not seek money, fame, or popularity by sharing the gospel. He demonstrated the sincerity of his motives by showing that he and Silas had suffered for sharing the gospel in Philippi. People become involved in ministry for a variety of reasons, not all of them good or pure. When their bad motives are exposed, all of Christ's work suffers.

OCTOBER 10

Jeremiah 14:11–16:15; 1 Thessalonians 2:10–3:13; Psalms 80:1-19; Proverbs 25:1-5

JEREMIAH 14:17
Was Jeremiah or God crying in Jeremiah 14:17?

Actually it was both. Jeremiah was so in tune with God that he expressed God's great compassion and sorrow for his chosen people in his own tears. This was a symbol the people could understand.

JEREMIAH 16:5
Why did God tell Jeremiah not to mourn for the dead?

In Jeremiah's culture, it was unthinkable not to show grief publicly. The absence of mourning showed the people how complete their devastation would be. So many people would die that it would be impossible to carry out mourning rituals for all of them.

1 THESSALONIANS 2:15-16
Why were so many Jews opposed to Christianity?

(1) Although the Jewish religion had been declared legal by the Roman government, it still had a tenuous relationship with the government. At this time, Christianity was viewed as a sect of Judaism. The Jews were afraid that reprisals leveled against the Christians might be expanded to include them. (2) The Jewish leaders thought Jesus was a false prophet, and they didn't want his teachings to spread. (3) They feared that if many Jews were drawn away, their own political position might be weakened. (4) They were proud of their special status as God's chosen people, and they resented the fact that Gentiles could be full members within the Christian church.

1 THESSALONIANS 2:18
When Paul spoke of "Satan" in 1 Thessalonians 2:18, was this a symbol of some kind of suffering or trouble?

Satan is real. Paul was not using the word "Satan" here symbolically. Satan is called "the god of this age" (2 Cor. 4:4) and "the ruler of the kingdom of the air" (Eph. 2:2). We don't know exactly what hindered Paul from returning to Thessalonica—opposition, illness, travel complications, or a direct attack by Satan—but Satan worked in some way to keep him away. Many of the difficulties that prevent us from accomplishing God's work can be attributed to Satan (see Eph. 6:12).

OCTOBER 11

Jeremiah 16:16–18:23; 1 Thessalonians 4:1–5:3; Psalms 81:1-16; Proverbs 25:6-7

 JEREMIAH 17:5-8
What is the meaning of Jeremiah 17:5-8?

Two kinds of people are contrasted here: those who trust in human beings and those who trust in the Lord. The people of Judah were trusting in false gods and military alliances instead of God, and thus they were barren and unfruitful. In contrast, those who trust in the Lord flourish like trees planted by water (see Psalm 1). In times of trouble, those who trust in human beings will be impoverished and spiritually weak, so they will have no strength to draw on. But those who trust in the Lord will have abundant strength, not only for their own needs, but even for the needs of others.

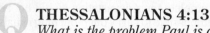 THESSALONIANS 4:13
What is the problem Paul is addressing in 1 Thessalonians 4:13?

The Thessalonians were wondering why many of their fellow believers had fallen asleep (died) and what would happen to them when Christ returned. Paul wanted the Thessalonians to understand that death is not the end of the story. When Christ returns, all believers—dead and alive—will be reunited, never to suffer or die again.

 1 THESSALONIANS 4:9
When will the dead be raised?

Knowing exactly *when* the dead will be raised, in relation to the other events at the second coming, is not as important as knowing why Paul wrote these words—to challenge believers to comfort and encourage one another when loved ones die. This passage can be a great comfort when any believer dies. The same love that should unite believers in this life will unite believers when Christ returns and reigns for eternity.

1 THESSALONIANS 5:2
What is the "day of the Lord"?

The "day of the Lord" is a future time when God will intervene directly and dramatically in world affairs. Predicted and discussed often in the Old Testament (Isa. 13:6-12; Joel 2:28-32; Zeph. 1:14-18), the day of the Lord will include both punishment and blessing. Christ will judge sin and set up his eternal kingdom.

OCTOBER 12

Q JEREMIAH 19:7-14
Did Jeremiah's prophecy in 19:7-14 come to pass?

The horrible carnage that Jeremiah predicted happened twice, in 586 B.C. during the Babylonian invasion under Nebuchadnezzar, and in A.D. 70 when Titus destroyed Jerusalem. During the Babylonian siege, food became so scarce that people became cannibals, even eating their own children. (See Lev. 26:29 and Deut. 28:53-57 for prophecies concerning this; and see 2 Kings 6:28-29; Lam. 2:20; 4:10 for accounts of actual occurrences.)

Q 1 THESSALONIANS 5:17, NRSV
How can I "pray without ceasing"?

We cannot spend all our time on our knees, but it is possible to have a prayerful attitude at all times. This attitude is built upon acknowledging our dependence on God, realizing his presence within us, and determining to obey him fully. Then we will find it natural to pray frequent, spontaneous, short prayers. A prayerful attitude is not a substitute for regular times of prayer but should be an outgrowth of those times.

Q 1 THESSALONIANS 5:19, TLB
What does it mean to "smother the Holy Spirit"?

By warning us not to "put out the Spirit's fire," Paul means that we should not ignore or toss aside the gifts the Holy Spirit gives. Here, he mentions prophecy (1 Thess. 5:20); in 1 Corinthians 14:39, he mentions tongues. Sometimes spiritual gifts are controversial, and they may cause division in a church. Rather than trying to solve the problems, some Christians prefer to smother the gifts. This impoverishes the church. Christians should not stifle the Holy Spirit's work in anyone's life but encourage the full expression of these gifts to benefit the whole body of Christ.

Q 1 THESSALONIANS 5:27
How could Paul's letter to the Thessalonians "be read to all the holy brethren"?

The Thessalonian church was young, and they needed help and encouragement. Both the persecution they faced and the temptations of their pagan culture were potential problems for these new Christians. Paul wrote, therefore, to strengthen their faith and bolster their resistance to persecution and temptation. For every Christian to hear this letter, it had to be read in a public meeting—there were not enough copies to circulate. Paul wanted to make sure that everyone had the opportunity to hear his message because he was answering important questions and offering needed encouragement.

OCTOBER 13

Jeremiah 22:1–23:20; 2 Thessalonians 1:1-12; Psalms 83:1-18; Proverbs 25:11-14

 ### JEREMIAH 23:9-14
How did the nation become so corrupt?

A major factor was false prophecy. The false prophets had a large, enthusiastic audience and were very popular because they made the people believe that all was well. By contrast, Jeremiah's message from God was unpopular because it showed the people how bad they were. There are four warning signs of false prophets that still apply today: (1) They may appear to speak God's message, but they do not live according to his principles. (2) They water down God's message in order to make it more palatable. (3) They encourage their listeners, often subtly, to disobey God. (4) They tend to be arrogant and self-serving, appealing to the desires of their audience instead of being true to God's Word.

 ### 2 THESSALONIANS
Why did Paul write 2 Thessalonians?

Paul wrote this letter from Corinth less than a year after he wrote 1 Thessalonians. He and his companions, Timothy and Silas, had visited Thessalonica on Paul's second missionary journey (Acts 17:1-10). They established the church there, but Paul had to leave suddenly because of persecution. This prompted him to write his first letter (1 Thessalonians), which contains words of comfort and encouragement. Paul then heard how the Thessalonians had responded to this letter. The good news was that they were continuing to grow in their faith. But the bad news was that false teachings about Christ's return were spreading, leading many to quit their jobs and wait for the end of the world. So Paul wrote to them again. While the purpose of Paul's first letter was to comfort the Thessalonians with the assurance of Christ's second coming, the purpose of his second letter is to correct false teaching about the second coming.

 ### 2 THESSALONIANS 1:4-6
Why were the Thessalonians suffering?

Paul had been persecuted during his first visit to Thessalonica (Acts 17:5-9). No doubt those who had responded to his message and had become Christians were continuing to be persecuted by both Jews and Gentiles. In Paul's first letter to the Thessalonians, he said that Christ's return would bring deliverance from persecution and judgment on the persecutors. But this caused the people to expect Christ's return right away to rescue and vindicate them. So Paul had to point out that while waiting for God's kingdom, believers could and should learn perseverance and faith from their suffering.

OCTOBER 14

Jeremiah 23:21–25:38; 2 Thessalonians 2:1-17; Psalms 84:1-12; Proverbs 25:15

Q JEREMIAH 24:2-10
What are the good and bad figs in Jeremiah 24:2-10?

The good figs represented the exiles to Babylon—not because they were good, but because their hearts would respond to God. He would preserve them and bring them back to the land. The poor figs represented those who remained in Judah or ran away to Egypt. Those people may have arrogantly believed they would be blessed if they remained in the land or escaped to Egypt, but the opposite was true because God would use the captivity to refine the exiles.

Q 2 THESSALONIANS 2:3
Who is the "man of lawlessness" in 2 Thessalonians 2:3?

Throughout history there have been individuals who epitomized evil and who were hostile to everything Christ stands for (see 1 John 2:18; 4:3; 2 John 1:7). These people, called antichrists, have lived in every generation and will continue to work their evil. Then just before Christ's second coming 2 Thessalonians 2:3 says, "the man of lawlessness . . . the man doomed to destruction" will arise. He will be Satan's tool, equipped with Satan's power (2 Thess. 2:9). This lawless man will be *the* antichrist. It is dangerous, however, to label any person as the antichrist and to try to predict Christ's coming based on that assumption. Paul mentions the antichrist, not so we might identify him specifically, but so we might be ready for anything that threatens our faith.

Q 2 THESSALONIANS 2:7
Who holds back the lawless one?

Three possibilities have been suggested: (1) government and law, which help to curb evil; (2) the ministry and activity of the church and the effects of the gospel; or (3) the Holy Spirit. The Bible is not clear on who this restrainer is, only that he will not restrain forever. We should not fear this time when the restraint is removed—God is far stronger than the lawless one, and God will save his people.

Q 2 THESSALONIANS 2:7
What does Paul mean by "the secret power of lawlessness is already at work"?

This means that the work that this antichrist will do is already going on. "Secret" means something no one can discover, but something God will reveal. "Lawlessness" is the hidden, subtle, underlying force from which all sin springs. Civilization still has a veneer of decency through law enforcement, education, science, and reason. Although we are horrified by criminal acts, we have yet to see the real horror of complete lawlessness. This will happen when "the one who now holds it back [possibly the Holy Spirit] . . . is taken out of the way."

OCTOBER 15

Q JEREMIAH 26:2-9
Why did the priests and false prophets want to kill Jeremiah?

Shiloh was where the tabernacle had been set up after the conquest of Canaan (Josh. 18:1). It was destroyed in 1050 B.C. by the Philistines. "I will make this house like Shiloh" means that Jerusalem and the temple would be destroyed. When Jeremiah said that Jerusalem, the city of God, would become an object of cursing and the temple would be destroyed (Jer. 26:6), the priests and false prophets were infuriated. The temple was important to them because the people's reverence for it brought them power. By saying that the temple would be destroyed, Jeremiah undermined their authority. Jesus also infuriated the religious leaders of his time by foretelling the destruction of Jerusalem and the temple (Matt. 24:2).

Q JEREMIAH 27:1ff.
Why did Jeremiah wear a yoke?

The year was 593 B.C., and Nebuchadnezzar had already invaded Judah once and had taken many captives. Jeremiah wore a yoke (a wooden frame used to fasten a team of animals to a plow) as a symbol of bondage. This was an object lesson, telling the people they must put themselves under Babylon's yoke or be destroyed.

Q JEREMIAH 27:19-21
When did the events of Jeremiah 27:19-21 occur?

Nebuchadnezzar invaded Judah in 597 B.C. for the second time. He took away many important people living in Jerusalem—including Daniel and Ezekiel. Although these men were captives, they had a profound impact on the exiles and leaders in Babylon. Jeremiah predicted that more people and even the precious objects in the temple would be taken. This happened in 586 B.C. during Babylon's third and last invasion.

Q 2 THESSALONIANS 3:11
Why does Paul warn the Thessalonians against laziness?

Some people in the Thessalonian church may have been falsely teaching that because Christ would return any day, people should set aside their responsibilities, quit work, do no future planning, and just wait for the Lord. But their lack of activity only led them into sin. They became a burden to the church, which was supporting them; they wasted time that could have been used for helping others; and they became "busybodies". These church members may have thought that they were being more spiritual by not working, but Paul tells them to be responsible and get back to work.

OCTOBER 16

Jeremiah 28:1–29:32; 1 Timothy 1:1-20; Psalms 86:1-17; Proverbs 25:17

JEREMIAH 29:10
When were the seventy years of captivity?

Scholars differ on the exact dates of this 70-year period in Babylon. Some say it refers to the years 605–538 B.C., from the first deportation to Babylon to the arrival of the first exiles back in Jerusalem after Cyrus's freedom decree. Others point to the years 586–516 B.C., from the last deportation to Babylon and the destruction of the temple until its rebuilding. A third possibility is that 70 years is an approximate number meaning a lifetime. All agree that God sent his people to Babylon for a long time, not the short captivity predicted by the false prophets.

1 TIMOTHY
What is the background of Paul's first letter to Timothy?

Paul first visited Ephesus on his second missionary journey (Acts 18:19-21). Later, on his third missionary journey, he stayed there for almost three years (Acts 19–20). Ephesus, along with Rome, Corinth, Antioch, and Alexandria, was one of the major cities in the Roman empire. It was a center for the commerce, politics, and religions of Asia Minor, and the location of the temple dedicated to the goddess Artemis (Diana). This letter was written to Timothy in A.D. 64 or 65, after Paul's first imprisonment in Rome (Acts 28:16-31). Apparently Paul had been out of prison for several years, and during that time he had revisited many churches in Asia and Macedonia. When he and Timothy returned to Ephesus, they found widespread false teaching in the church. Paul had warned the Ephesian elders to be on guard against the false teachers who inevitably would come after he had left (Acts 20:17-31). Paul sent Timothy to lead the Ephesian church while he moved on to Macedonia. From there Paul wrote this letter of encouragement and instruction to help Timothy deal with the difficult situation in the Ephesian church. Later, Paul was arrested again and brought back to a Roman prison. The church at Ephesus may have been plagued by the same heresy that was threatening the church at Colosse—the teaching that to be acceptable to God, a person had to discover certain hidden knowledge and had to worship angels (Col. 2:8, 18). Thinking that it would aid in their salvation, some Ephesians constructed mythical stories based on Old Testament history or genealogies. The false teachers were motivated by their own interests rather than Christ's. They embroiled the church in endless and irrelevant questions and controversies, taking precious time away from the study of the truth.

OCTOBER 17

1 TIMOTHY 2:9-15
Does 1 Timothy 2:9-15 show that Paul was against women?

To understand these verses, we must understand the situation in which Paul and Timothy worked. In first-century Jewish culture, women were not allowed to study. When Paul said that women should *learn* in quietness and full submission, he was offering them an amazing new opportunity. Paul did not want the Ephesian women to teach because they didn't yet have enough knowledge or experience. The Ephesian church had a particular problem with false teachers. The women were especially susceptible to the false teachings (2 Tim. 3:1-9), because they did not yet have enough biblical knowledge to discern the truth.

1 TIMOTHY 1:12
Are women never to teach in the assembled church?

Commentators point out that Paul did not forbid women from ever teaching. Paul's commended coworker, Priscilla, taught Apollos, the great preacher (Acts 18:24-26). In addition, Paul frequently mentioned other women who held positions of responsibility in the church. Phoebe worked in the church (Rom. 16:1). Mary, Tryphena, and Tryphosa were the Lord's workers (Rom. 16:6, 12), as were Euodia and Syntyche (Phil. 4:2). Paul was very likely prohibiting the Ephesian women, not all women, from teaching. In Paul's reference to women being silent, the word *silent* expresses an attitude of quietness and composure. (A different Greek word is usually used to convey "complete silence.") In addition, Paul himself acknowledges that women publicly prayed and prophesied (1 Cor. 11:5). The women in the Ephesian church, however, were abusing their newly acquired Christian freedom. Because they were new converts, they did not yet have the necessary experience, knowledge, or Christian maturity to teach those who already had extensive biblical education.

1 TIMOTHY 2:15
How is a woman "saved through childbearing"?

There are several ways to understand the phrase, being "saved through childbearing": (1) Man sinned and so men were condemned to painful labor. Woman sinned and so women were condemned to pain in childbearing (Gen. 3:16). Both men and women, however, can be saved through trusting Christ and obeying him. (2) Women who fulfill their God-given roles are demonstrating true commitment and obedience to Christ. One of the most important roles for a wife and mother is to care for her family. (3) The childbearing mentioned here refers to the birth of Jesus Christ. Women (and men) are saved spiritually because of the most important birth, that of Christ himself. (4) From the lessons learned through the trials of childbearing, women can develop qualities that teach them about love, trust, submission, and service.

OCTOBER 18

Jeremiah 31:27–32:44; 1 Timothy 3:1-16; Psalms 88:1-18; Proverbs 25:20-22

JEREMIAH 31:33
What is the "new covenant"?

The old covenant, broken by God's people, would be replaced by a new covenant. The foundation of this new covenant is Christ (Heb. 8:6). It is revolutionary, involving not only Israel and Judah, but even the Gentiles. It offers a unique personal relationship with God himself, with his laws written on individuals' hearts instead of on stone. Jeremiah looked forward to the day when the Messiah would come to establish this covenant. Under the new covenant God would write his law on their hearts rather than on tablets of stone as were the Ten Commandments. In Jeremiah 17:1 their sin was engraved on their hearts so that they wanted above all to disobey. This change seems to describe an experience very much like the new birth, with God taking the initiative.

1 TIMOTHY 3:8-10
What is a "deacon"?

Deacon means "one who serves." This position was possibly begun by the apostles in the Jerusalem church (Acts 6:1-6) to care for the physical needs of the congregation, especially the needs of the Greek-speaking widows. Deacons were leaders in the church, and their qualifications resemble those of the overseers. In some churches today, the office of deacon has lost its importance. New Christians are often asked to serve in this position, but that is not the New Testament pattern. Paul says that potential deacons should first be tested before they are asked to serve.

1 TIMOTHY 3:16
What is the "mystery of godliness" mentioned in 1 Timothy 3:16?

In this short hymn, Paul affirms the humanity and divinity of Christ. By so doing he reveals the heart of the gospel, "the mystery of godliness" (the secret of how we become godly). "Appeared in a body"—Jesus was a man; Jesus' incarnation is the basis of our being right with God. "Was vindicated by the Spirit"—Jesus' resurrection showed that the Holy Spirit's power was in him (Rom. 8:11). "Was seen by angels" and "was taken up in glory"—Jesus is divine. As a man, Jesus lived a perfect life, and so he is a perfect example of how to live. As God, Jesus gives us the power to do what is right. It is possible to live a godly life—through following Christ.

OCTOBER 19

Jeremiah 33:1–34:22; 1 Timothy 4:1-16; Psalms 89:1-13; Proverbs 25:23-24

 **JEREMIAH 33:22**
Did God give the promise of Jeremiah 33:22 to Abraham?

The promise of countless descendants was also given to Abraham (Gen. 15:5; 22:17). Not only is God remembering his promises to the nation's forefathers, he is also giving an even greater promise during the nation's darkest hour.

JEREMIAH 34:8
Why did Zedekiah free the slaves?

Babylon had laid siege to Jerusalem, and the city was about to fall. Zedekiah finally decided to listen to Jeremiah and try to appease God—so he freed the slaves. He thought he could win God's favor with a kind act, but what he needed was a change of heart. The people had been disobeying God's law from the beginning (Exod. 21:2-11; Lev. 25:39-55; Deut. 15:12-18). When the siege was temporarily lifted, the people became bold and returned to their sins (Jer. 34:11-17; 37:5, 11).

1 TIMOTHY 4:1, NIV
What were the teachings of those who abandoned the faith?

False teachers were and still are a threat to the church. Jesus and the apostles repeatedly warned against them (see, for example, Mark 13:21-23; Acts 20:28-31; 2 Thess. 2:1-12; 2 Pet. 3:3-7). The danger that Timothy faced in Ephesus seems to have come from certain people in the church who were following some Greek philosophers who taught that the body was evil and that only the soul mattered. The false teachers refused to believe that the God of creation was good, because his very contact with the physical world would have soiled him. Though these Greek-influenced church members honored Jesus, they could not believe he was truly human. Paul knew that their teachings, if left unchecked, would greatly distort Christian truth.

1 TIMOTHY 4:1-2
Why did Paul say that the false teachers were hypocritical liars who encouraged people to follow "deceiving spirits and things taught by demons"?

Satan deceives people by offering a clever imitation of the real thing. The false teachers gave stringent rules (such as forbidding people to marry or to eat certain foods). This made them appear self-disciplined and righteous. Their strict disciplines for the body, however, could not remove sin (see Col. 2:20-23).

OCTOBER 20

JEREMIAH 35:1ff.
What is the significance of the story of the Recabites?

The Recabites' code of conduct resembled that of the Nazirites, who took a special vow of dedication to God (Num. 6). For two hundred years, they had obeyed their ancestors' vow to abstain from wine. While the rest of the nation was breaking its covenant with God, these people were steadfast in their commitment. God wanted the rest of his people to remain as committed to their covenant with him as the Recabites were to their vow. God had Jeremiah tempt the Recabites with wine to demonstrate their commitment and dedication. God knew they wouldn't break their vow. There is a vivid contrast between the Recabites and the other Israelites: (1) The Recabites kept their vows to a fallible human leader; the people of Israel broke their covenant with their infallible divine Leader. (2) Jonadab told his family one time not to drink, and they obeyed; God commanded Israel constantly to turn from sin, and they refused. (3) The Recabites obeyed laws that dealt with temporal issues; Israel refused to obey God's laws that dealt with eternal issues. (4) The Recabites had obeyed for hundreds of years; Israel had disobeyed for hundreds of years. (5) The Recabites would be rewarded; Israel would be punished.

1 TIMOTHY 5:3
Why was it important for the church to take care of widows?

Because there were no pensions, no social security, no life insurance, and few honorable jobs for women, widows were usually unable to support themselves. The responsibility for caring for the helpless naturally falls first on their families, the people whose lives are most closely linked with theirs. Paul stresses the importance of families caring for the needs of widows, and not leaving it for the church to do, so the church can care for those widows who have no families. A widow who had no children or other family members to support her was doomed to poverty. From the beginning, the church took care of its widows, who in turn gave valuable service to the church.

PSALM 89:19
Who is the prophet mentioned in Psalm 89:19?

The prophet here may be Samuel, who anointed David as king of Israel (1 Sam. 16:1-13), or Nathan who was a prophet to Israel when David became king (2 Sam. 7:4-17).

OCTOBER 21

 **JEREMIAH 38:7,** KJV
Why is Ebed-melech called a "Cushite", and why was the king "sitting in the Benjamin Gate"?

Ebed-melech was probably an Ethiopian eunuch and a servant of Zedekiah. The ancient name for Ethiopia was *Cush*. The Benjamin Gate was one of Jerusalem's city gates where legal matters were handled. When Ebed-Melech heard of Jeremiah's plight, he went immediately to deal with the injustice. This incident shows that Ebed-Melech feared God more than man. He alone among the palace officials stood up against the murder plot. His obedience could have cost him his life. Because he obeyed, however, he was spared when Jerusalem fell (Jer. 39:15-18).

1 TIMOTHY 6:10, TLB
Does 1 Timothy 6:10 mean that it is wrong to be wealthy?

No, money is neither good nor bad in itself. Nor is it wrong for the believer to be wealthy. But many people have been turned away from God because of their love for money. It is called "the first step toward all kinds of sins", or "a root of all kinds of evil" (NRSV). The love of money is related to covetousness. More crimes have been committed for money than for almost any other reason. Pride in riches is forbidden and the wealthy are "to use their money to do good" (1 Tim. 6:18, TLB). Being rich in good works is infinitely better than being wealthy yet poor in good works. Ephesus was a wealthy city, and the Ephesian church probably had many wealthy members. Paul advised Timothy to deal with any potential problems by teaching that having riches carries great responsibility. Those who have money must be generous, but they may not be arrogant just because they have a lot to give. They must be careful not to put their hope in money instead of in the living God for their security. In this chapter Paul gives some guidelines about dealing with money: (1) realize that one day riches will all be gone (1 Tim. 6:7, 17); (2) be content with what you have (1 Tim. 6:8); (3) monitor what you are willing to do to get more money (1 Tim. 6:9-10); (4) love people more than money (1 Tim. 6:11); (5) love God's work more than money (1 Tim. 6:11); (6) freely share what you have with others (1 Tim. 6:18). (See Proverbs 30:7-9 for more on avoiding the love of money.)

OCTOBER 22

Jeremiah 39:1–41:18; 2 Timothy 1:1-18; Psalms 90:1–91:16; Proverbs 26:1-2

JEREMIAH 39:1
How long did Zedekiah rule Judah?

Zedekiah, son of Josiah and last king of Judah, ruled 11 years, from 597 to 586 B.C. Zedekiah's two older brothers, Jehoahaz and Jehoiakim, and his nephew Jehoiachin ruled before him. When Jehoiachin was exiled to Babylon, Nebuchadnezzar made 21-year-old Mattaniah the king, changing his name to Zedekiah. Zedekiah rebelled against Nebuchadnezzar, who captured him, killed his sons in front of him, and then blinded him and took him back to Babylon where he later died (see 2 Kings 24–25; 2 Chron. 36; Jer. 52).

JEREMIAH 38:11-12
Why did Nebuchadnezzar protect Jeremiah?

God had promised to rescue Jeremiah from his trouble (Jer. 1:8). The superstitious Babylonians, who highly respected magicians and fortune-tellers, treated Jeremiah as a seer. Because he had been imprisoned by his own people, they assumed he was a traitor and on their side. They undoubtedly knew he had counseled cooperation with Babylon and predicted a Babylonian victory. So the Babylonians freed Jeremiah and protected him. What a difference there is between Jeremiah's fate and Zedekiah's! Jeremiah was freed; Zedekiah was imprisoned. Jeremiah was saved because of his faith; Zedekiah was destroyed because of his fear. Jeremiah was treated with respect; Zedekiah was treated with contempt. Jeremiah was concerned for the people; Zedekiah was concerned for himself.

2 TIMOTHY 1:1
What is the background of Paul's second letter to Timothy?

This is a somber letter. Paul was imprisoned for the last time, and he knew he would soon die. Unlike Paul's first imprisonment in Rome, when he was in a house (Acts 28:16, 23, 30) where he continued to teach, this time he was probably confined to a cold dungeon, awaiting his death (2 Tim. 4:6-8). Emperor Nero had begun a major persecution in A.D. 64 as part of his plan to pass the blame for the great fire of Rome from himself to the Christians. This persecution spread across the empire and included social ostracism, public torture, and murder. As Paul was waiting to die, he wrote a letter to his dear friend Timothy, a younger man who was like a son to him (2 Tim. 1:2). Written in approximately A.D. 66/67, these are the last words we have from Paul.

OCTOBER 23

Jeremiah 42:1–44:23; 2 Timothy 2:1-21; Psalms 92:1–93:5; Proverbs 26:3-5

2 TIMOTHY 2:8-9
Why did the Gospel bring suffering to Paul?

Paul was in chains in prison because of the gospel he preached. When Paul said that Jesus was God, he angered the Jews who had condemned Jesus for blasphemy; but many Jews became followers of Christ (1 Cor. 1:24). He angered the Romans who worshiped the emperor as god; but even some in Caesar's household turned to Jesus (Phil. 4:22). When Paul said Jesus was human, he angered the Greeks who thought divinity was soiled if it had any contact with humanity; still many Greeks accepted the faith (Acts 11:20-21). The truth that Jesus is one person with two united natures has never been easy to understand, but it is being believed by people every day.

2 TIMOTHY 2:17
Who were Hymenaeus and Philetus?

They were heretics who had "wandered away from the truth" (2 Tim. 2:18). Hymenaeus is also mentioned in 1 Timothy 1:20. He weakened people's faith by teaching that the resurrection had already occurred. In 1 Timothy 1:20 Paul says that he handed Hymenaeus over to Satan, meaning that Paul had removed him from the fellowship of the church. Paul did this so that Hymenaeus would see his error and repent. The ultimate purpose of this punishment was correction.

2 TIMOTHY 2:18, TLB
What does it mean that "the resurrection of the dead has already occurred"?

The false teachers were denying the resurrection of the body. They believed that when a person became a Christian, he or she was spiritually reborn, and that was the only resurrection there would ever be. To them, resurrection was symbolic and spiritual, not physical. Paul clearly taught, however, that believers will be resurrected after they die, and that their bodies as well as their souls will live eternally with Christ (1 Cor. 15:35ff.; 2 Cor. 5:1-10; 1 Thess. 4:15-18).

PSALM 92:12
Why does the psalmist use images of trees in Psalm 92:12?

Palm trees are known for their long life. To flourish like palm trees means to stand tall and to live long. The cedars of Lebanon grew to 120 feet in height and up to 30 feet in circumference; thus, they were solid, strong, and immovable. The psalmist saw believers as upright, strong, and unmoved by the winds of circumstance. Those who place their faith firmly in God can have this strength and vitality.

OCTOBER 24

2 TIMOTHY 3:6-7, NKJV
Who were the "gullible women loaded down with sins"?

This phrase is also translated "silly, sin-burdened women" (TLB). Because of their cultural background, women in the Ephesian church had had no formal religious training. They enjoyed their new freedom to study Christian truths, but their eagerness to learn made them a target for false teachers. Paul warned Timothy to watch out for men who would take advantage of these women.

2 TIMOTHY 3:8-9
Who were Jannes and Jambres?

According to tradition, Jannes and Jambres were two of the magicians who counterfeited Moses' miracles before Pharaoh (Exod. 7:11-12). Paul explained that just as Moses exposed and defeated them (Exod. 8:18-19), God would overthrow the false teachers who were plaguing the Ephesian church.

2 TIMOTHY 3:11, TLB
How did Timothy know about Paul's troubles?

In Lystra, Timothy's hometown, Paul had been stoned and left for dead (Acts 14:19); it is likely that Timothy witnessed this event. This was only one incident among many. In 2 Corinthians 11:23-33 Paul summarized his lifetime of suffering for the sake of the gospel. Paul mentioned his suffering here to contrast his experience with that of the pleasure-seeking false teachers.

2 TIMOTHY 3:16
What is the meaning of the phrase "All Scripture is God-breathed"?

This is a more literal translation of the Greek words that are often rendered "All Scripture is given by inspiration of God" (NKJV). The Bible is not a collection of stories, fables, myths, or merely human ideas about God. It is not a human book. Through the Holy Spirit, God revealed his person and plan to certain believers, who wrote down his message for his people (2 Peter 1:20-21). This process is known as *inspiration.* The writers wrote from their own personal, historical, and cultural contexts. Although they used their own minds, talents, language, and style, they wrote what God wanted them to write. Scripture is completely trustworthy because God was in control of its writing. The Bible is "God-breathed." Its words are entirely authoritative for our faith and lives.

OCTOBER 25

Jeremiah 48:1–49:22; 2 Timothy 4:1-22; Psalms 95:1–96:13; Proverbs 26:9-12

JEREMIAH 49:7
Who were the wise men of Edom?

Because the Israelites descended from Jacob and the Edomites from his twin brother, Esau, both nations descended from their father, Isaac. There was constant conflict between these nations, and Edom rejoiced at the fall of Jerusalem (see the book of Obadiah). Teman, a town in the northern part of Edom, was known for its wisdom and was the hometown of Eliphaz, one of Job's friends (Job 2:11). But even the wisdom of Teman could not save Edom from God's wrath.

2 TIMOTHY 4:8
What is the "crown of righteousness" Paul is expecting?

In Roman athletic games, a laurel wreath was given to the winners. A symbol of triumph and honor, it was the most coveted prize in ancient Rome. This is probably what Paul was referring to when he spoke of a "crown." But his would be a crown of righteousness.

2 TIMOTHY 4:10
Who was Demas?

Demas had been one of Paul's co-workers (Col. 4:14; Philem. 24), but he had deserted Paul because he "loved this world." In other words, Demas loved worldly values and worldly pleasures. There are two ways to love the world. God loves the world as he created it and as it could be if it were rescued from evil. Others, like Demas, love the world as it is, sin and all. Mentioning Demas reminded Paul of more faithful co-workers. Only Luke was with Paul, and Paul was feeling lonely. Tychicus, one of his most trusted companions (Acts 20:4; Eph. 6:21; Col. 4:7; Tit. 3:12), had already left for Ephesus. Paul missed his young helpers Timothy and Mark. Mark had left Paul and Barnabas on the first missionary journey, and this had greatly upset Paul (Acts 13:13; 15:36-41). But later Mark proved to be a worthy helper, and Paul recognized him as a good friend and trusted Christian leader (Col. 4:10; Philem. 24).

2 TIMOTHY 4:13
If Paul was in prison why did he need his coat?

Paul's arrest probably occurred so suddenly that he was not allowed to return home to gather his personal belongings. Because he was a prisoner in a damp and chilly dungeon, Paul asked Timothy to bring him his coat. Even more than the cloak, Paul wanted his scrolls and parchments. The scrolls may have included books of the Old Testament; the parchments may have included copies of his own letters or have been blank sheets for writing.

OCTOBER 26

JEREMIAH 50:1, TLB
Who were the Chaldeans?

Babylon is another name for the nation of the Chaldeans. At the height of its power, the Babylonian empire seemed immovable. But when Babylon had finished serving God's purpose of punishing Judah for her sins, it would be punished and crushed for its own. Babylon was destroyed in 539 B.C. by the Medo-Persians (Dan. 5:30-31). Babylon is also used in Scripture as a symbol of all evil. This message can thus apply to the end times when God wipes out all evil, once and for all.

TITUS 1:1
Why did Paul write to Titus?

Paul wrote this letter between his first and second imprisonments in Rome (before he wrote 2 Timothy) to guide Titus in working with the churches on the island of Crete. Paul had visited Crete with Titus and had left him there to minister (Tit. 1:5). There was a strong pagan influence on this small island, because Crete may have been a training center for Roman soldiers. Therefore, the church in Crete needed strong Christian leadership.

TITUS 1:1
Who was Titus?

Titus, a Greek, was one of Paul's most trusted and dependable co-workers. Paul sent Titus to Corinth on several special missions to help the church in its troubles (2 Cor. 7–8). Paul and Titus also traveled together to Jerusalem (Gal. 2:3) and Crete (Tit. 1:5). Paul left Titus in Crete to lead the new churches springing up on the island. Titus is last mentioned by Paul in 2 Timothy 4:10, Paul's last recorded letter. Titus had leadership ability, so Paul gave him leadership responsibility, urging him to use his abilities well.

TITUS 1:12
Why would Paul say such terrible things about the people of Crete?

Paul was quoting a line from a poem by Epimenides, a poet and philosopher who had lived in Crete six hundred years earlier. Some Cretans had a bad reputation and were known for lying. Paul used this familiar phrase to make the point that Titus' ministry and leadership were very much needed.

OCTOBER 27

Jeremiah 51:1-53; Titus 2:1-15; Psalms 99:1-9; Proverbs 26:17

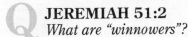

JEREMIAH 51:2
What are "winnowers"?

Winnowers worked at harvest time to separate the wheat from the chaff. When they threw the mixture into the air, the wind blew away the worthless chaff while the wheat settled to the floor. Babylon would be blown away like chaff in the wind. In Matthew 3:12, speaking to the Jews, John the Baptist says Jesus "will clear his threshing floor and will gather his wheat into the granary; but the chaff he will burn with unquenchable fire" (NRSV).

JEREMIAH 51:33
What is a "threshing floor," and what is "flailing"?

Grain was threshed on a threshing floor, where sheaves were brought from the field. The stalks of grain were distributed on the floor, a large level section of hard ground. There the grain was crushed to separate the kernels from the stalk; then the kernels were beaten, or flailed, with a wooden tool. Sometimes a wooden sledge was pulled over the grain by animals to break the kernels loose. Babylon would soon be "threshed" as God judged it for its sins.

JEREMIAH 51:36
Did God dry up Babylon's water supply?

This verse may refer to an event accomplished by Cyrus, who took Babylon by surprise by diverting the river that ran through the city far upstream and walking in on the dry river bed. More likely it is saying that Babylon will be deprived of life-giving water. Unlike Jerusalem, Babylon will not be restored.

TITUS 2:9-10
Why did Paul speak of slavery?

Slavery was common in Paul's day. Paul did not condemn slavery in any of his letters, but he advised slaves and masters to be loving and responsible in their conduct (see also Eph. 6:5-9). The standards set by Paul can help any employee/employer relationship. Employees should always do their best work and be trustworthy, not just when the employer is watching.

PROVERBS 26:17, TLB
What does "yanking a dog's ears" have to do with arguing?

Seizing the ears of a dog is a good way to get bitten, and interfering in arguments is a good way to get hurt. Many times both arguers will turn on the person who interferes. It is best simply to keep out of arguments that are none of your business.

OCTOBER 28

Jeremiah 51:54–52:34; Titus 3:1-15; Psalms 100:1-5; Proverbs 26:18-19

JEREMIAH 51:59-64
Why did Jeremiah send his message to Babylon through Seraiah?

Jeremiah could not visit Babylon, so he sent the message with Seraiah, the officer who cared for the comforts of the army. Seraiah was probably Baruch's brother (Jer. 32:12). In this last of Jeremiah's messages, we find again the twin themes of God's sovereignty and his judgment. Babylon had been allowed to oppress the people of Israel, but Babylon itself would be judged.

JEREMIAH 51–52
Chapter 51 seems to conclude the book of Jeremiah. What is the purpose of chapter 52?

This chapter provides more detail about the destruction of Jerusalem recorded in chapter 39 (similar material is found in 2 Kings 24:18–25:21). This appendix shows that Jeremiah's prophecies concerning the destruction of Jerusalem and the Babylonian captivity happened just as he predicted. It also constitutes a sort of preface to the Lamentations which follow, and it serves as a key to understanding that book.

JEREMIAH 52:13
What happened to the ark of the covenant after the temple was burned?

Before Nebuchadnezzar and his soldiers destroyed Jerusalem and burned the temple, the glory of God had departed from that scared house. So far as we know, the ark of the covenant was destroyed when the temple was burned. The possibility that the Ark still exists somewhere is very remote. The Ark without the glory and presence of God might be archaeologically significant but it would be spiritually useless.

TITUS 3:12
Where was Nicopolis?

The city of Nicopolis was on the western coast of Greece. Artemas or Tychicus would take over Titus' work on the island of Crete, so Titus could meet Paul in Nicopolis. Tychicus was one of Paul's trusted companions (Acts 20:4; Eph. 6:21; Col. 4:7). Titus would have to leave soon because sea travel was dangerous in the winter months.

OCTOBER 29

Lamentations 1:1–2:19; Philemon 1:1-25; Psalms 101:1-8; Proverbs 26:20

LAMENTATIONS 1:1
Why did Jeremiah write Lamentations?

This is the prophet Jeremiah's song of sorrow for Jerusalem's destruction. The nation of Judah had been utterly defeated, the temple destroyed, and captives taken away to Babylon. Jeremiah's tears were for the suffering and humiliation of the people, but those tears penetrated even deeper into his heart. He wept because God had rejected the people for their rebellious ways. Each year this book was read aloud to remind all the Jews that their great city fell because of their stubborn sinfulness.

LAMENTATIONS 2:9
What is the meaning of Lamentations 2:9?

This verse says that four powerful symbols and sources of security were lost: the protection of the *gates,* the leadership of the *king and princes,* the guidance of the *law,* and the vision of the *prophets.* With those four factors present, the people were lulled into a false sense of security and felt comfortable with their sins. But after each was removed, the people were confronted with the choice of repenting and returning to God or continuing on this path of suffering.

PHILEMON 1:1
What is the purpose of Paul's letter to Philemon?

Paul wrote this letter from Rome in about A.D. 60, when he was under house arrest (see Acts 28:30-31). Onesimus was a domestic slave who belonged to Philemon, a wealthy man and a member of the church in Colosse. Onesimus had run away from Philemon and had made his way to Rome where he met Paul, who apparently led him to Christ (Philem. 10). Paul convinced Onesimus that running from his problems wouldn't solve them, and he persuaded Onesimus to return to his master. Paul wrote this letter to Philemon to ask him to be reconciled to his runaway slave.

PHILEMON 1:1-2
Who were Philemon, Apphia, and Archippus?

Philemon was a Greek landowner living in Colosse. He had been converted under Paul's ministry. Apphia may have been Philemon's wife. Archippus may have been Philemon's son, or perhaps an elder in the Colossian church. In either case, Paul included him as a recipient of the letter, possibly so Archippus could read the letter with Philemon and encourage him to take Paul's advice. The Colossian church met in Philemon's home. The early churches often would meet in people's homes.

OCTOBER 30

Lamentations 2:20–3:66; Hebrews 1:1-14; Psalms 102:1-28; Proverbs 26:21-22

LAMENTATIONS 3
Was Lamentations written in poetic form?

In the original Hebrew, the first four chapters in Lamentations are acrostic poems. Each verse in each chapter begins with a successive letter of the Hebrew alphabet. Chapter 3 has 66 verses rather than 22 because it is a triple acrostic: the first three verses begin with the Hebrew equivalent of "A," the next three with "B," and so on. This was a typical form of Hebrew poetry. Other examples of acrostics are Psalms 37, 119, and 145, and Proverbs 31:10-31.

HEBREWS 1:1
What is the background of the book of Hebrews?

The book of Hebrews describes in detail how Jesus Christ not only fulfills the promises and prophecies of the Old Testament, but how Jesus Christ is better than everything in the Jewish system of thought. The Jews accepted the Old Testament, but most of them rejected Jesus as the long-awaited Messiah. The recipients of this letter seem to have been Jewish Christians. They were well-versed in Scripture, and they had professed faith in Christ. Whether through doubt, persecution, or false teaching, however, they may have been in danger of giving up their Christian faith and returning to Judaism. The authorship of this book is uncertain. Several names have been suggested, including Luke, Barnabas, Apollos, Priscilla, and Paul. Most scholars do not believe that Paul was the author, because the writing style of Hebrews is quite different from that of his letters. In addition, Paul identified himself in his other letters and appealed to his authority as an apostle, whereas this writer of Hebrews, who never gives his or her name, appeals to eyewitnesses of Jesus' ministry for authority. Nevertheless, the author of Hebrews evidently knew Paul well. Hebrews was probably written by one of Paul's close associates who often heard him preach.

HEBREWS 1:13-14
Why does Hebrews say that Christ is better than the angels?

False teachers in many of the early churches taught that God could be approached only through angels. Instead of worshiping God directly, followers of these heretics bowed to angels. Hebrews clearly denounces such teaching as false. Some thought of Jesus as the highest angel of God. But Jesus is not a superior angel; and, in any case, angels are not to be worshiped (see Col. 2:18; Rev. 19:1-10). Jesus is God, he alone deserves our worship. Angels are God's messengers, spiritual beings created by God and under his authority (Col. 1:16).

OCTOBER 31

Q LAMENTATIONS 4:10
Why were people in Jerusalem eating their children?

When a city was under siege, the city wall—built for protection—sealed the people inside. They could not get out to the fields to get food and water because the enemy was camped around the city. As food in the city ran out, the people watched their enemies harvest and eat the food in the fields. The siege was a test of wills to see which army could outlast the other. Jerusalem was under siege for two years. Life became so harsh that people even ate their own children, and dead bodies were left to rot in the streets. All hope was gone.

Q LAMENTATIONS 4:6
What was Sodom?

Sodom, the city destroyed by burning sulfur from heaven because of its wickedness (Gen. 18:20–19:29), became a symbol of God's ultimate judgment. Yet the sin of Jerusalem was even greater than the sin of Sodom!

Q HEBREWS 2:11-13
Is Hebrews 2:11-13 a quotation from Psalms?

Yes, various Psalms look forward to Christ and his work in the world. Here the writer quotes a portion of Psalm 22, a Messianic psalm. Because God has adopted all believers as his children, Jesus calls them his brothers and sisters.

Q HEBREWS 2:16-17, TLB
What does it mean that Jesus is "our merciful and faithful High Priest before God"?

In the Old Testament, the high priest was the mediator between God and his people. His job was to regularly offer animal sacrifices according to the law and to intercede with God for forgiveness for the people's sins. Jesus Christ is now our high priest. He came to earth as a human being; therefore, he understands our weaknesses and shows mercy to us. He has *once and for all* paid the penalty for our sins by his own sacrificial death (atonement), and he can be depended on to restore our broken relationship with God. We are released from sin's domination over us when we commit ourselves fully to Christ, trusting completely in what he has done for us.

Q PSALM 103:1-22
What does it mean to "bless the LORD"?

Everything everywhere is to praise the Lord: all angels—mighty ones and heavenly hosts—and all his works! Praising God means remembering all he has done for us, fearing him and obeying his commands, and doing his will.

NOVEMBER 1

Ezekiel 1:1–3:15; Hebrews 3:1-19; Psalms 104:1-23; Proverbs 26:24-26

EZEKIEL 1:1
Who was Ezekiel?

Ezekiel, born and raised in the land of Judah, was preparing to become a priest in God's temple when the Babylonians attacked in 597 B.C. and carried him away along with ten thousand other captives (2 Kings 24:10-14). The nation was on the brink of complete destruction. Five years later, when Ezekiel was thirty (the normal age for becoming a priest), God called him to be a prophet. During the first six years when Ezekiel ministered in Babylonia (Ezek. 1:3), Jeremiah was preaching to the Jews still in Judah, and Daniel was serving in Nebuchadnezzar's court. The Kebar River connected to the Euphrates in Babylonia and was the location of a Jewish settlement of exiles. Ezekiel's latest dated message from God (Ezek. 29:17) was given in 571 B.C. He was taken captive during the second Babylonian invasion of Judah. The Babylonians invaded Judah a third and final time in 586 B.C., completely destroying Jerusalem, burning the temple, and deporting the rest of the people (see 2 Kings 25). Ezekiel dates all his messages from the year he was taken captive (597). His first prophecy to the exiles occurred four years after he arrived in the land of Babylon (593 B.C.).

EZEKIEL 1:1
What is a "vision"?

God communicated to Ezekiel in visions. A vision is a miraculous revelation of God's truth. These visions seem strange to us because they are *apocalyptic*. This means that Ezekiel saw symbolic pictures that vividly conveyed an idea. Daniel and John were other Bible writers who used apocalyptic imagery. The people in exile had lost their perspective of God's purpose and presence, and Ezekiel came to them with a vision from God to show God's awesome glory and holiness and to warn the exiles of sin's consequences before it was too late.

EZEKIEL 1:5, TLB
What is the meaning of "the four living beings"?

Each of the four living creatures had four faces, symbolizing God's perfect nature. Some believe that the lion represented strength; the ox, diligent service; the man, intelligence; and the eagle, divinity. Others see these as the most majestic of God's creatures and say that they therefore represent God's whole creation. The early church fathers saw a connection between these beings and the four Gospels: the lion with Matthew, presenting Christ as the lion of Judah; the ox with Mark, portraying Christ as the servant; the human with Luke, portraying Christ as the perfect human; the eagle with John, portraying Christ as the Son of God, exalted and divine. The vision of John in Revelation 4 parallels Ezekiel's vision.

NOVEMBER 2

Ezekiel 3:16–6:14; Hebrews 4:1-16; Psalms 104:24-35; Proverbs 26:27

EZEKIEL 4:4-8
Why did God command Ezekiel to do such strange things?

Ezekiel's actions symbolically portrayed the fate of Jerusalem. He lay on his left side for 390 days to show that Israel would be punished for 390 years; then he lay on his right side for 40 days to show that Judah would be punished for 40 years. Ezekiel was not allowed to move, symbolizing imprisonment of the people within the walls of the city. We know that Ezekiel did not have to lie on his side all day because these verses tell of other tasks God asked him to do during this time. The small amount of food he was allowed to eat represented the normal ration provided to those living in a city under siege by enemy armies, and cooking over excrement was a symbol of Judah's spiritual uncleanness.

EZEKIEL 6:14
Why does God say "Then you will know that I am LORD?
Didn't the people know this?

The phrase "then they will know that I am the LORD" (or a variation on this phrase) occurs 65 times in the book of Ezekiel. The purpose of all God's punishment was not to take revenge, but to impress upon the people the truth that the Lord is the only true and living God. People in Ezekiel's day were worshiping man-made idols and calling them gods.

HEBREWS 4:1
Why does Hebrews say "be careful that none of you be found to
have fallen short"?

Some of the Jewish Christians who received this letter may have been on the verge of turning back from their promised rest in Christ, just as the people in Moses' day had turned back from the promised land. In both cases, the difficulties of the present moment overshadowed the reality of God's promise, and the people doubted that God would fulfill his promises.

HEBREWS 4:14
Is Jesus a High Priest?

To the Jews, the high priest was the highest religious authority in the land. He alone entered the Holy of Holies in the temple once a year to make atonement for the sins of the whole nation (Lev. 16). Like the high priest, Jesus mediates between God and us. As humanity's representative, he intercedes for us before God. As God's representative, he assures us of God's forgiveness. Jesus has more authority, he is superior to the Jewish high priests because he is truly God and truly man. Unlike the high priest who could go before God only once a year, Christ is always at God's right hand, interceding for us.

NOVEMBER 3

Ezekiel 7:1–9:11; Hebrews 5:1-14; Psalms 105:1-15; Proverbs 26:28

EZEKIEL 8:1
What is the date given in Ezekiel 8:1?

This prophecy's date corresponds to 592 B.C. The message of chapters 8–11 is directed specifically toward Jerusalem and its leaders. Chapter 8 records Ezekiel being taken in a vision from Babylon to the temple in Jerusalem to see the great wickedness being practiced there. The people and their religious leaders were thoroughly corrupt. While Ezekiel's first vision (chapters 1–3) showed that judgment was from God, this vision showed that their sin was the reason for judgment.

EZEKIEL 9:3
What are "Guardian Angels"?

The Guardian Angels are called "cherubim" in many translations. Cherubim ("cherub" is singular) are an order of powerful angelic beings created to glorify God. They are associated with God's absolute holiness and moral perfection. God placed cherubim at the entrance of Eden to keep Adam and Eve out after they sinned (Gen. 3:24). Representations of cherubim were used to decorate the tabernacle and temple. The lid of the ark of the covenant, called the atonement cover, was adorned with two gold cherubim (Exod. 37:6-9). It was a symbol of the very presence of God. The cherubim seen by Ezekiel left the temple along with the glory of God (chapter 10). Ezekiel then recognized them as the living creatures he had seen in his first vision (see chapter 1).

HEBREWS 5
What is the meaning of Hebrews 5?

This chapter stresses both Christ's divine appointment and his humanity. The writer uses two Old Testament verses to show Christ's divine appointment—Psalms 2:7 and 110:4. At the time this book was written, the Romans selected the high priest in Jerusalem. In the Old Testament, however, God chose Aaron, and only Aaron's descendants could be high priests. Christ, like Aaron, was chosen and called by God.

HEBREWS 5:12-13
Why were the Hebrew Christians called "infants"?

These Jewish Christians were immature. Some of them should have been teaching others, but they had not even applied the basics to their own lives. They were reluctant to move beyond age-old traditions, established doctrines, and discussion of the basics. They wouldn't be able to understand the high-priestly role of Christ unless they moved out of their comfortable position, cut some of their Jewish ties, and stopped trying to blend in with their culture.

NOVEMBER 4

Ezekiel 10:1–11:25; Hebrews 6:1-20; Psalms 105:16-36; Proverbs 27:1-2

Q EZEKIEL 10
What is occurring in Ezekiel 10?

Chapters 8–11 depict God's glory departing from the temple. In Ezekiel 8:3-4 his glory was over the northern gate. It then moved to the door (Ezek. 9:3), the south side of the temple (Ezek. 10:3-4), the eastern gate (Ezek. 10:18-19; 11:1), and finally the mountain east of the temple (Ezek. 11:23), probably the Mount of Olives. Because of the nation's sins, God's glory had departed.

Q EZEKIEL 11:1-4
Why does Ezekiel see twenty-five prominent men in 11:1-4?

God had abandoned his altar and temple (chapters 9–11); here his judgment was complete as his glory stopped above the mountain east of the city (Ezek. 11:23). The city gate was where merchants and politicians conducted business, so the 25 men may have represented the nation's rulers. Because of their leadership positions, they were responsible for leading the people astray. They had wrongly said that they were secure from another attack by the Babylonians. "This city is a cooking pot, and we are the meat" means they were the elite, the influential, the ones who would be protected.

Q EZEKIEL 11:7
Why does God call Jerusalem an "iron shield"?

Some translations use the word "cauldron" or "pot" rather than "iron shield." The city leaders thought Jerusalem was safe, like meat cooking in a pot. But Ezekiel said that the pot's contents would be poured out over the cooking fire, illustrating how precarious Jerusalem's position really was.

Q EZEKIEL 11:23
What is the name of the mountain in Ezekiel 11:23?

God's glory left Jerusalem and stood above a mountain on the east side of the city—almost certainly the Mount of Olives. Ezekiel 43:1-4 implies that God will return the same way he left, when he comes back to set up his perfect kingdom.

Q HEBREWS 6:19
What is the veil mentioned in Hebrews 6:19?

This curtain hung across the entrance from the Holy Place to the Most Holy Place, the two innermost rooms of the temple. This curtain prevented anyone from entering, gazing into, or even getting a fleeting glimpse of the Most Holy Place. The high priest could enter there only once a year to stand before God's presence and atone for the sins of the entire nation. But Christ is in God's presence at all times as the high priest who can continually intercede for us.

NOVEMBER 5

Q **EZEKIEL 12:1-10**
What is the meaning of God's message to Ezekiel in 12:1-10?

Zedekiah, Judah's last king (597–586 B.C.), was reigning in Jerusalem when Ezekiel gave these oracles or messages from God. Ezekiel showed the people what would happen to Zedekiah. Jerusalem would be attacked again, and Zedekiah would join the exiles already in Babylon. Zedekiah would be unable to see because Nebuchadnezzar would have his eyes gouged out (2 Kings 25:3-7; Jeremiah 52:10-11). Ezekiel played the role of a captive being led away to exile, portraying what was about to happen to King Zedekiah and the people remaining in Jerusalem. The exiles knew exactly what Ezekiel was doing because only six years earlier they had made similar preparations as they left Jerusalem for Babylonia. This was to show the people that they should not trust the king or the capital city to save them from the Babylonian army—only God could do that. And the exiles who hoped for an early return from exile would be disappointed. Ezekiel's graphic demonstration was proven correct to the last detail. But when he warned them, many refused to listen.

Q **HEBREWS 7:2-16**
What is the purpose of the story in Hebrews 7:2-16?

The writer of Hebrews uses this story from Genesis 14:18-20 to show that Christ is even greater than Abraham, father of the Jewish nation, and Levi (Abraham's descendant). Therefore, the Jewish priesthood (made up of Levi's descendants) was inferior to Melchizedek's priesthood (a type of Christ's priesthood). Melchizedek was a priest of God Most High (see Gen. 14:18). He is said to remain a priest forever (see also Ps. 110:4), because his priesthood has no record of beginning or ending—he was a priest of God in Salem (Jerusalem) long before the nation of Israel and the regular priesthood began. Jesus' high-priestly role was superior to that of any priest of Levi, because the Messiah was a priest of a higher order (Ps. 110:4). If the Jewish priests and their laws had been able to save people, why would God need to send Christ as a priest, who came not from the tribe of Levi (the priestly tribe), but from the tribe of Judah? The animal sacrifices had to be repeated, and they offered only temporary forgiveness; but Christ's sacrifice was offered once, and it offers total and permanent forgiveness. Under the new covenant, the Levitical priesthood was canceled in favor of Christ's role as high priest.

NOVEMBER 6

Ezekiel 14:12–16:42; Hebrews 7:18-28; Psalms 106:1-12; Proverbs 27:4-6

 **EZEKIEL 14:14**
Why wouldn't Noah, Daniel, and Job have been able to save Jerusalem?

Noah, Daniel, and Job were great men in Israel's history, renowned for their relationships with God and for their wisdom (see Gen. 6:8-9; Dan. 2:47-48; Job 1:1). Daniel had been taken into captivity during Babylon's first invasion of Judah in 605 B.C., eight years before Ezekiel was taken captive. At the time of Ezekiel's message, Daniel occupied a high government position in Babylon. But even these great men of God could not have saved the people of Judah because God had already passed judgment on the nation's pervasive evil.

EZEKIEL 16:3
What was "Canaan?" What was a "Hittite" and an "Amorite"?

"Canaan" was the ancient name of the territory taken over by the children of Israel. The Bible often uses this name to refer to all the corrupt pagan nations of the region. The Amorites and Hittites, two Canaanite peoples, were known for their wickedness. But here God implies that his people are no better than the Canaanites.

EZEKIEL 16:20-21
Did Israel offer children to idols?

Child sacrifice had been practiced by the Canaanites long before Israel invaded their land. But it was strictly forbidden by God (Lev. 20:1-3). By Ezekiel's time, however, the people were openly sacrificing their own children (2 Kings 16:3; 21:6). Jeremiah confirmed that this was a common practice (Jer. 7:31; 32:35). Because of such vile acts among the people and priesthood, the temple became unfit for God to inhabit. When God left the temple, he was no longer Judah's guide and protector.

HEBREWS 7:22-24, TLB
What is the "new arrangement"?

Sometimes called the "better covenant" (NIV), this new arrangement is also called the new covenant or testament. It is new and better because it allows us to go directly to God through Christ. We no longer need to rely on sacrificed animals and mediating priests to obtain God's forgiveness. This new covenant is better because, while all human priests die, Christ lives forever. Priests and sacrifices could not save people, but Christ truly saves.

NOVEMBER 7

Ezekiel 16:43–17:24; Hebrews 8:1-13; Psalms 106:13-31; Proverbs 27:7-9

Q EZEKIEL 16:44-50
Why is Jerusalem called the "sister" of Sodom and Samaria?

The city of Sodom, a symbol of total corruption, was completely destroyed by God for its wickedness (Gen. 19:24-25). Samaria, the capital of what had been the northern kingdom (Israel), was despised and rejected by the Jews in Judah. To be called a sister of Samaria and Sodom was bad enough, but to be called *more depraved* (NIV) than that meant that Judah's sins were an unspeakable abomination and that its doom was inevitable. The reason it was considered worse was not necessarily that Judah's sins were worse, but that Judah knew better. (See also Matt. 11:20-24.)

Q EZEKIEL 17:3
What does the eagle represent in Ezekiel 17:3?

The eagle here represents King Nebuchadnezzar of Babylon (see Ezek. 17:12), who appointed or "planted" Zedekiah as king in Jerusalem. Zedekiah rebelled against this arrangement and tried to ally with Egypt, the second eagle, to battle against Babylon. This took place while Ezekiel, miles away in Babylon, was describing these events. Jeremiah, a prophet in Judah, was also warning Zedekiah not to form this alliance (Jer. 2:36-37). Although many miles apart, the prophets had the same message because both spoke for God. God still directs his chosen spokesmen to speak his truth all around the world.

Q HEBREWS 8:4, NRSV
Why does Hebrews 8:4 say, "If he were on earth, he would not be a priest at all"?

Under the old Jewish system, priests were chosen only from the tribe of Levi, and sacrifices were offered daily on the altar for forgiveness of sins (see Heb. 7:12-14). This system would not have allowed Jesus to be a priest while he was living on earth, because he was from the tribe of Judah. But his perfect sacrifice ended all need for further priests and sacrifices.

Q HEBREWS 8:8-12
Where else are these words recorded?

This passage is a quotation of Jeremiah 31:31-34, which compares the new covenant with the old. The old covenant was one of law between God and Israel. The new is the covenant of grace—Christ's offer to forgive our sins and bring us to God through his sacrificial death. This covenant is new in extent—it goes beyond Israel and Judah to include all the Gentile nations. It is new in application because it is written on our hearts and in our minds. It offers a new way to forgiveness, not through animal sacrifice but through faith.

NOVEMBER 8

EZEKIEL 18:2, NRSV
Why were the captives of Judah repeating the proverb, "The parents have eaten sour grapes, and the children's teeth are set on edge"?

The people of Judah believed they were being punished for the sins of their ancestors, not their own. They thought this way because this was the teaching of the Ten Commandments (Exod. 20:5). Ezekiel taught that the destruction of Jerusalem was due to the spiritual decay in previous generations. But this belief in the corporate life of Israel led to fatalism and irresponsibility. So Ezekiel gave God's new policy for this new land because the people had misconstrued the old one. God does not punish us for someone else's sins; and we can't use their mistakes as an excuse for our sins. Each person is accountable to God for his or her actions. In addition, some people of Judah used the corporate umbrella of God's blessing as an excuse for disobeying God. They thought that because of their righteous ancestors (Ezek. 18:5-9) they would live. God told them that they would not; they were the evil sons of righteous parents and, as such, would die (Ezek. 18:10-13). If, however, anyone returned to God, he or she would live (Ezek. 18:14-18).

HEBREWS 9:7, NKJV
What was the "second part" of the tabernacle?

The high priest could enter the Holiest of All (Heb. 9:3; or the "second part," Heb. 9:7, NKJV), the innermost room of the tabernacle, one day each year to atone for the nation's sins. This Most Holy Place (NIV) was a small room that contained the ark of the covenant (a gold-covered chest containing the original stone tablets on which the Ten Commandments were written, a jar of manna, and Aaron's staff). The top of the chest served as the "atonement cover" (the altar) on which the blood would be sprinkled by the high priest on the Day of Atonement. The Most Holy Place was the most sacred spot on earth for the Jews. Only the high priest could enter—the other priests and the common people were forbidden to come into the room. Their only access to God was through the high priest, who would offer a sacrifice and use the animal's blood to atone first for his own sins and then for the people's sins (see also Heb. 10:19).

NOVEMBER 9

Ezekiel 20:1-49; Hebrews 9:11-28; Psalms 107:1-43; Proverbs 27:11

HEBREWS 9:15
How can Christ's death rescue people who sinned long before he lived?

People in Old Testament times were saved through Christ's sacrifice, although that sacrifice had not yet happened. In offering unblemished animal sacrifices, they were anticipating Christ's coming and his death for sin.

HEBREWS 9:22
Why does forgiveness require the shedding of blood?

This is no arbitrary decree on the part of a bloodthirsty God, as some have suggested. There is no greater symbol of life than blood; blood keeps us alive. Jesus shed his blood—gave his life—for our sins so that we wouldn't have to experience spiritual death, eternal separation from God. Jesus is the source of life, not death. He gave his own life to pay our penalty for us so that we might live. After shedding his blood for us, Christ rose from the grave and proclaimed victory over sin and death.

HEBREWS 9:26, NKJV
What is "the end of the ages"?

The "end of the ages" refers to the time of Christ's coming to earth in fulfillment of the Old Testament prophecies. Christ ushered in the new era of grace and forgiveness. We are still living in the "end of the ages." The day of the Lord has begun and will be completed at Christ's return.

HEBREWS 9:28, KJV
What will happen when Christ comes "the second time"?

When Christ comes again many purposes in the plan of God will be consummated: (1) Our salvation will be completed (Heb. 9:28; 1 Pet. 1:5); (2) He will reign in heaven and on earth as absolute sovereign (Rev. 11:15); (3) He will destroy the power and the reign of death (1 Cor. 15:25, 26); (4) He will be admired and praised by all the saints (2 Thess. 1:10); (5) Every dark and hidden thing will be revealed (1 Cor. 4:5); (6) The final judgment of the living and the dead will take place (John 5:22; 2 Tim. 4:1; Jude 15; Rev. 20 11-13); (7) The dead believers will rise first (1 Thess. 4:16); (8) The living believers will be caught up together with the risen dead believers in the clouds (1 Thess. 4:17); (9) The man of lawlessness will be destroyed (2 Thess. 2:8).

NOVEMBER 10

Ezekiel 21:1–22:31; Hebrews 10:1-17; Psalms 108:1-13; Proverbs 27:12

EZEKIEL 22:17-22, TLB
What is "slag" and "dross"?

Precious metals are refined with intense heat to remove the impurities. When heated, the slag, or dross (impurities) rises to the top of the molten metal and is skimmed off and thrown away. The purpose of the invasion of Jerusalem was to refine the people, but the refining process showed that the people, like worthless dross, had nothing good in them.

EZEKIEL 22:28, TLB
What does it mean to "repair the walls with whitewash"?

The wall spoken of here is not made of stones, but of faithful people united in their efforts to resist evil. This "wall of righteousness" (Ezek. 22:30) was in disrepair because there was no one who could lead the people back to God. The feeble attempts to repair the gap—through religious rituals or messages based on opinion rather than God's will—were as worthless as whitewash, only covering over the real problems. What the people really needed was total spiritual reconstruction!

HEBREWS 10:9
Did Jesus Christ's death cancel the law of the Old Testament?

Setting aside the first system in order to establish a far better one meant doing away with the system of sacrifices contained in the *ceremonial law*. It didn't mean eliminating God's *moral* law (the Ten Commandments). The ceremonial law prepared people for Christ's coming. With Christ's death and resurrection, that system was no longer needed. And through Christ we can fulfill the moral law as we let him live in us.

HEBREWS 10:12
Why does Hebrews 10:12 emphasize a single sacrifice for sin?

If the Jewish readers of this book were to return to the old Jewish system, they would be implying that Christ's sacrifice wasn't enough to forgive their sins, and that they needed something more. Adding anything to his sacrifice or taking anything from it denies its validity. Any system to gain salvation through good deeds is essentially rejecting the significance of Christ's death and spurning the Holy Spirit's work.

NOVEMBER 11

HEBREWS 10:26, NRSV
Why does Hebrews 10:26 say, "There no longer remains a sacrifice for sins"?

When people deliberately reject Christ's offer of salvation, they reject God's most precious gift. They ignore the leading of the Holy Spirit, the one who communicates to us God's saving love. This warning was given to Jewish Christians who were tempted to reject Christ for Judaism, but it applies to anyone who rejects Christ for another religion or, having understood Christ's atoning work, deliberately turns away from it (see also Num. 15:30-31 and Mark 3:28-30). The point is that there is no other acceptable sacrifice for sin than the death of Christ on the cross. If someone deliberately rejects the sacrifice of Christ after clearly understanding the gospel teaching about it, then there is no way for that person to be saved, because God has not provided any other name under heaven by which we can be saved (see Acts 4:12).

HEBREWS 10:38
What does living by faith in Hebrews 10:38 have to do with the need of patience in Hebrews 10:36?

The writer encourages his readers not to abandon their faith in times of persecution, but to show by their endurance (patience) that their faith is real. Faith means resting in what Christ has done for us in the past, but it also means trusting him for what he will do for us in the present and in the future (see Rom. 8:12-25; Gal. 3:10-13).

PSALM 109:1-4
Why did David pray for his enemies?

David was angry at being attacked by evil people who slandered him and lied. Yet David remained a friend and a man of prayer. He endured many false accusations (1 Sam. 22:7-13; 2 Sam. 15:3-4), as did Christ centuries later (Matt. 26:59-61; 27:39-44). David's prayer for his enemies is echoed in Jesus' prayer for those who nailed him to the cross (Luke 23:34). Also Peter, speaking of Judas's death, quoted Psalm 109:8 in Acts 1:20 saying, "It is written in the book of Psalms, 'May his place be deserted; let there be no one to dwell in it,' and, 'May another take his place of leadership' (NIV).

NOVEMBER 12

Ezekiel 24:1–26:21; Hebrews 11:1-16; Psalms 110:1-7; Proverbs 27:14

 **EZEKIEL 25:1ff.**
Why did God judge the nations around Judah?

Chapters 25–32 are God's word concerning the seven nations surrounding Judah. The judgments in these chapters are not simply the vengeful statements of Jews against their enemies; they are God's judgments on nations that failed to acknowledge the one true God and fulfill the good purposes God intended for them. The Ammonites were judged because of their joy over the desecration of the temple (Ezek. 25:1-7), the Moabites because they found pleasure in Judah's wickedness (Ezek. 25:8-11), the Edomites because of their racial hatred for the Jews (Ezek. 25:12-14), and the Philistines because they sought revenge against Judah for defeating them in battle (Ezek. 25:15-17).

 **EZEKIEL 26:1ff.**
What and where was Tyre?

Tyre was the capital of Phoenicia, just north of Israel. Part of the city was on the coastline, and part was on a beautiful island. Tyre rejoiced when Jerusalem fell, because Tyre and Judah always competed for the lucrative trade that came through their lands from Egypt in the south and Mesopotamia to the north. Tyre dominated the sea trading routes while Judah dominated the land caravan routes. After Judah was defeated, Tyre thought it had all the trade routes to itself. But this gloating didn't last long. In 586 B.C., Nebuchadnezzar besieged the city. It took him thirteen years to capture Tyre (586–571) because the city lay on the seacoast, so fresh supplies could be shipped in daily. Nebuchadnezzar could not conquer the part of Tyre located on the island; thus certain aspects of the description in Ezekiel 26:12, 14 exceed the actual damage done to Tyre by Nebuchadnezzar. But the prophecy predicted what would happen to the island settlement later during the conquests of Alexander the Great. Alexander threw the rubble of the mainland city into the sea until it made a bridge to the island. Then he marched across the bridge and destroyed the island (332 B.C.). Today the island city is still a pile of rubble, a testimony to God's judgment.

PSALM 110
Is Psalm 110 quoted in the New Testament?

This is one of the psalms that is most-quoted in the New Testament. In Matthew 22:41-45, Jesus recited the words of this verse and applied them to himself. Verses 1 and 6 look forward to Christ's final and total destruction of the wicked (Rev. 6–9); Psalm 110:2 prophesies Christ's reign on the earth (Rev. 20:1-7); Psalm 110:3-4 tells of Christ's priestly work for his people (Heb. 5–8); and Psalm 110:5-6 looks forward to the final battle on earth when Christ will overcome the forces of evil (Rev. 19:11-21).

NOVEMBER 13

EZEKIEL 27:1ff.
Why would God judge Tyre?

God orders Ezekiel to raise a lamentation over Tyre at a time when it was highly prosperous and there was no reason to suppose it would decay and disappear as a significant city of commerce. Pride and a sense of security caused its ruin.

EZEKIEL 28:2-3
Who is the "Daniel" in Ezekiel 28:2-3?

This was the prophet Daniel, a Jewish captive and an important official in Nebuchadnezzar's kingdom (Ezek. 14:14), who was already renowned for his wisdom. Daniel proclaimed that all his wisdom came from God (Dan. 2:20-23). By contrast, the king of Tyre thought that he himself *was* a god.

EZEKIEL 28:13
Is Ezekiel talking about Satan in Ezekiel 28:12-19?

Some of the phrases in this passage describing the human king of Tyre may describe Satan. Great care must be taken to interpret these verses with discernment. It is clear that, at times, Ezekiel describes this king in terms that could not apply to a mere man. This king had been in the Garden of Eden, had been "anointed as a guardian cherub" (Ezek. 28:14), and had access to the holy mountain of God (Ezek. 28:14), but was driven from there (Ezek. 28:16-17). Ezekiel, therefore, may have been condemning not only the king of Tyre, but Satan, who had motivated the king to sin.

EZEKIEL 28:26
Has the promise in Ezekiel 28:24-26 been fulfilled?

This promise that God's people will live in complete safety has yet to be fulfilled. While many were allowed to return from exile under Zerubbabel, Ezra, and Nehemiah, and although the political nation is restored today, the inhabitants do not yet live in complete safety. Therefore, this promise will have its ultimate fulfillment when Christ sets up his eternal kingdom. Then all people who have been faithful to God will dwell together in harmony and complete safety.

HEBREWS 11:31
Who was Rahab?

When Joshua planned the conquest of Jericho, he sent spies to investigate the fortifications of the city. The spies met Rahab, who had two strikes against her—she was a Gentile and a prostitute. But she showed that she had faith in God by welcoming the spies and by trusting God to spare her and her family when the city was destroyed.

NOVEMBER 14

 EZEKIEL 29:1ff.
Why did Ezekiel prophesy against Egypt?
There are seven prophecies in chapters 29–32, all dealing with judgment on Egypt. This is probably the first prophecy that was given by Ezekiel in 587 B.C. Hezekiah, Jehoiakim, and Zedekiah (kings of Judah) had all sought help from Egypt despite God's warnings. There are three key reasons for this prophecy: (1) Egypt was an ancient enemy of the Jews, having once enslaved them for four hundred years; (2) Egypt worshiped many gods; (3) Egypt's wealth and power made it seem like a good ally. Egypt offered to help Judah only because of the benefits it hoped to receive from such an alliance. When the Egyptians didn't get what they hoped for, they bailed out of their agreement without regard to any promises they had made.

 EZEKIEL 29:11-15
When did the forty-year period in Ezekiel 29:11-15 occur?
This 40-year period of desolation in Egypt is hard to pinpoint. Nebuchadnezzar attacked Egypt around 572 B.C. and carried many people off to Babylon, while others fled for safety to surrounding nations. Approximately 33 years later, Cyrus, king of the Persian empire, conquered Babylon and allowed the nations which Babylon had conquered to return to their homelands. Adding a possible seven-year regrouping and travel period, this could then make up that 40-year time period. Since that time, Egypt has never returned to its previous dominance as a world power. Upper Egypt was the region south of the Nile delta.

HEBREWS 11:32-35
Who are the people referred to in Hebrews 11:32-35?
The Old Testament records the lives of the various people who experienced these great victories. Joshua and Deborah conquered kingdoms (the book of Joshua; Judges 4–5). Nehemiah administered justice (the book of Nehemiah). Daniel was saved from the mouths of lions (Dan. 6). Shadrach, Meshach, and Abednego were kept from harm in the furious flames of a fiery furnace (Dan. 3). Elijah escaped the edge of the swords of evil Queen Jezebel's henchmen (1 Kings 19:2ff.). Hezekiah regained strength after sickness (2 Kings 20). Gideon was powerful in battle (Judg. 7). A widow's son was brought back to life by the prophet Elisha (2 Kings 4:8-37). These Jewish heroes did not receive God's total reward, because they died before Christ came (Heb. 11:39-40). In God's plan, they and the Christian believers (who were also enduring much testing) would be rewarded together. Once again Hebrews shows that Christianity supersedes Judaism.

NOVEMBER 15

Q EZEKIEL 31:1ff.
Why does Ezekiel mention Assyria in Egypt's judgment?

This message was given in 587 B.C. Ezekiel compared Egypt to Assyria, calling Assyria a great cedar tree. The Egyptians were to look at the fall of the mighty nation of Assyria (whose demise they had seen) as an example of what would happen to them. Just like Assyria, Egypt took pride in its strength and beauty; this would be its downfall. She would crash like a mighty tree and be sent to the place of the dead. There is no permanence apart from God, even for a great society with magnificent culture and military power.

Q EZEKIEL 32:18, TLB
What is the meaning of the phrase, "Send them down to the nether world among the denizens of death" in Ezekiel 32:18?

The Hebrews believed in an afterlife for all people, good and bad. The Egyptians had a preoccupation with the afterlife (the pyramids were built solely to ensure the pharaohs' comfort in the next life). Ezekiel's message assumed that the evil nations had already been sent there (to the "pit", NIV) and that Egypt would share their fate. The words here are more poetic than doctrinal (see Job 24:19; Ps. 16:10; Isa. 38:10; Matt. 25:46).

Q EZEKIEL 32:24-26
What were Elam, Meshech, and Tubal?

Elam was a nation of fierce warriors living east of Assyria. They were conquered by Nebuchadnezzar (Jer. 49:34-39) and eventually rebuilt themselves and became part of Persia. Meshech and Tubal were territories located in the eastern region of Asia Minor, now eastern and central Turkey. In chapters 38 and 39 they are described as allies of Gog, the chief prince of a confederacy. They are included with the evil nations who will be judged for fighting against God's people.

Q EZEKIEL 31
If Babylon was God's enemy, why isn't it mentioned in Ezekiel's judgments?

After reading Ezekiel's prophecies against all these foreign nations, we may wonder if he was blindly loyal to his own nation which was captive in Babylon. But Ezekiel spoke only when God gave him a message (Ezek. 3:27). Besides, God's prophets pronounced judgment on God's sinful people just as much as on God's enemies. Perhaps because (1) God wanted to foster a spirit of cooperation between the exiles and Babylon in order to preserve his people; (2) God was still using Babylon to refine his own people; (3) God wanted to use Daniel, a powerful official in Babylon, to draw the Babylonians to him.

NOVEMBER 16

Ezekiel 33:1–34:31; Hebrews 13:1-25; Psalms 115:1-18; Proverbs 27:21-22

EZEKIEL 33:1
Why does Ezekiel's tone change after chapter 32?

Chapter 33 sets forth a new direction for Ezekiel's prophecies. Up to this point, Ezekiel has pronounced judgment upon Judah (chapters 1–24) and the surrounding evil nations (chapters 25–32) for their sins. After Jerusalem fell, he turned from messages of doom and judgment to messages of comfort, hope, and future restoration for God's people (chapters 33–48). God previously appointed Ezekiel to be a watchman warning the nation of coming judgment (see Ezek. 3:17-21). Here God appointed him to be a watchman again, but this time to preach a message of hope. There are still sections full of warnings (Ezek. 33:23–34:10; 36:1-7), but these are part of the larger picture of hope. God will remember to bless those who are faithful to him. We must pay attention to both aspects of Ezekiel's message: warning and promise. Those who persist in rebelling against God should take warning. Those faithful to God should find encouragement and hope.

HEBREWS 13:13
What is the meaning of Hebrews 13:13?

The Jewish Christians were being ridiculed and persecuted by Jews who didn't believe in Jesus the Messiah. Most of the book of Hebrews told them how Christ is greater than the sacrificial system. Here the writer drives home the point of his lengthy argument: It may be necessary to leave the "camp" and suffer with Christ. To be outside the camp meant to be unclean—in the days of the exodus, those who were ceremonially unclean had to stay outside the camp. But Jesus suffered humiliation and uncleanness outside the Jerusalem gates when he died on their behalf. The time had come for Jewish Christians to declare their loyalty to Christ above any other loyalty, to choose to follow the Messiah whatever suffering that might entail. They needed to move outside the safe confinement of their past, their traditions, and their ceremonies to live for Christ.

HEBREWS 13:15
What is the "sacrifice of praise"?

Since these Jewish Christians, because of their witness to the Messiah, no longer worshiped with other Jews, they should consider praise their sacrifice—one they could offer anywhere, anytime. This must have reminded them of the prophet Hosea's words, "Forgive all our sins and receive us graciously, that we may offer the fruit of our lips" (Hos. 14:2).

NOVEMBER 17

Ezekiel 35:1–36:38; James 1:1-18; Psalms 116:1-19; Proverbs 27:23-27

EZEKIEL 35:1ff.
Didn't Ezekiel already prophesy against Edom?

Yes, his first prophecy against Edom is found in Ezekiel 25:12-14. In this prophecy, Ezekiel is probably using Edom to represent *all* the nations opposed to God's people. Chapter 36 says that Israel will be restored, while this chapter says that Edom (God's enemy) will be made "a desolate waste" (NIV). Edom's long-standing hostility against God's people resulted in God's judgment. Ezekiel prophesied not only against the people of Edom, but also against their mountains and land (Ezek. 35:8). Their home territory was Mount Seir. Mountains, symbols of strength and power, represented the pride of these people who thought they could get away with evil. Edom's desire for revenge turned against them. The Edomites received the punishment they were so hasty to give out.

EZEKIEL 36:21, NKJV
Why did God have concern for his holy name?

God was concerned about the salvation not only of his people, but also of the whole world. To allow his people to remain in sin and be permanently destroyed by their enemies would lead other nations to conclude that their pagan gods were more powerful than Israel's God (Isa. 48:11). Thus, to protect his holy name, God would return a remnant of his people to their land. God will not share his glory with false gods—he alone is the one true God. The people had the responsibility to represent God properly to the rest of the world.

JAMES 1:1
Who was James and why did he write his letter?

The writer of this letter, a leader of the church in Jerusalem (see Acts 12:17; 15:13), was James, Jesus' brother, not James the apostle. The book of James was one of the earliest letters, probably written before A.D. 50. After Stephen was martyred (Acts 7:55–8:3), persecution increased, and Christians in Jerusalem were scattered throughout the Roman world. There were thriving Jewish-Christian communities in Rome, Alexandria, Cyprus, and cities in Greece and Asia Minor. Because these early believers did not have the support of established Christian churches, James wrote to them as a concerned leader, to encourage them in their faith during those difficult times.

NOVEMBER 18

Q EZEKIEL 37:15-17
What is the meaning of the vision in Ezekiel 37?

This vision illustrates the promise of chapter 36—new life and a nation restored, both physically and spiritually. The dry bones are a picture of the Jews in captivity—scattered and dead. The two sticks represent the reunion of the entire nation of Israel that had divided into northern and southern kingdoms after Solomon. The scattered exiles of both Israel and Judah would be released from the "graves" of captivity and one day regathered in their homeland, with the Messiah as their leader. This vision has yet to be fulfilled. Ezekiel felt he was speaking to the dead as he preached to the exiles because they rarely responded to his message. But these bones responded! And just as God brought life to the dead bones, he would bring life again to his spiritually dead people.

Q EZEKIEL 38
What is occurring in Ezekiel 38?

In chapter 37, Ezekiel revealed how Israel (God's people) would be restored to their land from many parts of the world. Once Israel became strong, a confederacy of nations from the north would attack, led by Gog (see also Rev. 20:8). Their purpose would be to destroy God's people. Gog's allies would come from the mountainous area southeast of the Black Sea and southwest of the Caspian Sea (central Turkey), as well as from the area that is present-day Iran, Ethiopia, Libya, and possibly the Soviet Union. Gog could be a person (he sometimes is identified with Gyges, king of Lydia in 660 B.C.), or Gog could also be a symbol of all the evil in the world. Whether symbolic or literal, Gog represents the aggregate military might of all the forces opposed to God. Many say that the battle Ezekiel described will occur at the end of human history, but there are many differences between the events described here and those in Revelation 20. Regardless of when this battle will occur, the message is clear: God will deliver his people—no enemy can stand before his mighty power.

Q JAMES 1:27
Why does James specifically say to take care of widows and orphans?

In the first century, orphans and widows had very little means of economic support. Unless a family member was willing to care for them, they were reduced to begging, selling themselves as slaves, or starving. By caring for these powerless people, the church put God's Word into practice.

NOVEMBER 19

Ezekiel 39:1–40:27; James 2:18–3:18; Psalms 118:1-18; Proverbs 28:2

EZEKIEL 40
Is the temple described in Ezekiel 40 a literal or a figurative building?

The building of the temple envisioned a time of complete restoration to the exiles, a time when God would return to his people. A temple was built in Jerusalem in 520–515 B.C. (see Ezra 5–6), but fell short of Ezekiel's plan (Hag. 2:3; Zech. 4:10). This vision of the temple has been interpreted in four main ways: (1) This is the temple Zerubbabel should have built in 520–515 B.C. and is the actual blueprint Ezekiel intended. But due to disobedience (Ezek. 43:2-10), it was never followed. (2) This is a literal temple to be rebuilt during the millennial reign of Christ. (3) This temple is symbolic of the true worship of God by the Christian church right now. (4) This temple is symbolic of the future and eternal reign of God when his presence and blessing fill the earth. Whether the temple is literal or symbolic, it seems clear that this is a vision of God's final perfect kingdom. This gave hope to the people of Ezekiel's time who had just seen their nation and its temple destroyed with no hope of rebuilding it in the near future. The details given in this vision gave the people even more hope that what Ezekiel saw had come from God and would surely happen in the future. One argument against the view that Ezekiel's temple is a literal building of the future is that sacrifices are mentioned (Ezek. 40:38-43). If the sacrifices were to be reinstituted in the last days, then Christ's final sacrifice would not have been final. The New Testament makes it clear that Christ died once and for all (Rom. 6:10; Heb. 9:12; 10:10, 18). Our sins have been removed; no further sacrifice is needed.

   In Ezekiel's day, however, the only kind of worship the people knew was the kind that revolved around the sacrifices and ceremonies described in Exodus through Deuteronomy. Ezekiel had to explain the new order of worship in terms the people would understand. The next nine chapters tell how the temple is the focal point of everything, showing that the ideal relationship with God is when all of life centers on him. Ezekiel explained God's dwelling place in words and images the people could understand. God wanted them to see the great splendor he had planned for those who lived faithfully. This kind of temple was never built, but it was a vision intended to typify God's perfect plan for his people—the centrality of worship, the presence of the Lord, the blessings flowing from it, and the orderliness of worship and worship duties.

NOVEMBER 20

JAMES 4:2
Why does James emphasize lust and desire in 4:2?

Virtually all sins have their origin in covetousness, lusting after or desiring what is not ours. For example, Satan coveted the power of the Creator. Virtually all wars begin by one nation's coveting what another nation possesses. Judas Iscariot coveted money; as keeper of the common purse, he stole what was not his. The corruption found among people in public life is most frequently caused by the same sin.

JAMES 4:8
How can I come near to God?

The psalmist said, "But it is good for me to draw near to God" (Ps. 73:28, KJV) James gives five ways to do this: (1) *Submit to God* (James 4:7). Yield to his authority and will, commit your life to him and his control, and be willing to follow him. (2) *Resist the devil* (James 4:7). Don't allow Satan to entice and tempt you. (3) *Wash your hands . . . and purify your hearts* (that is, lead a pure life) (James 4:8). Be cleansed from sin, replacing your desire to sin with your desire to experience God's purity. (4) *Grieve and mourn and wail* in sincere sorrow for your sins (James 4:9). Don't be afraid to express deep heartfelt sorrow for what you have done. (5) *Humble yourself before the Lord,* and he will lift you up (James 4:10; 1 Pet. 5:6).

PSALM 118:22-23
Does Psalm 118:22-23 refer to Jesus Christ?

Yes, Jesus referred to this verse when he spoke of being rejected by his own people (Matt. 21:42; Mark 12:10-11; Luke 20:17). Although he was rejected, Jesus is now the "capstone," the most important part of the church (Acts 4:11; Eph. 2:20; 1 Pet. 2:6-7). The capstone is the center stone in the top of an arch, holding the whole arch together.

PSALM 118
Who was the author of Psalm 118?

The authorship, the time, and the circumstances of this psalm are not known specifically. Many attribute it to David. At least a segment of it has Messianic implications. Psalm 118:22-23 is picked up in whole or in part or referred to in Matthew 21:42, Mark 12:10, Luke 20:17, Acts 4:11, Ephesians 2:20, and 1 Peter 2:4, 7.

NOVEMBER 21

Ezekiel 42:1–43:27; James 5:1-20; Psalms 119:1-16; Proverbs 28:6-7

EZEKIEL 43:18-27
Does Ezekiel's vision in 43:18-27 indicate that there will again be animal sacrifices sometime in the future?

This vision was simultaneously flashing back to Mount Sinai where the law of the sacrifices was given and forward to Mount Calvary where Jesus Christ died as the unique lamb of God and final sacrifice. When the people returned from exile, they would seek forgiveness through the sacrificial system instituted in Moses' day. Today, Christ's death has made the forgiveness of our sins possible, making us acceptable to God (Heb. 9:9-15). God stands ready to forgive those who come to him in faith. It is perplexing whether there will be a literal restoration of animal sacrifices, which were done away with by Christ's work at Calvary. Some think that there will be offerings to serve as a memorial, corresponding to the Lord's Supper of this present age. Others, knowing that the Old Testament sacrifices have been superseded, consider these prophecies to be a description in Old Testament terms of the principle that Christ's blood will avail wholly during the kingdom age.

JAMES 5:6, NRSV
Who are the "innocent men" who have been condemned and killed, as mentioned in James 5:6?

The innocent men were defenseless persons, probably poor laborers. Poor people who could not pay their debts were thrown in prison or forced to sell all their possessions. At times, they were even forced to sell their family members into slavery. With no opportunity to work off their debts, poor people often died of starvation. God called this murder. Other translations identify the murdered one (following the singular in the Greek) as the "righteous man" (i.e., Jesus).

JAMES 5:14-15
Does James 5:14-15 refer to someone who is spiritually weak?

No, James is referring to someone who is incapacitated physically. In Scripture, oil was both a medicine (see the parable of the good Samaritan in Luke 10:30-37) and a symbol of the Spirit of God (as used in anointing kings, see 1 Sam. 16:1-13). Thus oil can represent both the medical and the spiritual spheres of life.

JAMES 5:15, KJV
Whose faith accomplishes the healing in James 5:15?

"The prayer of faith," does not refer to the faith of the sick person, but to the faith of the people praying. God heals, faith doesn't, and all prayers are subject to God's will. But our prayers are part of God's healing process. That is why God often waits for our prayers of faith before intervening to heal a person.

NOVEMBER 22

1 PETER 1:1-12
Why was 1 Peter written?

The apostle Peter wrote this letter to encourage believers who would likely face trials and persecution under Emperor Nero. During most of the first century, Christians were not hunted down and killed throughout the Roman empire. They could, however, expect social and economic persecution from three main sources: the Romans, the Jews, and their own families. All would very likely be misunderstood; some would be harassed; a few would be tortured and even put to death. The legal status of Christians in the Roman empire was unclear. Many Romans still thought of Christians as members of a Jewish sect; and because the Jewish religion was legal, they considered Christianity legal also—as long as Christians complied with the empire's laws. However, if Christians refused to worship the emperor or join the army, or if they were involved in civil disturbances (such as the one in Ephesus recorded in Acts 19:23ff.), they might be punished by the civil authorities. Many Jews did not appreciate being legally associated with Christians. As the book of Acts frequently records, Jews occasionally harmed Christians physically, drove them out of town, or attempted to turn Roman officials against them. Saul, later the great apostle Paul, was an early Jewish persecutor of Christians. Another source of persecution was the Christian's own family. Under Roman law, the head of the household had absolute authority over all its members. Unless the ruling male became a Christian, the wife, children, and servants who were believers might well face extreme hardship. If they were sent away, they would have no place to turn but the church; if they were beaten, no court of law would uphold their interests. Peter may have been writing especially for new Christians and those planning to be baptized. Peter wanted to warn them about what lay ahead, and they needed his encouraging words to help them face opposition.

1 PETER 1:11
What is the "Spirit of Christ"?

The Spirit of Christ is another name for the Holy Spirit. Before Jesus left his ministry on earth to return to heaven, he promised to send the Holy Spirit, the Counselor, to teach, help, and guide his followers (John 14:15-17, 26; 16:7). The Holy Spirit would tell them all about Jesus and would reveal his glory (John 15:26; 16:14). The Old Testament prophets, writing under the Holy Spirit's inspiration (2 Pet. 1:20-21), described the coming of the Messiah. The New Testament apostles, through the inspiration of the same Spirit, preached the crucified and risen Lord.

NOVEMBER 23

Ezekiel 45:13–46:24; 1 Peter 1:13–2:10; Psalms 119:33-48; Proverbs 28:11

1 PETER 1:18
What does "redeemed" mean?

The word *redeemed* comes from a Greek word which means "to buy back from bondage" or "to redeem." The noun form of the word is "redemption". The need to be redeemed or bought back springs from our bondage to Satan and to sin (John 8:34; Rom. 6:17, 23). It is God who redeems us by his grace. God has done this through the death of Jesus Christ (1 Cor. 1:30; Gal. 3:13; 4:4-5; Eph. 1:7; Tit. 2:14). Redemption is past, present, and future. We have been redeemed; we are being redeemed; and we will be redeemed. The final redemption occurs when that which we have embraced by faith becomes a historical reality.

1 PETER 2:2-8
Why does Peter call the church a building?

In describing the church as God's spiritual house, Peter drew on several Old Testament texts familiar to his Jewish Christian readers: Psalm 118:22; Isaiah 8:14; 28:16. Peter's readers would have understood the living stones to be Israel; then Peter applied the image of "stone" to Christ. Once again Peter showed that the church does not cancel the Jewish heritage, but fulfills it. Here Peter portrays the church as a living, spiritual house, with Christ as the foundation and cornerstone and each believer as a stone. No doubt Peter could not forget Jesus' words to him right after he confessed that Jesus was "the Christ, the Son of the living God": "You are Peter, and on this rock I will build my church, and the gates of Hades will not overcome it" (Matt. 16:16-18). What is the stone that really counts in the building of the church? Peter answers: Christ himself. Jesus Christ is called "the stone that causes men to stumble and a rock that makes them fall." Some will stumble over Christ because they reject him or refuse to believe that he is who he says he is. But Psalm 118:22 says that "the stone the builders rejected has become the capstone," the most important part of God's building, the church.

NOVEMBER 24

Ezekiel 47:1–48:35; 1 Peter 2:11–3:7; Psalms 119:49-64; Proverbs 28:12-13

Q EZEKIEL 47:1-12
What is the meaning of the river in Ezekiel 47:1-12?

This river is similar to the river mentioned in Revelation 22:1-2. Both rivers are associated with the river in the Garden of Eden (see Gen. 2:10). The river symbolizes life from God and the blessings that flow from his throne. It is a gentle, safe, deep river, expanding as it flows.

Q 1 PETER 2:11
Why are we called aliens and strangers in the world?

As believers, we are "aliens and strangers" in this world, because our real home is with God. Heaven is not the pink-cloud-and-harp existence popular in cartoons. Heaven is where God lives. Life in heaven operates according to God's principles and values, and it is eternal and unshakable. Heaven came to earth in the symbolism of the Jewish sanctuary (the tabernacle and temple) where God's presence dwelt. It came in a fuller way in the person of Jesus Christ, "God with us." It permeated the entire world as the Holy Spirit came to live in every believer. Someday, after God judges and destroys all sin, the kingdom of heaven will rule every corner of this earth. John saw this day in a vision, and he cried out, "Now the dwelling of God is with men, and he will live with them. They will be his people, and God himself will be with them and be their God" (Rev. 21:3).

Q 1 PETER 3:1-6
Why does Peter expect so much of women in 3:1-6?

In ancient times when a man became a Christian, he usually would bring his whole family into the church with him (see, for example, the story of the conversion of the Philippian jailer in Acts 16:29-33). By contrast, a woman who became a Christian usually came into the church alone. Under Roman law, the husband and father had absolute authority over all members of his household, including his wife. Demanding her rights as a free woman in Christ could endanger her marriage if her husband disapproved. Peter reassured Christian women who were married to unbelievers that they did not need to preach to their husbands. Under the circumstances, their best approach would be one of loving service: they should show their husbands the kind of self-giving love that Christ showed the church. By being exemplary wives, they would please their husbands. At the very least, the men would then allow them to continue practicing their "strange" religion. At best, their husbands would join them and become Christians too.

Daniel 1:1–2:23; 1 Peter 3:8–4:6; Psalms 119:65-80; Proverbs 28:14

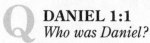

DANIEL 1:1
Who was Daniel?

Born during the middle of Josiah's reign (2 Kings 22–23), Daniel grew up during the king's reforms. During this time, Daniel probably heard Jeremiah, a prophet he quoted in Daniel 9:2. In 609 B.C., Josiah was killed in a battle against Egypt, and within four years, the southern kingdom of Judah had returned to its evil ways. In 605 B.C. Nebuchadnezzar became king of Babylonia. In September of that year, he swept into Palestine and surrounded Jerusalem, making Judah his vassal state. To demonstrate his dominance, Nebuchadnezzar took many of Jerusalem's wisest men and most beautiful women to Babylon as captives. Daniel was among this group.

DANIEL 1:7
Why were Daniel and his friends given new names?

Nebuchadnezzar changed the names of Daniel and his friends because he wanted to make them Babylonian—in their own eyes and in the eyes of the Babylonian people. New names would help them assimilate into the culture. Daniel means "God is my Judge" in Hebrew; his name was changed to Belteshazzar meaning "Bel, protect his life!" (Bel, also called Marduk, was the chief Babylonian god). Hananiah means "the LORD shows grace"; his new name, Shadrach, probably means "under the command of Aku" (the moon god). Mishael means "who is like God?"; his new name, Meshach, probably means "who is like Aku?" Azariah means "the LORD helps"; his new name, Abednego, means "servant of Nego/Nebo" (or Nabu, the god of learning and writing). This was how the king attempted to change the religious loyalty of these young men from Judah's God to Babylonia's gods.

1 PETER 3:18-20
What is the meaning of 1 Peter 3:18-20?

The meaning of these verses is not completely clear, and commentators have explained it in different ways. The traditional interpretation is that Christ, between his death and resurrection, announced salvation to God's faithful followers who had been waiting for their salvation during the whole Old Testament era. Matthew records that when Jesus died, "the bodies of many holy people who had died were raised to life. They came out of the tombs, and after Jesus' resurrection they went into the holy city and appeared to many people" (Matt. 27:52-53). A few commentators think that this passage says that Christ's Spirit was in Noah as Noah preached to those imprisoned by sin (but now in Hades). Still others hold that Christ went to Hades to proclaim his victory and final condemnation to the fallen angels imprisoned there since Noah's day (see 2 Pet. 2:4).

NOVEMBER 26

Daniel 2:24–3:30; 1 Peter 4:7–5:14; Psalms 119:81-96; Proverbs 28:15-16

DANIEL 2:31ff.
What is the meaning of Nebuchadnezzar's dream?

The head of gold on the statue in the dream represented Nebuchadnezzar, ruler of the Babylonian empire. The silver chest and two arms represented the Medo-Persian empire, which conquered Babylon in 539 B.C. The belly and thighs of bronze were Greece and Macedonia under Alexander the Great, who conquered the Medo-Persian empire in 334–330 B.C. The legs of iron represented the Romans, who conquered the Greeks in 63 B.C. The feet of clay and iron represented the breakup of the Roman empire, when the territory Rome ruled divided into a mixture of strong and weak nations. The type of metal in each part depicted the strength of the political power it represented. The rock cut out of the mountain depicted God's kingdom, which would be ruled eternally by the Messiah, the King of kings. The dream revealed Daniel's God as the power behind all earthly kingdoms.

1 PETER 5:1-2
Why did Peter call himself an apostle?

Peter, one of Jesus' 12 disciples, was one of the three who saw Christ's glory at the transfiguration (Mark 9:1-13; 2 Pet. 1:16-18). Often the spokesman for the apostles, Peter witnessed Jesus' death and resurrection, preached at Pentecost, and became a pillar of the Jerusalem church. But writing to the elders, he identified himself as a fellow elder, not a superior. He asked them to "be shepherds of God's flock," exactly what Jesus had told him to do (John 21:15-17). Peter was taking his own advice as he worked along with the other elders in caring for God's faithful people. His identification with the elders is a powerful example of Christian leadership, where authority is based on service, not power (Mark 10:42-45).

1 PETER 5:12
Who was Silvanus?

Silvanus, also called Silas, was one of the men chosen to deliver the letter from the Jerusalem council to the church in Antioch (Acts 15:22). He accompanied Paul on his second missionary journey (Acts 15:40–18:11), is mentioned by Paul in the salutation of Paul's letters to the Thessalonians (1 Thess. 1:1; 2 Thess. 1:1), and ministered with Timothy in Corinth (2 Cor. 1:19). Very likely, Silvanus helped Peter compose this epistle.

NOVEMBER 27

Daniel 4:1-37; 2 Peter 1:1-21; Psalms 119:97-112; Proverbs 28:17-18

2 PETER 1:1
When and why was 2 Peter written?

First Peter was written just before the time that the Roman Emperor Nero began his persecution of Christians. Second Peter was written two or three years later (between A.D. 66-68), after persecution had intensified. First Peter was a letter of encouragement to the Christians who suffered, but 2 Peter focuses on the church's internal problems, especially on the false teachers who were causing people to doubt their faith and turn away from Christianity. Second Peter combats their heresies by denouncing the evil motives of the false teachers and reaffirming Christianity's truths—the authority of Scripture, the primacy of faith, and the certainty of Christ's return.

2 PETER 1:13-14
When did Peter die?

Peter knew that he would die soon. Many years before, Christ had prepared Peter for the kind of death Peter would face (see John 21:18-19). At this time, Peter knew that his death was at hand. Peter was martyred for the faith in about A.D. 68. According to one tradition, he was crucified upside down, at his own request, because he did not feel worthy to die in the same manner as his Master.

2 PETER 1:16-21
What is the meaning of 2 Peter 1:16-21?

This section is a strong statement on the inspiration of Scripture. Peter affirms that the Old Testament prophets wrote God's messages. He puts himself and the other apostles in the same category, because they also proclaim God's truth. The Bible is not a collection of fables or human ideas about God. It is God's very words given *through* people *to* people. Peter emphasized his authority as an eyewitness as well as the God-inspired authority of Scripture to prepare the way for his harsh words against the false teachers. If these wicked men were contradicting the apostles and the Bible, their message could not be from God.

2 PETER 1:19
Why is Christ called the "morning star"?

When Christ returns, he will shine in his full glory like the morning star. Until that day we have Scripture as a light and the Holy Spirit to illuminate Scripture for us and guide us as we seek the truth. For more on Christ as the morning star, see Ephesians 5:14; Revelation 2:28; 22:16.

NOVEMBER 28

Daniel 5:1-31; 2 Peter 2:1-22; Psalms 119:113-128; Proverbs 28:19-20

DANIEL 5:1
Who is Belshazzar?

Sixty-six years have elapsed since chapter 1, which tells of Nebuchadnezzar's strike against Jerusalem in 605 B.C. Nebuchadnezzar died in 562 B.C. after a reign of 43 years. His son, Evil-Merodach, ruled from 562–560 B.C.; his brother-in-law Neriglissar reigned four years from 560–556 B.C. After a two-month reign by Labashi-Marduk in 556 B.C., the Babylonian empire continued from 556–539 B.C. under the command of Nabonidus. Belshazzar was the son of Nabonidus. He co-reigned with his father from 553–539 B.C. Nebuchadnezzar is called Belshazzar's "father." The term could also mean "ancestor." Archaeologists have recently discovered Belshazzar's name on several documents. He ruled with his father, Nabonidus, staying home to administer the affairs of the kingdom while his father tried to reopen trade routes taken over by Cyrus and the Persians. Belshazzar was in charge of the city of Babylon when it was captured.

DANIEL 5:31
Who was Darius?

This Darius is not to be confused with Darius I, mentioned in Ezra, Haggai, and Zechariah, or Darius II (the Persian), mentioned in Nehemiah. Darius the Mede is named only in the book of Daniel. Other records name no king between Belshazzar and Cyrus. Thus, Darius may have been (1) appointed by Cyrus to rule over Babylon as a province of Persia, (2) another name for Cyrus himself or for his son, Cambyses, or (3) a descendant of Xerxes I.

2 PETER 2:1
What was false about the "false teachers"?

Jesus had told the disciples that false teachers would come (Matt. 24:11; Mark 13:22-23). Peter had heard these words, and at this time he was seeing them come true. Just as false prophets had contradicted the true prophets in Old Testament times (see, for example, Jer. 23:16-40; 28:1-17), telling people only what they wanted to hear, so false teachers were twisting Christ's teachings and the words of his apostles. These teachers were belittling the significance of Jesus' life, death, and resurrection. Some claimed that Jesus couldn't be God; others claimed that he couldn't have been a real man. These teachers allowed and even encouraged all kinds of wrong and immoral acts, especially sexual sin.

NOVEMBER 29

Daniel 6:1-28; 2 Peter 3:1-18; Psalms 119:129-152; Proverbs 28:21-22

DANIEL 6
How old was Daniel at the time of chapter 6?

At this time, Daniel was over eighty years old and one of Darius's top three administrators. Daniel was working with those who did not believe in his God, but he worked more efficiently and capably than all the rest. Thus, he attracted the attention of the pagan king and earned a place of respect.

DANIEL 6:8-9
If the King signed a law, why couldn't he change it?

In Babylon, the king's word *was* the law. In the Medo-Persian empire, however, when a law was made, even the king couldn't change it. Darius was an effective government administrator, but he had a fatal flaw—pride. By appealing to his vanity, the men talked Darius into signing a law effectively making himself a god for 30 days. This law could not be broken—not even by an important official like Daniel. Another example of the irrevocable nature of the laws of the Medes and Persians appears in Esther 8:8.

DANIEL 6:16
Did the Persians normally keep lions?

Lions roamed the countryside and forests in Mesopotamia, and the people feared them and greatly respected their power. Some kings hunted lions for sport. The Persians captured lions, keeping them in large parks where they were fed and attended. Lions were also used for executing people. But God has ways of delivering his people (Dan. 6:22) that none of us can imagine. God can even shut the lions' mouths.

2 PETER 3:15-18
How did the false teachers twist Paul's teachings?

Peter and Paul had very different backgrounds and personalities, and they preached from different viewpoints. Paul emphasized salvation by grace, not law, while Peter preferred to talk about Christian life and service. The two men did not contradict each other, however, and they always held each other in high esteem. The false teachers intentionally misused Paul's writings by distorting them to condone lawlessness. No doubt this made the teachers popular, because people always like to have their favorite sins justified, but the net effect was to totally destroy Paul's message. Paul may have been thinking of teachers like these when he wrote in Romans 6:15: "What then? Shall we sin because we are not under law but under grace? By no means!" Peter warned his readers to avoid the mistakes of those wicked teachers by growing in the grace and knowledge of Jesus.

NOVEMBER 30

Daniel 7:1-28; 1 John 1:1-10; Psalms 119:153-176; Proverbs 28:23-24

 1 JOHN 1:1
Who wrote 1 John and why?

First John was written by John, one of Jesus' original 12 disciples. He was probably "the disciple whom Jesus loved" (John 21:20) and, along with Peter and James, he had a special relationship with Jesus. This letter was written between A.D. 85–90 from Ephesus, before John's exile to the island of Patmos (see Rev. 1:9). Jerusalem had been destroyed in A.D. 70, and Christians were scattered throughout the empire. By the time John wrote this letter, Christianity had been around for more than a generation. It had faced and survived severe persecution. The main problem confronting the church at this time was declining commitment: many believers were conforming to the world's standards, failing to stand up for Christ, and compromising their faith. False teachers were plentiful, and they were accelerating the church's downward slide away from the Christian faith. John wrote this letter to put believers back on track, to show the difference between light and darkness (truth and error), and to encourage the church to grow in genuine love for God and for one another. He also wrote to assure true believers that they possessed eternal life and to help them know that their faith was genuine—so they could enjoy all the benefits of being God's children.

 1 JOHN 1:7
How does Jesus' blood purify us from every sin?

In Old Testament times, believers symbolically transferred their sins to an animal, which they then sacrificed (see a description of this ceremony in Lev. 4). The animal died in their place to pay for their sin and to allow them to continue living in God's favor. God graciously forgave them because of their faith in him, and because they obeyed his commandments concerning the sacrifice. Those sacrifices anticipated the day when Christ would completely remove sin. Real cleansing from sin came with Jesus, the "Lamb of God, who takes away the sin of the world" (John 1:29). Sin, by its very nature, brings death—that is a fact as certain as the law of gravity. Jesus did not die for his own sins; he had none. Instead, by a transaction that we may never fully understand, he died for the sins of the world. When we commit our lives to Christ and thus identify ourselves with him, his death becomes ours. He has paid the penalty for our sins, and his blood has purified us. Just as Christ rose from the grave, we rise to a new life of fellowship with him (Rom. 6:4).

DECEMBER 1

Daniel 8:1-27; 1 John 2:1-17; Psalms 120:1-7; Proverbs 28:25-26

DANIEL 8:20
What do the two horns in Daniel 8:3 represent?

The two horns were the kings of Media and Persia. The longer horn represented the growing dominance of Persia in the Medo-Persian empire.

DANIEL 8:21
What does the goat in Daniel 8:5-7 represent?

The goat represented Greece, and its large horn, Alexander the Great. This is an amazing prediction because Greece was not yet considered a world power when this prophecy was given. Alexander the Great conquered the world with great speed and military strategy, indicated by the goat's rapid movement. Shattering both horns symbolized Alexander breaking both parts of the Medo-Persian empire.

DANIEL 8:8
What is the meaning of Daniel 8:8?

Alexander the Great died in his thirties at the height of his power. His kingdom was split into four parts under four generals: Ptolemy I of Egypt and Palestine; Seleucus of Babylonia and Syria; Lysimachus of Asia Minor; and Antipater of Macedon and Greece.

DANIEL 8:9
Was Israel really attacked as mentioned in Daniel 8:9 (TLB, "pleasant land" in KJV)?

Israel ("the Beautiful Land," NIV) was attacked by Antiochus IV Epiphanes (the small horn) in the second century B.C. He was the eighth ruler of the Seleucid empire (Babylonia and Syria). He overthrew the high priest, looted the temple, and replaced worship of God with a Greek form of worship. A further fulfillment of this prophecy of a powerful horn will occur in the future with the coming of the antichrist (see Dan. 8:17, 19, 23; 11:36; 2 Thess. 2:4).

DANIEL 8:17, NRSV
What is the "time of the end"?

The "time of the end," in this case, refers to the whole period from the end of the exile until the second coming of Christ. Many of the events that would happen under Antiochus IV Epiphanes will be repeated on a broader scale just before Christ's second coming. During these times, God deals with Israel in a radically different way, with divine discipline coming through Gentile nations. This period is sometimes referred to as the "times of the Gentiles" (Luke 21:24).

DECEMBER 2

Daniel 9:1–11:1; 1 John 2:18–3:6; Psalms 121:1-8; Proverbs 28:27-28

1 JOHN 2:18, NKJV
When is the "last hour" when "antichrists" come?
John is talking about the last days, the time between Christ's first and second comings. The first-century readers of 1 John lived in the last days, and so do we. During this time, antichrists (false teachers who pretend to be Christians and who lure weak members away from Christ) will appear. Finally, just before the world ends, one great antichrist will arise, symbolized as "the beast" (Rev. 13; 19:20; 20:10).

1 JOHN 2:19
Who were these "antichrists"?
The antichrists were not total strangers to the church; they once had been in the church, but they did not really belong to it. John does not say why they left; it is clear that their reasons for joining in the first place were wrong. Apparently the antichrists in John's day were claiming faith in God while denying and opposing Christ (1 John 2:23). To do so, John firmly states, is impossible. Because Jesus is God's Son and the Messiah, to deny Christ is to reject God's way of revealing himself to the world. A person who accepts Christ as God's Son accepts God the Father at the same time. The two are one and cannot be separated. Many cultists today call themselves Christians, but they deny that Jesus is divine.

1 JOHN 2:20
What is the "anointing"?
Anointing usually refers to the pouring out of special olive oil. Oil was used to consecrate kings and special servants for service (1 Sam. 16:1, 13), and also was used by the church when someone was sick (James 5:14). "You have an anointing from the Holy One" could read, "The Holy Spirit has been given to you by the Father and the Son." When a person becomes a Christian, he or she receives the Holy Spirit. One way the Holy Spirit helps the believer and the church is by communicating truth. Jesus is the truth (John 14:6), and the Holy Spirit guides believers to him (John 16:13).

1 JOHN 3:5
What does "He was manifested to take away our sins" mean?
Under the Old Testament sacrifice system, a lamb without blemish was offered as a sacrifice for sin. Jesus is "the Lamb of God, who takes away the sin of the world" (John 1:29). Because Jesus lived a perfect life and sacrificed himself for our sins, we can be completely forgiven (1 John 2:2). We can look back to his death for us and know that we need never suffer eternal death (1 Pet. 1:18-20).

DECEMBER 3

Daniel 11:2-35; 1 John 3:7-24; Psalms 122:1-9; Proverbs 29:1

DANIEL 11:6-7
When were the prophecies in Daniel 11:6-7 fulfilled?

These prophecies seem to have been fulfilled many years later in the Seleucid wars between Egypt and Syria. In 252 B.C., Ptolemy II of Egypt ("the South") gave his daughter Berenice in marriage to Antiochus II of Syria ("the North") to finalize a peace treaty between their two lands. But Berenice was murdered in Antioch by Antiochus II's former wife, Laodice. Berenice's brother, Ptolemy III, ascended the Egyptian throne and declared war against the Seleucids to avenge his sister's murder.

DANIEL 11:32
Who is the one who flattered "those who hate the things of God"?

This reference to those who have violated the covenant may include Menelaus, the high priest, who was won over by Antiochus and who conspired with him against the Jews who were loyal to God. The "people who know their God" may refer to the Maccabees and their sympathizers, but a further fulfillment may lie in the future.

1 JOHN 3:23, NKJV
What does it mean to "believe on the name of His Son Jesus Christ"?

In the Bible, a person's name stands for his or her character. It represents who he or she really is. We are to believe not only in Jesus' words, but also in his very person as the Son of God. Moreover, to believe "in the name" means to pattern your life after Christ's, to become more like him by uniting yourself with him. And if we are living like Christ, we will "love one another."

PSALM 122:5
What are the "thrones for judgment" in Psalm 122:5?

The "thrones for judgment" are the courts of justice by the town gate. In Bible times, the elders in a town sat to hear cases and administer justice at the gate (Ruth 4:1-2). Sometimes the king himself would sit at the gate to meet his subjects and make legal decisions (2 Sam. 19:8). Speeches and prophecies were also made at the city gate (Neh. 8:1; Jer. 17:19-20).

DECEMBER 4

Daniel 11:36–12:13; 1 John 4:1-21; Psalms 123:1-4; Proverbs 29:2-4

DANIEL 12:2
What is the meaning of Daniel 12:2?

This is a clear reference to the resurrection of both the righteous and the wicked, although the eternal fates of each will be quite different. Up to this time, teaching about the resurrection was not common, although Israelites believed that one day they would be included in the restoration of the new kingdom. This reference to a bodily resurrection of both the saved and the lost was a sharp departure from common belief. (See also Job 19:25-26; Ps. 16:10; and Isa. 26:19 for other Old Testament references to the resurrection.)

DANIEL 12:4
Why was the prophecy sealed and kept secret?

Closing up and sealing the scroll meant that it was to be kept safe and preserved. This was to be done so that believers of all times could look back on God's work in history and find hope. Daniel did not understand the exact meaning of the times and events in his vision. We can see events as they unfold, for we are in the end times. The whole book will not be understood until the climax of earth's history.

DANIEL 12:11 TLB
What is the "Horrible Thing" in Daniel 12:11?

"The abomination" (NIV) set up in the temple refers to the altar of Zeus, where Antiochus IV Epiphanes sacrificed a pig. Some think it will have another fulfillment in the antichrist and one of his horrible acts of evil (Matt. 24:15). However, this and the predictions at the early part of the chapter may refer specifically to Antiochus IV Epiphanes, and the rest of the prophecy may refer to the end times.

1 JOHN 4:1
What is the meaning of the phrase, "Do not believe every spirit, but test the spirits"?

This means that we shouldn't believe everything we hear just because someone says it is a message inspired by God. There are many ways to test teachers to see if their message is truly from the Lord. One is to check to see if their words match what God says in the Bible. Other tests include their commitment to the body of believers (1 John 2:19), their life-style (1 John 3:23-24), and the fruit of their ministry (1 John 4:6). But the most important test of all, says John, is what they believe about Christ. Do they teach that Jesus is fully God and fully man?

DECEMBER 5

HOSEA 1:1
Who was Hosea and why did he write his prophecy?

Hosea was a prophet to the northern kingdom of Israel. He served from 753 to 715 B.C. Under the reign of Jeroboam II, the northern kingdom had prospered materially but had decayed spiritually. The people were greedy and had adopted the moral behavior and idolatrous religion of the surrounding Canaanites. Hosea's role was to show how the people of the northern kingdom had been unfaithful to God, their "husband" and provider, and had married themselves to Baal and the gods of Canaan. He warned that unless they repented of their sin and turned back to God, they were headed for destruction. Hosea spoke of God's characteristics—his powerful love and fierce justice—and how their practical experience of these should affect their lives and make them return to God. Unfortunately, the people had broken their covenant with God, and they would receive the punishments God had promised (Deut. 27–28).

HOSEA 1:2-3
Did God really order his prophet to marry a woman who would commit adultery?

Some who find it difficult to believe God could make such a request view this story as an illustration, not an historical event. Many, however, think the story is historical and give one of these explanations: (1) According to God's law, a priest could not marry a prostitute or a divorced woman (Lev. 21:7). However, Hosea was not a priest. (2) It is possible that Gomer was not an adulterous woman when Hosea married her, and that God was letting Hosea know that Gomer would later turn to adultery and prostitution. In any case, Hosea knew ahead of time that his wife would be unfaithful and that their married life would become a living object lesson to the adulterous northern kingdom. Hosea's marriage to an unfaithful woman would illustrate God's relationship to the unfaithful nation of Israel.

1 JOHN 5:6
Why does 1 John 5:6 say Jesus "came by water and blood"?

This may refer to Jesus' baptism and his crucifixion. At this time, there was a false teaching in circulation that said Jesus was "the Christ" only between his baptism and his death—that is, he was merely human until he was baptized, at which time "the Christ" then descended upon him but then later left him before his death on the cross. But if Jesus died only as a man, he could not have taken upon himself the sins of the world, and Christianity would be an empty religion.

DECEMBER 6

Hosea 4:1–5:15; 2 John 1:1-13; Psalms 125:1-5; Proverbs 29:9-11

HOSEA 4:4-10
Who were the religious leaders Hosea accused?

When Jeroboam I rebelled against Solomon's son Rehoboam and set up a rival kingdom in the north, he also set up his own religious system (see 1 Kings 12:25-33). In violation of God's law, he made two golden calves and told the people to worship them. He also appointed his own priests, who were not descendants of Aaron. At first the residents of the northern kingdom continued to worship God, even though they were doing it in the wrong way; but very soon they also began to worship Canaanite gods. Before long they had substituted Baal for God and no longer worshiped God at all. It is not surprising that Jeroboam's false priests were unable to preserve the true worship of God.

HOSEA 4:8, TLB
Why did "the priests rejoice in the sins of the people"?

The priests relished the people's sins (NIV). Every time a person brought a sin offering, the priest received a portion of it. The more the people sinned, the more the priests received. Because they couldn't eat all of the offerings themselves, they sold some and gave some to their relatives. The priests profited from the continuation of sin; it gave them power and position in the community. So instead of trying to lead the people out of sin, they encouraged sin to increase their profits.

2 JOHN 1:1
Why was John's second epistle written?

This letter was written shortly after 1 John to warn about false teachers. The salutation, "to the chosen lady and her children," could refer to a specific woman, or to a church whose identity is no longer known. John may have written this from Ephesus.

2 JOHN 1:7
What does it mean to "not confess that Jesus Christ has come in the flesh"?

In John's day, many false teachers taught that spirit was good and matter was evil; therefore, they reasoned that Jesus could not have been both God and man, that he as God did not really live in human flesh. In strong terms, John warns against this kind of teaching.

DECEMBER 7

HOSEA 8:7
What does it mean to "sow to the wind"?

Crop yield is the result of good seed planted in good soil and given the proper proportions of sunlight, moisture, and fertilizer. A single seed can produce multiple fruit in good conditions. Israel, however, had sown its spiritual seed to the wind—it had invested itself in activities without substance. Like the wind that comes and goes, its idolatry and foreign alliances offered no protection. In seeking self-preservation apart from God, it had brought about its own destruction. Like a forceful whirlwind, God's judgment would come upon Israel by means of the Assyrians. When we seek security in anything except God, we expose ourselves to great danger. Without God there is no lasting security.

3 JOHN 1:1
Why did John write his third epistle?

This letter gives us an important glimpse into the life of the early church. Third John, addressed to Gaius, is about the need for showing hospitality to traveling preachers and other believers. It also warns against a would-be church dictator. Whereas 2 John emphasizes the need to refuse hospitality to false teachers, 3 John urges continued hospitality to those who teach the truth. Hospitality is a strong sign of support for people and their work. It means giving them of your resources so their stay will be comfortable and their work and travel easier.

3 JOHN 1:1
Who was Gaius?

We have no further information about Gaius, but he is someone whom John loved dearly. Perhaps Gaius had shared his home and hospitality with John at some time during John's travels. If so, John would have appreciated his actions, because traveling preachers depended on expressions of hospitality to survive (see Matt. 10:11-16).

3 JOHN 1:12
Who was Demetrius?

We know nothing about Demetrius except that he may have carried this letter from John to Gaius. The book of Acts mentions an Ephesian silversmith named Demetrius who opposed Paul (Acts 19:24ff.), but this is probably another man. In contrast to the corrupt Diotrephes, Demetrius had a high regard for truth. John personified truth as a witness to Demetrius's character and teaching. In other words, if truth could speak, it would speak on Demetrius's behalf. When Demetrius arrived, Gaius certainly opened his home to him.

DECEMBER 8

HOSEA 12:2-5
Who is Jacob mentioned in Hosea 12:2-5?

Jacob, whose name was later changed to Israel, was the common ancestor of all twelve tribes of Israel (both northern and southern kingdoms). Like the nations that descended from him, Jacob practiced deceit. Unlike Israel and Judah, however, he constantly searched for God. Jacob wrestled with the angel in order to be blessed, but his descendants thought their blessings came from their own successes. Jacob purged his house of idols (Gen. 35:2), but his descendants could not quit their idol worship.

JUDE 1:1
What is the theme of the book of Jude?

Jude's letter focuses on *apostasy*—when people turn away from God's truth and embrace false teachings. Jude (brother of James and half brother of Jesus) reminded his readers of God's judgment on those who had left the faith in the past. This letter is a warning against false teachers—in this case, probably Gnostic teachers. Gnostics opposed two of the basic tenets of Christianity—the incarnation of Christ and the call to Christian ethics. Jude wrote to combat these false teachings and to encourage true doctrine and right conduct.

JUDE 1:9
When did Michael argue with Satan over Moses' body?

This incident is not recorded in any other place in Scripture. Moses' death is recorded in Deuteronomy 34. Here Jude may have been making use of an ancient book called *The Assumption of Moses.* The book demonstrated that Moses was taken immediately into God's presence after his death. Two other saints in the Old Testament were also taken into God's presence (only they were taken before they died)—Enoch (Gen. 5:21-24) and Elijah (2 Kings 2:1-15). Moses and Elijah appeared with Jesus at the Transfiguration (Matt. 17:1-9).

JUDE 1:12
What is a "love feast"?

When the Lord's Supper was celebrated in the early church, believers ate a full meal before taking part in Communion with the sharing of the bread and wine. The meal was called a "love feast," and it was designed to be a sacred time of fellowship to prepare one's heart for Communion. However, the false teachers were joining these love feasts, becoming "blemishes" in what should have been a time of holy celebration.

DECEMBER 9

 ## JOEL 2:26-27
If the Jews would never again experience a disaster like this locust plague ("never again will my people be shamed"), how do we explain the captivity in Babylon, the Jews' slavery under the Greeks and Romans, and their persecution under Hitler?

It is important not to take these verses out of context. This is still part of the "blessings" section of Joel's prophecy (Joel 2:18–3:21). Only if the people truly repented would they avoid a disaster like the one Joel had described. God's blessings are promised only to those who sincerely and consistently follow him. God does promise that after the final day of judgment, his people will never again experience this kind of disaster (Zech. 14:9-11; Rev. 21).

 ## REVELATION 1:1
What is the book of Revelation about?

Revelation is a book about the future *and* about the present. It offers future hope to all believers, especially those who have suffered for their faith, by proclaiming Christ's final victory over evil and the reality of eternal life with him. It also gives present guidance as it teaches us about Jesus Christ and how we should live for him now. Through graphic pictures we learn that (1) Jesus Christ is coming again, (2) evil will be judged, and (3) the dead will be raised to judgment, resulting in eternal life or eternal destruction.

REVELATION 1:1
Who wrote Revelation?

According to tradition, John, the author of Revelation, was the only one of Jesus' original twelve disciples who was not killed for the faith. He also wrote the Gospel of John and the letters of 1, 2, and 3 John. When he wrote Revelation, John was exiled on the island of Patmos for his witness about Jesus Christ.

 ## REVELATION 1:13
Who is the one who is "like a son of man"?

This is Jesus himself. The title *Son of Man* occurs many times in the New Testament in reference to Jesus as the Messiah. John recognized Jesus because he lived with him for three years and had seen him both as the Galilean preacher and as the glorified Son of God at the transfiguration (Matt. 17:1-8). Here Jesus appears as the mighty Son of Man. His white hair indicates his wisdom and divine nature (see also Dan. 7:9); his blazing eyes symbolize judgment of all evil; the golden sash around his chest reveals him as the high priest who goes into God's presence to obtain forgiveness of sin for those who have believed in him.

DECEMBER 10

Amos 1:1–3:15; Revelation 2:1-17; Psalms 129:1-8; Proverbs 29:19-20

Q AMOS 1:1
Who was Amos?

Amos was a shepherd and fig grower from the southern kingdom (Judah), but he prophesied to the northern kingdom (Israel). Israel was politically at the height of its power with a prosperous economy, but the nation was spiritually corrupt. Idols were worshiped throughout the land, and especially at Bethel, which was supposed to be the nation's religious center. Like Hosea, Amos was sent by God to denounce this social and religious corruption. About 30 or 40 years after Amos prophesied, Assyria destroyed the capital city, Samaria, and conquered Israel (722 B.C.). Uzziah reigned in Judah from 792–740; Jeroboam II reigned in Israel from 793–753.

Q REVELATION 2:6
Who were the Nicolaitans?

The Nicolaitans were believers who compromised their faith in order to enjoy some of the sinful practices of Ephesian society. The name *Nicolaitans* is held by some to be roughly the Greek equivalent of the Hebrew word for "Balaamites." Balaam was a prophet who induced the Israelites to carry out their lustful desires (see Rev. 2:14 and Num. 31:16). Christ has strong words for those who look for excuses to sin.

Q REVELATION 2:7
What is the meaning of the "tree of life" in Revelation 2:7?

Two trees were in the Garden of Eden—the tree of life and the tree of the knowledge of good and evil (see Gen. 2:9). Eating from the tree of life brought eternal life with God; eating from the tree of knowledge brought realization of good and evil. When Adam and Eve ate from the tree of knowledge, they disobeyed God's command. So they were excluded from Eden and barred from eating from the tree of life. Eventually, evil will be destroyed and believers will be brought into a restored paradise. In the new earth, everyone will eat from the tree of life and will live forever.

Q REVELATION 2:17
What is "hidden manna"?

"Hidden manna" suggests the spiritual nourishment that the faithful believers will receive. As the Israelites traveled toward the promised land, God provided manna from heaven for their physical nourishment (Exod. 16:13-18). Jesus, as the bread of life (John 6:51), provides spiritual nourishment that satisfies our deepest hunger.

DECEMBER 11

AMOS 4:4
Why would Amos invite people to worship idols?

Amos sarcastically invited the people to sin in Bethel and Gilgal where they worshiped idols instead of God. Bethel was where God had renewed his covenant to Abraham with Jacob (Gen. 28:10-22). At this time, Bethel was the religious center of the northern kingdom, and Jeroboam had placed an idol there to discourage the people from traveling to Jerusalem in the southern kingdom to worship (1 Kings 12:26-29). Gilgal was Israel's first campground after entering the promised land (Josh. 4:19). Here Joshua had renewed the covenant and the rite of circumcision, and the people had celebrated the Passover (Josh. 5:2-11). Saul was crowned Israel's first king in Gilgal (1 Sam. 11:15).

AMOS 5:16
Why would the people call for farmers to mourn?

Failure to honor the dead was considered horrible in Israel, so loud weeping was common at funerals. Paid mourners, usually women, cried and mourned loudly with dirges and eulogies. Amos said there would be so many funerals that there would be a shortage of professional mourners, so farmers would be called from the fields to help. (See also Jer. 9:17-20.)

REVELATION 2:20, TLB
Who was "that woman Jezebel"?

A woman in the church in Thyatira was teaching that immorality was not a serious matter for believers. Her name may have been Jezebel, or John may have used the name Jezebel to symbolize the kind of evil she was promoting. Jezebel, a pagan queen of Israel, was considered the most evil woman who ever lived (see 1 Kings 19:1-2; 21:1-15; 2 Kings 9:7-10, 30-37).

REVELATION 2:20
Was there a problem in the church with food offered to idols?

In pagan temples, meat was often offered to idols. Then the meat that wasn't burned was sold to shoppers in the temple marketplace. Eating meat offered to idols wasn't wrong in itself, but it could violate the principle of sensitivity toward weaker Christian brothers and sisters who would be bothered by it (see 1 Cor. 8). Jezebel was obviously more concerned about her own selfish pleasure and freedom than about the needs and concerns of fellow believers.

DECEMBER 12

AMOS 9:11-12
Has the prophecy in Amos 9:11-12 been fulfilled?

God's covenant with David stated that one of David's descendants would always sit on his throne (2 Sam. 7:12-16). The exile made this promise seem impossible. But "in that day" God would raise up and restore the kingdom to its promised glory. This was a promise to both Israel and Judah, not to be fulfilled by an earthly, political ruler, but by the Messiah, who would renew the spiritual kingdom and rule forever. James quoted these verses (Acts 15:16-17), finding the promise fulfilled in Christ's resurrection and in the presence of both Jews and Gentiles in the church. "Possess the remnant of Edom" envisions the Messianic kingdom, which will be universal and include Gentiles. When God brings in the Gentiles, he is restoring the ruins. After the Gentiles are called together, God will renew and restore the fortunes of the new Israel. All the land that was once under David's rule will again be part of God's nation.

REVELATION 3:7
What is the "key of David"?

The key of David represents Christ's authority to open the door of invitation into his future kingdom. After the door is opened, no one can close it—salvation is assured. Once it is closed, no one can open it—judgment is certain.

REVELATION 3:10, TLB
What is the "Great Tribulation"?

"I will protect you from the time of Great Tribulation" (TLB) can also be translated, "I will also keep you from the hour of trial" (NIV). Some believe there will be a future time of great tribulation from which true believers will be spared. Others interpret this to mean that the church will go through the time of tribulation and that God will keep them strong in the midst of it. Still others believe this refers to times of great distress in general, the church's suffering through the ages.

REVELATION 3:12
What is the "New Jerusalem"?

The new Jerusalem is the future dwelling of the people of God (Rev. 21:2). We will have a new citizenship in God's future kingdom. Everything will be new, pure, and secure.

DECEMBER 13

Obadiah 1:1-21; Revelation 4:1-11; Psalms 132:1-18; Proverbs 29:24-25

OBADIAH 1:1
Who was Obadiah and when did he prophesy?

Obadiah was a prophet from Judah who told of God's judgment against the nation of Edom. Two commonly accepted dates for this prophecy are (1) between 853 and 841 B.C., when King Jehoram and Jerusalem were attacked by a Philistine/Arab coalition (2 Chron. 21:16ff.), or (2) 586 B.C., when Jerusalem was completely destroyed by the Babylonians (2 Kings 25; 2 Chron. 36). Edom had rejoiced over the misfortunes of both Israel and Judah, and yet the Edomites and Jews descended from two brothers—Esau and Jacob (Gen. 25:19-26). But just as these two brothers were constantly fighting, so were Israel and Edom. God pronounced judgment on Edom for its callous and malicious actions toward his people.

REVELATION 4:4
Who are the twenty-four elders in Revelation 4:4?

Because there were twelve tribes of Israel in the Old Testament and twelve apostles in the New Testament, the twenty-four elders in this vision probably represent all the redeemed of God for all time (both before and after Christ's death and resurrection). They symbolize all those—both Jews and Gentiles— who are now part of God's family. The twenty-four elders show us that *all* the redeemed of the Lord are worshiping him.

REVELATION 4:5
Why is there lightning and thunder coming from God's throne?

In Revelation, lightning and thunder are connected with significant events in heaven. They remind us of the lightning and thunder at Mount Sinai when God gave the people his laws (Exod. 19:16). The Old Testament often uses such imagery to reflect God's power and majesty (Ps. 77:18).

REVELATION 4:6
What are the "four living creatures"?

Just as the Holy Spirit is seen symbolically in the seven lighted lamps, so the "four living creatures" represent the attributes (the qualities and character) of God. These creatures were not real animals. Like the cherubim (the highest order of the angels), they guard God's throne, lead others in worship, and proclaim God's holiness. God's attributes symbolized in the animal-like appearance of these four creatures are majesty and power (the lion), faithfulness (the ox), intelligence (the man), and sovereignty (the eagle). The Old Testament prophet Ezekiel saw four similar creatures in one of his visions (Ezek. 1:5-10).

DECEMBER 14

JONAH 1:17
Was Jonah really swallowed by a great fish?

Many have tried to dismiss this miraculous event as fiction, but the Bible does not describe it as a dream or a legend. We should not explain away this miracle as if we could pick and choose which of the miracles in the Bible we believe and which ones we don't. That kind of attitude would allow us to question any part of the Bible and cause us to lose our trust in the Bible as God's true and reliable word. Jonah's experience was used by Christ himself as an illustration of Christ's death and resurrection (Matt. 12:39-40).

JONAH 4:1
Why did Jonah become angry when God spared Nineveh?

The Jews did not want to share God's message with Gentile nations in Jonah's day, just as they resisted that role in Paul's day (1 Thess. 2:14-16). They had forgotten their original purpose as a nation—to be a blessing to the rest of the world by sharing God's message with other nations (Gen. 22:18). Jonah thought that God should not freely give his salvation to a wicked pagan nation. Yet this is exactly what God does for all who come to him today in faith.

REVELATION 5:5-6
In Revelation 5:5 the elder saw Jesus as a lion, but in Revelation 5:6 John saw him as a lamb. Why?

Jesus Christ is pictured as both a Lion (symbolizing his authority and power) and a Lamb (symbolizing his submission to God's will). One of the elders calls John to look at the Lion, but when John looks he sees a Lamb. Christ the Lamb was the perfect sacrifice for the sins of all mankind; therefore, only he can save us from the terrible events revealed by the scroll. Christ the Lamb won the greatest battle of all. He defeated all the forces of evil by dying on the cross. The role of Christ the Lion will be to lead the battle where Satan is finally defeated (Rev. 19:19-21). Christ the Lion is victorious because of what Christ the Lamb has already done. We will participate in his victory not because of our effort or goodness, but because he has promised eternal life to all who believe in him.

DECEMBER 15

Micah 1:1–4:13; Revelation 6:1-17; Psalms 134:1-3; Proverbs 30:1-4

MICAH 1:1
Who was Micah?

Micah and Isaiah lived at the same time, about 750–680 B.C., and undoubtedly knew of each other. Micah directed his message mainly to Judah, the southern kingdom, but he also had some words for Israel, the northern kingdom. Judah was enjoying great prosperity at this time. Of the three kings mentioned, Jotham (750–732) and Hezekiah (715–686) had tried to follow God (2 Kings 15:32-38; 18–20), but Ahaz (735–715) was one of the most evil kings ever to reign in Judah (2 Kings 16). Moresheth was a Judean village, near Gath on the border with Philistia.

REVELATION 6:1
What is the significance of Christ's unrolling of the scroll in Revelation 6:1?

This is the first of three seven-part judgments. The trumpets (chapters 8–9) and the bowls (chapter 16) are the other two. As each seal is opened, Christ the Lamb sets in motion events that will bring about the end of human history. This scroll is not completely opened until the seventh seal is broken (Rev. 8:1). The contents of the scroll reveal mankind's depravity and portray God's authority over the events of human history.

REVELATION 6:8
Why do the four horsemen only control one fourth of the earth?

This indicates that God is still limiting his judgment—it is not yet complete. With these judgments there is still time for unbelievers to turn to Christ and away from their sin. In this case, the limited punishment not only demonstrates God's wrath on sin, but also his merciful love in giving people yet another opportunity to turn to him before he brings final judgment.

REVELATION 6:15-17
Are believers included among the people who try to hide from judgment in Revelation 6:15-17?

At the sight of God sitting on the throne, all human beings, great and small, will be terrified, calling for the mountains to fall on them so that they will not have to face the judgment of the Lamb. This vivid picture was not intended to frighten believers. For them, the Lamb is a gentle Savior. But those generals, emperors, or kings who previously showed no fear of God and arrogantly flaunted their unbelief will find that they were wrong, and in that day they will have to face God's wrath. No one who has rejected God can survive the day of his wrath, but those who belong to Christ will receive a reward rather than punishment.

DECEMBER 16

 MICAH 5:2
Who is the king that Micah prophesied to be born in Bethlehem?

This ruler (KJV) is Jesus, the Messiah. Micah accurately predicted Christ's birthplace hundreds of years before Jesus was born. The promised eternal King in David's line, who would come to live as a man, had been alive forever—"from of old, from ancient times." Although eternal, Christ entered human history as the man, Jesus of Nazareth.

 REVELATION 7:4-8
What is the meaning of the 144,000 in Revelation 7:4-8?

The number 144,000 is twelve times twelve times one thousand, symbolizing completeness—*all* God's followers will be brought safely to him; not one will be overlooked or forgotten. God seals these believers either by withdrawing them from the earth (this is called the rapture) or by giving them special strength and courage to make it through this time of great persecution. Even though many believers have to undergo persecution, the seal does not necessarily guarantee protection from physical harm—many will die (see Rev. 6:11)—but God will protect them from spiritual harm. No matter what happens, they will be brought to their reward of eternal life. Their destiny is secure. These believers will not fall away from God even though they may undergo intense persecution. This is not saying that 144,000 individuals must be sealed before the persecution comes, but that when persecution begins, the faithful will have already been sealed (marked by God) and they will remain true to him until the end.

 REVELATION 7:4-8
Why are the twelve tribes of Israel listed in Revelation 7:4-8?

This is a different list from the usual listing of the twelve tribes in the Old Testament, because it is a symbolic list of God's true followers. (1) Judah is mentioned first because Judah is both the tribe of David and of Jesus the Messiah (Gen. 49:8-12; Matt. 1:1). (2) Levi had no tribal allotment because of the Levites' work for God in the temple (Deut. 18:1), but here the tribe is given a place as a reward for faithfulness. (3) Dan is not mentioned because it was known for rebellion and idolatry, traits unacceptable for God's followers (Gen. 49:17). (4) The two tribes representing Joseph (usually called Ephraim and Manasseh, after Joseph's sons) are here called Joseph and Manasseh because of Ephraim's rebellion. See Genesis 49 for the story of the beginning of these twelve tribes.

DECEMBER 17

Nahum 1:1–3:19; Revelation 8:1-13; Psalms 136:1-26; Proverbs 30:7-9

NAHUM 1:1
Why did Nahum prophesy to Nineveh?

Nahum, like Jonah, was a prophet to Nineveh, the capital of the Assyrian empire, and he prophesied between 663 and 612 B.C. Jonah had seen Nineveh repent a century earlier (see the book of Jonah), but the city had fallen back into wickedness. Assyria, the world power controlling the Fertile Crescent, seemed unstoppable. Its ruthless and savage warriors had already conquered Israel, the northern kingdom, and were causing great suffering in Judah. So Nahum proclaimed God's anger against Assyria's evil. Within a few decades, the mighty Assyrian empire would be toppled by Babylon.

NAHUM 1:11
Who is the one "who plots evil against the LORD and counsels wickedness"?

This could have been (1) Ashurbanipal (669–627 B.C.), king of Assyria during much of Nahum's life and the one who brought Assyria to the zenith of its power; (2) Sennacherib (705–681), who openly defied God (2 Kings 18:13-35), epitomizing rebellion against God; (3) no one king in particular, but the entire evil monarchy. The point is that Nineveh would be destroyed for rebelling against God.

NAHUM 2:6
What were the "river gates"?

This reference to the opening of river gates could refer either to the enemy flowing into Nineveh like a flood (Nah. 1:8) or to an actual flood of water. Some scholars suggest that dam gates, which were found in archaeological excavations, were closed to dam up the river. When an enormous amount of water had been accumulated, the gates were opened, allowing the water to flood Nineveh.

REVELATION 8:13
What is the significance of the eagle in Revelation 8:13?

Habakkuk used the image of an eagle to symbolize swiftness and destruction (see Hab. 1:8, KJV). The picture here is of a strong, powerful bird flying over all the earth, warning of the terrors yet to come. While both believers and unbelievers experience the terrors described in Revelation 8:7-13, the "inhabitants of the earth" are the unbelievers who will meet spiritual harm through the next three trumpet judgments. God has guaranteed believers protection from spiritual harm (Rev. 7:2-3).

DECEMBER 18

HABAKKUK 1:1
Who was Habakkuk and why did he write his book?

Habakkuk lived in Judah during the reign of Jehoiakim (2 Kings 23:36–24:5). He prophesied between the fall of Nineveh (the capital of Assyria) in 612 B.C. and the Babylonian invasion of Judah in 588 B.C. With Assyria in disarray, Babylon was becoming the dominant world power. This book records the prophet's dialogue with God concerning the questions, "Why does God often seem indifferent in the face of evil? Why do evil people seem to go unpunished?" While other prophetic books brought God's word to people, this brought people's questions to God.

REVELATION 9:1
Who is the one who falls from heaven to earth in Revelation 9:1?

It is not known whether this "star" that fell from heaven is Satan, a fallen angel, Christ, or a good angel. Most likely it is a good angel, because the key to the shaft of the Abyss (bottomless pit) is normally held by Christ (Rev. 1:17-18), and it was temporarily given to this other being from heaven (see also Rev. 20:1). This being, whoever he may be, is still under God's control and authority. The Abyss represents the place of the demons and of Satan, the king of demons (Rev. 9:11). See also Luke 8:31 for another reference to the Abyss.

REVELATION 9:3-10
What are the locusts in Revelation 9:3-10?

The prophet Joel described a locust plague as a foreshadowing of the "day of the Lord," meaning God's coming judgment (Joel 2:1-10). In the Old Testament, locusts were symbols of destruction because they destroyed vegetation. Here, however, they symbolize an invasion of demons called to torture people who do not believe in God. They were not created by Satan, because God is the Creator of all; rather, they are fallen angels who joined Satan in his rebellion. God limits what they can do; they can do nothing without his permission. Their main purpose on earth is to prevent, distort, or destroy people's relationship with God. Because they are corrupt and degenerate, their appearance reflects the distortion of their spirits. While it is important to recognize their evil activity so we can stay away from them, we must avoid any curiosity about or involvement with demonic forces or with the occult.

DECEMBER 19

ZEPHANIAH 1:1
When did Zephaniah prophesy?

Zephaniah prophesied in the days of Josiah king of Judah (640–609 B.C.) who followed God. During his reign the Book of the Law was discovered in the temple. After reading it, Josiah began a great religious revival in Judah (2 Kings 22:1–23:25) with Zephaniah's help. Although this great revival turned the nation back to God, it did not fully eliminate idolatry and so lasted only a short time. Twelve years after Josiah's death, Judah was invaded by Babylon, and a number of people were sent into exile.

ZEPHANIAH 2:7
Who were the "remnant"?

All the prophets, even while prophesying doom and destruction, speak of a "remnant"—a small group of God's people who remain faithful to him and whom God will restore to the land. Although God said he would destroy Judah, he also promised to save a remnant, thus keeping his original covenant to preserve Abraham's descendants (Gen. 17:4-8). Because God is holy, he cannot allow sin to continue. But God is also faithful to his promises.

ZEPHANIAH 2:13-15
Why was the destruction of Nineveh so significant?

To predict the destruction of Nineveh ten years before it happened would be equivalent to predicting the destruction of Tokyo, Moscow, or New York. Nineveh was the ancient Near Eastern center for culture, technology, and beauty. It had great libraries, buildings, and a vast irrigation system that created lush gardens in the city. The city wall was sixty miles long, one hundred feet high, and over thirty feet wide, and it was fortified with fifteen hundred towers. Yet the entire city was destroyed so completely that its very existence was questioned until it was discovered, with great difficulty, by nineteenth-century archaeologists. Nineveh had indeed become as desolate and dry as the desert.

REVELATION 10:2
Is the scroll in Revelation 10:2 the same as the one in chapter 5?

No, there are two scrolls. The first contains a revelation of judgments against evil (Rev. 5:1ff.). The contents of the second scroll are not indicated, but it also may contain a revelation of judgment. The prophet Ezekiel had a vision in which he was told to eat a scroll filled with judgments against the nation of Israel (Ezek. 3:1ff). The taste was sweet, but the scroll's contents brought destruction—just like the scroll John was told to eat. God's Word is sweet to believers because it brings salvation, but bitter to unbelievers who are judged by it.

DECEMBER 20

HAGGAI 1:1
What was the historic setting of Haggai's prophecy?

The Jews who had returned from Babylon in 538 B.C. to rebuild the temple in Jerusalem were not able to finish their work because they were hindered by their enemies. After opposition put a halt to progress, no further work had been done on the temple for over fifteen years. In August, 520 B.C., Haggai delivered a message to encourage the people to rebuild the temple. Haggai was probably born in captivity in Babylon and returned to Jerusalem with Zerubbabel in 538 B.C. (Ezra 1–2). Haggai and Zechariah, two prophets who encouraged the temple rebuilding, are mentioned in Ezra 5:1.

REVELATION 11:3
What is the meaning of the number 1,260 in Revelation 11:3?

In the book of Revelation, numbers are likely to have symbolic rather than literal meanings. The forty-two months or 1,260 days equal three-and-a-half years. As half of the perfect number seven, three and a half can indicate incompletion, imperfection, or even evil. Notice the events predicted for this time period: there is trouble (cf. Dan. 12:7), the holy city is trampled (Rev. 11:2), the woman takes refuge in the desert (Rev. 12:6), and the devil-inspired beast exercises his authority (Rev. 13:5). Some commentators link the three-and-a-half years with the period of famine in the days of Elijah (Luke 4:25; James 5:17). Since Malachi predicted the return of Elijah before the Last Judgment (Mal. 4:5), and since the events in Daniel and Revelation pave the way for the second coming, perhaps John was making this connection. It is possible, of course, that the three and a half years are literal. If so, we will clearly recognize when the three and a half years are over! Whether symbolic or literal, however, they indicate that evil's reign will have a definite end.

REVELATION 11:3
Who are the "two witnesses" in Revelation 11:3?

These two witnesses bear strong resemblance to Moses and Elijah, two of God's mighty prophets. With God's power, Moses called plagues down upon the nation of Egypt (see Exod. 8–11). Elijah defeated the prophets of Baal (1 Kings 18). Both of these men appeared with Christ at his transfiguration (see Matt. 17:1-7).

DECEMBER 21

REVELATION 12:1-6, TLB
What is the meaning of the "great pageant" in heaven pictured in Revelation 12:1-6?

The woman represents God's faithful people who have been waiting for the Messiah; the crown of twelve stars represents the twelve tribes of Israel. God set apart the Jews for himself (Rom. 9:4-5), and that nation gave birth to the Messiah. The male child (Rev. 12:5) is Jesus, born to a devout Jew named Mary (Luke 1:26-33). Evil King Herod immediately tried to destroy the infant Jesus (Matt. 2:13-20). Herod's desire to kill this newborn king, whom he saw as a threat to his throne, was motivated by Satan (the red dragon), who wanted to kill the world's Savior. The heavenly pageant of Revelation 12 shows that Christ's quiet birth in the town of Bethlehem had cosmic significance.

REVELATION 12:7-9
What is the "war in heaven"?

Much more happened at Christ's birth, death, and resurrection than most people realize. A war between the forces of good and evil was under way. With Christ's resurrection, Satan's ultimate defeat was assured. Some believe that Satan's fall to earth took place at Jesus' resurrection or ascension and that the 1,260 days (three-and-a-half years) is a symbolic way of referring to the time between Christ's first and second comings. Others say that Satan's defeat will occur in the middle of a literal seven-year tribulation period, following the rapture of the church and preceding the second coming of Christ and the beginning of Christ's thousand-year reign. Whatever the case, we must remember that Christ is victorious—Satan has already been defeated because of Christ's death on the cross (Rev. 12:10-12).

REVELATION 13:1
Who was the "beast coming out of the sea"?

This creature was initially identified with Rome, because the Roman empire, in its early days, encouraged an evil life-style, persecuted believers, and opposed God and his followers. But the beast also symbolizes the antichrist—not Satan, but someone under Satan's power and control. This antichrist looks like a combination of the four beasts that Daniel saw centuries earlier in a vision (Dan. 7). As the dragon (Rev. 12:17) is in opposition to God, so the beast from the sea is against Christ and may be seen as Satan's false messiah. The early Roman empire was strong and also anti-Christ (or against Christ's standards); many other individual powers throughout history have been anti-Christ. Many Christians believe that Satan's evil will culminate in a final antichrist, one who will focus all the powers of evil against Jesus Christ and his followers.

DECEMBER 22

REVELATION 13:3
Is the event in Revelation 13:3 a true resurrection?

Throughout the Bible we see miracles performed as proofs of God's power, love, and authority. But here we see counterfeit miracles performed to deceive. This is a reminder of Pharaoh's magicians, who duplicated Moses' signs in Egypt. True signs and miracles point us to Jesus Christ, but miracles alone can be deceptive. That is why we must ask with respect to each miracle we see: Is this consistent with what God says in the Bible? The second beast here gains influence through the signs and wonders that he can perform on behalf of the first beast. The second beast orders the people to worship an image in honor of the first beast—a direct flouting of the second commandment (Exod. 20:4-6).

REVELATION 13:16-18
What is the mark mentioned in Revelation 13:16-18?

This mark of the beast is designed to mock the seal that God places on his followers (Rev. 7:2-3). Just as God marks his people to save them, so Satan's beast marks his people to save them from the persecution that Satan will inflict upon God's followers. Identifying this particular mark is not as important as identifying the purpose of the mark. Those who accept it show their allegiance to Satan, their willingness to operate within the economic system he promotes, and their rebellion against God. To refuse the mark means to commit oneself entirely to God, preferring death to compromising one's faith in Christ. The meaning of this number has been discussed more than that of any other part of the book of Revelation. The three sixes have been said to represent many things, including the number of man or the unholy trinity of Satan, the first beast, and the false prophet (Rev. 16:13). If the number seven is considered to be the perfect number in the Bible, and if three sevens represent complete perfection, then the number 666 falls completely short of perfection. The first readers of this book probably applied the number to the Emperor Nero, who symbolized all the evils of the Roman empire. (The Greek letters of Nero's name represent numbers that total 666.) Whatever specific application the number is given, the number symbolizes the worldwide dominion and complete evil of this unholy trinity designed to undo Christ's work and overthrow him.

DECEMBER 23

Zechariah 4:1–5:11; Revelation 14:1-20; Psalms 142:1-7; Proverbs 30:21-23

ZECHARIAH 4:14
Who are the two anointed ones in Zechariah 4:14?

The two anointed ones may be Joshua and Zerubbabel, dedicated for this special task. Also note that in Revelation 11:3, two witnesses arise to prophesy to the nations during the time of tribulation. These witnesses will be killed but will rise again.

REVELATION 14:1ff.
What is the interpretation of John's vision of the Lamb with the 144,000?

Chapter 13 described the onslaught of evil that will occur when Satan and his helpers control the world. Chapter 14 gives a glimpse into eternity to show believers what awaits them if they endure. The Lamb is the Messiah. Mount Zion, often another name for Jerusalem, the capital of Israel, is contrasted with the worldly empire. The 144,000 represent believers who have endured persecutions on earth and now are ready to enjoy the eternal benefits and blessings of life with God forever. The three angels contrast the destiny of believers with that of unbelievers.

REVELATION 14:6-7
What is the "eternal gospel"?

Some believe that this is a final, worldwide appeal to all people to recognize the one true God. No one will have the excuse of never hearing God's truth. Others, however, see this as an announcement of judgment rather than as an appeal. The people of the world have had their chance to proclaim their allegiance to God, and now God's great judgment is about to begin.

REVELATION 14:8
What does the city of Babylon represent in Revelation 14:8?

Babylon was the name of both an evil city and an immoral empire, a world center for idol worship. Babylon ransacked Jerusalem and carried the people of Judah into captivity (see 2 Kings 24 and 2 Chron. 36). Just as Babylon was the Jews' worst enemy, the Roman empire was the worst enemy of the early Christians. John, who probably did not dare speak against Rome openly, applied the name *Babylon* to this enemy of God's people (Rome)—and, by extension, to all God's enemies of all times.

DECEMBER 24

Zechariah 6:1–7:14; Revelation 15:1-8; Psalms 143:1-12; Proverbs 30:24-28

Q ZECHARIAH 6:9-15
What is the meaning of the vision in Zechariah 6:9-15?

This vision is about the Messiah, the King-Priest. In the days of the kings and after the exile, Judah's government was to be ruled by two distinct persons— the king, ruling the nation's political life, and the high priest, ruling its religious life. Kings and priests had often been corrupt. God was telling Zechariah that someone worthy of the crown would come to rule as both king ("rule on his throne") and priest ("a priest on his throne"). This was an unlikely combination for that day.

Q ZECHARIAH 7:1
What was the date of the message from God mentioned in Zechariah 7:1?

The fourth year of King Darius' reign was 518 B.C. For the previous seventy years, the people had been holding a fast in August to remember the destruction of Jerusalem. Because Jerusalem was being rebuilt, they came to the temple to ask if they had to continue this annual fast. God did not answer their question directly. Instead, he told them that their acts of justice and mercy were more important than their fasting. What he wanted from his people was true justice in their dealings and mercy and compassion for the weak.

Q REVELATION 15:5-8
Why is "the temple of the tabernacle of the testimony in heaven" opened?

The Holy of Holies was the innermost room in the temple (see Heb. 9:1-17), where the ark of the covenant resided (a symbol of God's presence among his people). This room was closed off from view by a great curtain. Only the High Priest could enter there, and only on the Day of Atonement. The Holy of Holies was thrown open once before—at Christ's crucifixion, when the curtain was ripped from top to bottom (Matt. 27:50-53). The wide-open entrance into the Holy of Holies symbolizes the open access to God's very presence which Christians have on the basis of Jesus' shed blood. Those of us who are united with the sinless Christ, our High Priest, can approach God boldly (Heb. 4:14-16), but unrepentant sinners will be destroyed by his presence (Nah. 1:2-6). The angels coming out of the temple are clothed in white with golden belts across their chests. Their garments, reminiscent of the High Priest's clothing, show that they are free from corruption, immorality, and injustice. The smoke that fills the temple is the manifestation of God's glory and wrath. There is no escape from this judgment.

DECEMBER 25

Zechariah 8:1-23; Revelation 16:1-21; Psalms 144:1-15; Proverbs 30:29-31

 ### REVELATION 16:12
Where is the Euphrates River?

The Euphrates River, located in present-day Iraq, was a natural protective boundary against the empires to the east (Babylon, Assyria, Persia). If it dried up, nothing could hold back invading armies. The armies from the east symbolize unhindered judgment.

 ### REVELATION 16:13-14
What are the "frogs" mentioned in Revelation 16:13-14?

These are spirits of demons performing miraculous signs. They come out of the mouths of the unholy trinity to unite the rulers of the world for battle against God. The imagery of the demons coming out of the mouths of the three evil rulers signifies the verbal enticements and propaganda that will draw many people to their evil cause.

 ### REVELATION 16:16?
Where is "Armageddon"?

This battlefield is near the city of Megiddo (southeast of the modern port of Haifa), which guarded a large plain in northern Israel. It is a strategic location near a prominent international highway leading north from Egypt through Israel, along the coast, and on to Babylon. Megiddo overlooked the entire plain southward toward Galilee and westward toward the mountains of Gilboa. Sinful people will unite here to fight against God in a final display of rebellion.

DECEMBER 26

ZECHARIAH 9:9
Who is the king in Zechariah 9:9?

The triumphal entry of Jesus riding into Jerusalem (Matt. 21:1-11) was predicted here more than five hundred years before it happened. Just as this prophecy was fulfilled when Jesus came to earth, so the prophecies of his second coming are just as certain to come true.

ZECHARIAH 9:9-10
If Zechariah 9:9 talks about Jesus, why does Zechariah 9:10 seem to speak of an eternal kingdom?

When we view two distant mountains, they appear to be close together, perhaps even to touch each other. But as we approach them, we can see that they are in fact far apart, even separated by a huge valley. This is the situation with many Old Testament prophecies. Verse 9 was clearly fulfilled in Christ's first coming, but verse 10 can now be seen to refer to his second coming. At that time all nations will be subject to Christ, and his rule will extend over the whole earth. In Philippians 2:9-10, we are told that at that time every knee will bow to Christ and every tongue will confess him as Lord.

ZECHARIAH 9:11, TLB
Why was the covenant in Zechariah 9:11 "sealed with blood"?

Covenants in Old Testament times were sealed or confirmed with blood, much as we would sign our name to a contract. The old covenant was sealed by the blood of sacrifices, pointing ahead to the blood Christ would shed at Calvary, his "signature" that confirmed God's new covenant with his people. Because God had made a covenant with these people, he delivered them from the "waterless pit," the cistern-like prison of exile.

REVELATION 17:1-18
What is the meaning of the images in Revelation chapter 17?

The destruction of Babylon mentioned in 16:17-21 is now described in greater detail. The "great prostitute," called Babylon, represents the early Roman empire with its many gods and the blood of Christian martyrs on its hands. The water stands for either sea commerce or a well-watered (well-provisioned) city. The great prostitute represents the seductiveness of the governmental system that uses immoral means to gain its own pleasure, prosperity, and advantage. In contrast to the prostitute, Christ's bride, the church, is pure and obedient (Rev. 19:6-9). The wicked city of Babylon contrasts with the heavenly city of Jerusalem (Rev. 21:10–22:5). The original readers probably rather quickly identified Babylon with Rome, but Babylon also symbolizes any system that is hostile to God (see Rev. 17:5).

DECEMBER 27

ZECHARIAH 10:4
What are the meanings of the images in Zechariah 10:4?

Zechariah's prophecy, more than five hundred years before Christ's first coming, called Christ a "cornerstone" (see also Isa. 28:16), a "tent peg" (Isa. 22:23), a "bow" that wins the battle, and a "ruler" who was a man of action (see also Gen. 49:10; Mic. 5:2). This Messiah would be strong, stable, victorious, and trustworthy—all in all, the answer to Israel's problems. Only in the Messiah will all the promises to God's people be fulfilled.

ZECHARIAH 11:4-17
Why did God tell Zechariah to become a shepherd?

In this message, God told Zechariah to act out the roles of two different kinds of shepherds. The first type of shepherd demonstrated how God would reject his people (the sheep) because they rejected him (Zech. 11:4-14). The second type of shepherd demonstrated how God would give over his people to evil shepherds (Zech. 11:15-17). (See Ezek. 34 for a detailed portrayal of the evil shepherds of Israel.)

ZECHARIAH 11:17, NRSV
What is the significance of the two shepherd's staffs in Zechariah 11:17?

Zechariah took two shepherd's staffs and named them "Favor" and "Unity". He broke the first one ("Favor") to show that God's gracious covenant with his people was broken. He broke the second one ("Union") to show that "the family ties between Judah and Israel" were broken (Zech. 11:14).

ZECHARIAH 11:12-13
Why was Zechariah paid "thirty shekels of silver"?

To pay this shepherd 30 pieces of silver was an insult. This was the price paid to an owner for a slave gored by an ox (Exod. 21:32). This is also the amount Judas received for betraying Jesus (Matt. 27:3-10). The priceless Messiah was sold for the price of a slave. "Throw it into the treasury" can also be translated "throw it to the potter" (NIV, KJV) Potters were in the lowest social class. The "lordly price" (NRSV, a sarcastic comment) was so little that it could be thrown to the potter. It is significant that the 30 pieces of silver paid to Judas for betraying Jesus were returned to the temple and used to buy a potter's field (Matt. 27:3-10).

DECEMBER 28

ZECHARIAH 13:1
What is the meaning of the fountain mentioned in Zechariah 13:1?

This fountain is the never-ending supply of God's mercy, forgiveness, and cleansing power, it is similar to the never-ending stream flowing out from the temple (Ezek. 47:1). The fountain is used in Scripture to symbolize God's forgiveness. In John 4, Jesus tells of his "living water" that satisfies completely.

ZECHARIAH 13:7
Who are the shepherd and sheep in Zechariah 13:7?

Just before his arrest, Jesus quoted from this verse, referring to himself and his disciples (Matt. 26:31-32). He knew beforehand that his disciples would scatter when he was arrested. The Roman "sword" was the military power that put Christ to death.

REVELATION 19:7, TLB
What is the "wedding banquet of the Lamb"?

This is the culmination of human history—the judgment of the wicked and the wedding of the Lamb and his bride, the church. The church consists of all faithful believers from all time. The bride's clothing stands in sharp contrast to the gaudy clothing of the great prostitute of Revelation 17:4 and 18:16. The bride's clothing is the righteousness of the saints. These righteous acts are not religious deeds done by believers to their merit, but they reflect the work of Christ to save us (Rev. 7:9, 14). In Revelation 19:7-9 the church is pictured as both the bride (Rev. 19:7-8) and the quests invited to the wedding feast (Rev. 19:9). As those given to Christ, we are the bride; as those called to be part of God's Kingdom, we are the invited guests.

REVELATION 19:20, KJV
What is the "lake burning with fire and brimstone"?

The fiery lake of burning sulfur (NIV) is the final destination of the wicked. This lake is different from the abyss (bottomless pit) referred to in Revelation 9:1. The antichrist and the false prophet are thrown into the fiery lake. Later, their leader, Satan himself, will be thrown into that lake (Rev. 20:10), and finally death and Hades (Rev. 20:14). Afterward, everyone whose name is not recorded in the book of life will be thrown into the lake of fire (Rev. 20:15).

DECEMBER 29

Zechariah 14:1-21; Revelation 20:1-15; Psalms 148:1-14; Proverbs 31:8-9

 ZECHARIAH:14:1-21
Why will there still be an Old Testament feast during the Messiah's kingdom?

This Feast of Tabernacles is the only feast still appropriate during the Messiah's reign. The Passover was fulfilled in Christ's death; the Day of Atonement, in acceptance of Christ's salvation; the Feast of Firstfruits in his resurrection; and Pentecost, with the arrival of the Holy Spirit. But the Feast of Tabernacles, a festival of thanksgiving, celebrates the harvest of human souls for the Lord. Jesus may have alluded to it in John 4:35.

 REVELATION 20:2-4
When do the one thousand years in Revelation 20:2-4 occur?

The one thousand years are often referred to as the *millennium* (Latin for *one thousand*). There are three major positions on how and when the millenium will occur: postmillennialism, premillennialism, and amillennialism. (1) *Postmillennialism* looks for a literal thousand-year period of peace on earth ushered in by the church. At the end of the thousand years, Satan will be unleashed once more, but Christ will return to defeat him and reign forever. Christ's second coming will not occur until after the thousand-year period. (2) *Premillennialism* also views the thousand years as a literal time period, but holds that Christ's second coming initiates his thousand-year reign, which occurs before the final removal of Satan. (3) *Amillennialism* sees the thousand-year period as symbolic of the time between Christ's ascension and his return. It is the reign of Christ in believers' hearts and in his church. This period will end with the second coming of Christ. These different views about the millennium need not cause division and controversy in the church, because each view acknowledges what is most crucial to Christianity—Christ will return, defeat Satan, and reign forever! Whatever and whenever the millennium is, Jesus Christ will unite all believers; therefore, we should not let this issue divide us.

 REVELATION 20:5-6
What is the first resurrection?

Christians hold two basic views concerning this first resurrection. (1) Some believe the first resurrection is spiritual (in our hearts at salvation), and that the millennium is our spiritual reign with Christ between his first and second comings. During this time, we are priests of God because Christ reigns in our hearts. Then, the second resurrection is the bodily resurrection of all people for judgment. (2) Others believe that the first resurrection occurs after Satan has been set aside. It is a physical resurrection of believers who then reign with Christ on the earth for a literal one thousand years. The second resurrection occurs at the end of this millennium in order to judge unbelievers who have died.

DECEMBER 30

Malachi 1:1–2:17; Revelation 21:1-27; Psalms 149:1-9; Proverbs 31:10-24

MALACHI 1:1
Who was Malachi; when and why did he prophesy?

Malachi, the last Old Testament prophet, preached after Haggai, Zechariah, and Nehemiah—about 430 B.C. The temple had been rebuilt for almost a century, and the people were losing their enthusiasm for worship. Apathy and disillusionment had set in perhaps because the exciting Messianic prophecies of Isaiah, Jeremiah, and Micah had not been fulfilled. Many of the sins that had brought the downfall of Jerusalem in 586 B.C. were still being practiced in Judah. Malachi confronted the hypocrites with their sin by portraying a graphic dialogue between a righteous God and his hardened people.

REVELATION 21:2-3
What is the new Jerusalem?

The "Holy City, the new Jerusalem" is described as the place where God will "wipe every tear from their eyes." Forevermore, in her there will be no death, pain, sorrow, or crying (Rev. 21:4). This is "the city which has foundations, whose builder and maker is God" (Heb 11:10, NKJV), where God lives among his people for eternity. Instead of our going up to meet him, he comes down to be with us, just as God became man in Jesus Christ and lived among us (John 1:14). The new Jerusalem is a picture of God's future home for his people. The twelve tribes of Israel (Rev. 21:12) probably represent all the faithful in the Old Testament; the twelve apostles (Rev. 21:14) represent the church. Thus, both believing Gentiles and Jews who have been faithful to God will live together in the new earth.

REVELATION 21:15-17
Why does the book of Revelation give the exact measurements of the new Jerusalem?

The city's measurements are symbolic of a place that will hold all God's people. These measurements are all multiples of twelve, the number for God's people: there were twelve tribes in Israel, and twelve apostles who started the church. The walls are 144 (twelve times twelve) cubits (two hundred feet) thick; there are twelve layers in the walls, and twelve gates in the city; and the height, length, and breadth are all the same, twelve thousand stadia (fourteen hundred miles). The new Jerusalem is a perfect cube, the same shape as the most holy place in the temple (1 Kings 6:20). These measurements illustrate that this new home will be perfect for us.

DECEMBER 31

Malachi 3:1–4:6; Revelation 22:1-21; Psalms 150:1-6; Proverbs 31:25-31

MALACHI 3:1
Who is the messenger in Malachi 3:1?

There are actually two messengers in this verse. The first ("My messenger . . . to prepare the way") is usually understood to be John the Baptist (Matt. 11:10; Luke 7:27). The second messenger is Jesus, the Messiah, ("The Messenger of God's promises," TLB) for whom John the Baptist prepared the way.

MALACHI 4:5-6
Who is the "prophet like Elijah"?

Elijah was one of the greatest prophets who ever lived (his story is recorded in 1 Kings 17–2 Kings 2). With Malachi's death, the voice of God's prophets would be silent for four hundred years. This last prophecy of the Old Testament promises that a prophet would come, like Elijah, to herald Christ's coming (Matt. 17:10-13; Luke 1:17). This prophet was John the Baptist. John prepared people's hearts for Jesus by urging people to repent of their sins. Christ's coming would bring unity and peace, but also judgment on those who refused to turn from their sins.

REVELATION 22:2
What is the "tree of life"?

This *tree of life* is like the tree of life in the Garden of Eden (Gen. 2:9). After Adam and Eve sinned, they were forbidden to eat from the tree of life because they could not have eternal life as long as they were under sin's control. But because of the forgiveness of sin through the blood of Jesus, there will be no evil or sin in this city. We will be able to eat freely from the tree of life when sin's control over us is destroyed and our eternity with God is secure. Moreover, this "tree of life" bears twelve kinds of fruit so that fruit is available each month. This means that life in the new Jerusalem will be abundant and never-ending.

REVELATION 22:16
What did Jesus mean in saying "I am the Root and the Offspring of David, the Bright and Morning Star?

Jesus is both David's "Root" and "Offspring." As the Creator of all, Jesus existed long before David. As a human, however, he was one of David's direct descendants (see Isa. 11:1-5; Matt. 1:1-17). As the Messiah, he is the "bright Morning Star," the light of salvation to all.